Considerations and Characteristics of the Millennial Leader in Today's Global Society

Tymon M. Graham
TMGraham Consulting, LLC, USA

A volume in the Advances in Logistics, Operations, and Management Science (ALOMS) Book Series

IGI Global
PUBLISHER of TIMELY KNOWLEDGE

Published in the United States of America by
IGI Global
Business Science Reference (an imprint of IGI Global)
701 E. Chocolate Avenue
Hershey PA, USA 17033
Tel: 717-533-8845
Fax: 717-533-8661
E-mail: cust@igi-global.com
Web site: http://www.igi-global.com

Library of Congress Cataloging-in-Publication Data

Names: Graham, Tymon, 1988- editor.
Title: Considerations and characteristics of the millennial leader in today's global society / Tymon Graham, editor.
Description: Hershey PA : Business Science Reference, [2023] | Includes bibliographical references and index. | Summary: "This book will provide narrative and insight on the millennial leaders, leadership qualities needed of future leaders, with an investigation into other millennial leaders who have ascended, and how managers, supervisors and senior leaders can help in the changes of the organizational life cycle"-- Provided by publisher.
Identifiers: LCCN 2022018288 (print) | LCCN 2022018289 (ebook) | ISBN 9781668447116 (hardcover) | ISBN 9781668447123 (paperback) | ISBN 9781668447130 (ebook)
Subjects: LCSH: Leadership. | Generation Y. | Mentoring in business. | Conflict of generations in the workplace.
Classification: LCC HD57.7 .C66625 2023 (print) | LCC HD57.7 (ebook) | DDC 658.4/092--dc23/eng/20220707
LC record available at https://lccn.loc.gov/2022018288
LC ebook record available at https://lccn.loc.gov/2022018289

This book is published in the IGI Global book series Advances in Logistics, Operations, and Management Science (ALOMS) (ISSN: 2327-350X; eISSN: 2327-3518)

British Cataloguing in Publication Data
A Cataloguing in Publication record for this book is available from the British Library.

Advances in Logistics, Operations, and Management Science (ALOMS) Book Series

ISSN:2327-350X
EISSN:2327-3518

Editor-in-Chief: John Wang, Montclair State University, USA

MISSION

Operations research and management science continue to influence business processes, administration, and management information systems, particularly in covering the application methods for decision-making processes. New case studies and applications on management science, operations management, social sciences, and other behavioral sciences have been incorporated into business and organizations real-world objectives.

The **Advances in Logistics, Operations, and Management Science** (ALOMS) Book Series provides a collection of reference publications on the current trends, applications, theories, and practices in the management science field. Providing relevant and current research, this series and its individual publications would be useful for academics, researchers, scholars, and practitioners interested in improving decision making models and business functions.

COVERAGE

- Computing and information technologies
- Networks
- Marketing engineering
- Production Management
- Decision analysis and decision support
- Operations Management
- Organizational Behavior
- Services management
- Information Management
- Political Science

IGI Global is currently accepting manuscripts for publication within this series. To submit a proposal for a volume in this series, please contact our Acquisition Editors at Acquisitions@igi-global.com or visit: http://www.igi-global.com/publish/.

The Advances in Logistics, Operations, and Management Science (ALOMS) Book Series (ISSN 2327-350X) is published by IGI Global, 701 E. Chocolate Avenue, Hershey, PA 17033-1240, USA, www.igi-global.com. This series is composed of titles available for purchase individually; each title is edited to be contextually exclusive from any other title within the series. For pricing and ordering information please visit http://www.igi-global.com/book-series/advances-logistics-operations-management-science/37170. Postmaster: Send all address changes to above address.

Titles in this Series

For a list of additional titles in this series, please visit:
http://www.igi-global.com/book-series/advances-logistics-operations-management-science/37170

Strategies and Applications of Islamic Entrepreneurship
Ahmad Rafiki (Universitas Medan Area, Indonesia) Alfatih Gessan Pananjung (Bahrain Institute of Banking and Finance, Bahrain) and Muhammad Dharma Tuah Putra Nasution (Universitas Pembangunan Panca Budi, Indonesia)
Business Science Reference • © 2023 • 313pp • H/C (ISBN: 9781668475195) • US $250.00

Entrepreneurship Ecosystems and Their Opportunities and Challenges
Mohammed El Amine Abdelli (University of Brest, France) Shajara Ul-Durar (University of Sunderland, UK) and Hala Wasef Hattab (British University in Egypt, Egypt)
Business Science Reference • © 2023 • 337pp • H/C (ISBN: 9781668471401) • US $250.00

Climate Change Management and Social Innovations for Sustainable Global Organization
Sumita Dave (Amity University, Raipur, India) Monica Sainy (Amity University, Raipur, India) Disha Sharma (Amity University, Raipur, India) and Anupam Singh (University of Stirling, UK)
Engineering Science Reference • © 2023 • 313pp • H/C (ISBN: 9781668495032) • US $250.00

Technological Innovation Driving Sustainable Entrepreneurial Growth in Developing Nations
Nana Yaw Asabere (Accra Technical University, Ghana) Glenn Kwabena Gyimah (Accra Technical University, Ghana) Amevi Acakpovi (Accra Technical University, Ghana) and Florence Plockey (Accra Technical University, Ghana)
Business Science Reference • © 2023 • 452pp • H/C (ISBN: 9781668498439) • US $250.00

Emerging Technologies and Digital Transformation in the Manufacturing Industry
Fernando Ortiz-Rodriguez (Tamaulipas Autonomous University, Mexico) Sanju Tiwari (Tamaulipas Autonomous University, Mexico) Luis Manuel Hernández-González (INDEX, Mexico) and Agustin Tiburcio (INDEX, Mexico)
Business Science Reference • © 2023 • 291pp • H/C (ISBN: 9781668480885) • US $250.00

IGI Global
PUBLISHER of TIMELY KNOWLEDGE

701 East Chocolate Avenue, Hershey, PA 17033, USA
Tel: 717-533-8845 x100 • Fax: 717-533-8661
E-Mail: cust@igi-global.com • www.igi-global.com

Table of Contents

Detailed Table of Contents

these positions. This chapter explores the key skills and characteristics required for millennials to excel as leaders, highlighting the unique challenges and opportunities they face in today's rapidly evolving business environment.

When it comes to the workplace, millennials yearn for a work-life balance and to be in a learning environment where they can develop more than professional life skills. Anyone born between 1981 to 1996 is considered a "millennial." Millennials are also known as "Gen Y," and are relatively well aware of the digital presence in the society they grew up in since they grew up with the growth of the digital era. Millennials face different challenges as they enter the workforce since many of the workforce leaders are a generation or two ahead. Due to their career interest and degrees advancement, millennial leaders are known to enter the workforce earlier than other generations. This generation is known to turn down any career opportunity or job offer that does not align with their life values. Of all the challenges this generation faces in their lives, the "imposter syndrome" has become a blaring feeling that makes them feel invalid about the spaces they exist in.

It is noted that those born between the years of 1981 and 1996 are deemed millennials. For the sake of this text, the authors define leadership as a person who is committed to a purpose with the ability to influence people to accomplish or achieve a goal. As the largest living generation, the millennial generation brings a sense of diversity, inclusivity, and disruption to the normal operation of life, liberty, and the pursuit thereof. This chapter reviews the different generations, what leadership means to millennials, millennial leaders who exemplify characteristics important to millennials, preferences of millennial leaders, and what millennial leaders bring to the table, roles, jobs, and spaces.

Ascension is defined by the act of rising to an important position. This chapter identifies rationales, opportunities, and principles for millennial leaders to consider during the ascension phase. Essential points in this chapter include strategizing ascension,

Preface

In today's rapidly evolving global society, leadership is not a static concept; it's a dynamic force that constantly adapts to the changing tides of time and technology. As leaders ascend the executive ranks, we find ourselves in a pivotal era where the torch is being passed from one generation to the next. This transition is not merely a symbolic gesture; it's a fundamental shift in the very fabric of leadership.

In this reference book, *Considerations and Characteristics of the Millennial Leader in Today's Global Society*, we embark on a journey to explore the unique qualities, challenges, and contributions of the millennial leader. As we delve into this fascinating subject, we will uncover the profound impact these individuals are making on the educational and corporate landscapes.

The millennial leader, defined by birth years spanning from 1980 to 1999, represents a generation poised to take the helm as their predecessors gracefully step into retirement. Their ascent is not a matter of mere happenstance; it is a necessity born out of the ever-changing demands of our organizations and the critical need for fresh perspectives and innovations.

It is often found that many tend to discuss the millennial student, the millennial employee, and the millennial operative, while providing viewpoints both positive and negative, yet lack the direct lived experience of the millennial. In the years to come, millennials will begin to assume leadership spaces currently held by long standing members of the Baby Boomer and Generation X groups.

For over a decade, and as a millennial, I often sat as the youngest in the room or at the decision-making table. I was the voice of millennials often hearing the words that place the millennial at a grave disadvantage. As such, it is always an honor to enlighten others of the strategies when working with millennials. The millennial generation has seen the good, the bad, and the ugly in all shapes and forms. The generation has seen terrorist attacks, bombings, mass shootings, and a global pandemic. The generation has seen celebratory athletic wins, monumental elections, and the Black Lives Matter movement. Additionally, the millennial generation has had a higher access to educational attainment and social integration.

The pages of this book are dedicated to illuminating the paths millennial leaders take on their journey to the upper echelons of leadership. We will examine the challenges they face, the invaluable lessons they learn, and the qualifications they must possess to succeed in a world that never stops evolving.

Leadership is not a solitary endeavor but a collective responsibility. This text is not just for the millennial leader but for anyone in a position to guide, mentor, or influence the leaders of tomorrow. It is a resource for managers, supervisors, and senior executives seeking to navigate the changing tides of the organizational life cycle with wisdom and foresight.

The content herein will traverse a diverse range of topics, from the qualities that define successful millennial leaders to the competencies that set them apart. We will explore transformational leadership, leadership development theory, and the emergence of the "New Age Leadership" paradigm. Moreover, we will address the challenges unique to millennial leadership and provide insights into the vital role succession planning plays in ensuring the continuity of leadership excellence.

This book allows for much narrative, thought, and research surrounding the millennial generation from a global perspective. This text, *Considerations and Characteristics of the Millennial Leader in Today's Global Society* brings together 14 authors and scholars to contribute to a body of work highlighting both easy and challenging considerations and characteristics of leaders in the millennial generation. This text is brought forth in order to create an additional global platform for millennial research as it relates to leadership and competence. Each chapter addresses an aspect of millennial leadership overlooked or often highlighted with controversial viewpoints.

Our intended audience is as diverse as the subject matter itself. This book is tailored to professionals in both the educational and corporate sectors, recognizing that the principles of effective leadership are universal. Whether you are a seasoned executive, a first-time leader, or someone charting a nontraditional leadership route, you will find valuable insights and practical guidance within these pages.

ORGANIZATION OF BOOK

Chapter 1

In the opening chapter of our book, we embark on a journey to comprehend the concept of millennial leadership. We recognize that leadership, a dynamic and challenging field, has evolved over the years. With an increasingly diverse workforce comprising multiple generations, it is imperative to explore how millennial leaders can contribute positively to our global society. Through a qualitative approach and an extensive literature review, this chapter lays the foundation for our exploration of millennial leadership.

Chapter 2

In Chapter 2, we delve into the modern era's complexities, shaped by rapid technological advancements and globalization. Traditional leadership approaches no longer suffice in our fast-paced world. The rise of the millennial generation has transformed leadership across industries. This chapter explores the essential skills and characteristics that enable millennial leaders to excel in this evolving business landscape, shedding light on the challenges and opportunities they face.

Chapter 3

Chapter 3 brings our focus to the millennial workforce, born between 1981 and 1996, who seek a balance between work and life and yearn for continuous learning. We delve into the unique challenges faced by millennials as they enter the workforce, including the generational gap with older leaders. We also examine how their career choices align with their values and the prevalence of the "imposter syndrome" in their lives.

Chapter 4

Chapter 4 explores the perspectives of millennial leaders. We define leadership as a commitment to a purpose with the ability to influence people toward a goal. We examine what leadership means to millennials, highlight exemplar millennial leaders, and uncover their preferences, roles, and contributions. This chapter provides insights into how millennial leaders are reshaping our societal and organizational landscapes.

Chapter 5

Chapter 5 focuses on the ascension phase of millennial leaders. Ascension involves rising to important positions, and this chapter identifies the rationales, opportunities, and principles millennial leaders should consider during this crucial phase. It explores how millennials make choices based on lifestyle and work-life balance, emphasizing their impact on the greater good.

Chapter 6

Chapter 6 examines the unique position of African diasporic millennial leaders in the midst of dual pandemics (race and COVID-19) and technological revolutions. It explores their navigation of multiple enterprises and the impact of Panther Parenting. We delve into Ubuntu-based principles and the narratives of prominent millennial leaders, analyzing their distinctive qualities.

Chapter 7

In Chapter 7, we highlight the importance of mentoring in the development and succession planning of millennial leaders. We discuss how mentoring not only enhances leadership skills but also increases organizational commitment and retention among millennials. This chapter offers insights into mentorship program development, addressing diversity and evolving mentoring formats.

Chapter 8

Chapter 8 delves into the benefits and challenges faced by millennial leaders, particularly in the educational setting. We explore the unique characteristics of millennial leadership and provide examples and solutions to address these challenges. This chapter offers valuable insights for anyone working with millennial leaders.

Chapter 9

Chapter 9 examines the skills millennial leaders need in the digital age. We explore five key themes, including visionary and crisis leadership, inclusivity, resilience, and the ability to communicate and share knowledge. This chapter sheds light on how millennial leaders can lead with purpose and adapt to a rapidly changing world.

Chapter 10

Chapter 10 reviews the effects of positive social psychology interventions on the wellbeing and performance of millennial leaders within organizational contexts. We explore various variables, outcomes, and contexts related to these interventions, highlighting their potential to enhance performance and wellbeing. This chapter underscores the importance of happiness in the workplace for millennial leaders.

Chapter 11

In the final chapter, we focus on millennial business leaders and their unique leadership qualities. Through a comprehensive review of literature and case studies, we analyze how these leaders are reshaping organizations and driving positive change. This chapter provides valuable insights into the transformative power of millennial leadership in today's ever-changing global landscape.

In the midst of unprecedented change and uncertainty, it is our hope that this book will serve as a beacon of knowledge and inspiration for millennial leaders and those who seek to support their growth and development. Together, we will navigate the complexities of leadership in the 21st century and ensure that there are capable hands to sustain our organizations in the years to come.

Tymon M. Graham
TMGraham Consulting, LLC, USA

Acknowledgment

The research surrounding leadership can be thought-provoking, yet still controversial. Notwithstanding, as a millennial I remain undaunted in the work to not only show and prove, but also reach back and assist the next generation. The gravity and breath of this text reaches beyond the educational realm and beyond the boarders of the United States of America. Each chapter written provides for an intentional look at the millennial group in all its facets. I would particularly like to thank the chapter reviewers who spent time reading, evaluating, and providing considerate ideas and helpful recommendations to the work of this text:

July Carrillo

Shakti Chaturvedi

Thea Dirton

Ranson Sifiso Gwala

Velicia Hawkins-Moore

Jasmine K S

Shardul Shankar

Bhavna Taneja

Michael Weaver

I owe much gratitude to and wish to acknowledge those whose scholarly work and practical efforts has provided an avenue for me to navigate and further narrate the millennial ideals on various platforms. The ongoing efforts to keep dialogue to highlight millennial excellence is much appreciated and applauded, for we stand on the shoulder of giants.

I am grateful to Nina Eddinger, Jocelynn Hessler, and everyone at IGA Global for their commitment to making sure this text comes to fruition. I hope that readers will see this text as one that highlights virtuous ideals, international views, genuine discovery, challenges of the millennial leader, and the truths within.

Many thanks to my family, friends, mentors, and colleagues for their knowledge, wisdom, and support of me both personally and professionally. Because of you, I am!

Chapter 1
Millennial Leadership in Global Society and Future Prospects

Neeta Baporikar
https://orcid.org/0000-0003-0676-9913
Namibia University of Science and Technology, Namibia & SP Pune University, India

ABSTRACT

Leadership has always been an interesting but challenging and dynamic area of management studies. Be it the theories on leadership or the evolution of leadership or what makes good leadership, studies are numerous. But with the changing workforce, and organizations having more than four generations at work, it becomes more interesting and challenging to lead this group. Among the existing generations, the millennial generation workforce calls for more studies due to changing patterns of work, culture, technology roles, etc. Hence adopting a qualitative approach with an in-depth literature review; the aim of this chapter is to understand the concept of millennial leadership and the future prospects for millennial leaders to make a positive contribution to global society.

INTRODUCTION

Leadership theories and the academic literature can sometimes seem difficult for practitioners to understand because of complex conceptualizations, obscure terms, and its enormousness (Baporikar, 2023). Yet taken as a whole, the literature makes a great deal of sense and has much to offer. Indeed, the truths are often quite simple,

DOI: 10.4018/978-1-6684-4711-6.ch001

elegant, and straightforward. However, leadership is a process ordinary people use to bring forth the best from themselves and others; it is not reserved for a few charismatic men and women (Kouzes & Posner, 2007). Leadership first requires personal growth that develops through inner self-leadership; then moves outward as the leader influences, guides, supports, and leads others. Individuals ultimately demonstrate leadership through their actions and influence on those around them; however, leadership begins with how an individual develops personally (Baporikar, 2018). Although discussions of leadership have continued for many centuries (Burns, 1978; Hackman & Johnson, 2009; Kouzes & Posner, 2007; Northouse, 2010), the concept has evolved in definition and understanding (Burns, 1978) as researchers' proposed different explanations for how leadership works. The actual success of the leader may be the result of the *leadership style* engaged (Hackman & Johnson, 2009; Northouse, 2010). Leadership style is a consistent pattern of behavior, exhibited by a leader over time, when trying to influence followers, which also affects human resource performance and organizational results (Baporikar, 2021).

Karl Mannheim (1952, as cited in Pilcher, 1994) presented the seminal work on generational theory and created the term *generational cohort*. Mannheim argued that generations emerge when political and historical events create an impact on society. Today's workforce comprises multiple generations, each trying to understand the differences in their perspectives on work, perspectives influenced by events that occurred earlier in their collective lives that contribute to their generational identity (Alsop, 2008; Elam, Stratton, & Gibson, 2007; Kunreuther, Kim, & Rodriguez, 2008; Twenge, 2006). Recent emphasis in the literature on workforce differences related to generational cohorts likely stems from the first occurrence of four generations in the workforce at the same time (Green, 2008; Piktialis, 2007). Only very recently has any interest emerged regarding the impact of generational differences on leadership, as the leadership differences become recognized as one of many diversity issues that leaders face in today's rapidly changing organizations and research also confirms that different generations have different leadership styles (Salahuddin, 2010).

Recent research has indicated there is an organizational impact of generational cohort differences on leaders and leadership (Sessa, Kabacoff, Deal, & Brown, 2007). The current lack of identification and understanding of Millennials as leaders leaves management making assumptions that, if incorrect, could impact the future of their organizations. Despite identified differences in leadership styles for Veterans, Baby Boomers, and Generation Xers (Green, 2007); there is a gap in the corresponding research for millennial leaders (Sessa et al., 2007). With the retirement of Veteran leaders and the beginning of retirement for Baby Boomer leaders, Generation X and Millennials will begin to fill more leadership positions in organizations. Better understanding the leadership style of millennial leaders will help organizations adapt to this group of workers in hiring, motivating, incentivizing, and retaining these future leaders (Piktialis, 2007; Tulgan, 2009). To succeed as future leaders, Millennials need training, mentoring, coaching, and proper placement in their organizations (Baldonado & Spangenburg, 2009; Lowe, Levitt, & Wilson, 2008). The leaders from the millennial generational cohort will be a dominant factor in the workforce in a few years, making it important that today's leaders begin to understand tomorrow's leaders. The leadership styles of Veterans, Baby Boomers, and Generation Xers have been described in the literature (Green, 2007), yet the leadership style of the newest group of leaders, Millennials, is not yet addressed in scholarly literature, due to their recent entry in leadership positions. Therefore, research is needed to understand and describe the leadership style of millennial leaders. Thus the central research question (Creswell & Creswell, 2017) this study addresses is as follows: What is millennial leadership and what are their prospects?

Hence, adopting a qualitative approach with an in-depth literature review the aim of this chapter is to understand the concept of millennial leadership and the future prospects for millennial leaders to make a positive contribution to global society.

LITERATURE REVIEW

Defining Leadership

One of the issues addressed by Yukl (2002) was the search for a universal definition of leadership, given that it was easy to illustrate the act of leading, but difficult to describe leadership. Most definitions of leadership implied that leadership involved intentional influence exerted by one person over another to organize and manage activities and relationships in a group or organization.

Given below are salient definitions from management literature.

- Leadership was described earlier as "power exercised when persons mobilize institutional, political, psychological, and other resources to arouse, engage, and satisfy the motives of followers" (Burns, 1978, p. 18).
- DuBrin (1995) stated that leadership was the "key dynamic force that motivates and coordinates the organization in the accomplishment of its objectives" (p. 2).
- Jacobs and Jaques (1987) described leadership as a process of giving meaningful direction to collective effort, and creating a willing effort to achieve purpose.
- Kouzes and Posner (2007) defined leadership as a relationship between those who aspired to lead and those who chose to follow.

- Yukl (2012) defined *leadership* as "the process of influencing others to understand and agree about what needs to be done, how it can be done effectively, and the process of facilitating individual and collective efforts to accomplish the shared objectives" (p. 7).
- Webb, Bruyere, Halladay, & Walker, (2021), define leadership as "positively influencing others to engage in behaviours that contribute to a shared goal to protect" (p. 3).

Many more definitions discuss leadership in terms of individual traits, leader behavior, interaction patterns, role relationships, follower perceptions, influence over followers, influence on task goals, and influence on organizational culture. But many of these definition differences in the scholarly research may be due to the methodology of investigation and data interpretation (Ashford & Sitkin, 2019; Munley, 2011; Yukl, 1989).

However, the two areas which provide the background for this study are *generational theory* and *leadership theory and practice*. These key bodies of theory are summarized below.

Generational Research

Differences in the beliefs, values, preferences, and attitudes of each generation affect how each generation views leadership (Howe & Strauss, 2000). Thus, generational leadership changes affect organizations. Currently, for instance, Veterans leaving and Baby Boomers retiring at increasing rates create opportunities for Generation Xers and Millennials to move into leadership positions at an accelerating pace (Sessa et al., 2007). As generational shifts take place in the workforce, the attitudes of the individuals in the workforce change (Piktialis, 2007), the expectations of leaders change, and the leaders themselves change. Generational research documents recent changes in the workforce, as organizations shift from primarily rank and hierarchy structures to global, flatter organizations with more employee decision making (France, Leahy, & Parsons, 2009, 2009; Howe & Strauss, 2000; Kunreuther et al., 2008). Changes in leadership styles reflect the generational shift in values from Veterans' and Baby Boomers' loyalty to the organization and desire to succeed, to Generation X's and Millennials' expectation of stimulation, feedback, and free agency. Generational research finds that social and environmental influences have more impact on individuals than other factors such as family or genealogy (Twenge, 2006). Thus, the *generational cohort* is not a new concept, but a more popular area of study in recent years because humans are living longer (Piktialis, 2007). Each age group has its personality, influenced by events that occurred during those individuals' developmental years. As each group reached certain ages, the characteristics of that group influenced their actions. One theory, based on social constructivism, posited that the lifestyles of future generations could be predicted based on observing the cycles of past and current generations (Strauss & Howe, 1991). The social aspects of how generational groups must get along with each other in society have also become a predominant theme in the literature (Lancaster & Stillman, 2002; Zemke, Raines, & Filipczak, 2000).

Generational Differences at Work

Recent research focus on generational differences in the workforce (Howe & Strauss, 2000; Kunreuther et al., 2008; Lancaster & Stillman, 2002) is the result of the Millennial cohort's entry into the workforce over the past 10 years, thereby creating four distinct generations in the workforce (Green, 2007, 2008; Piktialis, 2007):

- *Veterans* (born 1925-1945)
- *Baby Boomers* (1946-1964)
- *Generation X* (1965-1979)
- *Millennial* (1980-2000)

Each generation has different goals and styles (Lancaster & Stillman, 2002). These four generations have unique work ethics, different perspectives on work, distinct and preferred ways of managing and being managed, idiosyncratic styles, and unique ways of viewing such work-world issues as quality, service, and well…just showing up for work (Zemke et al., 2000). Research studies on generational trends in the workforce most often look at issues related to the Veteran generation leaving the workforce (Piktialis, 2007), Baby Boomers beginning to retire (Piktialis, 2007), Generation Xers looking for their role (Haserot, 2007), and Millennials entering the workforce in large numbers with high expectations and excellent educations (Howe & Strauss, 2000). Studies on *leadership preferences* by generation show differences in the type of leadership preferred by the different generational cohorts (Dulin, 2008; Haserot, 2007), based on their values (Green, 2007). Awareness of this unprecedented multigenerational workforce has sparked interest in how Millennials behave in the work environment and interact with other generational groups (Alsop, 2008; Elam et al., 2007; Kunreuther et al., 2008; Twenge, 2006).

Leadership Theory and Practice

Also informing the question of Millennials as leaders is the literature on leaders and leadership. The success of any leader depends on followers' perceptions of the leader's abilities (Hackman & Johnson, 2009; Kouzes & Posner, 2007). Identifying the four most important qualities they seek in a leader, followers want a leader to be honest, forward looking, inspiring, and competent (Kouzes & Posner, 2007). Together these qualities, excluding forward looking, comprise credibility, which is the foundation of leadership in admired leaders (Kouzes & Posner, 2007). The same generational beliefs, values, preferences, and attitudes that affect other aspects of performance will affect both leaders' and followers' views and perceptions (Howe & Strauss, 2000). Therefore, context is an important aspect of leadership (Green, 2007) that causes individuals to interpret the actions of leaders relative to their own perceptions, influenced by their generational cohort (Bell, 2008).

Although there is no single, established definition of leadership, there are many studies on different aspects of leadership. Understanding leadership and individual leaders' approaches often starts with an assessment of leaders' attributes, such as intelligence, communication skills, perseverance, motivation, risk taking, perspective, integrity, self-confidence, adaptability, positive attitude, and responsibility. Differences in beliefs, values, preferences, and attitudes of generational cohorts influence how each generational cohort views leadership (France et al., 2009; Howe & Strauss, 2000), which manifests through different leadership styles (Salahuddin, 2010; Zemke et al., 2000).

Leadership style is the preferred method of influencing others toward accomplishing goals (Kruglanski, Pierro, & Higgins, 2007). Descriptions of leadership style include terms such as *autocratic, charismatic, democratic* or *participatory, laissezfaire, servant,* and/or *transformational* (Bolman & Deal, 2003; Gardner, 1990). *Situational leadership* refers to the use of several styles at different times, invoked by a leader based on the specific situation (Bolman & Deal, 2003). Regardless of the leadership style, leaders must engage and inspire those they lead and serve, thus creating an organizational culture and climate that promotes teamwork and collaboration amid the challenges and opportunities for the multigenerational workforce in organizations.

Millennials are entering the workforce during a time of increased worker diversity (Kunreuther et al., 2008), a trend influenced by globalization and the presence of more women and minorities in the workforce (Tulgan, 2009; Zemke et al., 2000); yet generational differences are often overlooked as a diversity factor (Arsenault, 2004). At the same time, organizations are becoming flatter and more employee-driven (Arsenault, 2004; Green, 2008). As a result of these changes, leadership in organizations is changing from the hierarchical approach used by Veterans (Crumpacker & Crumpacker, 2007) to a more collaborative approach preferred by Baby Boomers and Generation Xers (Green, 2007). However, a gap remains in the literature in identifying a defining leadership style for Millennials as a cohort (Dulin, 2008; Sessa et al., 2007; Tulgan, 2004).

The continued lack of knowledge about how the Millennial cohort describes themselves as leaders (Dulin, 2008) makes it difficult to mentor and train Millennials as they advance in the workforce, which then prevents Millennial leaders from meeting their own expectations as leaders (Martin & Tulgan, 2001). Research in the literature documents specific leadership styles for each of the three older generational cohorts currently in the workforce (Crumpacker & Crumpacker, 2007; Green, 2007). Yet no similar research identifies a specific leadership style of Millennials (Dulin, 2008; Sessa et al., 2007; Tulgan, 2004).

UNDERSTANDING MILLENNIAL LEADERSHIP IN GLOBAL SOCIETY

The term *Millennial* first appeared in the work of two later generational theorists, Strauss and Howe (1991), who contributed to the explanations of what generations were, how they interacted, and history's role in defining and influencing future generations. Each generation lives through a shared set of social and historical events that help form attitudes and beliefs around that generation's ideas related to their life experiences (Dulin, 2008; Strauss & Howe, 1991). Because of their common experiences, generational cohorts often bring shared values, beliefs, preferences, and attitudes to work (Dulin, 2008; Howe & Strauss, 2000; Lancaster & Stillman, 2002; Martin & Tulgan, 2001; Zemke et al., 2000). As an interdisciplinary study, generational theory relates to the fields of history, sociology, psychology, economics, anthropology, biology, and many other disciplines. Generational theory defines generations and ties them to historical events (Johnson, & Lopes, 2008).

Thus, *Millennials* refer to those born between 1980 and 2000 who are entering the workforce as the most optimistic, educated generational cohort group (Zemke et al., 2000), already taking many organizations by surprise as employers look for ways to attract and retain this talent pool (Howe & Strauss, 2000; Martin & Tulgan, 2001). These individuals, who have become accustomed to stepping up to leadership positions in school, volunteer organizations, and in their part-time jobs, enter the workforce with high expectations and a desire to make a difference (Tulgan, 2009). Yet, the current members of the organizations into which these young people are stepping are questioning these newcomers as future leaders and how they fit into the leadership roles to which they aspire (Martin & Tulgan, 2001). The Millennial generation will have a marked impact on organizations as the mix of generations in the workforce changes, and Millennials become prominent in the workforce in numbers even larger than the Baby Boom generation that raised them. The shift in generational cohorts affects the dynamics of the workforce (Crumpacker & Crumpacker, 2007). The resulting change in generational mix is a diversity factor and an influence on leadership that is often overlooked (Arsenault, 2004; Sessa et al., 2007). Because the older generations have been in the workforce longer, data are available on their leadership styles; but with Millennials only recently entering the workforce, there is a need for research identifying leadership styles of their generational cohort, as identified by Arsenault (2004) and Dulin (2008).

Millennials have started their jobs as the most optimistic, eager, enthusiastic group of workers to enter the workforce (Elam et al., 2007; Howe & Strauss, 2000; Tulgan, 2009). They are graduating from college in large numbers each year as the best-educated generation (Zemke et al., 2000) with résumés listing part-time jobs, internships, community-service work, and leadership positions in school organizations (Alsop, 2008). They are ambitious, having grown up in a child-centered environment, at home in a world dominated by technology and instant gratification, influenced by their Baby Boomer parents (Elam et al., 2007; Howe & Strauss, 2000). They are willing to work hard and expect immediate gratification and quick advancement in return (Tulgan, 2009).

Characteristics of Millennials

The Millennial Generation are individuals born between 1980 and 2000 (Jefferies & Hunte, 2003). This generation has lived with technology from an early age (Tapscott, 2009). The most watched-over generation in our history (Jefferies & Hunte, 2003), they respect the rules and accept authority, are smart, and are optimistic about the future (Alsop, 2008; Zemke et al., 2000). The Millennial cohort is a group with worldwide impact because of the availability of technology and communications, and more freedom and access to move across borders and travel than prior generations. Descriptions of this generation include optimistic, street smart, civically responsible, social, and achievement oriented (Jefferies & Hunte, 2003; Lancaster & Stillman, 2002; Tulgan, 2009).

Generational profiles are cyclical and tend to be repeated since the 17th century (Howe & Strauss, 2000). Because of these generational patterns, the Millennial generation resembles the Veteran generation in many ways, such as moral values, preference for love and respect over money, and a return to etiquette and manners (Zemke et al., 2000). Howe and Strauss (2000) referred to both Veteran and Millennial generations as *hero generations*. These two generational groups, considered special, were protected from harm, expected to behave, and pressured to achieve. A generation of this type follows an upheaval in values and culture and a prior generational cohort that appeared to be disappointing (Howe & Strauss, 2000).

Millennials are also technologically literate, good at multitasking, and purposeful (Kyles, 2005). This generation has had more exposure to technology than any previous generation, with access to personal computers and cell phones since early childhood (Lancaster & Stillman, 2002). The Internet has also provided Millennials with the ability to travel virtually. Since many of Millennials' parents had smaller numbers of children and better earnings, they were more committed to rearing Millennials. Parents of some Millennials had a tendency to become overly involved in their children's jobs and personal activities. The way in which parents of Millennials hovered over their children resulted in the introduction of the term *helicopter parents* (Lipkin & Perrymore, 2009). Media reinforced the renewed interest in child nurturing with a return to family-friendly movies in the 1980s (Strauss & Howe, 1991).

Large numbers of Millennials join organizations and volunteer for community service, showing a renewed interest in giving back to the community (Alsop, 2008). The impact of violent events globally, like the terrorist attacks of September 11, 2001, and gang violence (Lancaster & Stillman, 2002) may have helped foster a return of valor and patriotism (Alsop, 2008).

The Millennial generation has a reputation for being open, self-assured, hopeful, well educated, and goal oriented. Millennials have benefited from each of the three older generations, receiving allegiance and trust in organizations from Veterans, confidence and optimism from Baby Boomers, and a healthy dose of skepticism from Generation X (Lancaster & Stillman, 2002). Millennials refocused the allegiance and trust in organizations learned from Veterans to allegiance and trust in relationships. The confidence and optimism they learned from Baby Boomers helped Millennials turn the skepticism they learned from Generation X into an ability to look at the present more realistically than Baby Boomers while still maintaining a positive outlook about the future (Lancaster & Stillman, 2002; Zemke et al., 2000). Millennials have grown up in a diverse, global society and are both tolerant of others and focused on service, with the potential to become the next greatest generation (Strauss & Howe, 1991).

Work Attitudes-Beliefs-Preferences-Values

The Millennials had a significant impact on organizations, primarily because of their different perspective on values, beliefs, preferences, and attitudes about how and where they work. The socialization of Millennials reflected parental nurturing, protection, and praise far greater than any previous generation. Millennial cohort members exhibit confidence and optimism, combined with demands for immediate feedback and nearly continual recognition and value the close relationships they have built with their parents, other family members, and friends, staying in constant contact with them (Zemke et al., 2000).

However, Millennials enter the workforce with high expectations and excellent educations and expect to find satisfying jobs (Alsop, 2008). Millennials want to work in teams, are goal oriented, confident, and service oriented (Elam et al., 2007), which may not be what their bosses expect. They are ambitious, and skilled in the use of technology (Elam et al., 2007; Howe & Strauss, 2000). They are willing to work hard, expecting immediate gratification and quick advancement in return (Tulgan, 2009). This is not always the work environment they enter when they finally find a job where they will be working with Generation Xers, Baby Boomers, and possibly some Veterans who are still in the workforce. They also prefer a polite relationship with authority. Like leaders who pull people together. Believe in collective action and a will to get things changed.

As individuals become leaders over time and through experience, they develop as leaders through observation of other leaders, including role models, feedback, and practice (Ancona, 2010). Good leaders learn to identify their own goals, values, and ambitions, becoming self-aware and capable of self-leadership (Kouzes & Posner, 2007; 2000; 2017).

PROSPECTS FOR MILLENNIAL LEADERS

Credibility is the foundation of effective leadership; people want leaders who are honest, forward looking, competent, and inspiring (Kouzes & Posner, 2007). Leadership is a process by which an individual influences others to accomplish a stated objective while directing the organization in a more cohesive and coherent way. Leaders accomplish this by applying leadership attributes, such as visioning, personal mastery, self-awareness, interpersonal skills, encouraging the heart, knowledge and skills, positive emotions, creating followership, and stewardship (Kouzes & Posner, 2007; Senge, 2017). Nevertheless, when people are deciding if they respect a person as a leader, they do not think about the leader's attributes; more likely, they observe that person's actions, to learn who that person really is. An individual uses observation to tell if a person is an honorable and trusted leader or a self-serving person who misuses authority to look good and gain promotion (Kouzes & Posner, 2007). Self-serving leaders are not as effective because their employees do not respect them, and will obey them, rather than follow them (Allio, 2007). Good leadership is based on honorable character and selfless service to one's organization (Kouzes & Posner, 2007).

Role Models for Leaders

Role models are often key factors in the successful development of young, aspiring leaders (Singh, Vinnicombe, & James, 2006). Although the developing leader may not personally know the role model, the idealization of having similar beliefs and preferences makes the developing individual look to the role model as an example (Gibson, 2003) and influences the choices that individuals make (Morrisette & Schraeder, 2010). Individuals also identify negative role models, whom they learn to avoid emulating (Gibson, 2003). Regardless of the intent of the role-model target, role models develop from the perceptions of the individual. The simple act of identification makes a person a role model, whatever the role model's actions and the appeal of a role model is the individual's desire to enhance their similarity, because he or she represents a vision the individual desires to attain. By providing an example of valued goals, role models help individuals define and develop their self-concepts (Gibson, 2003).

The way a person behaves as a leader differs by generational cohort in a similar manner to generational leadership style preferences (Hackman & Johnson, 2009).

Millennials show a dedication to teamwork like Baby Boomers, the can-do attitude of Veterans, and the technological skill of the Generation Xers (Hackman & Johnson, 2009). However, their defining leadership style as a group has not been identified in the literature. Two factors that contributed to the minimal amount of research on workers from this generation in the literature were the tendency to study full-time workers in larger organizations, thus overlooking younger, often part-time workers (Dulin, 2008; Loughlin & Barling, 2001); and the focus of most generational differences studies on family influence rather than on work-related influences of the younger work group (Sessa et al., 2007).

LEADERSHIP VIEWS OF MILLENNIALS

Millennial employees are very high tech but they want personal relationships with their colleagues. They prefer leaders who are mentors and are willing to guide them, yet at the same time are willing to listen to them (Dulin, 2008). Millennials are accustomed to the participative relationship they had and still have with their parents (Hicks & Hicks, 1999. Hence, their preferred leadership values include trust, passion, social consciousness, collaboration, doing the right thing, doing what they say, and continuous learning (Dulin, 2008), as depicted in Figure 1, followed by a discussion.

- **Passion:** According to millennial generation leaders must have passion to lead and that millennial leaders are passionate. There is also need of passion as it would be difficult to lead without a passion for the purpose, goal, or vision that was to be accomplished. Hence, millennial leaders feel passion drives leaders and they as leaders must be passionate to inspire others to follow them. They also want to feel passionate about the organizations in which they are leading others.
- **Trust:** Trust and honesty is essential to be an effective leader. Hence, trust is important in a millennial leader's view of a leader. They want to have confidence in the sincerity of the relationship and the authenticity of the

Figure 1. Millennial preferred leadership values
Source: Self-Developed

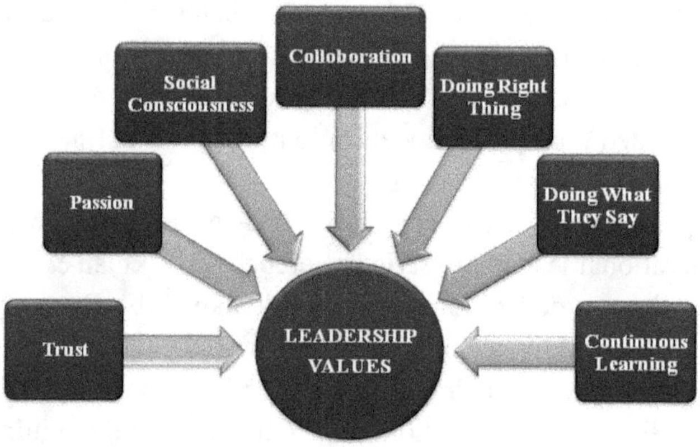

leader. If a person in a leadership role cannot be trusted, he or she will not maintain the support of his or her followers for long and consequently will not be able to accomplish his or her goals. Further, the relationship of trust has to be reciprocal because leaders need to know they can trust their followers and count on them for their support.

- **Collaboration:** Employees in general and more so in knowledge driven economy prefer in leaders and leadership an involving collaboration and sharing of knowledge. There is the importance of using networking and social media as part of collaborative work efforts when needed to research information or request immediate feedback. This includes the value of including the ideas of others, especially their peers. Millennial leaders expect to be invited to contribute their ideas and feel discounted when they are not given an opportunity to state their views. Additionally, many feel that with the rising magnitude of social media as tools for collaboration and the advancements in technology have changed the way their generation communicates, such as networking within and outside the organization for additional ideas, use of e-mail, blogging, Facebook, Twitter, YouTube and hence there is the need to be adaptable and allow for role changes during collaboration.
- **Social consciousness:** Leadership is about others and the greater good, not personal interests, in the view of millennial leaders. Millennial leaders admire leaders who have social interests and respect for others more so than those who are successful for what they have accomplished. Different aspects of social consciousness include volunteerism on a local level, global efforts

for fund raising and volunteerism, mentoring youth, servant leadership and developing young leaders.

- **Leaders do the right thing:** In general there is an expectation that leaders *do the right thing*, often adding *for the right reasons*. Millennial are absolute in their view that about leaders doing the right thing, and they also feel that leaders from previous generations had sometimes not done the right things, or had done what they thought was right at the time, but that it later became evident that some actions of leaders from previous generations were for the wrong reasons. Some reasons for leaders doing the right thing were because the leader had the right values; the leader was setting an example or showing others how to do.
- **Leaders do what they say:** Several studies in leadership have discussed the importance of seeing leaders carry through on their commitments, rather than saying they would do something then not doing so. Consistency in action is important aspects of leadership for several reasons like leaders need to keep their commitments to be respected, leaders should be able and willing to do things they talk about doing and leaders who are not showing followers how to make good choices are not good enough for leading.
- **Continuous learning:** Essential as many of the millennial were young and leadership was new to them and also being a good leader always involves learning and evolving. Continuous learning is a hallmark of a good leader and this means requires constantly learning new skills and adapting to situations as being a leader requires experience, mentors are valuable in assisting with learning, being a good leader is an evolutionary process, learning involves continuous improvement and learning involves others, including elders, mentors, and peers.

Other salient values include:

- **Leadership is about inspiring others:** Millennial leaders expect to be inspired by their leaders, and believe that leading others to accomplish a goal or a vision requires motivating and inspiring others.
- **Leading by example:** Millennial leaders expect leaders to set the example of what they expect from their followers and to demonstrate how to be a good leader by their own actions.
- **Leaders are selfless and look out for the good of others:** Millennial leaders admire leaders who have an interest in social responsibility and respect for others more than those who are just successful for what they have accomplished personally. Millennials also expect their leaders to invest in helping them through mentoring and guidance; however, they do not want to be micromanaged or told exactly what to do.

Thus it is clear that millennial have a style of leadership that is different from previous generational cohorts as collaborative, inclusive, and passionate, believe in doing the right thing, sharing responsibility, participative, casual, creative, innovative, rely on technology and social media for information and networking.

FUTURE AREAS FOR RESEARCH

This research is a snapshot in time, not a longitudinal study. Although generational beliefs and attitudes are based on events that occur at an earlier development period, it is possible that, over time, Millennials could have different views on leadership. There could be potential benefits of longitudinal research on generational and Millennials to understand any changes in their leadership style as they gain more experience as leaders. There are opportunities for research with a focus in each of these areas based on region, culture ethnicity and location. In recent years, the number of women graduating from college and moving into professional roles has outpaced that of men. A study that compares the leadership styles of female and male millennial leaders for possible leadership style differences could add valuable information to the body of knowledge on Millennials as leaders, as well as gender differences in leadership styles.

Recent initial research in the literature indicates that ethnic/racial diversity does not impact the results of Millennials' leadership style (Bordas, 2012). Additional research in this area would also be valuable, especially in the areas of beliefs, values, preferences, and attitudes. Millennial leaders were often impacted by divorce during their formative years and as a result many of them lived in single-parent or blended families. The changing relationship with parents and siblings often led to different family dynamics that changed their views of leadership within the family and impacted the millennial generation's priorities when looking at their beliefs and values (Crumpacker & Crumpacker, 2007). Future research on how divorce and family dynamics impacted Millennials' leadership style and their commitment to take on leadership roles at work may add valuable insight into how their generation will perform as leaders in organizations.

Coaches as role models during the millennial leaders' formative years warrant research. The role of mentors for Millennials would contribute valuable knowledge on the expectations of these leaders. Millennials expect to have multiple mentors and to have them available as advisors to guide them with decision making. A good understanding of these expectations would help with the knowledge gap and preparation for the leaders and their organizations. Another topic for future research closely related to leadership training would be to explore how Millennials learn. Millennials are technology oriented, skilled at multitasking, and known for their short attention spans (Tapscott, 2009). One aspect of Millennials' lack of leadership training may be the lack of training presented in a format that interests them or is suited to their learning styles and/or ability to learn. This warrants further research considering multimedia, collaborative, interactive, on-demand, flexible, and other types of training targeted to Millennials. The role of religion as a factor in leadership may be another area for future research. Millennials often cited servant leaders as examples of role models and made references to Gods as role models or as inspiring them. The changing view of work-life balance deserves future research.

SOLUTIONS AND RECOMMENDATIONS

Millennials, the generation that spans 1981 to 2000 have created quite a buzz in the workforce and various professions over the past two decades. Much attention is focused on their attributes, how to retain them, and how they seem to want to change the rules. This group of individuals is described as goal-oriented, open to change, and innovative. However, they're also perceived as possessing a sense of entitlement and being willing to hop from one job to next. As of 2022, Millennials are the largest generation within workforce, yet few of them are in leadership roles. As the older members of this cohort begin to take the reins and develop interest in moving into upper leadership positions, differences must be put aside and strategies for cohesiveness among generations encouraged reducing the challenges and enhancing the opportunities for effective Millennials leadership. For that to happen some of the recommendations and solutions include:

Promote Collaboration and Shared Responsibility

Providing Millennials with opportunities to enter into leadership roles, introducing them to professional organizations, and explaining the local and national impact these roles play are critical. However, it requires collaboration among the generations. Not only must Millennials be open to understanding past, but older generations must be willing to re-evaluate established practices, be open to new viewpoints, and offer guidance to those just beginning their leadership journeys. More organizations are addressing this issue by offering professional development resources as well as implementing leadership and mentoring programs to get them connected early. Both current leaders and Millennials have important roles to play in ensuring this generation has a seat and voice at the leadership table as regardless of the generation, all leaders have a responsibility to help shape the future of the profession. Organizations success has always been a team effort when it comes to hard reality. There is a need to use that teamwork mentality to promote the growth of generations to come. As nations seek to develop leadership becomes more and more crucial and hence, there should be a sense of duty to safeguarding leadership role as advocates for the rights of those who can't speak for themselves. Using collaboration with shared responsibility culture there is needed to ensure that the youngest voices of any profession are stronger and louder than previous generations. It is more than a choice; it's a commitment to the legacy of leading future generations.

Suggestions to Leaders Developing Millennials

Millennials must lean in and find their place at the leadership table, and all generations must be engaged and willing to collaborate to preserve the gains that have been made over the past several decades. Some tips for success when developing Millennials within your organization.

- Identify what they're passionate about and help facilitate it.
- Provide autonomy.
- Engage in mentorship.
- Embrace the differences.

Suggestions to Millennials Interested in Leadership

Although being a millennial leader has its challenges, much can be gained from pursuing these positions. You'll not only begin to understand professions and workplace on a global level, you'll also be presented with opportunities to have a voice in changes being made within the profession. Some tips for success for Millennials when interested in leadership.

- Embrace rejection.
- Establish a circle of mentors.
- Engage the generations as you lead.
- Take advantage of all learning opportunities.

CONCLUSION

Most Millennial leaders are casual in their attitude and approach to work, collaborative and inclusive, and rely on technology including social media for access to information and networking with peers. Truth and integrity are important values to millennial leaders, in addition to a desire for leaders to exhibit good moral values. Work life balance and the relationship of work to family, friends, and volunteerism are also key concerns for the millennial generation. Millennial leaders value the wisdom of experience and guidance from mentors. To be successful as leaders, they expect to have multiple mentors easily accessible and depend on their mentors for guidance. Millennial leaders' leadership development was influenced by their early leadership experiences, leadership training, observing negative examples, and learning from experience. Early leadership experiences involved family, school, or sports situations where a family member, teacher, or coach had an impact on the individual view of a leader.

REFERENCES

Allio, R. (2007). Bad leaders: How they get that way and what to do about them. *Strategy and Leadership*, *35*(3), 12–17. doi:10.1108/10878570710745785

Alsop, R. (2008). *The trophy kids grow up: How the millennial generation is shaking up the workplace*. Jossey-Bass.

Arsenault, P. M. (2004). Validating generational differences: A legitimate diversity and leadership issue. *Leadership and Organization Development Journal*, *25*(1/2), 124–141. doi:10.1108/01437730410521813

Ashford, S. J., & Sitkin, S. B. (2019). From problems to progress: A dialogue on prevailing issues in leadership research. *The Leadership Quarterly*, *30*(4), 454–460. doi:10.1016/j.leaqua.2019.01.003

Baldonado, A., & Spangenburg, J. (2009). Leadership and the future: Gen Y workers and two-factor theory. *The Journal of American Academy of Business, Cambridge*, *15*(1), 99–103.

Baporikar, N. (Ed.). (2018). *Global Practices in Knowledge Management for Societal and Organizational Development*. IGI Global. doi:10.4018/978-1-5225-3009-1

Baporikar, N. (2021). Human Resource Management for Managing Cultural Diversity. In I. Management Association (Ed.), Research Anthology on Empowering Marginalized Communities and Mitigating Racism and Discrimination (pp. 976-1004). IGI Global. doi:10.4018/978-1-7998-8547-4.ch046

Baporikar, N. (Ed.). (2023). *Leadership and Governance for Sustainability*. IGI Global. doi:10.4018/978-1-6684-9711-1

Bell, E. (2008). Exploring employee perception of the work environment along generational lines. *Performance Improvement*, *47*(9), 35–45. doi:10.1002/pfi.20032

Bolman, L. G., & Deal, T. E. (2003). *Reframing organizations: Artistry, choice, and leadership* (3rd ed.). Jossey-Bass.

Bordas, J. (2012). *Salsa, soul, and spirit: Leadership for a multicultural age* (2nd ed.). Berrett-Koehler.

Burns, J. M. (1978). *Leadership*. Harper & Row.

Creswell, J. W., & Creswell, J. D. (2017). *Research design: Qualitative, quantitative, and mixed methods approaches*. Sage publications.

Crumpacker, M., & Crumpacker, J. (2007). Succession planning and generational stereotypes: Should HR consider age-based values and attitudes a relevant factor or a passing fad? *Public Personnel Management, 36*(4), 349–369. doi:10.1177/009102600703600405

DuBrin, A. J. (1995). *Leadership: Research findings, practice, skills*. Houghton Mifflin.

Dulin, L. (2008). Leadership preferences of a generation Y cohort: A mixed-methods investigation. *Journal of Leadership Studies, 2*(1), 43–59. doi:10.1002/jls.20045

Elam, C., Stratton, T., & Gibson, D. (2007). Welcoming a new generation to college: The millennial students. *Journal of College Admission, 195*, 20–25.

France, D., Leahy, M., & Parsons, M. (2009). Attracting, developing, and retaining talent. *Research Technology Management, 52*(6), 33–44. doi:10.1080/08956308.2009.11657598

Gardner, J. W. (1990). *On leadership*. The Free Press.

Gibson, D. E. (2003). Developing the professional self-concept: Role model construals in early, middle, and late career stages. *Organization Science, 14*(5), 591–610. doi:10.1287/orsc.14.5.591.16767

Green, D. (2007). Leading a postmodern workforce. *Academy of Strategic Management Journal, 6*, 15–26.

Green, D. (2008). Value transformation in 21st century organizations. *Journal of Organizational Culture. Communication and Conflict, 12*(2), 95–102.

Hackman, M., & Johnson, C. (2009). *Leadership: A communication perspective* (5th ed.). Waveland Press.

Haserot, P. (2007). Generational transformation, leadership, development, and much more. *Of Counsel, 26*(7), 5-9.

Hicks, R., & Hicks, K. (1999). *Boomers, Xers, and other strangers*. Tyndale House.

Howe, N., & Strauss, W. (2000). *Millennials rising: The next great generation*. Random House.

Jacobs, T., & Jaques, E. (1987). Leadership in complex systems. In J. Zeider (Ed.), *Human productivity enhancement: Organizations, personnel, and decision making* (Vol. 2, pp. 7–65). Praeger.

Jefferies, F. L., & Hunte, T. L. (2003). Generations and motivation: A connection worth making. *Journal of Behavioral and Applied Management*, *6*(1), 37–70.

Johnson, J. A., & Lopes, J. (2008). The intergenerational workforce, revisited. *Organization Development Journal*, *26*(1), 31–36.

Kouzes, J. M., & Posner, B. Z. (2007). *The leadership challenge* (4th ed.). Jossey-Bass.

Kruglanski, A., Pierro, A., & Higgins, E. (2007). Regulatory mode and preferred leadership styles: How fit increases job satisfaction. *Basic and Applied Social Psychology*, *29*(2), 137–149. doi:10.1080/01973530701331700

Kyles, D. (2005). Managing your multigenerational workforce. *Strategic Finance*, *87*(6), 52–55.

Lancaster, L., & Stillman, D. (2002). *When generations collide: Who they are. Why they clash. How to solve the generational puzzle at work*. Harper Collins.

Lipkin, N. A., & Perrymore, A. J. (2009). *Y in the workplace: Managing the "me first" generation*. The Career Press.

Loughlin, C., & Barling, J. (2001). Young workers' work values, attitudes, and behaviors. *Journal of Occupational and Organizational Psychology*, *74*(4), 543–559. doi:10.1348/096317901167514

Lowe, D., Levitt, K., & Wilson, T. (2008). Solutions for retaining generation Y employees in the workplace. *Business Renaissance Quarterly*, *3*(3), 43–57.

Martin, A. (2006). The demise of the heroic leader. *Leader to Leader*, *42*, 55–56.

Martin, C., & Tulgan, B. (2001). *Managing generation Y: Global citizens born in the late seventies and early eighties*. HRD Press.

Morrisette, S., & Schraeder, M. (2010). Leadership development approaches. *Journal for Quality and Participation*, *32*(4), 32–34.

Munley, A. E. (2011). Culture differences in leadership. *The IUP Journal of Soft Skills*, *5*(1).

Northouse, P. (2010). *Leadership theory and practice* (5th ed.). Sage.

Northouse, P. G. (2021). *Leadership: Theory and practice*. Sage publications.

Piktialis, D. (2007). Adaptations to an aging workforce: Innovative responses by the corporate sector. *Generations (San Francisco, Calif.)*, *31*(1), 76–82.

Pilcher, J. (1994). Mannheim's sociology of generations: An undervalued legacy. *The British Journal of Sociology*, *45*(3), 481–494. doi:10.2307/591659

Salahuddin, M. (2010). Generational differences impact on leadership style and organizational success. *Journal of Diversity Management*, *5*(2), 1–6. doi:10.19030/jdm.v5i2.805

Senge, P. (2000). The leadership of profound change. *SPC Ink*, 1-3.

Senge, P. M. (2017). The leaders' new work: Building learning organizations. In *Leadership perspectives* (pp. 51–67). Routledge. doi:10.4324/9781315250601-6

Sessa, V. I., Kabacoff, R. I., Deal, J., & Brown, H. (2007). Generational differences in leader values and leadership behaviors. *The Psychologist Manager Journal*, *10*(1), 47–74. doi:10.1080/10887150709336612

Singh, V., Vinnicombe, S., & James, K. (2006). Constructing a professional identity: How young female managers use role model. *Women in Management Review*, *26*(1), 67–81. doi:10.1108/09649420610643420

Strauss, W., & Howe, N. (1991). *Generations: The history of America's future, 1584 to2069*. William Morrow.

Tapscott, D. (2009). *Grown up digital: How the net generation is changing your world*. McGraw-Hill.

Tulgan, B. (2009). *Not everyone gets a trophy: How to manage Generation Y*. Jossey-Bass.

Twenge, J. (2006). *Generation me: Why today's young Americans are more confident, assertive, entitled – and more miserable than ever before*. Free Press.

Webb, S. A., Bruyere, B., Halladay, M., & Walker, S. (2021). A framework for conceptualizing leadership in conservation. *Oryx*, 1–7.

Yukl, G. (1989). Managerial leadership: A review of theory and research. *Journal of Management*, *15*(2), 251–290. doi:10.1177/014920638901500207

Yukl, G. (2012). Effective leadership behavior: What we know and what questions need more attention. *The Academy of Management Perspectives*, *26*(4), 66–85. doi:10.5465/amp.2012.0088

Zemke, R., Raines, C., & Filipczak, B. (2000). *Generations at work: Managing the clash of veterans, boomers, Xers, and nexters in your workplace*. AMA.

KEY TERMS AND DEFINITIONS

Baby Boomers: Individuals born after World War II between 1946 and 1964, who grew up in an era of opportunity, progress, and optimism; also referred to as Boomers.

Generational Cohort: A collection of people in a delineated population, who experience the same significant historical and social events in a given period of time, occurring between the ages of 5 and 18, that influence and define them.

Generational Differences: The unique values and behaviors that characterize distinct generational cohorts.

Generation X: Individuals born between 1965 and 1979, which grew up in the shadow of the Baby Boomers, technologically savvy, raised in the age of dual-career families; also referred to as the 13th Generation, Baby Busters, Post-Boomers, and the Lost Generation.

Leader: One who influences a group of individuals to achieve a common goal in an organizational position directly and personally responsible for leading individual direct reports, a project, a team, and/or a function and managing budget.

Leadership: An ability to influence followers to adjust their behavior as they encounter receptiveness or opposition from the leader in various situations. The perception that an individual is leading others and is able to self-identify as a leader may be subject to the individual's own view of the role of a leader.

Leadership Style: A leader's preferred manner and exhibited approach used to provide direction, accomplish goals, and engage, motivate, and inspire followers, which may be self-described.

Millennials: Individuals born between 1980 and 2000, who have always had computer technology available and grew up in a global world of multitasking, text messaging, and instant messaging; also referred to as Generation Y, Echo Boomers, Nexters, Internet Generation, Generation Next, Generation Rx), and Trophy Kids because everyone in their generation was rewarded just for participating.

Veterans: Individuals born between 1925 and 1945, which grew up influenced by the Great Depression and World War II; also referred to as the Silent Generation, Traditionalists, and the WW II Generation.

Chapter 2
Thriving in Leadership:
Essential Skills for the Millennial Generation

Jasmine K. S.
https://orcid.org/0000-0002-8251-4261
R.V. College of Engineering, India

ABSTRACT

The modern era is characterized by rapid technological advancements, globalization, and societal changes. In today's fast-paced and constantly changing world, traditional leadership approaches are often insufficient to navigate the complexities of the modern business landscape. In recent years, the rise of the millennial generation has transformed the landscape of leadership in various industries. The millennial generation has emerged as a dynamic force reshaping the global workforce and leadership landscape. As this generation continues to move into leadership roles, there is a growing need to identify and understand the essential skills and characteristics that enable them to thrive in these positions. This chapter explores the key skills and characteristics required for millennials to excel as leaders, highlighting the unique challenges and opportunities they face in today's rapidly evolving business environment.

INTRODUCTION

As the Millennial generation continues to ascend into positions of leadership, the world of business and organizations undergoes a transformation unlike anything witnessed before. Born between the early 1980s and the mid-1990s, Millennials bring forth a unique set of perspectives, values, and technological prowess that

DOI: 10.4018/978-1-6684-4711-6.ch002

distinguishes them from their predecessors. To thrive in leadership roles, this dynamic generation must embrace and cultivate a distinct set of essential skills that cater to the demands and challenges of the modern professional landscape.

In this chapter, we delve into the key skills and attributes that are crucial for Millennials seeking to excel as leaders. Drawing from extensive research and industry insights, we shed light on the distinctive qualities that define effective leadership in the Millennial era. Moreover, we explore how these skills align with the ever-evolving expectations of employees, customers, and stakeholders. With their reputation for being tech-savvy, collaborative, and socially conscious, Millennials are poised to make a lasting impact on the world of leadership. However, their success hinges on developing and honing a specific set of skills that transcend traditional management approaches. By embracing innovative strategies, harnessing their inherent strengths, and adapting to the fast-paced nature of today's business environment, Millennial leaders can navigate complex challenges and drive meaningful change.

There are nine essential skills that empower Millennial leaders to thrive in their roles such as cultivating effective communication, fostering a diverse and inclusive work culture, leveraging digital technologies, embracing continuous learning, and displaying adaptability in the face of uncertainty. By mastering these skills, millennial leaders can inspire their teams, drive innovation, and foster a sense of purpose that resonates with both their employees and the broader society. This chapter can serves as a guide to equip Millennials with the necessary skills and insights to thrive as leaders in the ever-evolving professional landscape. By understanding and embodying the unique attributes that define their generation, Millennials have the opportunity to shape the future of leadership and redefine what it means to lead in the 21st century.

The Chapter will summarize the key findings on the leadership qualities of successful millennial leaders, Implications for organizations and leadership development programs and future trends and the evolving nature of leadership in the millennial era.

BACKGROUND

The existing research works in the area of leadership skills in millennials reveals that millennials possess unique leadership attributes driven by their distinct upbringing and exposure to technology. Many studies agree that millennials are adept at utilizing digital tools, which contributes to their collaborative and adaptable leadership style. Their emphasis on work-life balance and social responsibility has also shaped their leadership approach, focusing on employee empowerment and inclusivity.

The employee job and supervisor satisfaction are predicted by perceived managerial effectiveness in reducing boring aspects of work, as well as perceived managerial support of employee coping mechanisms (Martin et al.,2023). The study provides a systematic testing of ethical leadership and organizational citizenship behavior (OCB) by examining the underlying mechanisms of leader motivation language on ethics through which ethical leadership influences followers' OCB at the team level(Abu et.al,2022). The support for the mediating role of a proactive orientation is linked with authentic leadership to creative performance, above, and beyond the effects of ethical leadership. With a highlight on the moderating role of LMX on the authentic leadership-proactive orientation relationship (Sumanth et al.,2023). There are practically significant differences between millennial leaders and Generation X leaders. Millennial leaders display less leadership behaviour than those of Generation X(Easton, C. and Steyn, R..2023). New hires through effective onboarding programs ensures employees meet their potential, thereby contributing to employer–employee success(Chillakuri,2020). The characteristics of the cohort Generation Z and need to identify strategies for maximizing their talent is critical for the organization to accommodate this cohort group. With Generation Z entering the workforce, the nature of entry-level jobs is changing; hence, HR needs to redesign their strategies to attract and engage Generation Z(Chillakuri, B. and Mahanandia, R.,2018).

The summary of literature survey suggests that millennials excel in transformational leadership, characterized by their ability to inspire and motivate team members to achieve higher performance levels. They exhibit high emotional intelligence, which enables them to navigate complex interpersonal dynamics effectively. However, the survey also highlights certain challenges faced by millennial leaders. Some studies indicate that millennials may struggle with decision-making in high-pressure situations due to a fear of failure or the desire for consensus-driven solutions. Moreover, traditional hierarchical structures may not always align with their preference for a more flexible and horizontal approach to leadership.

A FEW ASPECTS ON CHARACTERISTICS OF A MILLENNIAL LEADER

This section deals with some key aspects defining the millennial generation and their impact on leadership such as technological proficiency, collaborative and inclusive leadership, purpose-driven leadership, Entrepreneurial mindset etc

The Significance of Emotional Intelligence in Millennial Leadership

In the context of millennial leadership, emotional intelligence plays a significant role in their approach to leading and managing teams. Millennials value authentic and genuine relationships. Emotional intelligence allows millennial leaders to build strong connections with their team members by understanding their emotions, empathizing with their experiences, and showing genuine care and support. This fosters trust, loyalty, and a sense of belonging within the team.

Emotional intelligence enables millennial leaders to be strong in the following Areas:

- **Effective communication and conflict resolution:** Emotional intelligence enables millennial leaders to communicate effectively, both verbally and non-verbally. They are attuned to the emotions and reactions of others, allowing them to adjust their communication style accordingly. Millennial leaders with high emotional intelligence can navigate difficult conversations, address conflicts, and provide constructive feedback in a way that promotes understanding and collaboration.
- **Empowering and motivating teams:** Millennial leaders with emotional intelligence understand the individual needs, strengths, and motivations of their team members. They are skilled at providing the necessary support, guidance, and recognition to empower their teams and boost their motivation. By recognizing and addressing the emotional needs of their team, millennial leaders can create a positive and motivating work environment.
- **Resilience and stress management:** Millennial leaders face various challenges and pressures in the fast-paced and competitive work environment. Emotional intelligence helps them develop resilience and effectively manage stress. They are more self-aware of their emotions, understand their triggers, and employ coping mechanisms to handle stress effectively. This ability allows them to lead by example and maintain a composed and positive demeanor during challenging situations.
- **Promoting a positive work culture:** Emotional intelligence contributes to creating a positive work culture within millennial-led organizations. Leaders who exhibit emotional intelligence are adept at managing their own emotions and promoting a positive atmosphere. They encourage open communication, respect diverse perspectives, and prioritize the well-being of their team members. This results in increased employee satisfaction, engagement, and productivity.
- **Adaptability and innovation:** Emotional intelligence allows millennial leaders to be more adaptable and open to change. They can navigate uncertainties, embrace new ideas, and inspire their teams to be innovative. By understanding their own emotions and those of others, they can effectively manage resistance to change and promote a culture of continuous improvement and creativity.

Leveraging Social Media and Digital Platforms for Leadership Influence

Leveraging social media and digital platforms for leadership influence has become increasingly important in today's digital age. These platforms provide millennial leaders with powerful tools to connect with their audience, build their personal brand, and influence others in various ways namely, thought leadership and content creation, Collaborating with influencers and industry peers, Staying updated and leveraging trend etc.

Millennial leaders can leverage their social media presence to amplify the messages and values of their organization. By sharing updates, success stories, and initiatives related to their company, they can extend the reach and impact of the organization's brand and mission. This helps in creating a positive perception of the organization among their followers. Social media platforms also allow millennial leaders to collaborate and network with other influencers and industry peers. By engaging in conversations, participating in online events, or co-creating content, they can expand their reach, gain insights, and leverage the collective influence of their network.

Embracing a Collaborative Leadership Style and Fostering Diverse and Inclusive Teams

Millennial leaders prioritize collaboration and teamwork in their approach to leadership. They value input from their team members, seek diverse perspectives, and emphasize collective decision-making. By fostering a collaborative environment, millennial leaders encourage open communication, knowledge sharing, and cross-functional cooperation. This approach enhances problem-solving, creativity, and efficiency within the team. Collaborative leaders empower their team members, distribute responsibilities, and create a sense of ownership, leading to higher levels of employee satisfaction and engagement (Easton, C., & Steyn, R., 2023).

To embrace a collaborative leadership style and foster diverse and inclusive teams, millennial leaders can:

- Encourage open and transparent communication within the team.
- Establish platforms and processes that promote collaboration and knowledge sharing.
- Actively seek input and feedback from team members and value their contributions.
- Foster a culture of trust, respect, and psychological safety.
- Provide opportunities for professional development and growth.
- Create initiatives that celebrate diversity and promote inclusivity.

- Actively recruit and retain a diverse workforce.
- Address biases and promote fairness in decision-making processes.

Embracing a Growth Mindset and Encouraging Innovation

Millennial leaders prioritize a growth mindset, which is the belief that abilities and intelligence can be developed through effort, practice, and learning. They understand that skills and knowledge can be improved over time and view challenges as opportunities for growth rather than obstacles.

Millennial leaders recognize the importance of innovation in driving organizational success and staying ahead in a rapidly changing world. They encourage their teams to think creatively, challenge the status quo, and explore new ideas and solutions. By creating an environment that supports experimentation, risk-taking, and learning from failures, millennial leaders foster a culture of innovation.

Purpose-Driven Leadership in Millennials by Aligning Personal Values With Organizational Goals

Millennials seek purpose and meaningful work experiences, and as leaders, they prioritize the alignment of their personal values with the mission and values of the organization. By aligning personal values with organizational goals, purpose-driven millennial leaders create a sense of fulfillment and meaning in their leadership roles. They inspire and motivate their teams, make values-based decisions, foster a positive work culture, and contribute to the greater good of the organization and society (Felix et al., 2019).

They communicate the larger purpose behind the work, helping team members understand how their individual contributions align with the organization's mission. This sense of purpose and connection drives engagement, commitment, and high-performance within the team. They also prioritize values-based decision-making. They consider the ethical implications, social impact, and long-term consequences of their decisions. They strive to make choices that align with their personal values and contribute to the greater good of the organization and society as a whole with a focus on creating a positive work culture that reflects their values.

Agile Leadership in a Rapidly Evolving World for Overcoming Resistance and Managing Change Effectively

Agile leaders view change as an opportunity rather than a threat. They understand that in a rapidly evolving world, change is inevitable and necessary for growth and success. They cultivate a mindset that embraces change and encourages their teams to be adaptable and resilient.

To overcome resistance, agile leaders communicate the purpose and rationale behind the change. They ensure that stakeholders understand the need for change and involve them in the decision-making process. By involving individuals affected by the change, leaders can address concerns, gather feedback, and foster a sense of ownership and commitment to the transformation. They encourage a culture of experimentation and learning within their teams. They create a safe space for team members to try new approaches, learn from failures, and iterate on ideas. By fostering a learning mindset, leaders can overcome resistance by demonstrating that change is a continuous process of improvement by empowering their employees to be proactive and take ownership of their work.

Table1 gives a brief idea on various generations' perspectives on millennial leaders.

Table 1. Comparative study on generations and perspectives

People	Audience	Perspectives	Viewpoints	Period of Birth
Traditionalists	Business Owners	Inexperience	Traditionalists may view millennial leaders as inexperienced due to their relatively young age and limited work history.	
Baby Boomers	Co-workers	Ambitious	Baby Boomers may perceive millennial leaders as ambitious and driven to make an impact in their careers.	1945 and 1964
Generation X	Subordinates	Collaboration	Generation X employees may appreciate millennial leaders' collaborative approach, valuing teamwork and open communication.	1965 and 1980
Generation Y/ millennials	Clients	Innovative	Generation Y clients might see millennial leaders as innovative and open to new ideas, bringing fresh perspectives.	1981and 1996
Generation Z	Peers	Tech-savvy	Generation Z peers may admire millennial leaders for their tech-savviness and ability to navigate digital platforms.	1997 and 2012
HR Professionals	Organizational	Diversity and Inclusion	HR professionals recognize millennial leaders' emphasis on diversity, inclusivity, and creating equitable work environments.	
Industry Experts	Consultants	Disruptive	Industry experts may perceive millennial leaders as disruptive forces, challenging traditional norms and driving change.	
Government Officials	Policy Makers	Socially Conscious	Government officials may view millennial leaders as socially conscious and advocates for important societal issues.	
Investors	Financial Industry	Risk-takers	Investors may see millennial leaders as risk-takers, unafraid to pursue innovative ventures and disrupt established markets.	
Academics	Researchers	Work-Life Balance	Academics may appreciate millennial leaders' emphasis on work-life balance and their efforts to redefine work culture.	

Each generation has unique perspectives on leadership shaped by their experiences and values. Traditionalists, born before 1945, often value hierarchical structures and respect for authority. Baby boomers, born between 1945 and 1964, appreciate a strong work ethic and may prefer traditional leadership styles. Generation X, born from 1965 to 1980, seeks independence, work-life balance, and results-oriented leadership. Millennials, born from 1981 to 1996, value collaboration, feedback, and purpose-driven leadership. Generation Z, born from 1997 to 2012, prioritizes diversity, inclusion, and tech-savvy leaders (Berge, Z.L. and Berge, M.B.,2019). Generation Alpha, born from 2013 onwards, is growing up in a highly connected digital world, suggesting even higher expectations for tech-savvy leadership. These perspectives highlight the need for leaders to adapt their styles to effectively engage and lead multi-generational teams.

This mind map shown in Figure 1, illustrates key leadership skills and branches out into more specific skills within each category.

Figure 1. Mind map for leadership skills

Each category can be explained as follows:

- **Communication:** This skill encompasses active listening, empathy, and strategic thinking. Active listening involves attentively listening to others, while empathy allows leaders to understand and relate to their team members. Strategic thinking involves considering long-term goals and developing plans accordingly.
- **Decision-Making:** This category includes skills such as making informed decisions and thinking strategically. Leaders need to make effective

decisions based on available information, considering potential outcomes and consequences.

- **Influencing:** Influencing skills involve negotiation and the ability to persuade others. Leaders must be able to communicate persuasively and negotiate with various stakeholders to achieve desired outcomes.
- **Team Building:** This category emphasizes skills related to building and managing teams. It involves conflict resolution, fostering collaboration, and motivating team members to achieve shared goals (Martin et al., 2023).

The mind map provided here is not exhaustive, and leadership skills can vary depending on the context and situation. However, it provides a starting point for understanding and developing essential leadership skills.

This mind map, Figure 2 focuses on leadership skills that are particularly relevant and valuable for millennial leaders. Here's a brief explanation of each category:

Figure 2. Mind map for leadership skills for millennial leaders

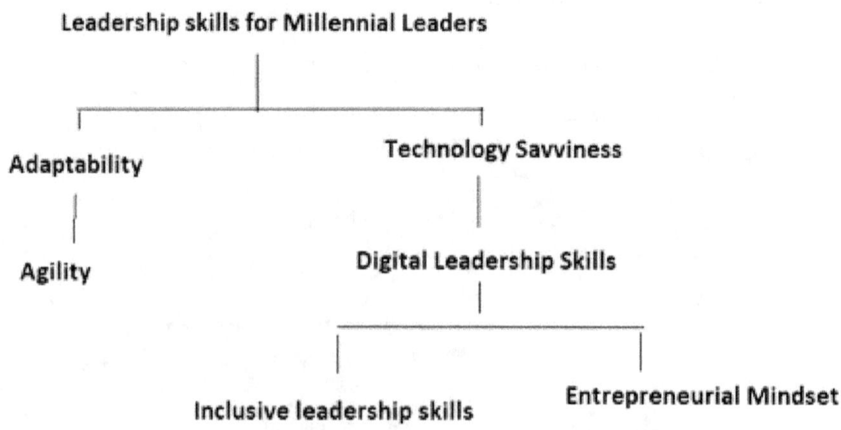

- **Adaptability:** Millennial leaders should possess the ability to adapt quickly to changing circumstances, embrace innovation, and navigate uncertainty with resilience.
- **Agility:** This skill involves being flexible, open to new ideas, and responsive to market dynamics. Millennial leaders should be able to quickly adjust their strategies and approaches to meet evolving business needs.
- **Technology Savviness:** Given their familiarity with technology, millennial leaders should leverage their digital skills to lead effectively in a tech-driven world. This includes being proficient in utilizing digital

tools, understanding emerging technologies, and promoting digital transformation within their organizations.

- **Inclusive Leadership:** Millennial leaders should emphasize inclusivity and diversity, creating an environment where all team members feel valued, respected, and included. This involves fostering a culture of belonging and leveraging diverse perspectives for better decision-making and innovation.
- **Entrepreneurial Mindset:** Millennial leaders often possess an entrepreneurial mindset characterized by a willingness to take calculated risks, think outside the box, and drive innovation. This mindset encourages creativity, experimentation, and a proactive approach to problem-solving (Felix et al., 2019).

The block diagram, Figure 3 has three main sections representing different categories of leadership skills: Personal Skills, Interpersonal Skills, and Strategic Skills. Each section consists of several blocks representing specific skills within that category.

Figure 3. Block diagram demonstrate diverse leadership skill set for millennial leaders

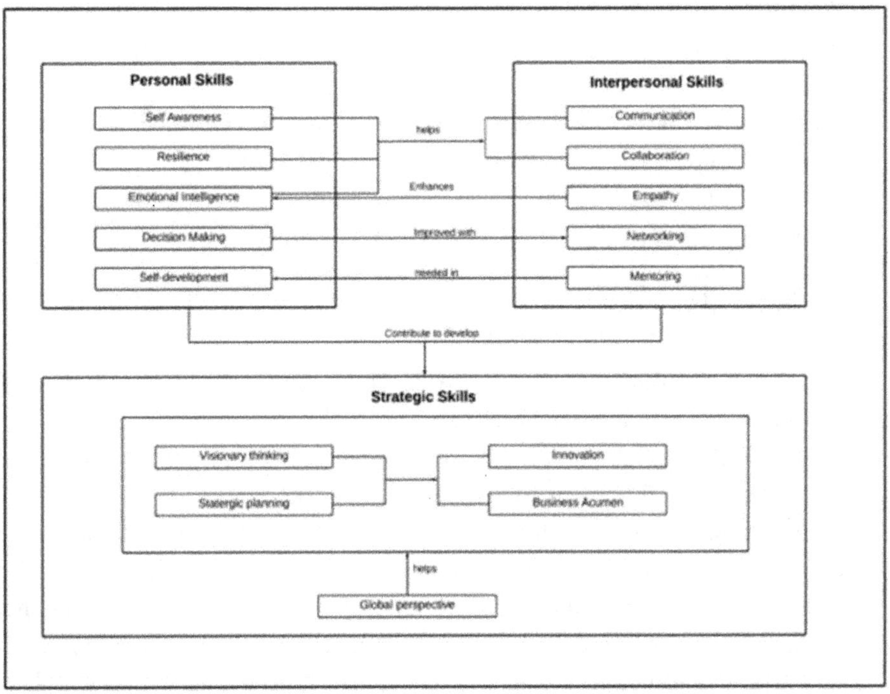

Personal Skills

- **Emotional Intelligence:** Ability to understand and manage emotions, empathize with others, and build strong relationships.
- **Self-Awareness:** Knowledge and understanding of one's own strengths, weaknesses, values, and biases.
- **Resilience:** Ability to adapt to challenges, bounce back from setbacks, and maintain a positive mindset.
- **Decision Making:** Skill in making effective and timely decisions based on available information and critical thinking.
- **Self-Development:** Commitment to continuous learning, personal growth, and acquiring new knowledge and skills.

Interpersonal Skills

- **Communication:** Proficiency in conveying ideas clearly, listening actively, and fostering open dialogue.
- **Collaboration:** Ability to work effectively in teams encourages diverse perspectives, and resolve conflicts.
- **Empathy:** Capacity to understand and relate to the emotions and experiences of others, fostering inclusivity and a supportive work environment (Abu et.al, 2022).
- **Networking:** Skill in building and maintaining professional relationships, seeking mentors, and expanding professional networks.
- **Coaching and Mentoring:** Ability to support and develop the potential of others, providing guidance and constructive feedback.

Strategic Skills

- **Visionary Thinking:** Capability to develop a clear and inspiring vision for the future and articulate it effectively.
- **Strategic Planning:** Proficiency in setting goals, formulating strategies, and implementing action plans to achieve desired outcomes.
- **Innovation:** Capacity to think creatively, embrace change, and encourage a culture of experimentation and risk-taking.
- **Business Acumen:** Understanding of key business principles, financial literacy, and the ability to make informed decisions in the context of organizational objectives.
- **Global Perspective:** Awareness of global trends, cultural diversity, and the ability to lead in a globalized world (Felstead, A. and Henseke, G.,2017).

CONCLUSION

The literature demonstrates that millennial leaders prioritize continuous learning and development, leveraging mentoring and coaching opportunities. They value feedback and appreciate workplaces that promote a growth mindset and foster a culture of openness. While some research suggests that millennials may encounter skepticism from older generations about their leadership capabilities, the overall consensus is that they possess strong leadership potential, especially when provided with the necessary support and guidance.

In conclusion, millennials exhibit a unique leadership style characterized by adaptability, collaboration, and a focus on transformational leadership. Despite certain challenges, their commitment to continuous learning and employee empowerment positions them well to become influential leaders in the modern workforce. Organizations that embrace and nurture millennial leaders are likely to benefit from their innovative and inclusive approach to leadership, resulting in enhanced performance and increased employee satisfaction.

REFERENCES

Chillakuri, B. (2020). Understanding Generation Z expectations for effective onboarding. Journal of Organizational Change Management, *33*(7), 1277-1296.

Abu Bakar, H., & Connaughton, S. L. (2022). Ethical leadership, perceived leader–member ethical communication and organizational citizenship behavior: Development and validation of a multilevel model. *Leadership and Organization Development Journal*, *43*(1), 96–110. doi:10.1108/LODJ-07-2021-0356

Berge, Z. L., & Berge, M. B. (2019). The economic ABCs of educating and training generations X, Y, and Z. *Performance Improvement*, *58*(5), 44–53. doi:10.1002/pfi.21864

Chicca, J., & Shellenbarger, T. (2018). Connecting with generation Z: Approaches in nursing education. *Teaching and Learning in Nursing*, *13*(3), 180–184. doi:10.1016/j.teln.2018.03.008

Chillakuri, B., & Mahanandia, R. (2018). Generation Z entering the workforce: The need for sustainable strategies in maximizing their talent. *Human Resource Management International Digest*, *26*(4), 34–38. doi:10.1108/HRMID-01-2018-0006

Easton, C., & Steyn, R. (2023). Millennial leaders and leadership styles displayed in the workplace. *South African Journal of Business Management*, *54*(1), a3139. doi:10.4102ajbm.v54i1.3139

Gale, F. S. (2015). Forget millennials: Are you ready for gen Z? *Chief Learning Officer*, *14*(7), 38–48.

Grow, J. M., & Yang, S. (2018). Generation-Z enters the advertising workplace: Expectations through a gendered lens. *Journal of Advertising Education*, *22*(1), 7–22. doi:10.1177/1098048218768595

Gupta, T. (2018). Changing the face of instructional practice with twitter: generation-Z perspectives. In *Communicating Chemistry through Social Media* (pp. 151–172). American Chemical Society. doi:10.1021/bk-2018-1274.ch009

Lanier, K. (2017). 5 Things HR professionals need to know about generation Z: Thought leaders share their views on the HR profession and its direction for the future. *Strategic HR Review*, *16*(6), 288–290. doi:10.1108/SHR-08-2017-0051

Lazányi, K., & Bilan, Y. (2017). Generetion Z on the labourmarket - do they TrustOthers within TheirWorkplace? *Polish Journal of Management Studies*, *16*(1), 78–93. doi:10.17512/pjms.2017.16.1.07

Martin, D. R., Winchatz, M. R., Knight, K., & Burrows, L. (2023). Managing Workplace Boredom: Employee Coping Strategies, Supervisor Communication, and Job Satisfaction. *Journal of Leadership & Organizational Studies*, *30*(3), 314–326. doi:10.1177/15480518231168209

Puiu, S. (2017). Generation Z — an educational and managerial perspective. *Young Economists Journal/Revista Tinerilor Economisti, 14*(29), 62-72.

Robertson, S. (2018). Generation Z characteristics & traits that explain the way they learn. *JKCP.* https://info.jkcp.com/blog/generation-z-characteristics

Sumanth, J. J., Černe, M., Hannah, S. T., & Škerlavaj, M. (2023). Fueling the Creative Spark: How Authentic Leadership and LMX Foster Employees' Proactive Orientation and Creativity. *Journal of Leadership & Organizational Studies*, *30*(3), 356–374. doi:10.1177/15480518231180064

Chapter 3
The Original Imposter:
Differentiating Between Being an Imposter and Being an Original

July P. Carrillo
Virginia State University, USA

ABSTRACT

When it comes to the workplace, millennials yearn for a work-life balance and to be in a learning environment where they can develop more than professional life skills. Anyone born between 1981 to 1996 is considered a "millennial." Millennials are also known as "Gen Y," and are relatively well aware of the digital presence in the society they grew up in since they grew up with the growth of the digital era. Millennials face different challenges as they enter the workforce since many of the workforce leaders are a generation or two ahead. Due to their career interest and degrees advancement, millennial leaders are known to enter the workforce earlier than other generations. This generation is known to turn down any career opportunity or job offer that does not align with their life values. Of all the challenges this generation faces in their lives, the "imposter syndrome" has become a blaring feeling that makes them feel invalid about the spaces they exist in.

INTRODUCTION

As people, we can often be our own worst critics. When we receive a compliment, we can begin to consider everything that goes against the given compliment. We can begin to feel out of place. After all, we are human. These contradictive feelings can sometimes make people consider that they are imposters. Imposter syndrome

DOI: 10.4018/978-1-6684-4711-6.ch003

is the faulty feeling of not measuring up, or [that] you do not deserve a compliment or accomplishment" (Brawbaw, 2021). The millennial generation faces several challenges but primarily experiences feelings of imposter syndrome. Millennials experience imposter syndrome in relationships, friendships, personal projects, and the workplace. Millennials consume the current workforce, and in the year 2022, are millennials truly imposters, or are they establishing a new norm as originals for the next generation?

Anyone born between 1981 to 1996 is considered a "Millennial." Millennials are known as "Gen Y" and are relatively well aware of the digital presence in the society they grew up in since they grew up with the growth of the digital era. Millennials face different challenges as they enter the workforce since many of the workforce leaders are a generation or two ahead. When it comes to the workplace, millennials yearn for a work-life balance and being in a learning environment where they can develop more than professional life skills. Due to their career interest and degrees advancement, millennial leaders are known to enter the workforce earlier than other generations. This generation is known to turn down any career opportunity or job offer that does not align with their life values. Of all the challenges this generation faces in their lives, the "imposter syndrome" has become a blaring feeling that makes them feel invalid about the spaces they exist in.

THE IMPOSTER SYNDROME

One of the biggest challenges millennial leaders face is "imposter syndrome." The imposter syndrome is a social phenomenon of doubt in hard-won success and often feeling fraudulent in specific spaces. About 70% of young millennials are high achievers and feel a level of imposter syndrome. Millennial leaders who experience imposter syndrome have a fear of failure or success. Bencie & Khadim (2022) shared a recent survey in Forbes magazine that people's biggest issue in leadership is the feeling of inadequacy whereas in a $366 Billion global industry, 77% of people felt leadership was their biggest concern. For example, college students who experience symptoms of imposter syndrome feel a deep insecurity about not being able to sufficiently complete tasks. "Millennial students either study too hard to prove their ability to themselves and others or become paralyzed by inadequacy, refusing to take risks", (McAllum, 2016). As cited by Brawbaw (2021), Dr. Young, a long-time imposter syndrome researcher, believes there are five different types and associated symptoms:

- **The Perfectionist:** Someone who feels they need to do everything perfectly or else they have failed. And if they are not perfect, they have an overwhelming feeling of self-doubt. Statements associated with this type of imposter syndrome:
    - Being accused of being a micromanager.
    - Difficulty delegating.
    - Feeling inadequate for not having the highest review.
    - Requiring work to be 100% perfect, 100% of the time.
- **The Superhero:** Someone who feels like they are a fraud, either at work or in a relationship, so they work extra hard to hide their supposed inadequacy. Often, the overload in work or stress of not measuring up is damaging to their mental health. Statements associated with this type of imposter syndrome:
    - The need to overwork past hours and tasks.
    - Stressed about completing work.
    - Prioritizing work over personal interests.
    - Feeling inadequate despite degrees and achievements.
- **The Natural Genius:** Someone who judges their worth by how easily something comes to them. They feel ashamed if they need to work to master a task or make a friend. Statements associated with this type of imposter syndrome:
    - Lack of progress.
    - The need to have a "perfect record."
    - Trophy child.
    - Avoid challenges to keep success momentum at an all-time high.
- **The Soloist:** Someone who feels that they need to do everything themselves. If they need to ask for help, they feel incompetent. Statements associated with this type of imposter syndrome:
    - Desire to accomplish projects alone.
    - Refuse to connect with others for assistance.
    - Feed the need of the project instead of the need of the person.
- **The Expert:** Someone who judges their worth by how much they know. They constantly feel like they are not smart enough and fear being exposed as unknowledgeable. Statements associated with this type of imposter syndrome:
    - Pass any career opportunity unless every requirement is met
    - Pursuit of numerous certifications and trainings to validate skillset
    - Enjoy being seen as the expert.

These high achievers cannot often accept their successes and consider a false inability to succeed in life due to the pressures from parents, people, and peers.

Experiencing imposter syndrome have millennials question their career interest and ask themselves why they are doing what they are doing. Alternatively, how they are managing their money. A common theme for millennial leaders is understanding and accepting their place with a looming doubt of how they will eventually fail at their endeavor.

CONNECTION IS CURRENCY

Millennials are considered a social generation. Their social behavior is contingent on their engagement with others and the communities they build. Something as simple as building communication channels with others in their community regarding products, locations, eateries, or anything similar builds on their quest for having a maximized experience with products and services. Millennials are known for "sharing their habits on Facebook, Snapchat, and other social sites, and the opinions they offer on Yelp, TripAdvisor, and Amazon reflect their eagerness for connection, as do their electronic alerts to friends and followers (via Foursquare et al.) that show off where they are, where they are coming from and where they are headed-online alerts that reflect and affect behavior in the physical world" (Solomon, 2017). Millennials do not move in silence. Their connection with people, products, and places serves as currency for them. The connection they form with others regarding their interests and likes is a form of validation that alleviates any feeling of being an "imposter."

A contributor to millennials feeling and identifying as high-achievers is the level of praise and criticism they experienced growing up. Millennials were raised in the trophy generation, where their parents unexpectedly sent mixed messages of over-praise and criticism (Carter, 2019). These experiences brought feelings of stress, anxiety, and even depression. Millennial students either put too much effort into studying or become frozen by inadequacy, resulting in them refusing to take risks. Due to the imposter experiences, millennials often believe they have something to prove and the need to have their talents validated. Millennials want to accomplish important goals. Millennials cope with their self-esteem by trying to perfect the task or procrastinating. This generation also tries to perfect their projects to compensate for the fear of failure. The high anxiety tagged with feeling like an imposter either sets a millennial's deadlines back, or they are overly prepared to accomplish their goal. Typically, people more prone to feeling the imposter syndrome are also more gauged with procrastination, which also brings on stress. Despite being the largest generation, these experiences are also referred to this generation as "Generation Stress." An APA survey in 2013 concluded that millennials were the most self-reported, stressed-out generation (Dahl, 2013).

REAL-LIFE IMPOSTERS

The imposter syndrome can hit any societal status. Celebrities such as Maya Angelou, Kate Winslet, Paul McCartney, and others have shared their doubts about being an imposter in their respective careers (Johny, 2022). They perform and create because their work is their passion and interest. A few celebrities who have identified with imposter syndrome reflect on their recognition; they share feelings of nervousness that someone would look at them as frauds one day. The psychological phenomenon has celebrities and others believing their success is not worth the recognition or success.

In 2016, a group of therapists created an online blog group, The Kip Team, which took time to interview a variety of people to ask about their feelings and regards towards imposter syndrome. As research has shown, the people that were interviewed shared similar feelings of low self-esteem and a lack of confidence overall. They believed they were frauds in one way or another and described having a difficult time accepting compliments from anyone regardless of the praise from colleagues and supervisors. Participants were asked what imposter syndrome felt like, its effects on them, and the actions imposter syndrome prompted them to take. Responses included were, "I never negotiated my salary because I was scared I would get 'caught' [and] thought I should prove myself before asking for more money." Another participant shared feeling the need to say 'yes' to every additional workload in a job while others contemplated rejecting promotions because they did not believe they deserved the offer or new job. When it comes to communicating with superiors at work, someone shared their feelings of severe anxiety and being unable to "be assertive with [my] boss, [feeling] defensiveness." One interviewed person shared, "I find it very hard to describe [imposter syndrome]. You could say that it was motivating and demotivating at the same time. I feel like I'm constantly chasing a ghost version of myself that I will never actually catch, but I seem to be getting closer to every day."

Lupita Nyong'o shared in an interview with *Time Out*, (September 2016):

"What [is] it called when you have a disease and it keeps recurring? I go through [acute impostor syndrome] with every role. I think winning an Oscar may in fact have made it worse. Now I [have] achieved this, what am I going to do next? What do I strive for? Then I remember that I did [not] get into acting for the accolades; I got into it for the joy of telling stories."

Actresses such as Penélope Cruz feel they will be fired every time she is making a movie, and Emma Watson said, "It [is] almost like the better I do, the more my feeling of inadequacy actually increases" and added that she thought someone would find out she was a fraud and undeserving of anything she achieved. Ma (2017) said Sigourney Weaver shared, "Have I ever doubted myself? *Have I ever not?* I feel self-doubt whether I [am] doing something hard or easy." —*Esquire*, January 2010. In January 2013, *The Wall Street Journal* interviewed Justice Sonia Sotomayor, and in her interview, she said, "I am not a classic impostor-syndrome person because I have that initial insecurity, but I am capable of stepping outside of it and proving to myself it is wrong."

What about the men? At the start of studying the imposter syndrome phenomenon, psychologists believed this mainly existed in women (2022). While many of the research and recorded interviews of people with imposter syndrome are from women, the Imposter Syndrome Institute (2022) shared that women were the primary group that was open to sharing their opinion. One researcher shared that with his experience studying imposter syndrome," countless men suffer terribly from their fraud fear" (2022), including police officials, attorneys, CEOs, and even an entire team of aerospace engineers. Another researcher, as shared by Lebowitz (2016), said the scientific community began to realize the universal experience of imposter syndrome and its impact on women and men equally. Men hid their fears and could not unravel the burdens they felt within from imposter syndrome. Cuddy shares that "impostorism causes us to self-criticize constantly, to "choke at the worst possible moments, [and to] disengage — thereby virtually ensuring that we will underperform at the very things we do best and love most," as shared by Lebowitz (2022). Male celebrities have their fair share of imposter syndrome, as well:

Paul McCartney, the winner of 18 Grammies, has felt like an impostor. "You never think you are good. I really ought to think I am fantastic because I have this pile of achievements ... but I am still going, "Oh, can I do it ... ?" A line from one of his songs says, "Everybody else busy doing better than me." He goes on to add that he still thinks that way and tries to convince himself that "that is probably not true."

Furthermore, it is not just men who have the inability to seek help. Johny (2022) quoted Clance, "The 'impostors' rarely seek help and strive for perfection in each of their tasks…." Officially, imposter syndrome has not been diagnosed as a mental disorder but is usually linked with depression (Johny, 2022). An article from the Harvard Business Review (2022) pinpointed the responsible psychologists named Pauline Rose Clance and Suzanne Imes, who coined this experience as the "imposter phenomenon" in their 1978 study.

FAKE IT UNTIL YOU MAKE IT

Social belonging is an essential aspect of millennials in social and career spaces. Millennials do not feel their skill sets are what make them inadequate which later leads to feeling like imposters. Their "I am not good enough" feeling in the workplace is attributed to other factors like older coworkers. Since millennials are known to quickly move into their careers after school, they find themselves in workplaces with much older coworkers or simply the youngest in their field. The age gaps allow for judgment, and millennials tend to feel tested on their abilities. As a generation that overcompensates to feel adequate, their "unhealthy diet, caffeine overdose, lack of sleep, and the absence of a time management system" (Ong, 2022) also contribute to the stress this generation experiences.

In many cases, a person experiencing imposter syndrome features success through how much work they put forth and the need, not the desire, to visibly work harder than others. In other cases, they believe their success is purely luck (Ferrari, 2005). For college students experiencing imposter syndrome intellectual phoniness as described by Clance & Imes (1978), a perfect example would be cheating on an exam, earning a good grade, and feeling shame or guilt for their success. The same student who cheats or plagiarizes would be the student that would most likely feel the pressure of having to perform above their peers and despite not being caught, would feel undeserving of their success. As the nation's largest living generation

People use a variety of different moral characteristics that help define their social identity which creates moral identity (Maftei et al., 2021). People will define moral identity with anything they deem important and positive for their identity whether construed or measured by social traits. In the end, a person with what they would consider a good moral identity would feel good about themselves. When people begin to experience imposter syndrome, a desire to change and show their best will come. Unfortunately, showing the best they have to offer also means hiding their anxiety and low-self esteem (Maftei et al., 2021) which prevents a person from being honest and therefore unable to holistically define their moral identity. From the moment a person with imposter syndrome begins to experience these feelings, they only expose their "bests" that fit others instead of themselves. A person's "bests" become external symbols.

Millennials are caught in vulnerable conversations measuring themselves to others with job titles, family and marital status compared to age, and the overall ability to do the job they are in. Comparative situations not only bring stress to this generation but also builds a toxic work environment that heightens the imposter feeling in this generation. This generation will consequently try to be a perfectionist and overproduce to feel significant in the workplace, creating difficult habits to break for the day-to-day lifestyle. In addition, this behavior can eventually unmask the harsh realities a millennial tried to mask, thus adding to their never-ending reasons for feeling like an imposter.

Individuals in the millennial generation who experience imposter syndrome have a significant fear of failure and a fear of success. These feelings arise when millennials are faced with new challenges in any space of their lives. To mask their feelings, their urge to be perfectionists or procrastinators takes over (Maftei, Dumitriu, & Holman, 2021). Previous research highlights a significant link between procrastination and impostor syndrome. Because of the high anxiety that impostors feel, they complete their tasks in two ways: either postponing the task or preparing intensely to accomplish it (Maftei, Dumitriu, & Holman, 2021).

PASSION OVER PAIN

If we consider the phrase "the 'me' in 'millennial'", we can remind ourselves of the main trait within the generation. Students from the millennial generation rely on their success on external factors on less on what they may have contributed (Morreale & Staley, 2016) and typically lack academic responsibility. Since then, instructors learned the need to cultivate academic responsibility and highlight the importance of the student/teacher roles, the purpose of the class or assignment, and professional feedback to students when they disapprove of any interaction. While the approach takes more time and is even 'parent-like", the adaption adds a layer to learning that can positively affect the student's holistic experience and carry over to the workforce (Morreale & Staley, 2016).

Despite their internal struggles, millennials are highly driven and extremely passionate about their values. For millennials, if the environment or experience is not up to their expectations, they will remove themselves, follow their core values, and eventually choose happiness. Solomon cites that "young millennials were revered, praised, sheltered, befriended and carefully guided by their parents to lead well-structured lives based on adherence to clear and mutually agreed-upon rules. This has produced a generation of young people that is, by most measures, accomplished, self-confident, group-oriented and optimistic" (2017).

The social awareness aspect of millennials is key to understanding the space and time they grew up in and why they hold their values so close to their hearts. Millennials will choose "equality, climate change, peace, justice, poverty, and prosperity" (Cheng, 2019). With the growth of social media and the internet, millennials grew up learning about others and their state of life. This parallelism has allowed them to reflect on their own lives and the impact they can make on society. Millennials will share their social mobility through various social media applications, and "this enables them to share and receive information, making millennials the most connected generation" (Cheng, 2019). As the most connected generation, they embrace friendships with people from all walks of life and are not shy about their support for diversity and inclusion on all levels.

RETAINING MILLENNIALS IN THE WORKPLACE

The year is 2022, and most workplaces are filled with millennials at various work levels. If millennials are known to choose purpose-filled careers and quickly move from one job to another, then how do employers help the job-hopping experience? Management can expect a millennial to be at a job for an average of 1.7 years (Sharma, 2019) which makes for high turnovers. Typically, people leave a place of employment for salary, unmatched work expectations, or to find better opportunities. On the other hand, millennials want to feel like they belong in their workplace and that their work has a purpose. The "trophy generation" needs to feel they are accomplishing deeds and tasks and making an impact by the end of their work days. Any company understanding the need to implement a "millennial change" can begin to consider different retention strategies to validate, empower, and ultimately show the millennial employee that they matter to the company.

According to Sharma (2019), there are three (3) primary goals in retaining millennial employees, starting with how to help build horizontal and vertical career opportunities within the company, maintain the workplace as a desirable location, and help build a robust social network within the company for the millennial employee. Like many improvement efforts, the most impactful change is the change that starts within. Any company looking to improve its efforts in millennial retention needs to build on its internal branding with training and implementing changes within its organization. "Millenial students are immersed in a digital world governed by codes and scripts" (Morreale & Staley, 2016, p. 357). Companies boosting their digital footprint in the workplace will help retain the same generation that grew up with the rise of technology. With purpose in the workplace taking precedence over any other value, millennials thrive in a supportive, flexible work environment that believes in and executes work-life balance. Aleksandr Korotkov, CEO of Uservice Blockchain Technology, said, as Fries (2018) shared, "Millennials place a high value on self-care, convenience and time with loved ones… they believe that work balance is good for happiness and emotional health".

OVERCOMING IMPOSTER SYNDROME

While there are many reasons millennials experience symptoms of imposter syndrome, millennials have found ways to overcome their struggles and maintain their sense of peace. The Cleveland Clinic (2022) listed recommendations from Dr. Albers, such as separating feelings from facts that lead to feelings of imposter syndrome. Even sharing their thoughts and emotions with others is a great way for millennials to realize how normal their feelings are and should help them from comparing themselves to others. "Comparing your own life to a carefully curated influencer's social media feed, for example, is a trap for feeling like you do [not] measure up" (Pogored, 2022).

A counselor named Dr. Rupa Murgai believes almost everyone in their life experiences some form or symptoms of imposter syndrome (Johny, 2022). She even stated, "It has been prevalent for a long time now, and self-doubt is natural to all human beings" (Johny, 2022). Based on her research, Dr. Murgai offers the following tips to keep the human mind ahead of the imposter syndrome:

- Positive self-talk for personal encouragement
- Being practical, not setting very high standards
- Self-awareness to know oneself from a realistic perspective
- Replace fear of failure with being comfortable with who you are
- Talk about and share your feelings, thoughts
- The digital file that makes you happy about yourself and your achievements
- Open communication with bosses
- Learner attitude brings in flexibility, dissipates rigid thoughts

Part of a millennial's upbringing included consistent praise of any big or small accomplishment from their parents. Johny (2022) stated, "Unrelenting criticism or huge emphasis on achievement during childhood leaves 'impostors' in constant pursuit of validating their talents and achievements." Another method for millennials to overcome imposter syndrome is taking notes of their accomplishments, such as any recognition from workplace superiors and praises from close friends and family they can often refer to.

CONCLUSION

Millennials are no longer the youngest generation in the workplace. This generation experienced the rise of technology and the virtual community's new-age lines of communication. Also known as "Gen Y," these individuals are a massive group familiar with technology and anything that helps command clear communication to meet the right expectations. Whether they are looking for clarity in the workplace or they are looking to validate the perfect purchase, the reviews and outlines for products and services are critical to millennials. For millennials, having these certainties help alleviate the symptoms associated with imposter syndrome because they can openly share thoughts, communicate, and meet workplace and relationship standards. Before our society's oversharing capabilities, people made purchases based on the few specs associated with the items, referrals from friends and families, or simply the brand name spoke for itself. Millennials are breaking traditional boundaries in the workplace, their connection to society and the world, and even the norm of how to conduct an average day in adult life. The values they look for from others as they build relationships are a means to, directly and indirectly, communicate effectively, reciprocate the exact expectations and validate themselves for the worries of feeling like an imposter. While the millennial generation feels like imposters and believes their work does not have direct value, they do not know that their generation is making the most considerable impact and making companies reconsider company policies and practices and discovering more ways to elevate their company while supporting the millennial employee. Whether through diet and exercise, millennials are finding products and direct ways to help alleviate the burdens they experience from the imposter syndrome.

REFERENCES

Bencie, L., & Khadim, B. (2022, October 7). Imposter syndrome causes a decline in leadership. *IACSP Journal*. https://iacspjournal.com/uncategorized/imposter-syndrome-causes-a-decline-in-leadership/

Brabaw, K. (2021, November 2). FYI: Perfectionism is definitely a type of impostor syndrome. *Women's Health*. https://www.womenshealthmag.com/health/a27018815/what-is-impostor-syndrome/?utm_source=google&utm_medium=cpc&utm_campaign=arb_ga_whm_md_pmx_us_urlx&gclid=Cj0KCQjw0oyYBhDGARIsAMZEuMvzIBPlhWwLT7thnmgg1ff4iBA-CCKR5-dnq16um9Z0trSo59nVe3caAtBQEALw_wcB

Carter, C. M. (2019, January 13). Why so many millennials experience impostor syndrome. *Forbes*. https://www.forbes.com/sites/christinecarter/2016/11/01/why-so-many-millennials-experience-imposter-syndrome/?sh=11f1a17d6aeb

Cheng, M. (2022, April 14). 8 characteristics of Millennials That Support Sustainable Development Goals (sdgs). *Forbes*. https://www.forbes.com/sites/margueritacheng/2019/06/19/8-characteristics-of-millennials-that-support-sustainable-development-goals-sdgs/?sh=7f99a0b029b7

Clance, P., & Imes, S. A. (1978). The impostor phenomenon in high achieving women: Dynamics and therapeutic intervention. *Psychotherapy: Theory, Research and Practice, 15*, 241-247.

Dahl, M. (2013, February 8). *Millennials are the most stressed-out generation, new survey finds*. NBCNews.com. https://www.nbcnews.com/health/health-news/millennials-are-most-stressed-out-generation-new-survey-finds-flna1b8296642

Ferrari, J. R. (2005). Impostor Tendencies and Academic Dishonesty: Do They Cheat Their Way to Success? *Social Behavior and Personality, 33*(1), 11–17. https://doi-org.vsu.idm.oclc.org/10.2224/sbp.2005.33.1.11. doi:10.2224bp.2005.33.1.11

Fries, K. (2018, January 31). 7 Ways Millennials Are Changing Traditional Leadership. *Forbes*. https://www.forbes.com/sites/kimberlyfries/2018/01/18/7-ways-millennials-are-changing-traditional-leadership/?sh=217d541d7dae

Johny, R. M. (2022, April 8). *BuzzFix: Is impostor syndrome special to millennials or are we all just human?* News18. https://www.news18.com/news/buzz/buzzfix-is-impostor-syndrome-special-to-millennials-gen-z-or-are-we-all-just-human-4952846.html

Lebowitz, S. (2016, January 12). Men are suffering from a psychological phenomenon that can undermine their success, but they're too ashamed to talk about it. *Business Insider*. https://www.businessinsider.com/men-suffer-from-impostor-syndrome-2016-1

Ma, J. (2017, January 12). 25 famous women on impostor syndrome and self-doubt. *The Cut*. https://www.thecut.com/2017/01/25-famous-women-on-impostor-syndrome-and-self-doubt.html

Maftei, A., Dumitriu, A., & Holman, A. (2021). "They will discover I'm a fraud!" the impostor syndrome among psychology students. *Studia Psychologica, 63*(4), 337–351. doi:10.31577p.2021.04.831

McAllum, K. (2016). Managing Imposter Syndrome among the "Trophy kids": Creating teaching practices that develop independence in millennial students. *Communication Education, 65*(3), 363–365. doi:10.1080/03634523.2016.1177848

Morreale, S. P., & Staley, C. M. (2016). Millennials, teaching and learning, and the elephant in the college classroom. *Communication Education, 65*(3), 370–373. doi:10.1080/03634523.2016.1177842

Ong, L. (2022, June 6). Dealing with imposter syndrome at work: A Millennial's two cents. *Calm Collective Asia Blog*. https://www.blog.calmcollective.asia/blog/dealing-with-imposter-syndrome-at-work-a-millennials-two-cents

Pogored. (2022, April 4). *What's imposter syndrome and how to overcome it.* Cleveland Clinic. https://health.clevelandclinic.org/a-psychologist-explains-how-to-deal-with-imposter-syndrome/

Sharma, D. (2019). *How to recruit, incentivize and retain millennials*. SAGE/Response Business Books.

Solomon, M. (2017). *5 characteristics of Millennials - Michigan Scouting*. Michigan Scouting. https://michiganscouting.org/wp-content/uploads/2017/11/Five-Characteristics-of-Millennials.pdf

Stop telling women they have imposter syndrome. Harvard Business Review. (2022, August 4). Retrieved August 27, 2022, from https://hbr.org/2021/02/stop-telling-women-they-have-imposter-syndrome#:~:text=Imposter%20syndrome%20is%20loosely%20defined,they're%20deserving%20of%20accolades

Team, T. K. (2017, March 30). Real stories: Imposter Syndrome. *Medium*. https://medium.com/kip-blog/real-stories-imposter-syndrome-15bce02a5c1e

What about men. (2022, March 14). Impostor Syndrome Institute. https://impostorsyndrome.com/what-about-men/

Chapter 4
The True Millennial Leader

Tymon M. Graham
https://orcid.org/0009-0001-8494-3174
Edward Waters University, USA

ABSTRACT

It is noted that those born between the years of 1981 and 1996 are deemed millennials. For the sake of this text, the authors define leadership as a person who is committed to a purpose with the ability to influence people to accomplish or achieve a goal. As the largest living generation, the millennial generation brings a sense of diversity, inclusivity, and disruption to the normal operation of life, liberty, and the pursuit thereof. This chapter reviews the different generations, what leadership means to millennials, millennial leaders who exemplify characteristics important to millennials, preferences of millennial leaders, and what millennial leaders bring to the table, roles, jobs, and spaces.

INTRODUCTION

It is noted by Dimock (2019) that those birthed between the years of 1981 and 1996 are deemed millennials. For the sake of this text, we define leadership as a person who is committed to a purpose with the ability to influence people to accomplish or achieve a goal. As the largest living generation, the millennial generation brings a sense of diversity, inclusivity, and disruption to the normal operation of life, liberty, and the pursuit thereof (Dimock, 2019).

In real life, millennials are social butterflies and thrive in community spaces. As a social generation, millennials use social skills in all aspects of their lives from

DOI: 10.4018/978-1-6684-4711-6.ch004

work, family, friends, colleagues, and even shopping. The opinions of others matter enough to influence a millennials' decision but not to follow a majority but rather as a form of validation to their considerations. In return, millennials will share their experiences, opinions, or recommendations and feedback to various life encounters like shopping and socializing (Howe & Strauss, 2003).

This chapter will discuss what makes a millennial leader and serve as an introduction to the true millennial leader, leadership, the millennial leader's needs, and how to cultivate the millennial leader within the workplace.

The Generations

Each generation is classified by age, time period, and even cohort. The age of an individual is simply age in numbers. The time period refers to events that happens or has happened during that persons life. The cohort refers to the group of people with shared experiences or events. Those in the same cohort may have similar attitudes and behaviors that further underscore the cohort an individual is within (DeVaney, 2015).

As baby boomers begin to exit the workforce and leadership roles millennials have been tapped to move forward but are constantly compared to the assumptions of the ideal leadership strategies of prior generations. Additionally, millennials are stereotyped with an inclusion of the postmillennial group or generation z which begins with those born in 1997 or later (Fry, 2018). According to Fry (2018), "prior to the millennial generation, is the generation X which are those birthed between 1965 to 1980 and baby boomers who were birthed between 1946 and 1964".

According to Fry (2018) the chart shown in Figure 1 provides context to the generational definitions.

Bialik & Fry (2019) tells us that "Millennials are now the second-largest generation in the U.S. electorate (after Baby Boomers), a fact that continues to shape the country's politics given their Democratic leanings when compared with older generations." Millennials have increased the awareness and brought forward the diversity within American society. With an increased percentage of educated millennials than previous generations, we see a more critical and strategic delivery of work product in the workplace (Bialik & Fry, 2019).

The Millennial

Millennials have seen the effects of the college loan debt and the recession. Millennials have seen social protest and social change. As a group, millennials are delaying marriage but starting businesses (DeVaney, 2015).

Figure 1. The generations defined

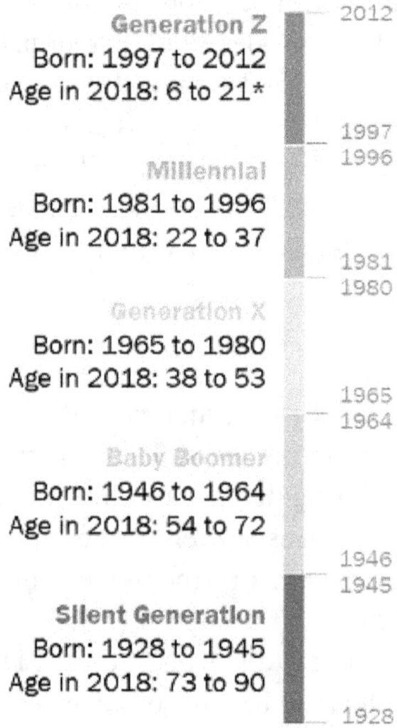

As noted prior, the millennial as an age group is born between 1981 and 1996. Additionally, within the millennial time period the group has seen terrorist attacks such as those on the World Trade Center on September 11, 2001, and the rise of the internet and digital age. Burstein (2013) states "the power for the young to influence and create new technology has grown tremendously in the last decade" (page 54). Even as early as first and second grade we have seen millennials connected and using technology. It should be no surprise that many embed this into their work in the workforce and leadership throughout. To that end founders of several companies to include YouTube, Facebook, Twitter, and Instagram are millennials (DeVaney, 2015).

What is Leadership to Millennials?

Millennial leadership is seen on a global scale in the likes of Dr. Wesley Bellamy, political and non-profit leader, higher education administrator and voice of black youth; Symone Sanders, political strategist, news commentator; and Colin Kaepernick, a civil rights activist, author, and NFL quarterback.

Dr. Wesley J. Bellamy is seen as a transformational millennial leader. After initially launching and running an initial campaign for City Council in Charlottesville, VA though unsuccessful there was a meaningful lesson learned. Bellamy built success from collaborative spaces for children, families, and friends from all walks of life and surpassing every boundary. On Saturday June 8, 2013, Bellamy hosted a "Move The City Forward" Community Cookout at Lee Park that essentially cost him the election. With a heavy following in place for change within the city and on the high of this initial campaign, Dr. Bellamy did not see what was coming next. Upon the brink of the cookout, fewer people were in attendance than in any other event he had hosted (Bellamy, 2019). Why? Because culture eats strategy for breakfast!

Lee Park, home of the Robert E. Lee statue was a reminder to many of the confederacy and a heart wrenching space of racism within the city of Charlottesville. Bellamy's followers, much those of color, found it to be a "slap in the face" for their chosen future leader who requests their votes and support to hold a cookout for comfort in a park holding a root of racism. They did not mind telling him their opinions either. Instantly the campaign of the community favorite was tarnished heavily by a culture ignored (Bellamy, 2019).

Dr. Bellamy later served as a leading force in the removal of the Robert E. Lee statue in Charlottesville, Virginia, a clear notion that underscores the zero tolerance of hate and the need to increase a common culture of care (Bellamy, 2019).

Leadership to millennials is noted as leadership of care of the people. Needless to say, Dr. Bellamy's future campaigns were successful. The care of peoples can change the scope and outcome of the work being put forth.

Ms. Symone Sanders has been a very vocal, authentic, and strategic cornerstone of the last decade representing millennials well with her work ethic, value-add dialogue, and strategic mindset. According to The Institute of Politics at Harvard University (n.d.), "at 25, she became the youngest presidential press secretary on record and was named to Rolling Stone Magazine's list of 16 young Americans shaping the 2016 election".

She began as the national press secretary to the then presidential candidate, Senator Bernie Sanders during his 2016 campaign run. Emerging as a millennial who can relate and draw in younger voters, Ms. Sanders eventually became a senior advisor to President Joseph R. Biden during his 2020 presidential campaign. Eventually, she joined Vice President Kamala Harris' team as chief spokesperson and senior advisor (Wright & Vazquez, 2021). Even post her time at the White House, Ms. Sanders has used her ability to relate the public, specifically millennials.

Ms. Sanders speaks widely and clearly of the power of millennial leadership and millennial impact in not only our United States but the nation and world. On her campaign tours to increase the young voting population, Ms. Sanders presented herself as herself. There was no gimmick, no trade off, nor a hidden agenda in her connection to the young voter. Even on her engagements and as a frequent commentator on Cable News Network (CNN), she as very vocal in expressing the thoughts, interests, and political views of millennials in a very clear, conscious, and even sometimes comedically fashion, even when not verbalized by millennials (Hardy, 2020).

Leadership to millennials is the ability to be authentic. As a very vocal and transparent leader, Ms. Sanders is known just as her authored book is entitled, she speaks truth to power and empowers millennials to be their true selves. No matter the setting, whether appearing in traditional business attire or trendy attire, the fashionista, Ms. Sanders does not stray away from presenting herself in her own way of authenticity and bright energy.

Mr. Colin Kaepernick widely known for his skill, accuracy, and mobility on the turf also drew national support and criticism when he refused to stand during the playing of the national anthem in 2016 (Tensley, 2021). This one act of taking a knee during the anthem in order to take a stand against sparked a divide within the country (Jubenville, 2016). In-fact, according to Brandon Tensley (2021) "he's expanded the scope of protest".

Tensley (2021) in the text by journalist Dave Zirin, The Kaepernick Effect: Taking a Knee, Changing the World states:

"It was the warning for a future that came to pass after the police murder of George Floyd, coming on the heels of the murders of Ahmaud Arbery and Breonna Taylor. It was the warning that people were poised and ready to fight."

In a time of police brutality, it is important for speak out and use our voices. Colin Kaepernick has been instrumental in using his platform to speak out for those who feel they cannot. Even after gaining public attention from multiple constituents both athletic and non-athletic based, Kaepernick did not stop from moving forward with what he believed.

In 2018, Nike released its 30th Anniversary Campaign intitled "Just Do It" with Colin Kaepernick as the face of the campaign. Though some were not happy with Nike's selection, there were many who praised the selection. Additionally, Nike's commercial starring the athlete and activist to support social causes won an Emmy in 2019 (Vera, 2019). Eventually, it has been noted that the Kaepernick jersey has risen to the top of the most-purchased jerseys on various websites. (Jubenville, 2016).

Leadership to millennials, is the ability to use your voice for the voiceless.

According to Jubenville (2016), "witnessing 20-something professional athlete Colin Kaepernick divide the country by sitting or taking a knee during the pre-game singing of America's national anthem has made one fact about our society abundantly clear: People fundamentally misunderstand the mindset of millennials".

Colin Kaepernick understands the millennial mindset and refuses to take a back seat. He has taken more than a few opportunities to use his voice widely and clearly to be a catalyst.

According to Post (2022), these are some key principles that guide what millennials are looking for in a leader:

1. Mission-based role assignment.
2. Acknowledgment of life outside of work.
3. Attention as an individual, not a group.
4. Encouragement to work toward something greater than themselves.

As a millennial leader, the workplace needs are different than those of other generations. Millennials desire to find and achieve a purpose in their lives. With finding purpose, there must be an alignment within their work. An unfulfilled millennial leader with leave a specific workplace environment to seek their purpose and roles that support their purpose. To this note, there must be a purpose alignment to roles and assignments of a millennial.

Post (2022) provides five leadership styles that were not considered a decade ago, however, are necessary and are directly applicable to the modern-day millennial evolution. These five leadership traits are innovative leadership, servile leadership, empathetic leadership, transformative leadership, and leadership committed to diversity. Innovative leaders think outside box and hire outside of the box. The protocol and processes under leaders employing innovative leadership are unorthodox and can possibly be seen as unconventional (Post, 2022). As an innovative leader, hiring outside of the box can be done by hiring a leader possessing three important things. These three things are competency, soft skills, and bench strength. Those hired must have competency to do the work of the position for hire. The soft skills such as effective communication, problem-solving ability, and work ethic are much needed of millennial leaders for work success. Lastly, as an innovative leader, hiring a millennial with bench strength provides for cross-organizational success. Though majority seen in regard to sports, bench strength speaks to one's ability to impact various aspects of the organization and in-turn enhancing departments outside of their own to in-turn serve as a capability to ascend to positions of increased responsibility within the organization when able and/or required (Post, 2022)

Servile leadership style is one of investing in the whole team member or whole employee to ensure both personal and professional successes. This style is achieved through mentorship and continuous education opportunities that grow the individual. According to Post (2022) "companies that strive for empathetic leadership, the ability to listen and understand employees ultimately improves the workplace culture for productivity and, in turn, success". Transformative leadership encourages and inspires employees. The transformation happens within employees and shows the value of employees to aid in a mutually beneficial professional relationship. Within a leadership committed to diversity, leadership looks to welcome all backgrounds, generations, and believes to grow and enhance the overall company culture and operation. Millennials within the workforce are providing transformation boldly.

Many millennials are first-time leaders. As stated in Graham, et al. (2021), "As a first-time leader, one must realize that relationships are at the core of leadership. Leaders are defined by the type of relationship developed with organizational members."

Graham, et al., (2021) states, that as a first-time leaders remember these:

- **Follow the leader:** Being directly behind the leader is a place of privilege because you can see the before and after of leadership without being the focal point.
- **Occupy your seat:** There aren't any assigned seats in the world but let your flexibility land you in new spaces which open up new opportunities.
- **Failure isn't fatal; move on:** As a first-time leader, you will make mistakes but a timeless leader won't make the same mistake twice. Learn and re-strategize your moves towards success.
- **Take time to learn the environment and build relationships with stakeholders:** A great leader recognizes that relationships are at the core of leadership.
- **Identify in- and out-groups:** Knowledge of these internal groups will aid your navigational skills within the organization's political environment.
- Build a work profile with early quick wins. This can be attained through **surveying the landscape** for "low hanging fruit".
- Don't forget politics are everywhere. As a first-time leader you must work to understand **Who's in Power and Who's connected to Power**.
- Before assuming a role, get to know the **pre-existing leaders**. Buy into their vision. If not there may be friction.
- **Allies, Mentors, and Sponsor** are important yet different roles for a first-time leader to keep in their circle. Understand each and use to the best of your ability.
- Take the time to write down monthly (or as they come) of tidbits of knowledge that you learn from your colleagues, supervisors and leaders. These will come in handy when you begin to **Groom New Leaders** (p. 12-13).

When engaging in leadership or assuming a leadership role, Maxwell (2005) reminds us of nine principles to perform while not only being a leader but also working for and supporting a leader.

Maxwell (2005), lists the 9 principles as:

1. Lead yourself exceptionally well.
2. Lighten your leader's load.
3. Be willing to do what others won't.
4. Do more than manage – lead!
5. Invest in relationship chemistry.
6. Be prepared every time you take your leader's time.
7. Know when to push and when to back off.
8. Become a go-to player.
9. Be better tomorrow than you are today.

The Preferences of the Millennial Leader

Millennial leaders seek many preferences of leaders, managers, and supervisors. Among those are transparency, work-life balance, and listening and communicating.

Transparency

As millennial leaders enter the workplace or a culture, one of transparency is a preference as it can be seen clearly during this time of social media. The straightforwardness and communication of millennials is expected to be reciprocated in and out of the workplace.

Llopis (2022), tells us "They desire their leaders to be proactive in sharing where the company is headed and forthright about its future." Llopis (2022), later states "The reason most leaders are not transparent is because they believe they will be viewed as less authoritative; that the credentials they worked so hard to attain will lose their power, leverage and gravitas." In the eyes of millennials this is less of the case. Millennials seek transparency as a precursor method of trust. All in all, transparency is better than promises made by leadership. The transparency is equivalent to action seen. The ability of providing more honesty and less corporate norm heightens the level of transparency in millennial leaders (Wylonis, 2021).

Work/Life Balance

Research tells us that millennials assume approximately 50 percent of the workforce and millennials as younger works require and in fact demand flexibility. This is a drastic difference than workers of previous generations. The notion of fulfillment of work life and home life cause requires the understanding of the work/life balance. Alesso-Bendisch (2020), states "If bosses make small investments in the right places, they can dramatically change the quality of job satisfaction and employee productivity."

Setting boundaries is key to the success of millennials in the workplace. Boundaries preempt the ability to create an efficient work life balance. Managers and supervisors should seek to understand work/life balance, create the ideal work environment, address and realize what family life looks like, help millennials to find and understand their vocation and purpose, and provide a holistic workplace with a focus on mental health, wellness and technology (Alesso-Bendisch, 2020). The work/life balance is important as employee performance depends on it.

The Value of Listening and Communicating

A key cornerstone of preferences is listening and communicating. If a leader does not understand the millennial mind, values, and voice on a team, there could be friction. As a young leader, a millennial seeks to give to the cause or initiative to reach a goal and be fully engaged in the process. The daily motivation is a driver of success. Managers and supervisors must listen to the feedback and input provided by millennials and be prepared to respond and act in a way that grows and challenges the leader but also reinforces the confidence and value in their position on the team (Donahue, 2021).

Millennials value effective communication and feedback. Some time it may seem that as a manager you are must over communicate, the communicate does provide clarity. Furthermore, consistent communication is a benefit for all parties. Even in providing feedback, some harp on the notion that millennials need praise and coddle however, it is more noted that the millennial leader is more driven by the ability to improve their skill and work. Now, just like any other professional, the method and delivery of feedback may determine reaction (Donahue, 2021). Donahue (2021), tells us "While millennials may require encouraging feedback, most Gen-Z will request straightforward feedback." According to DeVaney (2015), "employers and managers need to provide meaningful work, allow the millennials to provide input, and help the millennial feel that he or she is a good fit on a good team".

What Do Millennial Leaders Bring?

Sousssi (2020), notes that millennials are often framed with negative connotations however bring mimicable traits. Millennials are often willing to speak out, bring a natural entrepreneurial drive, project confidence and are inclusive in the workplace. Millennials are seen as those who do not mind "rocking the boat" in various spaces. As those who come into spaces asking the question of "why", not to be disrespectful or ill-mannered to those in power, millennials often move to be disruptive in spaces to speak truth for positive change that often have been an equal notation of what others may feel but may be silenced. As natural entrepreneurs, millennials don't mind navigating new spaces such as, starting an organization or busines. Millennials don't minds seeking out opportunities for innovation and change. Millennials take risks. That is hands down an easy way to say it! The skillfulness of the natural entrepreneurial and innovative mind provides for millennials to navigate projects and manage projects well. Though many millennials project confidence, this is naturally found when experienced colleagues help and sow into the leader for knowledge and growth. As a group who have been raised on sharing, group collaborations, and inclusion, millennials work with others regardless of backgrounds and work with inclusion in mind. This inclusion can come in ways of project member inclusion or creating a work environment that is welcoming (Soussi, 2020).

While the aforementioned are all great traits that millennials bring, Woodward (2020), notes 5 skills that millennials can develop that will in-turn make them better leaders and upset the stereotypes placed on them as a generation. Woodward (2020), notes that millennials should develop skills in the area of problem solving, follow through, receiving feedback, giving credit, and disconnecting from technology.

Millennials come with an entrepreneurial spirit and can be natural risk takers however, in the age of helicopter parents, some have not been provided the opportunity to solve their own problems or devise solutions to large scale problems. The ability to think critically on ones own and not asking for help will provide millennials with the tools to implement problem solving skills on both small and large scall problems. Though it may be commendable to solve problems without asking for help, there are times to ask for help (Woodward, 2020). Woodward (2020), states "To demonstrate true leadership potential, you'll need to both take the initiative to find solutions on your own, and know when to ask for help and communicate your progress so you and your team can cross the finish line together".

Millennials must possess patience and follow-through skills. It is a common reputation of millennials to be job-hoppers and not see projects from inception to completion. As a millennial leader, follow through is important to the leadership development and project management scope. In the adverse, organizations and companies must also consider how the todays workplace may provide for employee dissatisfaction and not immediately place a reoccurring job change on the fact that a group of leaders fall into a millennial category (Woodward, 2020). Millennials are willing to leave a place when leadership does not align with organizational and/or personal goals or standards (Fries, 2018).

Some believe that millennials need constant praise as a feedback motivator for continued work product success while, many will find that negative feedback is more motivating. The fact that feedback is given provides for the notion that a leader is invested in the success of the employee. On the side of the millennial, one cannot be fearful of feedback or stand in opposition or disagreement (Woodward, 2020). Woodward (2020), states "Letting people know you are open to receiving criticism can help them feel more free to give honest feedback without fearing how you'll respond". In fact, to take it a step further, listening to feedback, digesting the feedback, and making strides to implement the feedback is imperative.

Millennials have been stereotyped to want praise and credit for all pieces of work, both big and small. It is suggested to provide credit to others on the team as well as engaging in team-based projects to build trust and outwardly show true leadership. Another stereotype is the notion that millennials cannot disconnect from technology. While technology has increasingly become a larger part of our culture and way of life across generations, keeping ones laptop closed or not engaging on the cellular phone during meetings provide that opportunity to be present and fully engage in the tasks and conversations at hand (Woodward, 2020).

CONCLUSION

The true millennial leader often shows up to places and spaces as their whole self. When realizing the true millennial leader, we find that the leader has been stereotyped and often criticized but nevertheless come with a certain set of skills and experiences useful to organizations across the spectrum. This is the generation of transparency, outspokenness, and curiosity. As other generations engage with these millennial leaders, they consistently find a more entrepreneurial and technologically savvy generation, providing for opportunities to strategize for a more open, informative, engaging, communicative, and balanced atmosphere.

REFERENCES

Alesso-Bendisch, F. (2020). Millennials want a healthy work-life balance. here's what bosses can do. *Forbes*. https://www.forbes.com/sites/ellevate/2020/07/23/millennials-want-a-healthy-work-life-balance-heres-what-bosses-can-do/?sh=7d37e6127614

Bellamy, W. (2019). *Monumental: it was never about a statue*. BlackGold Publishing.

Bialik, K., & Fry, R. (2019). *Millennial life: How young adulthood today compares with prior generations*. Pew Research Center's Social & Demographic Trends Project. https://www.pewresearch.org/social-trends/2019/02/14/millennial-life-how-young-adulthood-today-compares-with-prior-generations-2/

Burstein, D. D. (2013). *Fast Future: How the millennial generation is shaping our world*. Beacon Press.

DeVaney, S. (2015). Understanding the millennial generation. *Journal of Financial Service Professionals*, *69*(6), 11–14.

Dimock, M. (2019). *Defining generations: Where millennials end and generation Z begins*. Pew Research Center. https://www.pewresearch.org/fact-tank/2019/01/17/where-millennials-end-and-generation-z-begins/

Donahue, J. (2021, November 30). *How to better lead millennials in 2021*. Jenn Donahue. https://www.jenndonahue.com/news-and-views/how-to-better-lead-millennials-in-2021

Fries, K. (2018). 7 Ways millennials are changing traditional leadership. *Forbes*. https://www.forbes.com/sites/kimberlyfries/2018/01/18/7-ways-millennials-are-changing-traditional-leadership/

Fry, R. (2018). *Millennials are the largest generation in the U.S. labor force. Fact Tank: News in the Numbers*. Pew Research Center. Available: https://www.pewresearch.org/fact-tank/2018/04/11/millennials-largest-generation-us-labor-force

Graham, T. M., Coleman, C., & Coleman, J. (2021). Teachable moments and strategies for first-time leaders. In M. Guah (Ed.), *Handbook of research on innate leadership characteristics and examinations of successful first-time leaders* (pp. 1–15). IGI Global. doi:10.4018/978-1-7998-7592-5.ch001

Hardy, J. (2020). *Symone Sanders viewed as millennial force for candidates*. TheGrio. https://thegrio.com/2020/02/04/symone-sanders-viewed-as-millennial-force-for-candidates/

Howe, N., & Strauss, W. (2003). *5 characteristics of millennials*. Michigan Scouting. https://michiganscouting.org/wp-content/uploads/2017/11/Five-Characteristics-of-Millennials.pdf

Jubenville, C. B. (2016). Colin Kaepernick and millennials. *The Washington Times*. https://www.washingtontimes.com/news/2016/sep/8/colin-kaepernick-and-millennials/

Llopis, G. (2022). 5 powerful things happen when a leader is transparent. *Forbes*. https://www.forbes.com/sites/glennllopis/2012/09/10/5-powerful-things-happen-when-a-leader-is-transparent/?sh=3efd86f84a3a

Maxwell, J. C. (2005). *The 360 degree leader: Developing your influence from anywhere in the organization*. Thomas Nelson Inc.

Post, J. (2022). Millennials and modern leadership styles. *business.com*. https://www.business.com/articles/leadership-styles-millennials/

Soussi, N. (n.d.). *4 Skills millennials bring to leadership positions*. Simon Sinek. https://simonsinek.com/discover/4-skills-millennials-bring-to-leadership-positions/

Tensley, B. (2021). *Analysis: How 'the kaepernick effect' has propelled a new generation of athletes to take a stand against racial injustice*. CNN. https://www.cnn.com/2021/10/28/politics/the-kaepernick-effect-race-deconstructed-newsletter/index.html

The Institute of Politics at Harvard University. (n.d.). *Symone Sanders*. Harvard University. https://iop.harvard.edu/fellows/symone-sanders

Vera, A. (2019). *Colin Kaepernick's Nike ad wins emmy for outstanding commercial*. CNN. https://www.cnn.com/2019/09/15/entertainment/nike-ad-emmy-win-trnd

Woodward, R. (2020). *5 Skills millennials can develop to become better leaders*. Simon Sinek. https://simonsinek.com/discover/5-skills-millennials-can-develop-to-become-better-leaders/

Wright, J., & Vazquez, M. (2021). *Symone Sanders, Harris' chief spokesperson, to leave White House*. CNN. https://www.cnnphilippines.com/world/2021/12/2/Symone-Sanders-Kamala-Harris-spokesperson-White-House-US.html

Wylonis, C. (2021). *Millennials are all in on transparency, and companies need to follow suit*. BenefitsPRO. https://www.benefitspro.com/2021/05/26/millenials-are-all-in-on-transparency-and-companies-need-to-follow-suit/?slreturn=20220707101647

Chapter 5
Considerations for Millennial Ascension

Michael N. Weaver
The University of Texas at Austin, USA

Curtis L. Coleman
Virginia State University, USA

ABSTRACT

Ascension is defined by the act of rising to an important position. This chapter identifies rationales, opportunities, and principles for millennial leaders to consider during the ascension phase. Essential points in this chapter include strategizing ascension, realizing opportunity within one's current role, and building credentials. In addition, the chapter also reassesses one's professional network, academic journey, and the notion of chasing a specific title. For millennials, the next step in their career is a cognitive choice that places ideals of lifestyle and work-life balance at the forefront of their decision to ascend. Millennial ascension is more about the impact on who they are serving over the effects on one's own career or finances.

INTRODUCTION

When should I leave? What is my next move? What are my must-haves in the next position? What am I willing to leave behind to ascend? What will I gain? What will I lose? All are common questions when considering a professional transition to the next level in your career. In these deep moments of thought and reflection, leaders tend to seek counsel from peers, colleagues, or friends on their aspirations to ascend. Some of your colleagues will suggest waiting a year before changing position or

DOI: 10.4018/978-1-6684-4711-6.ch005

leaving the organization while others will argue against leaving before a full two years have been completed. Both perspectives of the argument have valid points, but the decision should be ultimately based on what your professional and personal needs are now. Particularly, among millennials, job changes happen often. The Bureau of Labor Statistics (2020) found 2.8 years is the median tenure for ages 25-34. To most specialists in the workforce, millennials may seem professionally impatient when compared to former generations. "Millennials do not develop organization commitment the same way that Baby Boomers have over the years" (Gouldner, 2016, p. 2). However, millennials see opportunities in advancing, transitioning, and moving to various locations. Unlike their generation x or baby boomer counterparts, who may decide to stay in with one company for 10 or more years.

"ALTHOUGH THERE IS NO MOVEMENT, THERE IS STILL ACTION!"

We see ascension as the act of rising to a higher and more important position. Technically the adjective rising is an action. If one aspires to ascend, although they may not be in the act of moving transitioning jobs or careers, they can prepare themselves for the next position in a plethora of ways. For example, continuing education and training, gaining access to a related professional network, and identifying a mentor are phenomenal ways to move up and advance your career professionally. More importantly, all the examples don't require you to make a major change but will put you in space mentally and professionally for advancement.

Build Your Credentials: Employers, both current and future, often would like to see professionals in the field seek opportunities to develop themselves and others beyond the view of their job description and bullet point duties listed on their employee work performance form. If you feel your job or supervisor limits your impact, then seek out related opportunities within your field with other organizations that will not jeopardize your current standing within your job. For example, one can see out membership and volunteer opportunities with an association or non-profit connected to their line of work. It's also common for people in these groups to seek chairperson, executive, and leadership roles within these external organizations which not only looks good on your resume, but it holistically rounds out your experiences with internal and external experiences.

When reviewing your network, one should assess their connection to people within their current work environment, professionals in other organizations, and well-known leaders within the field. Majority of your leaders are connected to others in the field. As a result, sometimes people will follow up with former members of your teams to check references or see what others say about your work ethic and character. Therefore, the old age rule that goes “It’s not what you know, it’s who you know” still bares merit. If you aren’t connected, find a way to strategically connect with these individuals. In our social and technology driven society, people often hire individuals based on a combination of referrals and who they are connected to from former or current organizations. Thus, one should also connect with individual via social media platforms. These platforms can be pivotal in landing your next position. In our social and technology driven society, performing well at your job is simply not enough. Others must also witness your great advances and progress within the field. Documentation just an important as completing job functions. One must be a show horse and a work horse in the field to receive proper acknowledgement and recognition from their peers and colleagues.

During this season of ascension, some have decided to continue or restart their educational journey. The act of enrolling in an academic program should not be taken lightly. Thus, researching programs, credentials, and trainings should be done prior to starting a course. In addition, seek out guidance from those who have similar credentials. One should ask those with a higher background question like how long did it take you to complete your training or program, and do you think it was a good return on your investment? Regarding financial assistance, one should also see if your employer is willing to fully fund your education or at least offer aid to offset out of pocket expenses. Remember, your educational background is valuable, and employers see value in training others for both performance outcomes and leadership opportunities. However, some employee financial assistance programs may come with a stipulation of years of service to the company or the training your seeking may have to be directly connected to the work they require of you. Despite the stipulation, paid training and education is always beneficial if you plan to remain in your field or even transcend beyond it.

METHOD OF WORK VS. TITLE CHASE

Millennials are the largest living generation in the workplace (Alter, 2020). As a millennial looking for an essential leadership position with a lofty salary, I was certainly chasing a title in my earlier years within my field. Most of my conversations and venting sessions with colleagues were filled with statements like “they think they know everything”, “I can do that better than them”, and “they don’t listen to us.” Although some of my statements may have been correct, at the time, I didn’t have the body of work to support the positions I believed I could adequately handle. Before seeking out advancement, one should internally reflect on their body of work that supports advancing to the next role.

What large projects have you been solely responsible for? What strategies for advancement have you led and implemented? What developments have been most successful? What have you learned from your failures? And more importantly, who and what teams have you lead successfully? Ultimately, your body of work should support the title you're chasing. After your own reflection, seek out guidance from trusted colleagues who can review your professional background objectively.

The Body of Work Needed to Ascend: For those who were not hired because of nepotism, most of your future jobs will demand a wide variety of works completed prior to ascension. When examining projects to complete and new strategies to implement, should observe the current work climate to see what projects they can quickly participate in as a team member. As a team member of a special project, observe the relationship between old members, the committee chairperson, and the reporting supervisor for the committee. The results from this observation will provide insight on whether you should rejoin the committee, strive for a leadership within the committee, and more importantly who works well within a committee dynamic. After you've gained some experience as a team member, it's time to request your own leadership role to streamline a special project. Taking initiative will showcase your innovative thinking while separating you from your peers.

Once you have been positioned to lead strategic efforts for small teams, committees, or an appointed group, your work ethic and leadership qualities will speak for themselves. In these moments, people will begin to recognize your body of work and identify you as a leader. Please note, a leadership position, does not equal leadership recognition. Your colleagues, peers, and superiors will determine that based on how you make others feel, how you motivate others, and how well you and your committee perform. Team leadership is an essential characteristic that employees look for in the recruitment process. Look for opportunities to showcase your leadership skills both internally and externally within your field. A well-rounded leader, with successes from both within and outside of the company would be privilege for any hiring manager or supervisor looking to ascend the next person. Thus, your body of work should not only include your actual job duties and responsibilities. Your body of work must transcend job performance norms to advance and ascend.

ENTITLEMENT AND COMPARISON

As a millennial leader, there will be times where one may feel they deserve a promotion, or their productivity thus far should warrants an increase in title or pay.

This is called workplace entitlement, and it seldomly works in favor of the employee looking for it. While annual salary-based increases may be common in the workplace or profession, company rewards come in many different shapes and sizes (e.g. company trips, discounts, memberships, amenities, and public praises). One should also avoid comparing their career or job performance to their peers, especially to those who ascended and may have taken a different or non-traditional route.

For millennials, the next step in their career is a cognitive choice that places ideals of lifestyle and work life balance at the forefront of their decision to ascend. A good job or promotion is no longer defined by increase in pay (Tanner, 2010). Millennials will not agree to sacrifice their time, family goals, and lifestyle ideals for the sake of their job or even the next job.

TIME TO ASCEND

As baby boomers leave the workplace, the opportunity to ascend is at its peak for millennial leaders (Crumbley, 2021). To ascend to the next position, receive a promotion, or move to another organization, one must become an expert at something. One can accomplish this by observing work-related gaps within the organization or in the field. The act of becoming an expert makes your experience and unique skills more than valuable to the organization. As a result, this will increase the organization's motion to retain you while also crafting you an attractive new hire for another organization. Additionally, millennial leaders should consider going beyond their work (Legg, 2020). Leaders are praised and noticed for accomplishing more than just their assigned duties and responsibilities. Don't just execute, but also take initiative.

Growth is optional and change is inevitable. In our social and technology-driven world, change and growth often happen simultaneously. As a leader who transitioned to executive leadership roles quickly, I will not urge you to be patient and wait for growth. However, I will advise you to be proactive by planning your growth. As you assume your next leadership role, visualize what your next ascension will be. What new skills and experiences will that role require? What networks and people do you need access to? How will you ascend and rise to the next leadership role?

For millennials, the next step in their career is a cognitive choice that places ideals of lifestyle and work life balance at the forefront of their decision to ascend. A good job or promotion is no longer defined by increase in pay (Tanner, 2010). Millennials will not agree to sacrifice their time, family goals, and lifestyle ideals for the sake of their job or even the next job.

New Position. Now What?

Now that you have ascended to the next and higher-level role, it's time to strategize how you will make your mark and begin engaging with your new stakeholders. Brozek (2020) created a way for companies to strategize and develop strategy using thought leadership. According to Brozek (2020), thought leadership encourages framing new goals, creating sub-groups to accomplish goals, and identifying innovative solutions with major impacts. Additionally, a new leader must activate the group to implement and produce while also assessing and measuring productivity for long term results (Brozek, 2020).

Figure 1. The Sirius decisions thought leadership development model

AN EXAMPLE OF WHAT WE HAVE SEEN AS TIMES CHANGE

One area that we have seen a rise in millennial leadership is the field of diversity. With the murders of George Floyd and Breonna Taylor, the hiring of chief diversity officers (CDO) has become an emerging trend on postsecondary campuses nationwide (Arnold & Kowalski-Braun, 2011; Leon, 2014; Pennamon, 2017; Wilson, 2013). As such, diversity roles have become more and more attractive and ought after for millennial leaders in order to impact change. Present day, higher education has grown tremendously in terms of diversity, yet it still faces the challenges of making the space more equitable and inclusive.

Millennials have aimed to ascend to take on these roles, even as challenging as the role and time in history currently stands. The discussions held around diversity often focus on whether leaders, teachers, or administrators should be in the lead role of institutional diversity efforts (Winkle-Wagner & Locks, 2020). Furthermore, the CDO has proven to be a popular solution for many institutions to promote and coordinate diversity on college campuses. In most cases, these individuals and their units are the "face" of diversity efforts and carry formal administrative titles like vice provost, vice chancellor, associate provost, vice president, assistant provost, dean, or special assistant to the president for multicultural, international, equity, diversity, and inclusion (Williams & Wade-Golden, 2006; Worthington et al., 2014; Wilson, 2013). There are many synonymous titles of the CDO, but the work and mission of the role is the same across the board. For these specific roles with a shorter history of existence, millennials have less ability to aim for a title, yet understand that the position placement on the organizational chart and scope of work is needed for success in their work products.

The emergence of the chief diversity officer (CDO) position as a senior administrative role in companies and universities signals the critical need to expand representation across higher education among students, faculty, and administrators, as well as within the curriculum (Worthington et al., 2014). Like other professional areas of higher education, it is vital that Chief Diversity Officers have a space to access resources and have a community of people to lean on. Millennials understand they must secure credentials through various forms of professional development to be successful in the CDO position.

Many millennials think the role of the CDO is simple, but it can be quite complex at times. Individuals who fill these roles have a tremendous responsibility and must navigate through unpredictable channels in order to enact change (Wilson, 2013). The quest to educate members of a community on matters related to diversity has often been left up to a few individuals, mostly CDO's. The weight of this position is heavy yet vital to the success of diversity initiatives for institutions and these leaders must be able to have a comprehensive understanding of the organization's culture (Arnold & Kowalski-Braun, 2011; Wilson, 2013). Educating the campus community is just one facet of the many responsibilities carried by the Senior Diversity Officer.

In 2017 Douglas and Little conducted an interview with then Chief Diversity of University of Missouri System and Vice Chancellor for Inclusion, Diversity, and Equity at the University of Missouri about the role and experiences of the CDO. In response to the question of what is a CDO and what preparations, skillsets, and relevant experience does a CDO require, Dr. McDonald responded:

"I describe a Chief Diversity Officer as one that's providing collaborative leadership in the area of diversity and inclusion and helps move an organization forward... helps them think strategically."

The sole focus of the Chief Diversity Officer should be focusing on the outcomes and changes needed for the campus. It is difficult to have dual responsibilities with diversity work (Douglas & Little, 2017). The CDO is someone who serves with some level of accountability regarding the work that they move forward. Though there's a level of shared responsibility with organizational diversity and inclusion efforts, it is important and valuable to have someone who can coordinate and lead.

Ultimately, the CDO is a change agent and ensures that their institution is a place where everyone's voice or idea can be heard (Pennamon, 2017). Though there are some who are weary of CDOs, the CDO has the potential to turn a hostile situation into a non-hostile one through outreach and collaborative efforts (Wilson, 2013). Bolman and Deal (2003) recognized leaders who fail at leading their organization through change tend to lack mobility in four essential frames: structural, human resource, political, and symbolic. Comprehension and utilization of these frames is critical for leaders to be effective when their organization is experiencing change. The CDO must be skilled at managing people and navigating through bureaucracy to create the institutional change sought.

Anything that's worth having never comes easy, the same is true when it comes to the Chief Diversity Officer. While these positions have been consistently mentioned in diversity plans, senior leadership and others have been resistant, falsely criticizing these roles as "ghettoizing diversity" by putting the full burden on the shoulders of one person (Williams & Wade-Golden, 2006). This section explores the various challenges that Chief Diversity Officers face.

When considering what a millennial CDO needs to be successful, two things come to mind: the conditions in place at the institution, and the expectations that leaders and constituents have for what is to be accomplished. For most CDOs, they report or have direct access to the university president or chancellor. However, very few CDOs have a staff or the support necessary to meet the demands of diversity work (Leon, 2014). In a 2014 study conducted by Raul Leon, one of the participants noted "the job is certainly larger than what the staff is capable of handling, specifically referring to the level of work and intensity that is needed to truly make change." Achieving the goal of a diverse, inclusive, and equitable cannot be done by one person alone and without the proper staff support, no change can be made.

Another major area of struggle is tokenism. The tokenized status of persons in educational contexts is not a new concern (Niemann, 2016). However, with pressures of the country advocating and fighting for diversity, equity, and inclusion, universities rushed to ensure diversity had a presence on campus and that presence unfortunately comes at the expense of people of color (Simmonds-Jordan, 2021). Stroshine and Brandl (2011) note:

"According to tokenism theory, tokens (those who comprise less than 15% of a group's total) are expected to experience a variety of hardship in the workplace, such as feelings of heightened visibility, isolation, and limited opportunities for advancement."

Many American universities appoint African Americans and millennials to ceremonial posts such as Chief Diversity Officer (Starcher, 2012). Though presidents, board of regents, and government officials attempt to portray the role as important and vital, it generally a box checked off to say there is a person of color on the cabinet with a vice president title. However, organizations fail to realize the impact of hiring a token to cover up their blind spots (Simmonds-Jordan, 2021) as it does more harm than it does good.

"But the Negro in this country... the future of the Negro in this country... is precisely as bright or as dark as the future of the country. It is entirely up to the American people and not representatives. It is entirely up to the American People whether or not they are going to face and deal with and embrace the stranger they have maligned so long." (James Baldwin, 1979)

The quote above applies similarly to higher education or any organization for that matter. The future of people of color in higher education leadership is as bright or dark as the field allows it to be. It is up to campus communities, alumni, state officials, and university leadership to determine if they will choose to fix what has been broken for so long. The review of literature showed that there is still more to learn about the chief diversity officer and because the height of the CDO happened recently, the literature is ripe.

CONCLUSION

According to Karima et al. (2022), the focus on leadership discussion and research has shifted from explanatory to perspective. For millennials, positive leadership is about identifying people's natural strength and abilities, empowering others to increase productivity, and modeling good work life balance behavior. Thus, millennials are not easily swayed by the ascension alone. Millennial ascension is more about impact to who they are serving over impact to one's own career or finances.

REFERENCES

Alter, C. (2020, January 23). How millennial leaders will change America. *Time*. https://time.com/5770140/millennials-change-american-politics/

Arnold, J., & Kowalski-Braun, M. (2011). The journey to an inaugural chief diversity officer: Preparation, implementation and beyond. *Innovative Higher Education*, *37*(1), 27–36. doi:10.100710755-011-9185-9

Bolman, L. G., & Deal, T. E. (2003). *Reframing organizations: Artistry, choice, and leadership (Jossey-Bass Higher and adult education series)*. Jossey Bass Inc.

Brozek, C. (2020, May 5). *Five ways to make your thought leadership content stand out when the whole world is turning to digital*. Forrester. https://www.forrester.com/blogs/how-to-create-great-b2b-marketing-thought-leadership-content/

Crumbley, J. L., III. (2021). *Millennial Leadership: A Phenomenological Assessment into the Preparedness of the Millennial Leader* [Doctoral dissertation, Northcentral University].

Douglas, T.-R. M. O., & Little, M. (2017). Voice From the Field. *The Journal of Negro Education*, *86*(3), 381–391. doi:10.7709/jnegroeducation.86.3.0381

Gouldner, K. (2016). Millennial mindset: How to attract millennials to an aging industry. *GEN*, *75*(66), 65.

Karima, S., Uusiautti, S., & Määttä, K. (2022). Defining the core of successful millennial leadership. *European Journal of Workplace Innovation*, *7*(1), 109–131. doi:10.46364/ejwi.v7i1.917

Legg, D. (2020, June 16). How long should you wait to switch positions within a company after you start? *The Washington Post*. https://jobs.washingtonpost.com/article/how-long-should-you-wait-to-switch-positions-within-a-company-after-you-start/

Leon, R. A. (2014). The chief diversity officer: An examination of CDO models and strategies. *Journal of Diversity in Higher Education*, *7*(2), 77–91. doi:10.1037/a0035586

Niemann, Y. F. (2016). The Social Ecology of Tokenism in higher education. *Peace Review*, *28*(4), 451–458. doi:10.1080/10402659.2016.1237098

Pennamon, T. (2017). The Emergence of the Community College Chief Diversity Officer. *Diverse Issues in Higher Education*, 17–19.

Simmonds-Jordan, N. A., & Mills, B. (2021, October 14). Why a black chief diversity officer is not the answer when it comes to inclusion. *C Level Magazine*. http://c-levelmagazine.com/why-a-black-chief-diversity-officer-is-not-the-answer-when-it-comes-to-inclusion

Starcher, R. L. (2012). How Higher Education in the U.S. Can Inform Missions' Diversification Efforts. *Mission Studies: Journal of the International Association for Mission Studies*, *29*(2), 201–212. doi:10.1163/15733831-12341237

Stroshine, M. S., & Brandl, S. G. (2011). Race, gender, and tokenism in policing. *Police Quarterly*, *14*(4), 344–365. doi:10.1177/1098611111423738

Tanner, L. (2010). Who are the Millennials? Defence Research and Development Canada Ottawa (Ontario) Centre for Operational Research and Analysis.

U.S. Bureau of Labor Statistics. (2020, September 22). *Employee tenure summary*. U.S. Bureau of Labor Statistics. https://www.bls.gov/news.release/tenure.nr0.htm

Williams, D. A., & Wade-Golden, K. C. (2006). What is a Chief Diversity Officer? Inside Higher Ed.

Williams, D. A., & Wade-Golden, K. C. (2007). The Chief Diversity Officer. *College & University Professional Association for Human Resources*, 38–48.

Wilson, J. L. (2013). Emerging Trend: The Chief Diversity Officer Phenomenon within Higher Education. *The Journal of Negro Education*, *82*(4), 433–445. doi:10.7709/jnegroeducation.82.4.0433

Winkle-Wagner, R., & Locks, A. M. (2020). *Diversity and inclusion on campus: Supporting students of color in higher education*. Routledge.

Wolfe, B. L., & Dilworth, P. P. (2015). Transitioning normalcy. *Review of Educational Research*, *85*(4), 667–697. doi:10.3102/0034654314565667

Worthington, R. L., Stanley, C. A., & Lewis, W. T. (2014). National Association of Diversity Officers in Higher Education Standards of professional practice for chief diversity officers. *Journal of Diversity in Higher Education*, *7*(4), 227–234. doi:10.1037/a0038391

Chapter 6
African American Millennial Leaders:
The Impacts of Panther Parenting and Ubuntu Paradigm

Velicia Hawkins-Moore
Prairie View A&M University, USA

Dahleah Moore
University of Houston-Downtown, USA

ABSTRACT

African diasporic millennial leaders are uniquely situated to embark on critical leadership roles at the end of a millennia, in the middle of dual pandemics (race and COVID 19), an at the beginning of a technological/geopolitical revolution. This chapter examines the ways that African diasporic millennial leaders navigate multiple enterprises the impact of panther parenting. Managers engage the components of Ubuntu paradigm and the relationship with: Ubuntu-based axiological evaluation mechanism. Ubuntu-grounded ontological management tool. Ubuntu-constructed epistemological training instrument. Ubuntu-founded methodological device. It examines the narratives and insights of several prominent millennial leaders in popular culture. It analyzes the unique blend of leadership qualities specific to African diasporic millennial leaders. African diasporic governance standards are founded on Ubuntu principles like panther parenting. It explores the ways contemporary managers engage emerging millennial leaders during the evolution of organizational life cycles.

DOI: 10.4018/978-1-6684-4711-6.ch006

INTRODUCTION

Leadership in the new millennium involves transparency, flexibility, and a collective sense of community (Post, 2022). African diasporic millennial leaders (born between 1980 and 1999) espouse these tenets through direct dialogue, transparency in governance, and an Ubuntu-based organization philosophy (Robinson, 2021). There is some variability in how the age range for millennials (Generation Y) is computed. This 19-year age range, however, is widely accepted within the scientific community (Olsen, 2009). Ubuntu orientation refers to the predilection of individuals (in this case, millennial leaders) to 1) "iitaba" (believe) in Ubuntu (ciLuba). 2) belong to/be members of "abantu" (humanity; human beings: ciLuba), and 3) be a practitioner of; a worker of (Meena mudimu) the principles of Ubuntu (Imhotep, 2020). While this study includes limited references to theoretical and community-based ideologies, it is primarily organized as praxis research. At its core, this investigation offers practical insights and actionable steps. This study is divided into three sections.

The first section examines the narratives and insights of several prominent millennial leaders in popular culture. This section uses broad-based presuppositions to understand and explain the thematic observations in the lives of African diasporic millennial leaders. It draws logical and rational assumptions regarding an Ubuntu foundation from observable processes and patterns in the lives of millennial leaders throughout the African diaspora. An Ubuntu frame abductively utilizes implicit assumptions about communal leadership methodologies and goals. These postulates are then situated within a traditional Africana framework.

The second section analyzes the unique blend of leadership qualities specific to African diasporic millennial leaders. African diasporic millennial governance standards and attributes differ from Western ideations of authority because they are founded on Ubuntu principles like *Panther Parenting* (D. Moore, 2021), Ujamaa (cooperative economics) (Nyerere, 1974), and Sankofa (Hawkins-Moore, 2022). Inductive reasoning occurs when observations are synthesized to develop a general principle (Sauce, Matzel, 2017).

The final section is a deductive exploration of how contemporary managers, supervisors, and senior leaders can engage emerging millennial leaders during the evolution of organizational life cycles. Primarily, Ubuntu paradigm, these modern management strategies, and dynamic governance tools are increasingly crucial as African diasporic millennial leaders assume executive roles in organizations.

The study of African diasporic millennial leadership is critical as the world navigates into intra/post-COVID-19 routines. The current sociocultural landscape is punctuated by the nuances of the global "new normal." This is coupled with the bold and impassioned regard for humanity and inclusivity brought about by the revolutionary social resistance of 2019-20. The incessant murders of unarmed

Black men and women have triggered a conscious uprising, an igniting of the eternal flame of overt defiance, and a consummate rejection of a deficit model in Black and Afrocentric leadership.

NARRATIVES

Many successful African diasporic millennial leaders benefit from a distinctive, idiosyncratic parenting style called *Panther Parenting* (D. Moore, 2021). These systematic stratagems are revealed in the collective narratives of some of the most successful African diasporic millennial leaders. *Panther Parenting* consists of an authoritative (versus authoritarian) parenting foundation. *Panther Parents* are like *Tiger Parents* (Chua, 2011) in their elevated level of parental investment and commitment to children's success. However, *Panther Parents* of African diasporic millennial leaders differ significantly from *Tiger Parents* in the nature and intensity of the attachment to goals and the methodology utilized to create a sense of buy-in, onus, and autonomy for the children (D. Moore, 2021). A more extensive and substantive examination of the essence of *Panther Parenting* is provided in section two of this article. These traits are standard throughout the list of millennial leaders highlighted for this study.

Abductive reasoning is a method of forming logical inferences from a set of fragmented, partial, and often incomplete observations (Beckwith, 2018). Although the concept of abductive reasoning itself has been hotly debated, the general understanding is that it derives a set of best practices from incomplete observations (Kapitan, 1992). In the case of African-descended millennial leaders, various interviews, articles, and reports have been collected to extract an understanding and an interpretation of their cohesive and communal thought patterns, beliefs, and insights.

The aspect of leadership that sets successful, diasporic, millennial sports, entertainment, and media personalities apart is transferability (Banks, 2019). The diasporic millennial leaders selected for this study have been identified by their ability to maximize the impact of their transferable (portable) talents and competencies. These diasporic millennial leaders shift the factual specificity of their abilities and skillsets to occupy nuanced spaces. They build unique quasi-fanbases with supporters. They evolve to meet the socio-political and cultural needs of the most marginalized and historically minoritized throughout the diasporic community. They galvanize the masses by capitalizing on the minutiae of everyday life. They have become experts at defining those issues which are finite, as well as the all-encompassing. They construct empires of revolution from careers in athletics. They engineer mechanisms for social and civic change, from professions in the entertainment industry. They grow militias of faithful followers from news, dance, and media fanatics.

Abby Phillip (born in 1988) is an African American is a senior political correspondent at CNN and anchor of the highly-rated news show *Inside Politics* on Sunday mornings. Her parents (June and Carlos Phillip) are initially from Trinidad, but they moved to Washington D.C, so that her father could attend Howard University. Abby later attended Harvard University, where she studied for a Bachelor's degree in Government. After Abby's birth, the family moved back to Trinidad and returned to America when Abby was about eight years old (T&T Loop Lifestyle News, 2021). Later the family moved to Germantown, Maryland. After only four years working at CNN, her sense of purpose and dedication led to a promotion to her current position and saw her named the host of the popular news segment. She showed leadership qualities as the "on-air" voice for Black Millennials during the January 6th uprising at the U.S Capitol (Abby Phillip, CNN, November 29, 2021). Typically, first-generation African Americans would not be included in a *Panther Parenting study*. The connection to and history of resistance to American colonization, racism, and oppression helped establish the tenets of *Panther Parenting*. However, the case of Abby Phillip is unique in that she embraces her multicultural family yet has a deep appreciation of her nuanced role in the information industry and her connection (as an Afro-descended woman) to America and the rest of the world (T&T Loop Lifestyle News, 2021).

African diasporic millennial leaders raised by *Panther Parents* often exhibit elevated confidence, conviction, and self-awareness. These leaders benefit from this "strength-based parenting perspective" (Iruka, 2013). Leaders like Abby Phillip have often been equipped with the necessary tools to disrupt patterns and practices that perpetuate microaggressions and misogynistic bias and prejudice (Iruka, 2013). Their exposure to this distinctive parenting style has enhanced their powers of optimism and confidence. Abby is quoted in a 2021 article as follows "I think the way I move forward in my career is saying to myself, I am just going to do this as long as I can, and if I hit a dead-end, then I cannot go any further. But I will do this for as long as I can" (T&T Loop Lifestyle News, 2021). African-descended millennial leaders draw strength, fortification, and affirmation from their intricate and grounded familial relationships. They transfer that style, assurance, and validation to marketable managerial skills like self-actualization, team building, and assertiveness. African diasporic millennial leaders quickly become significant and consequential components of global industry. They exhibit the most complex and essential future-focused leadership attributes.

Naomi Osaka (born in 1997) identifies as a Black and Asian professional tennis player. Her mother is Japanese, and her father is Haitian. When Naomi was three years old, her family moved from Japan to Long Island, New York, near her father's family. When she turned 21 years old, she won her first Grand Slam, becoming the first Japanese player to win a singles title in a Grand Slam tournament. Osaka's father

(Leonard Francois) asserts that he drew inspiration from Richard Williams (Venus and Serena Williams' father). He contends that Richard gave him the "blueprint" to coach and train his daughter despite neither father having any formal training or experience in the professional tennis world. Naomi showed the epitome of millennial leadership ability as she advocated for her mental health concerns when she chose to withdraw from the French Open in 2021 (Naomi Osaka).

African-descended millennial leaders, like Naomi Osaka, tend to exude intrinsic ambition and a moral compass and constitution driven by social-justice aspirations. Contemporary research suggests that historical sociological and anthropological studies of child and youth development might have ignored or understudied growth and progressive assets among historically minoritized youth (Bialystok, Majumder, & Martin, 2003). Despite constant *othering* and exclusion, African-descended millennial leaders who benefit from *Panther Parenting* reject being ostracized and instead create spaces that are exclusive, private, intimate, and serene. These physical and figurative places are conducive to success, and they add a layer of defense and protection against trauma, confusion, abuse, and mistreatment.

Beyonce (born in 1981) was ranked among the 15 most impactful millennials in 2017. She is a world-renowned singer, songwriter, and actress. The 2020 release of her musical/visual album, *Black is King*, highlighted her writing, directing, and executive producing skills. It also paid homage to Africa and the African diasporic cultural connections. She has used her music to pay tributes to her parents in many ways. Her parents are known for having been instrumental in her success. She was raised in Houston, Texas, and began a singing career at nine. Beyonce' was the essence of millennial leadership as she navigated a very public marriage, career, and parenting. African diasporic millennial leaders raised by *Panther Parents* frequently show high work ethic and flexibility (Trier-Bieniek, 2016).

Simone Biles (born in 1997) is hailed as the most decorated American gymnast. Biles went to live with her maternal grandfather at the age of three. She and her younger sister spent some time in foster care before they were adopted by Ron (a U.S. Airforce Veteran) and his wife Nellie when Simone was five years old. Although Nellie is not biologically related to Simone, *other mothering (Hill-Collins,2000)* is a critical component of *Panther Parenting* in the African diasporic community. Simone recounts the practice (started by Nellie) of mapping out her twelve-month goals at the beginning of each school year. This pattern began not long after her ADHD diagnosis and her gymnastics lessons (Simone Biles, 2021). Simone exuded millennial leadership as she shared her struggles and psychological traumas stemming from sexual abuse. Many times, African diasporic millennial leaders raised by *Panther Parents* will present higher than average levels of resiliency and leadership.

Symone Sanders (born in 1989) served as Vice President Kamala Harris' chief spokesperson through December 2021. Sanders' mother, Terri, was the former

Executive Director of the Great Plains Black History Museum. Her mother currently serves as publisher of Nebraska's only black-owned newspaper. Her father is retired from the U.S. Army Corps of Engineers. Sanders explored facets of her African diasporic identity by performing in the cast of *African Redemption: The Life and Legacy of Marcus Garvey.* Symone embodied millennial leadership as she worked first with the Bernie Sanders campaign and then with the Kamala Harris team. In many cases, millennial leaders raised by *Panther Parents* possess a heightened sense of self-awareness and autonomy.

Serena Williams (born in 1981) is one half of the famous "Williams Sisters" duo in international tennis. Serena grew up in Compton, Las Angeles. She, her sister, and her father traversed the rough inner-city streets searching for a dream of tennis stardom. Serena began to play tennis around the age of four. In her HBO series *Being Serena,* she bravely assumes the mantle of millennial leadership as she confronts the crisis of Black maternal mortality and her near-miss with death during the birth of her daughter Olympia. Williams expresses a connection with her African diasporic roots in a widely shared Instagram post chronicling the origins of African hair braiding (Fasanella, 2019). Her foundation is also building schools in Jamaica, Uganda, Zimbabwe, and Kenya. Typically, millennial leaders raised by *Panther Parents* show extreme emotional intelligence and conscientiousness.

LEADERSHIP QUALITIES

African diasporic millennial leaders' qualities have not always been framed as assets. For example, Serena Williams' physique has undoubtedly aided her numerous tennis victories, yet she has come under countless media assaults for not appearing feminine enough (Davis, Gopal, 2022). However, in the 21st century, African diasporic millennial leaders have embraced nontraditional strategies in leadership. One example of this embrace is Serena Williams' withstanding the personal assaults to not only build an unrivaled tennis career, but to become a vocal spokesperson for African descended women in healthcare. She used her own traumatic experience during labor and delivery to highlight significant healthcare disparities involving black women in America (Lockhart, 2018). These stratagem assist in doing the work of combating exclusion and creating opportunities for future African diasporic leaders. These characteristics are audacity, perfectionism/competitiveness, laser focus, communal tethering, and self-care/fulfillment (Haynie, 2016).

Audacity

"Just a reminder to set boundaries. Audacity is at an all-time high" (DJ Intel, Twitter 2020)

African diasporic millennial leaders have embraced the ability to harness unmitigated gall and courageous, valiant forms of arrogance as ammunition against exclusion, injustice, and glass ceilings (McKenzie, 2017). This boldness is manifested in how millennial leaders communicate their agreement, satisfaction, gratification, and fulfillment (Graves, 2020). African diasporic millennial leaders use their sense of fearlessness to confront the hard truths regarding African diasporic agency and onus. Black millennial leaders contend with their obligations to contribute to the collective versus their need to realize their hopes, ambitions, and goals. Fred Bonner and Bequita Pegram identified the term *Code-stitching* in their 2001 article in the online magazine, *Diverse Issues in Higher Education.* They use the word to frame how BIPOC (Black, Indigenous, People of Color) can navigate potentially racially hostile spaces while maintaining a true sense of connection and appreciation for their native culture (Pegram, Bonner, 2021). In this way, African diasporic millennial leaders have begun to explore their aestheticism boldly.

Code-stitching allows for the inclusion of body language, verbal, and non-verbal messaging, as well as codified cultural norms and exemplars. *Code-stitching* allows diasporic millennial leaders to move beyond superficial languaging. It enables African diasporans to lean into holistic cultural connectivity. It allows them to authentically take up space in the most bold, prolific manner imaginable. These leaders engage this form of audacity as a means of harnessing creative energies, channeling collective powers, and mobilizing the full potential of the diasporic community.

Panther parenting facilitates millennial leader's ability to draw from different aspects of their personas to meet the individual needs of specific situations. The 1980s brought about a significant paradigm shift in the ways that African American parenting is understood. (McLoyd, Hardaway, Jocson, 2019) These same principles can explain the ways that diasporic millennial leaders have grown to embody the manifestations of Panther Parenting. Although some of the tenets of Panther Parenting can be traced to the ideologies of the Black Panther Party (Hill-O'Neal, C. Dec. 2015. Personal Communication) Panther Parenting as an academic construct is holistically separate from the Political Party and the movement.

One example of this level of audacity in African descended diasporic leaders concerns both Simone Biles, and Naomi Osaka. In the article The Audacity: When Black Women Decide for Themselves, author Khristi Adams (2021) explores the ways that white society struggles with Black women who prioritize them selves and their own physical, mental, and emotional health and well-being. She highlights the disparities in treatment of Black and white athletes and entertainers. She highlights the necessity of a significant level of audacity to counter to toxic implications of the implicit and explicit bias and prejudice that they would encounter. The author refers to the attribute, audacity, as a much-needed core strength. It is a powerful secret weapon, to be wielded in times of attack and distress. *Code-stitching* is an effective technique for applying this level of audacity. It can be displayed visually, verbally, or vicariously. It can be strategically aimed at an intended recipient and a community response can also accompany it.

PERFECTIONISM/COMPETITIVENESS

"I Understood the Assignment" (Tay Money, 2021)

The movement to animate African diasporic millennial leadership involves a constant balancing act. Leaders vacillate between motivating and mobilizing the troops and fighting self-defeatist, perfectionist ideals. Leaders connect their fan base with resources and support that can contribute to elevated levels of personal and communal success. Understanding the proverbial *assignment* as a millennial leader requires a strong sense of autonomy, while still being centered and grounded by the collective needs and desires of the community. Understanding and appreciating the *assignment* of African diasporic millennial leadership includes exhibiting the ability to strive for black excellence while simultaneously extending oneself the grace that is experienced through introspection, and self-reflection.

Perfectionism in the context of African descended millennial leaders refers to a combination of individuals sense of community and their role in it (Stewart, 2019). It explores millennial leaders' ideations surrounding cultural identity, cultural competence, community and individual expectations, and definitions. Perfectionism concerns a counterbalance between presuppositions and beliefs, knowledge and thought, fact and ever evolving opinions. Perfectionism in African diasporic millennial leadership surrounds occupying a shifting counterspace (Vaccaro, Swanson, Marcotte, Newman).

In 2017 Socorro Morales sought to re-define the notion of counterspace. The term is used to identify a safe-space where the re-imagining of perceived deficits of people of color are effectively and efficiently challenged. Leaders are afforded an opportunity to seek solutions to age-old problems in climates free from hostility and antagonism. This iteration of perfectionism moves diasporic millennial leaders from the periphery and centers their ideals, standards, and goals. Rather than an impossible, unobtainable version of perfection, diasporic millennials serve in this capacity as shapers of contemporary cultural content, academic discourse and dialogue, and ancestral artistic artifacts.

In his 2007 piece, Elwood Watson recounts some aspects of Tupac Shakur's upbringing that enabled him to ascend to levels of excellence and enabled him to compete with his own success and the entertainment industry that sought to contain him (Watson, 2007). The Panther Party exercised a profound connection to building a solid and diverse knowledge base. The ability to excel academically (and consequently socially and culturally) is predicated on an ability to understand a diverse set of theoretical concepts and abstract ideas Watson, 2007). Perfection is a personal level that is obtained. It is not assessed by another person's level of attainment. In a Panther Parenting Paradigm perfection and competition are internal processes. They build intrinsic fortitude and are driven by innate motivations.

The competitive aspect of diasporic millennial leadership involves a healthy level of exchange. Competition comprised of the consistent application of unapologetic, unmatched pressure. Pressure hat builds alliances, pressure that compels each leader to bring forth their best effort. This form of competition serves as a recourse to anti-intellectualism. It counters misnomers and misrepresentations. By increasing the level of rigor, precision and intent millennial diasporic leaders ease the impact of myopic and irrational organizational growth (Wilford, 2020)

During the COVID-19 lockdowns, many millennial leaders seized the moment as an opportunity to strengthen and perfect their crafts. During their alone time (Matsumoto, 2020) leaders explored variations of facets within their genres or engaged new ones. Ordinarily, perfectionism is considered a hindrance and an added, unattainable standard. However, for African diasporic millennial leaders, the drive for flawlessness and the genuine competitive spirit continues to produce heightened talent and excellence. Fueled by the greats from every industry in America, millennial leaders hold their predecessors in high esteem. They acknowledge the contributions of the Black leaders who came before them, and they establish innovative ways to build on the foundational tenets of the black community (Ellis, accessed Dec. 2021).

LASER FOCUSED

"Get Into It" (Tabatha Brown, 2018)

African diasporic millennial leaders have learned to find value in their uniqueness, in their crafts and within themselves outside their proximity to whiteness. They maintain an intense level of concentration and attention to detail borne of their love of competition and their quest for greatness. The Macmillan dictionary formally defines the phrase *get into it* as an invitation to explore, become excited about, delve into a deeper understanding of a subject or topic. African descended diasporic millennial leaders have adapted the phrase to showcase a specific issue which they are particularly proficient in and proud of their progress and level of acumen. It is often indicative of moment when the leadership can/will display a heightened sense of achievement. This concept takes on an idiosyncratic quality when viewed through an African descended diasporic millennial leader lens. These leaders benefit from a strength derived from actively rejecting and negating the historical false equivalence of Black inferiority and racist propagandistic tropes and mechanisms (Darity, Mullen, 2022).

Panther parenting precepts are in alignment with certain aspects of being fully engaged, and highly attentive. Diasporic millennial leaders use their sense of hyper focus, commitment, and enthusiasm to embody the sentiments of Dr Russell Barkley's theory of *Parents as Shepherds and not Engineers (1997)*. This ideology asserts that the sciences involving neuro-imaging, behavior genetics, developmental psychology and neuro-psychology prove that psychological traits that emerge as a child matures are impacted by environmental factors, but they are also impacted by their genetics. Dr Barkley describes children as a "genetic mosaic of their extended family". As a shepherd/parent, individuals are responsible for exposing youth to nourishing activities, but ultimately youth are not blank slates, empty vessels, tabula rasa (Barkley, 2022). The connection to generations of genetic material and appropriate intellectual stimuli have contributed to generations of youth exposed to the principles of Panther Parenting.

Being laser focused or hyper-focused and exhibiting a lack of flexibility and diversification can easily be a weakness in the business world and entertainment industry. Nevertheless, African diasporic millennial leaders take characteristics that some view negatively and turn them into their superpowers (Time Staff, 2015). The level of focus, the intensity of alignment, and the concentration of energy allow these leaders to promote the salience of socio-political, and cultural concerns. They use their influence within popular culture to shift emphasis, and attention to detail to prominent legal and ethical problems in the contemporary climate (Campbell, 2015).

The 2021 release of the contemporary Rap artist Doja Cat's blockbuster hit, *Get into It Yuh.* Supports a sentiment made popular by vegan food connoisseur and NAACP Image Award winner Tabitha Brown (Brown, 2021). The catchy phrase is an invitation of sorts. It is a clarion call for all interested parties to connect to the current events. African diasporic millennial leaders allow the phrase to shape their ideations of success and wholeness. The phrase advises all within earshot to become wholly invested, fully present, and actively attentive. By embracing the new and unknown, leaders encourage connecting with the unfamiliar. Getting into the nuanced can feel like existing in a space that requires vulnerability, intentionality, and accountability.

Amanda Gorman, a Black American poet, and activist, was born in 1998. She attended Harvard University, and one of the foci of her work is the African diaspora. She was catapulted into fame when she read her poem *The Hill We Climb* during the inauguration of 2020. Although her celebrity increased dramatically after the recitation, she does not want to be considered an overnight success. She highlights the years of demanding work and intestinal fortitude devoted to overcoming her obstacles and building upon her strengths. Amanda Gorman displays the true essence of African diasporic millennial leadership, as she never strayed far from her focus (Editorial Team, BHM.org, 2021).

COMMUNAL TETHERING/TIES

"I Can do All Things Through Black People Rhythmically Yelling...AYYYEEEE" (The Undefeated Internet, 2019)

The ability to draw strength from the collective while simultaneously pouring back into that talent pool, resources and cultural capital is a delicate balance. African diasporic Millennial leaders benefit from a deep-seated connection to family, community, and often, the Earth. Their expert abilities and talents emanate from an ethereal place buried deep below the surface of any superficial practice or training. The exuberant, youthful leaders bear the weight of the calling on their lives by treating it as a ministry of sorts. In this way (and only in this way) is the load made bearable. By allowing the community response to share in the burden of production, the leader is free to participate in the exchange of thoughts, resources, and energies. In her in-depth Netflix Documentary *Homecoming,* the multi-Platinum-selling artist Beyonce' explains the distribution of responsibility between herself and her fictitious alter-ego Sasha Fierce (. By allowing the ministry itself or the artistic genius to bear the weight of the responsibility for the management and control, the person is not weighed down with the totality of the responsibility (Kananen, 2020).

Beyoncé also shares a special connection and a communal tethering to her distinctive fan club, the Beyhive (Avdeeff, Mangaoang, Woehrel, Viñuela, Tinsley, Kooijman, Iddon, 202). This official grouping of her dedicated fan base has a reputation for fiercely and consistently defending her against perceived media misconceptions, and antagonistic agency attacks. The Communal tethering between the performer (Beyoncé') and her group of loyal admirers is a symbiotic one. The artist acknowledges the contributions (purchasing power and artistic loyalty) of her adoring audience by paying homage to them in song, performance, and special seating. The Beyhive (completely defined by group identity) I return uplift and support the performer by collectively patronizing and spreading awareness of the artists humanitarian and charitable endeavors. Diasporic millennial leaders take up space in ways that transform their philanthropic expanse into a pseudo-ecosystem of sorts. The expanse of these leaders' domains is ubiquitous and the effects transcend racial and ethnic boundaries.

The synergistic reverberations of *"Black People Rhythmically Yelling... AYYYEEEE"* is reminiscent of traditions explored in the early Black church, and even further back, during African tribal and ritualistic practices. Social Scientist Ralph Wiley deconstructs the notion of primal (not primitive) verbal utterances that defy the conventions of language. In his book Why Black People Tend to Shout, he attempts to explain these rhythmic, guttural expressions as Wiley (1991) proposes that Black people tend to shout ''because, when joy, pain, anger, confusion and frustration, ego and thought, mix it up, the way they do inside Black people, the uproar is too big to hold inside. The feeling must be aired'' (p. 1). Wiley further explains, ''Black people tend to shout because they want the answers to questions that go unasked'' (p. 2). Earl Wright expounds upon Wiley's considerations by suggesting that the collective negation of the value of Black culture, Black contributions, and Black identity as a whole, have left the Black community *speechless*, but not voiceless. The historical violence and terror rained upon Blackness have left this millennial generation of leaders sometimes without sufficient verbiage to convey the degree of their angst and disillusionment. They have adopted (and adapted) their ancestral practice of articulating both agreement and dismay though self-affirming shouts (Wright, 2001). They compensate for inadequate vernacular with poetic cry's and cheers. A pulsing call and response cadence take up where mere words fall short. A jaunty bellow fills the space of unspoken and unsteady vocabulary. The chants and cheers, the jaunts and jeers of Black people supporting the efforts and endeavors of their diasporic millennial guideposts have become a familiar staple within the circles of African descended leaders.

SELF-CARE

"Y'all Not Gonna Stress Us Out-Every Black Woman Everywhere" (BlackTwitter, 2021)

The mantra of the self-care generation, as sung by Solange Knowles (born in 1986), entitled Borderline (an Ode to Self-Care), may give significant insight into the African diasporic millennial leaders' commitment to and emphasis on the topic of personal protection and awareness. Close examination of the sociolinguistics surrounding the formation of concepts (real and imagined) that support specific self-care aimed at the needs of diasporic millennial leaders, reveals important contributions from trusted, prominent, figures in the media and entertainment. Film maker Ryan Coogler use his vast body of artistic works to engage the philosophies, racial histories and ethic ideologies impacting Black and Indigenous people of color. Beyond the documented past injustices and self-care hurdles, Coogler examines the persistent contemporary problems that plague the diasporic millennial leaders battle for wellness and mindfulness (Wanzo, 2022).

These leaders often displayed behaviors that exposed how deeply conscious and painfully aware of the consequences of neglecting self-care they were. Shanta Smith's (Ed.D.)

2020 article on the urgency of radical self-care for Black women leaders. She points to the necessity of intentionality is self-care strategies. One important distinction can be between creating rules (to guide the people that you engage and interact with), versus boundaries (to relegate and govern your own behavior). Diasporic millennial leader Allyson Felix had a very public battle with her sponsor Nike, in what she calls their typical strategy of punishing pregnancy in sports (Gregory, 2021). Felix defied the odds by breaking the World Record a mere ten months after giving birth to her daughter (Camryn). She then left her lucrative endorsement deal with Nike to become the first big name athlete to sign with Athleta. Athlete is the first sportswear brand specifically for women athletes. Simone Biles would later follow Felix's move. Beyond her athletic prowess, Allyson Felix used her platform to champion the causes associated with Black women's maternal mortality disparities in America. The most decorated athlete in the world used her voice and influence to become an advocate for Black maternal health and well-being (Gregory, 2021).

Major push-factors inhibiting an emphasis on self-care in African diasporic millennial leadership include complex and compound psychological traumas, generational stress disorders, continuing racially motivated injustices, and cognitive dissonance (Quaye, Karikari, & Allen, Okello, Carter, 2019). The unlearning of these toxic traits has become a lucrative industry and a saving grace (Smith, 2020). Actively protecting one's own well-being both physically and mentally is one important facet of achieving Black boy joy, Black girl magic, and Black LGBTQI/ Gender non-conforming triumph.

Primary pull factors for self-care as a non-negotiable involves communal demographic, psychographic, and geographic characteristics (e.g. race, ethnicity, political interests, cultural beliefs, physical origins, ancestral origins). The dangerous and destructive historical narratives perpetuating self-hatred and imposter syndrome among diasporic millennial leaders are being mitigated en masse.

Despite the biases and stereotypes that millennial leaders are consistently faced with, they continue to show up in spaces as their authentic selves. They continue to create safe spaces for others like them to grow, create, and explore. They refuse to shift their energy from positive to negative. They insist on bringing their best selves to the table to negotiate a formidable path forward and continue investing in a world that has been hostile, cruel, and unaccommodating. (Suyanto, Mu'ah, Purwanti, & Sayyid, 2019).

UBUNTU PARADIGM IN DIAPORIC MILLENNIAL MANAGEMENT: HOW MANAGERS, SUPERVISORS, AND SENIOR LEADERS ENGAGE UBUNTU PARADIGM TO NAVIGATE CHANGES IN THE ORGANIZATIONAL LIFE CYCLE

African diasporic millennial leaders have unique and specific characteristics that make them highly qualified leaders (Fry, Parker, 2018). Their abilities to shift between their media/entertainment personas and spokespersons for their fan base in the culture provide a distinctive leadership advantage (Grace, Rosenberg, 2016). These leaders have dominated their sport, entertainment, and media fields. They capitalized on these successes by becoming brand ambassadors, spokespersons for passion projects and personal causes. They created industries, major commodities and products. Upper and mid-level managers must show more flexibility with work structure, offering remote, blended, and hybrid options. Managers must support diasporic millennial leaders as they participate in collaborations and exchanges within the workplace. African diasporic millennial leaders are accustomed to enriching meaningful work tasks and to supervisors who are willing to endorse such options. Aspects of Panther parenting have prepared millennial leaders to seek reciprocity in a work environment. Panther Parenting has shaped them into individuals who require mutually fulfilling structures of management that assure them room for growth. Managers can aid millennial leaders by a focusing on a social-emotional learning model that incorporates a mental and physical health component. Managers must make this more than just a talking point, they should incorporate components of this into each workday. Panther Parenting has uniquely equipped African diasporic millennial leaders to transition to culturally responsive work places. Managerial staff can create a culturally responsive environment for employees of color. They can eliminate glass ceilings and other hindrances to promotion and elevation within the company (Arneil, Alcantara1, Alvarez, 2020). Many of these transformative stratagems can be accomplished by implementing the four facets of Ubuntu Paradigm: Ubuntu Ontology, Ubuntu Axiology, Ubuntu Epistemology, and Ubuntu Methodology.

Ubuntu Ontology

Ubuntu Ontology serves as the basis for culturally responsive and transformational leadership among African diasporic millennial leaders. It can best be described as a leadership model's academic or pedagogical ethos that targets an intersectional population. The foundational components of the Ubuntu Paradigm offer a didactic platform uniquely equipped to meet African diasporic millennial leaders' social and professional needs. The broad umbrella of leadership outside the African diaspora continues to subject millennial leaders to uniform notions of identity and Westernized ideas of power and authority. These leaders face a daily battle to mitigate the impact of the perceived stigmas of youth (deemed inexperience) and culture (African diasporic). A deep engagement with the principles of Ubuntu Ontology can transform leadership by dismantling long-standing and racially biased promotion and advancement barriers.

The practical application of this component focuses on the person-physical environment relationship and the spiritual relationship (Chigangaidze, 2021). In general, an ontological perspective relies on a set of concepts that make up a broader subject area. In the case of effectively managing millennials, Ubuntu ontology identifies the functional properties of diasporic millennial management and the ways that those attributes can best be applied. Managers of diasporic millennial leaders must avoid common microinvalidations (Montanez, 2020):

- Managers should avoid the concepts "I don't see race", "I am race neutral"- These sentiments only serve to highlight the place of privilege from which non POC engage race/ethnicity. Having the privilege of not thinking about or considering race is often not an option for diasporic millennial leaders. The climactic racial tensions of 2020 shined a spotlight on the heightened challenges that African descended millennial professionals and leaders face in the workforce. These leaders faced dual pandemics of COVID 19 and maintaining professionalism and productivity in the face of racial trauma and state sanctioned violence in real time. Managers must use intentional and specific languaging when building safe work spaces and non-hostile creative environments.
- Managers must refrain from attempting to form superficial bonds or connections with diasporic millennial leaders by asserting that they "have friends/ children/ partners of that race". The myth of proximity as a cure for

prejudice and racism has been debunked since slavery was practiced openly in America. Slave masters had sons, daughters, grandchildren, siblings, etc. These familial relations did not negate the racism and dehumanizing practice of owning people and treating them like chattel. The analogy that cannibals and serial killers had children, family members, and friends that they did not murder or consume. This does not make their treacherous acts any less reprehensive. Highlighting having an acquaintance, friend, or family member the same race as a BIPOC diasporic millennial leader likewise dos not absolve managers of racial bias or inappropriateness.

- Managers cannot openly confuse workers of the same race/ethnicity. This is seen as a complete lack of attention to detail and respect for individuality and personhood. Refusing to take the time to recognize individuals for who they are and for what they contribute to the team can create a negative shift in the work dynamic (Ferlazzo, 2019). Managers must eliminate the *white gaze* (and its lasting impact) from functioning work environments. The function of the *white gaze* is as a tool for centering and essentializing whiteness and white interests. It shapes the way creatives, inventors, and artisans operate. It is symbolic for the ways in which whiteness consumes priority and dominates how leaders think and operate within society. (Gassam Asare, 2021) Managers must move work, art, and production out of the white ether.

The person-physical environment in Ubuntu Ontology involves creating safe (physical) spaces and stigma-free zones. This notion is the tangible manifestation of Carl Rogers's mental/psychological concept, unconditional-positive regard (Rogers, 1963). As a critical component of a transformative leadership model, African diasporic millennial leaders have access and buy-in to a place that affords them respite and an informal sense of togetherness, cohesion, and congruence (Chigangaidze, 2021). In African diasporic settings, these leaders often include familial elements of the community like "breaking bread." This concept is more than simply the sharing of food; it is an act of communicating and relationship building through playful banter, the dropping of insightful nuggets of wisdom, and the process of active listening in a judgment-free way (Carey, 2016).

Ubuntu's definition of spirituality relates to moral uprightness; it is not a reference to a specific religious practice or even to general religiosity (Battle, 2021). Desmond Tutu describes the "freedoms of individuality and community" as almost synonymous (Battle, 2021). The stigma-defeating impact of a relationship of connectivity, belonging, and moral uprightness transcends the normative influence of Western ideations of leadership. Managers should draw from the diasporic millennial leaders' commitment to the greater good. They can increase the spirit of productivity and community by rejecting antiquated notions of a top down management style. They should capitalize on the magnanimous vibrancy, collaborative nature, and flexible disposition that diasporic millennial leaders often create.

Beyond the traditional conventions of the African-centered leadership model, an Ubuntu-based Ontology would involve a connection to the larger *truth.* It relies on relationships with the greater community. Historically Black Colleges and Universities (HBCUs) reject deficit thinking; in exchange for asset-based approaches, they have become resources and points of access and entry for African diasporic millennial leaders at various racial and ethnic intersections. Managers would do well to understand the significance of the HBCU community and its efficacy in developing Black talent. HBCUs help competent and adept diasporic millennial leaders to segue from student to junior executive seamlessly. Ubuntu Ontology utilizes relationships as an anti-stigmatization device. Managers could likewise use authentic rapport establishment as a means of reversing the effects of unfair censure. HBCUs hold the unique distinction of being an integral part of the ^{6th} region of the African Union (King, Kuschminder, 2023). 2019 was designated "The Year of Return'' by Ghana's President Nana Akufo-Addo. His declaration served as an open invitation for diasporic, African descended people around the globe, particularly those affiliated with HBCUs, to make their pilgrimage or a literal "Sankofa '' to Africa. (Kiunguyu, 2020). Reconnecting with continental Africans makes these leaders even more adept for global leadership positions. It positions them in ways that gives them first hand exposure, immersion in diverse environments, and a means of understanding geopolitical constructs from a first-person perspective.

Managers should also consider the HBCU community as pipelines for the talent pool that is diasporic millennial leaders. The HBCU network across America and the Caribbean is vast. The number of schools operating individual study abroad programs, international university collaborations, and transcontinental research partnerships is impressive and increasing at a significant rate. A multilateral partnership between HBCUs has resulted in the inception of a top-tier, research-centered satellite campus in West Africa. The first such endeavor of this kind initiated by HBCUs in the Global Knowledge Economy is revolutionary. Managers of millennials can partner with such initiatives early in order to solidify relationships and gain access to the increasing talent pool. This partnership between Morgan State University and African University College of communication (in Ghana, West Africa) will allow similar leadership development initiatives to increase exponentially. African diasporic millennial leaders would be exposed to ideas about and reciprocal relationships with HBCUs. In their 2017 article, Derek Wilson and Veeda Williams highlight the power of Ubuntu in developing frameworks like these that work to foster optimistic self-images and overall positive mental health models. Early career leaders who struggle at the intersections of race, gender, and ethnic background benefit from the "connectedness, competency, and consciousness" created by Ubuntu Ontology

(Wilson, Williams, 2013), The formation of a "Wakanda'' like branch/satellite campus in West Africa is allowing the scope of psycho-social research and academic scholarship to expand, while also permitting the HBCUs to evolve within a global context authentically. This can all be accomplished while remaining true to their overarching mission and without losing the uniqueness of the HBCU experience. Intersectional African diasporic millennial leaders can connect with these HBCUs as a component of Ubuntu Ontology academically, through Black Greek Letter Organizations (BGLOs), or other community stakeholders. For example, "In the summer of 2019, fraternity brothers from the Montclair Kappa League of Kappa Alpha Psi Incorporated took a group of six high school mentees from New Jersey to Ghana, West Africa (Watch the Yard, n.d.). The Montclair Kappa League hosts an annual international travel series, and the Kappas wanted to make sure that youth from the area they serve had a chance to experience" (Hawkins-Moore, 2021). Linking these students to a greater sense of self is a pathway to teaching them to dream (Giovanni, 1968). A solid connection to identity, hopefulness, goals, and pride can be effective countermeasures to stigmatization and an integral component of a feeder pattern system to develop future generations of African diasporic millennial leaders.

A fundamental commitment to Ubuntu Ontology in the African diasporic millennial leadership model can mitigate the negative impacts of imposter syndrome (Young, 2019). Ubuntu Ontology exists as a specific pedagogical foundation that supports African diasporic millennial leaders by moving beyond posturing and performative measures towards a substantive inclusive framework.

Ubuntu Axiology

Managers can engage in racially just practices in leadership while attending to the specific psycho-social needs of African diasporic millennial leaders through the appropriate application of the critical components of Ubuntu Axiology. An Axiology, in the case of Ubuntu, addresses communal value sets. "This is a humanistic approach to engaging and empowering *active learning*...It is grounded in the belief that all students are humans who can excel in their academics if their humanity is placed front and center of their learning" (Ukpokodu 2016, p.154). The African diasporic millennial leaders are the learners in this model and, as such, draw strength, identity, and support from a common theme of humanity first in professional, executive, and other leadership roles.

Ubuntu Axiology is the component of the Ubuntu Paradigm that connects the morals, standards, and values within a community. The paradigm is derived from a broad understanding of traditional African belief systems. An Afro-centric philosophical framework like Afrocentricity is a logical precursor to a practical application of Ubuntu as a framework for African diasporic millennial leaders (De

Bruyn, 2017). The paradigm benefits from being centered on an overarching, African-centered cosmology. "Afrocentricity is a paradigmatic intellectual perspective that privileges African agency within African history and culture trans continentally and trans-generationally" (Asante 1998).

The most important steps that managers can take to embrace Ubuntu Axiology in their interactions with African diasporic millennial leaders is to avoid the use of microinsults in day-to-day relations:

- Commenting on how someone is not like others of their ethnicity- According to a 2022 Pew Research Center Report, race and racial dynamics remains a constant point of contention for many BIPOC in America. Racial constructs are difficult to navigate both within and outside of racial groups. Negating the race of a diasporic millennial leader is not likely to make them feel more accepted by non POC managers. In fact, attempting to draw some disconnect between a diasporic millennial and the larger Black community can serve as a further point of contention, thereby widening the gap of discomfort and unrelatability with management (Cox, Tamir, 2022).
- Commenting on how articulate or well-spoken someone is given their race- Racial capital in the Black community is often tied to the way one looks, acts, or sounds. While Blackness is not a monolith, there are certain dialects, mannerisms, nomenclatures, and colloquialisms that are expressly reserved for the use and application of BIPOC. Invalidating an aspect of an individual's identity by implying that their entire race is made up of one rigid, inflexible, static, undifferentiated whole is beyond insulting. Actions like this expose the marginalizing capacity of management who refuse to avail themselves of readily available didactical constructs (Ajayi-Hackworth, 2021).
- Touching a colleague's hair without permission- Managers of diasporic millennial leaders have an opportunity to educate themselves (as well as other colleagues) regarding the dehumanizing impact of invading the personal space of others. The privilege of expanding the knowledge base of teammates regarding personal (as well as legal) ramifications surrounding the blatant disregard of Black personhood. The 2014 study concerning the politics of Black hair, femininity, blackness, and professionalism confirms an international radicalization and politicization of black hair (Yohannes, 2014).
- Excluding capable people from worthwhile career growth opportunities- One of the many structural hurdles that Managers must mitigate is designed to shape and limit the life-choices and opportunities of BIPOC. This strategy began with the denial of basic human rights for POC in America. Dr Amos Wilson infers (in his treatise concerning a Liberation Psychology) that the privileges associated with the atrocities connected to enslavement in America

super cede monetary gains. The implied power to gatekeep career growth opportunities is a component of the psychosis generated by those conditions maintained and enhanced by antebellum conditions in America. Diasporic millennial leaders could be one of the first generations to benefit from the dismantling of the colonization of intellectual property (through the patent system) and other facets of accumulated wealth protected by systems of inequality in America (Jameson, 2013).

- Excluding people from meetings relevant to their work- In office/corporate politics the outcomes of important meetings are typically predetermined. The decisions are seldom left up to chance and the individuals whose lives are being manipulated are usually not in on the decision-making process. Managers are often aware that both formal and informal *meetings before the official meeting* are both strategic and systemic. (Miller, 2018) Diasporic millennial leaders are often the beneficiaries of Panther Parenting strategies. Gaining a penchant for autonomy and a strong sense of resiliency enables them to mitigate whiteness (and the harm that it causes). Being relegated to inconsequential meetings and precluded from engaging in consultations pertinent to their careers will often result in subversive repercussions from diasporic millennial leaders (Darby, 2020).
- Unnecessarily giving white members of the team more support – Managers have a responsibility to disassociate themselves and their companies from practices that cater or pander to *white fragility.* These sentiments serve to preserve and maintain systems of disproportion an inequity in America. Diasporic millennial leaders are impacted by the narrative of meritocracy because it erases race and attempts to make white privilege a nonfactor (Montanez, 2020). The practice of centering whiteness, equating anything dealing with equity and diversity to a discriminatory practice against white people inhibits group cohesion, hampers academic and industrial productivity, and decreases functional and commercial progress (McGhee, 2021).

Ubuntu Axiology is more than a transformative academic narrative. It can be used to reconstruct a culturally responsive social and educational paradigm amid dual pandemics (COVID-19 and Civil Rights). Managers must consistently weigh existential "cost" of D.E.I (diversity, equity, and inclusion) in wok spaces. It involves the deconstruction of paternalistic theoretical constructs. These subjective ideologies have been paramount in perpetuating stigma-generating tropes surrounding African diasporic millennial leaders. Managers can be allies by applying African-centered nomenclature to ideas that build the self-esteem and self-image of African diasporic millennial leaders. This is one example of facilitation using an Ubuntu Axiological interpretation.

The pedagogical structure of *Cogito ergo sum*, "I think; therefore, I am, "is predicated on the Latin cosmology, which essentializes the autonomy and agency of individuals (Descartes, 1637). Managers should practice bottom-up management strategies. This policy allows for equal and equitable access to decision-making and policy development. According to Rene Descartes, the construct of personhood, ability, and identity lie in the subjective notion of individuality (Descartes, 1637). Conversely, Ubuntu (humanity) Pedagogy can delegitimize the presupposition of *Cogito* as a holistic academic ethos. In the Xhosa tradition, *umuntu ngumuntu ngabantu* translates to "I am because (you) we are'' (Metz, 2019). This pedagogy is grounded in a communal, idiosyncratic epistemology (Tavernaro-Haidarian, 2018). Managers can benefit by acknowledging the mutual benefits of professionally linked goals and destinies. Ubuntu acknowledges the "tethering" of fortunes, success and historical identities. Pedagogically it centers on the phenomenological doctrines and collective agreements of BIPOC (Swanson, 2007).

It is essential to write into existence the critical work and impact of the Ubuntu Axiological stratagem. Managers who effectively implement this practice benefit from the long-term, psycho-social effects of adopting an Ubuntu epistemology with fidelity and intentionality and rejecting the current isolationist theory (Cogito) that informs modern Western leadership models today By doing so, managers can 1) eliminate pedagogical identity/learning barriers and 2) mitigate stagnation in advancement and promotion. Moreover, it can 3) enhance the perpetuation of ubuntu-based ideologies across social/emotional, academic, and professional spheres and spaces. It can facilitate African diasporic millennials in being unapologetic about when, where and how they "show up" to traditionally hostile and uninviting spaces. It can promote their ability to holistically occupy and operate within those spaces while simultaneously resisting stigmatization associated with their leadership styles or their audacity to exist. This pedagogy can enable African diasporic millennial leaders to navigate hostile and threatening spaces as their authentic, unapologetic selves.

Ubuntu Axiology problematizes normative theories of leadership/education (Cogito pedagogy) by decentering the status quo in professional realms, political circles, schools, and schooling. It further uses mindfulness to counter the perpetuation and extension of institutional racism in the workplace. Dismantling these barriers will impede the perpetuation of misconceptions about various socio-cultural, and professional intersections. Lastly, it disrupts and disincentivizes the progenitors of racist, misogynistic, and ableist policy and governance by holding leadership accountable, creating a sense of onus and buy-in from the traditionally underrepresented, historically minoritized, and marginalized within society. An Ubuntu Axiological focal point for African diasporic millennial leaders is essential in the area of restorative justice because the exclusionary tactics and social justice atrocities perpetrated by global policing of Black bodies and persistent governmental inadequacies surrounding social justice have created a flashpoint within personal and professional settings, mental health spheres, schools, and schooling. The criminality of systemic under-educating, miseducating, and de-educating African diasporic millennials can only be rectified by implementing a comprehensive ethnically and culturally responsive pedagogy and paradigm (Ubuntu).

Ubuntu Epistemology

Ubuntu Epistemology concerns the knowledge base within a specific demographic of individuals. The origins, scope, and nature of these leaders' knowledge can be understood and disseminated in a globalized format and as a catalyst for systemic change. In 2020, the African American community was impacted more than any other. The passion displayed during the revolutionary civil unrest early in the year was matched by the elation expressed during the launch of the first Historically Black College and University (HBCU) Branch Campus in Ghana, West Africa. Both strategies are critical in the fight against anti-Blackness in the workforce and educational settings (Wilson, HBCU Africa Homecoming, 2020). Both actions are essential in the quest to create conditions that are conducive to the production and proliferation of Black excellence in leadership, appreciation of critical black millennial thought and theory, and inclusion (and agency) in both professional and academic settings and communities as a whole. Both tactics are necessary for the systematic rebuilding, reimagining, and reconstruction of the concept of authentic and legitimate representation of African diasporic millennial leadership.

The Epistemology of Ubuntu is the foundation for goals aimed at defeating anti-Blackness in professional leadership spaces. It is based on a concern for creating safe, communal, reimagined spaces for Black leadership. This epistemology signifies the interconnectedness of humanity to humanity. This was a crucial step toward African descendants' ancestral identity recovery. The goal of an Ubuntu-based Epistemology is to create a linear (rather than a hierarchical) structure of critical engagement and cultural exchange (HBCU Africa Homecoming, 2020). The academic community across the diaspora understood that African diasporic self-efficacy, esteem, pride, confidence, and ultimately their joy would rely on the knowledge of self and the connection to lineage, heritage and ancestry (HBCU Africa Homecoming, 2020). This "tethering" to culture is a part of the process of creating spaces in corporate governance, private industry, as well as academia.

Ubuntu Epistemology explores the methodology used to determine that which is known (to be true, factual) versus that which can only be inferred (as an opinion) in diasporic communities. Verbiage, language, vernacular, and vocabular are the primary mechanisms by which fact is separated from fiction. BIPOC are often subjected to tropes, embellishments, and exaggerations aimed at defaming them and/or their cultures. Managers of African diasporic millennial leaders are uniquely positioned to intervene in ways that protect these leaders from micro assaults in the workplace, specifically involving the use of racially insensitive language and policy:

- Use anonymous data collection methods to assess and audit company diversity and inclusion policies and strategies- Managers can maintain the integrity of any polling system by protecting the privacy of African diasporic millennial leaders as they participate in critical data gathering, analysis, dissemination regarding company DEI policy and progress (Montanez, 2020) .Lastly, managers must actively reject vanity metrics in favor of substantial (albeit uncomfortable) statistical information to be used in furthering the actual goals of the company.
- Engage in consistent transparent practices and motives- African diasporic millennial leaders are concerned with parity in mission statements and actual day-to-day practices (Montanez, 2020). Managers can cultivate a spirit of transparency, trust, and authenticity by recognizing the lived experiences of BIPOC and acknowledging them as subject matter experts. By centering the policy input of African diasporic millennial leaders they become critical proponents to the betterment of a company in a post-colonial white power structure.
- Ensure BIPOC in the workplace have diversity equity, inclusion, justice, and decolonization- Diversity addresses issues surrounding access. Access in a work place refers to having the liberty and ability to occupy spaces within the company. Equity attempts to identify the members of the organization who are not present in decision making spaces. It tries to understand the factors and mechanisms that inhibit the participation of these groups and any systemic procedures that perpetuate these conditions. Inclusion points to the need for each group (and member of the groups) to have a voice. It asserts the need for inclusive environments and for individuals to feel safe and valued in work spaces. Justice situates the voices, ideas, opinions, and values of the individuals within societal hierarchies. It highlights the need to give equal value to members of dominant socio-cultural groups and those outside of the main stream. Decolonization exposes the hidden motives, rationales, and incentives surrounding the business model and the ultimate career and professional design (Decolonize Your Mind, 2022).

Ubuntu Epistemology contextualizes the value, origins, scope, and rationality of the knowledge base within an Ubuntu Paradigm. This knowledge can easily be described as a commodity, an asset, or a thing of value for African diasporic millennial leaders. Cassi Pittman Claytor identifies several unique components of Black cultural capital. One of the most significant elements is "cultural flexibility, cultural duality or biculturalism"(Pittman Claytor, 2020). This facet of cultural capital allows African diasporic leaders to maneuver between distinctly different worlds and acquiesce to the norms, values, and standards associated with those contrasting spaces. In the new millennium, Black leaders have galvanized to form grass-roots movements to protect their rights and employ anti-stigma devices as a means of sociocultural survival (Robinson, 2017). Ubuntu-based tenets like self-definition and wholeness reify an internalized locus of control. African diasporic millennial leaders can leverage that capital by acclimating themselves to diverse bodies of literature, pursuing degrees from prestigious HBCUs, and pursuing entrepreneurial endeavors (Hannon, 2018). This behavior, situated within an Ubuntu Epistemological frame, can lead to the actualization of transformative justice for African diasporic millennial leaders. Transformative justice is concerned with safety, accountability, community action, healing, and, most importantly-transformation (Garnand, 2021). As a component of a Paradigmatic frame, Ubuntu Epistemology supports Black millennial leaders as they maneuver through the anti-Black fervor of the new millennium.

More recently, the inclusion of a phenotypical theoretical construct (Ubuntu Pedagogy) has been applied to the same underpinnings of social justice and transformative justice in tertiary education settings. Ubuntu Epistemology allows for applying the arguments, assertions, and presuppositions of studies surrounding the efficacy and positive impact of African diasporic millennial leadership models. Ubuntu Epistemology further narrows the scope of the paradigm by allowing Managers the ability to examine the findings/results through an African-centered lens. More specifically, this episteme facilitates the inception of a racially responsive tool that bridges the void between managers and Africa diasporic millennial leaders.

The Year of Return campaign was prosperous in revamping, reimagining, and reinventing non-hostile, racially and ethnically accommodating professional, leadership, and educational paradigms (HBCU Africa Homecoming, 2020). The first HBCU Branch Campus is a safe space that promotes development free of anti-Black themes, motives, and content. This endeavor allows African diasporic millennial leaders to collectively consider the long-term, intergenerational consequences of co-opting ethnic culture and the transnational linguicide that Black and indigenous people have endured for years. The total restructuring of Black millennial leadership paradigms requires the inclusion of theory, context, and curriculum that is relatable, relevant, and realistic (HBCU Africa Homecoming, 2020). Themes, genres, and motifs must consider the ethnic students' connection to the content and the content's connection to the real world. The desired outcomes of the full implementation of the Ubuntu Paradigm include: addressing anti-Blackness and the subsequent stigmatization in leadership development programs, reinventing Black and indigenous safe spaces in corporate settings, and creating conditions within the business and leadership realm that are conducive to the professional promotion and academic advancement of Black and indigenous leaders—engaging the global knowledge economy and embracing transnational endeavors that will lead students back to their roots and forward to their destinies.

Ubuntu Methodology

Ubuntu Methodology can be used to establish cohesive support systems and connect with global partners to promote the diversity and agency of African diasporic millennial leaders. Ubuntu Methodology is part of an African-centered, philosophical framework dedicated to exploring the nature, objectives, and origins of what is known to be accurate, how it is valued, and how knowledge about Africology is defined, organized, and disseminated. Michael Battle noted that Ubuntu begins with the collective and moves outward to the individual (Battle, 2009). Through this lens, African diasporic millennial leaders can establish individual boundaries that protect them from the expectations associated with Western ideas of leadership (individuality, competition, and self-centeredness) while building coalitions with individuals who are similarly aligned with the objectives of Ubuntu. In a contemporary, digital frame, Ubuntu Methodology centers on the global-social unit. In a social media sphere, Ubuntu Methodology utilizes technology, digital media information sites, and telecommunications applications (i.e., WhatsApp, Skype, Facebook Messenger, etc.) to express the collective power and the communal aspirations of the global, diasporic community. These safe spaces can be shaped in such a way as to share critical anti-stigma content and serve as a repository for data, services, and supports. In the twenty-first century, the village orientation of Ubuntu has evolved to envelop cyberspace, utilize high-tech modalities, and to develop automated and computer-based information sharing, and emotionally uplifting strategies.

Contextualizing the Role of Ubuntu Methodology within the larger Ubuntu Paradigmatic frame helps managers to systematize and standardize a pedagogy of resistance (Hanks, 2007). It specifically explores how managers can aid African diasporic millennial leaders to mobilize and galvanize through social media platforms to counter oppressive, racist, and holistically toxic ideologies and policies aimed at African diasporic aspiring leaders. Managers can assist these leaders in using Ubuntu Methodology in a technology-based framework to coordinate actionable tactics that address the interwoven ideologies of African descended people worldwide (including anti-racism, equity, and solidarity). During the ongoing opioid crisis, suicide epidemic, and political and social unrest, these ideas' relevance is constantly being transmitted to highlight the disparities and disadvantages that are often on full display.

Ubuntu methodology combines the theoretical and the empirical. It seeks to understand the ways that Ubuntu as a world view influences populations and demographics, rather that the ways that people engage Ubuntu (Garmon, Mgijima, 2012) Some actionable, specific methods that managers can employ to create and maintain more equitable work environments by applying an Ubuntu-based frame (lens) include:

- The establishment of a pipeline for historically marginalized and stigmatized African diasporic millennial leaders to participate in early engagement programs.
- Level-set early career diasporic leaders so that they are not compelled to overmanage themselves, make themselves small, or try to blend in/ mimic others.
- Respect (and assist) the establishment of healthy work boundaries and personal rules. Serve as a positive influence or a component of a career support network.

Ubuntu methodology provides a broad overview of the various forms of knowledge and knowledge production through an Ubuntu ideology. Through digital platforms, it creates a way to closely examine the images of the United Stated bureaucratic structure and the implications within a globalized capacity. It exposes the various ways that social stigmas impact aspiring Black millennial leaders. Social media (particularly Black Twitter) allows Africans and diasporic African descendants to confront and engage nuanced dialectical challenges in new and dynamic ways. They can use digital spaces to develop an apolitical consciousness and understanding of each other. This can serve as an intervention and foster defenses against marginalization and "othering." That process can be transparent and will elapse in real-time in public spaces. This diasporic camaraderie shapes and informs the textual and visual messages across continents and can build confidence, a positive self-image, and better overall mental well-being.

Members of the African Diaspora and Africans across the continent can unify through social networks and microblogging to spread knowledge and information. These individuals are able to form a global philanthropic community. A community that is multifaceted, multilayered, and multilateral can produce ethnically responsive leaders. These transnational actors can then coalesce and use web-based services to confront the hypocrisy of antagonistic, domestic, and international policy that limits African diasporic millennial representation. They share, blog, and retweet memes, videos, and images offering motivating and uplifting leadership content.

Ubuntu Methodology bridges the digital divide and creates safe-virtual spaces against racism, sexism, and ableism. The relationship between the African American community and the African Diaspora is long and intricate. The depth and breadth of the complexities of this relationship were amplified by social media networks (specifically Black Twitter). African diasporic millennial leaders can develop support networks using a framework for Ubuntu Methodology through a contemporary, diasporic, digital/social media lens. They can also better understand how the international optics of African American and African diasporic leaders are shaped by the strategic use of diasporic internet communities. Ubuntu (humanity) in the Zulu tradition is expressed as "ubuntu ngumuntu ngabantu," which loosely translates to "I am Because of Who We All Are" (Mugumbate, Nyanguru, 2013. p.84). The African Diasporic community has harnessed the power of technology, fluid information flow, and innovative "smart" devices. Their use has been weaponized for the cause of equity and liberation. These are the nuanced tools of the cultural revolution.

CONCLUSION

Professional and social equity and innovation does not occur in a vacuum; neither do the mechanisms that shape leadership opportunities and professional advancements. Professional and psychological paradigms worldwide are in a constant state of change (BeeBe, 2014). African diasporic millennial leaders will remain competitive in a global knowledge economy and private and corporate industry if they proactively and consistently create safe spaces and avenues of active resistance. "Many developing countries have higher education systems that lack capacity and quality" (Wilkins, 2017). African diasporic millennial leaders benefit from rapidly industrializing countries. These spaces offer entry-level and aspiring managers, supervisors, and directors leadership opportunities. Although many global south nations have experienced a severe shortage of high-quality colleges and universities (Wilkins, Huisman, 2012), these same institutions benefit from the collaborative networks of African diasporic millennial leaders. Historically, HBCUs have increasingly faced dwindling enrollment (Brown, 2013), yet African-centered leadership models attract potential students, faculty, and administrators. The symbiotic and synergistic solution to both problems may be hidden. These early-career leaders could greatly benefit the larger society if an investment in culturally relevant and socially just leadership models is made early on in their academic careers and perpetuated throughout their occupational lifespan.

REFERENCES

Adams, K. (2021). *The audacity: When Black women decide for themselves.* FaithandLeadership.com

Ajayi-Hackworth, F, (2021). A Point of View: You Don't Sound Black. *TheInclusionSolution.Me.*

Gabriel, A. G. & Alvarez, J. (2020). How Do Millennial Managers Lead Older Employees? *The Philippine Workplace Experience.* SAGE. journals.sagepub.com/home/sgo doi:10.1177/2158244020914651

Asante, M. K. (1998). The African American as African. *Diogenes, 46*(184), 39–50. doi:10.1177/039219219804618405

Avdeeff, M. Mangaoang, A., Fogarty Woehrel, M., Viñuela, E., Tinsley, O.N., Kooijman, J., & Iddon, M. (2020). Beyoncé: At Work, On Screen, and Online. Bloomington: Indiana University Press.

Banks, L. (2019). *Emerging Scholars, Transforming the future. 2019 Annual Report.* The Leadership Alliance.

Barkley, R. A. (2022). Parents as Shepherds, Not Engineers, Journal. *The ADHD Report, 30*(8), 11–14. doi:10.1521/adhd.2022.30.8.11

Battle, M. (2021). *How Tutu's Spirituality Incorporated Christian Mysticism with the African Notion of Interdependency.* Religion News Service.

Beckwith, A. (2018). C.S.Peirce and Adduction Inference. Johnson County Community College Honors Journal, 10(1).

Bialystok, E., Majumder, S., & Martin, M. M. (2003, March). there a bilingual advantage? *Applied Psycholinguistics, 24*(1), 27–44. doi:10.1017/S014271640300002X

Brown, M. C. II. (2013). The declining significance of historically Black colleges and universities: Relevance, reputation, and reality in Obamamerica. *The Journal of Negro Education, 82*(1), 3–19. doi:10.7709/jnegroeducation.82.1.0003

Brown, T. (2021). *Feeding the Soul (Because It's My Business).* Finding Our Way to Joy, Love, and Freedom.

Campbell, S. (2015). *5 Ways, Criticism and Rejection Builds your Capacity to Succeed.* Entrepreneur.com

Carey, H. (2016). *Ubuntu: My life in other people.* Matador.

Chigangaidze, R. K. (2021). Utilising Ubuntu in social work practice: Ubuntu in the eyes of the multimodal approach. *Journal of Social Work Practice*. doi:10.1080/02650533.2021.1981276

Chua, A. (2011). *Battle Hymn of the Tiger Mother*. Bloomsbury Publishing PLC.

Cox, K., & Tamir, C. (2022). *Race is Central to Identity for Back Americans and Affects How They Connect With Each Other.* PewResearch.

Darby, J. (2020). *Black Millennials: Identity, Ambition, and Activism*. Lexington Books.

Darity, W. A., Mullen, A. K., & Mullen, A. K. (Andrea K. (2020). From here to equality: reparations for Black Americans in the twenty-first century. The University of North Carolina Press.

Davis, S. & Gopal, T. (2022). Serena Williams became the greatest tennis player of all-time even as she endured racist and sexist attacks in the media. *Insider.com*.

De Bruyn, S. (2017). *An Afrocentric Inquiry on Lived Experiences of Ubuntu Among Isizulu-Speaking Persons From Different Geographic Areas, South Africa*. School of Applied Human Sciences at the University of KwaZulu- Natal.

Descartes, R. (1637). *Discourse on the Method of Rightly Conducting the Reason, and Seeking*. Truth in the Sciences.

Ellis, A. (n.d.). *What Jay-Z's 4:44 Means for Black Millennial Leaders*. Aerialellis. https://aerialellis.wordpress.com/tag/black-millennial-leaders/

Graves, L. (2020). *Black Millennial Movement Seeks to Offer Different Perspective Among Black Leaders.* KATU (Channel 2).

Fasanella, K. (2019). Serena Williams Shares the History of Hair Braiding in a Touching Photo with her Daughter. *Allure.com*.

Ferlazzo, L. (2019). *When People Say They Don't See Race 'I Ask Them if They Don't See Me'*. EducatonWeek.org.

Fry, R., & Parker, K. (2018). *Early benchmark Shows 'Post-Millennials' on Track to be Most Diverse, Best-Educated Generation Yet*. Pew Research Center.

Garmon, C. W., & Mgijima, M. (2012). *Using Ubuntu: A New Research Trend for Developing Effective Communication across Cultural Barriers*. Communication Faculty Publication. https://digitalcommons.wku.edu/comm_fac_pub/1

Garnand, I. (2021). *How Transitional, Restorative, and Transformative Justice Will Address Racial Injustice*. [University Honors Theses, U.C. Law].

Gassam, A. (2021). Understanding the White Gaze and How it Impacts Your Workplace. *Forbes.com.*

Giovanni, N. (1968). Dreams. Black Feeling, Black Talk, Black Judgment. HarperCollins Publishers.

Grace, C. & Rosenberg, S. (2016). Nielsen Report, Young, Connected, and Black. *African American Consumer Report.*

Gregory, S. (2021). Motherhood Could Have Cost Olympian Allyson Felix. She Wouldn't let it. *Time.com.*

Hanks, T. L. (2008). The Ubuntu Paradigm: Psychology's Next Force? *Journal of Humanistic Psychology*, *48*(1), 116–135. doi:10.1177/0022167807303004

Hannon, K. (2018). Black Women Entrepreneurs; The Good and Not-so-Good News. *Forbes.*

Hawkins-Moore, V. (2022). *Ubuntu Epistemology, Sankofa Scale, Africana Womanism, and African American Male Theory in Leadership: African American Mentoring*. IGI Global.

Haynie, D. (2016). Millennial Leaders Around the World. *U.S. News*. https://www.usnews.com/news/best-countries/slideshows/10-millennial-leaders-around-the-globe

Hill-Collins, P. Black Women and Motherhood. In *Black Feminist Thought*. Routledge.

Kananen, J. (2020). Why Did Beyonce Create Alter-Ego Sasha Fierce? *Showbiz Cheatsheet*. https://www.cheatsheet.com/entertainment/why-did-beyonce-create-alter-ego-Sasha-fierce.html/

Iruka, I. U. (2013). The Black family: Re-imagining family support and engagement. In *Being Black is not a risk factor: A strengths-based look at the state of the Black child* (pp. 18–23). National Black Child Development Institute.

Jameson, R. (2013). Amos Wilson: Toward a Liberation Psychology. *The Journal of Pan African Studies*, *6*(2).

Kapitan, T. (1992). Peirce and the Autonomy of Abductive Reasoning. *Erkenntnis (1975-), 37*(1), 1–26. https://www.jstor.org/stable/20012421

King, R., & Kuschminder, K. (Eds.). (2022). *Handbook of Return Migration*. Edward Elgar Publishing. DOI., doi:10.4337/9781839100055

Kiunguyu, K. (2020). *Ghana's Year of Return Campaign Dramatically Boosts the Country's Destination Profile*. ThisIsAfrica.me

Kunjufu, J. (2005). *Keeping black boys out of special education*. African American Images.

Lockhat, P.R. (2018). What Serena Williams's scary childbirth story says about medical treatment Of Black women. *Vox.com*.

Time Staff. (2015). 12 New Faces of Black Leadership. *Time Magazine*. https://time.com/3668782/12-faces-of-black-leadership/

Matsumoto, S. (2020). Black Millennial Movement Seeks to Empower Young Leaders. *OBP In The News*. https://www.opb.org/article/2020/08/26/black-millennial-movement-seeks-to-empower-young-leaders/

McGhee, H. (2021). *The Sum of Us: What Racism Costs Everyone and How We Can Proser*. One World Publishing.

McKenzie, L. M. (2017). *The Stereotypes and Biases that Plague Millennial leaders: Best Practices and Strategies for Job Promotion*. [Thesis, Pepperdine University].

McLoyd, V. C., Hardaway, C., & Jocson, J. (2019). *African American Parenting from: Handbook of Parenting, Volume 4: Social Conditions and Applied Parenting*. Routledge. https://www.routledgehandbooks.com/doi/10.4324/9780429398995-3

Metz, T. (2019). *The African Ethic of Ubuntu*. 1000-Word Philosophy. An Introductory Anthology.

Miller, J. (2018). *The Secret to a Good Meeting: The Meeting before the Meeting*. TheLadders.com

Montanez, R. (2020). 5 Strategies for Engaging a Workforce Inclusive of Millennial Talent. *Forbes.com*.

Morales, S. (2017). *Re-defining Counterspaces: New Directions and Implications for Research and Praxis. Issue No.8*. Center for Critical Race Studies.

Mugumbate, J., & Nyanguru, A. (2013). Exploring African Philosophy: The Value of Ubuntu in Social Work. *African Journal of Social Work, 3*(1).

Nyerere, J. K. (1974). From Uhuru to Ujamaa. *Africa Today*, *21*(3), 3–8. https://www.jstor.org/stable/4185420

Olson, M. E. (2009). The “Millennials”: First year in practice. *Nursing Outlook, 57*(1), 10-17.

Pegram, B., & Bonner, F. (2021). Code-Stitching to Code Stitching: Theorizing an Alternative Framework. *Diverse Issues in Higher Education.*

Claytor, P., & Pittman, C. (2020). *Black Privilege: Modern Middle-Class Blacks with Credentials and Cash to Spend.* Stanford University Press. www.sup.org/books/title/?id=25892 doi:10.1515/9781503613188

Post, J. (2022) What Does Modern Leadership Really Mean? *Business.com.*

Quaye, S., Karikari, S., Allen, C., Okello, W., & Carter, K. (2019). Strategies for Practicing Self-Care from Racial Battle Fatigue. *JCSCORE*, *5*(2), 94–131. doi:10.15763/issn.2642-2387.2019.5.2.94-131

Robinson, C. K. (2017). In the Trump Era, Black Women Must be Allowed to Lead. *PeoplesWorld.org*

Robinson, C. (2021). *How this Millennial Democracy Director Influences the Political Landscape, Especially for Black Women. Forbes.com.* ForbesWomen.

Rogers, C. R. (1963). Toward a Science of the Person. *Journal of Humanistic Psychology*, *3*(2), 72–92. doi:10.1177/002216786300300208

Sauce, B. & Matzel, L. (2017). *Inductive Reasoning*. Springer. . doi:10.1007/978-3-319-47829-6_1045-1

Smith, S. (2020). Why Radical Self-Care Cannot Wait: Strategies for Black Women Leaders Now. *Urban Education Journal UPENN Graduate School of Education, 18*(1).

Stewart, T. J. (2019). “Where We Are, Resistance Lives”: Black Women, Social Media, and Everyday Resistance in Higher Education. [JCSCORE]. *Journal Committed to Social Change on Race and Ethnicity*, *5*(2), 3–32. https://www.jstor.org/stable/48645354. doi:10.15763/issn.2642-2387.2019.5.2.1-31

Suyanto, U.Y., Mu’ah, M., Purwanti, I.S., & Sayyid, M. (2019). Transformational Leadership: Millennial Leadership Style. In *Industry 4.0.*

Swanson, D. M. (2007). Ubuntu: An African contribution to (re)search for/with a “humble Togetherness”. *Journal of Contemporary Issues in Education.*

Tavernaro-Haidarian, L. (2018). Deliberative epistemology: Towards an ubuntu-based Epistemology that accounts for a priori knowledge and objective truth. *South African Journal of Philosophy, 37(*2). doi:10.1080/025801362018.1470374

T&T Loop News. (2021). CNN Anchor with Trini Roots Listed Among Times Emerging leaders. *T & T Loop News*. https://tt.loopnews.com/content/cnn-anchor-trini-roots-listed-among-times-emerging-leaders

Trier-Bieniek, A. (2016). *The Beyonce's Effect: Essays on Sexuality, Race, and Feminism*. Farland & Company Inc. Publishers.

Ukpokodu, O. (2016). *Ubuntu Pedagogy- A humanistic approach to engaging and empowering students' active learning in urban schools*.

Vaccaro, S., & Marcotte, N. (2019). [JCSCORE]. Insights into the Sense of Belonging from Women of Color Interconnections of Cultural Competence, Expectations, Institutional Diversity, and Counterspaces. *Journal Committed to Social Change on Race and Ethnicity*, *5*(2), 33–65.

Wanzo, R. (2022). Resisting the Revolutionary Call. *New Political Science*, *44*(3), 450–456. doi:10.1080/07393148.2022.2119331

Watson, E. (2007). Tupac Shakur, 1971-1996. *BlackPast.org*

Wilford, L. (2020). *Leadership Strategies and Millennial Organizational Commitment*. [Dissertation, Walden University].

Wilkins, S. (2017). Ethical issues in transnational higher education: The case of international branch campuses[[DOI:]. *Studies in Higher Education*, *42*(8), 1385–1400. doi:10.1080/03075079.2015.1099624

Wilson, D., & Williams, V. (2013). Ubuntu: Development and Framework of a Specific Model of Positive Mental Health. *Psychology Journal, 10*. www.psychologicalpublishing.com

Wright, E. (2001). *Why Black People Tend To Shout! An Earnest Attempt To Explain The Sociological Negation Of The Atlanta Sociological Laboratory Despite Its Possible Unpleasantness*. Taylor & Francis.

Yohannes, S. (2014). *DON'T TOUCH MY HAIR A Qualitative Study on Professional Norms and Meanings of Black Female Hair in Swedish Public Administration*. University West.

Young, D. (2019). Impostor Syndrome is Having a Massive Effect on the Black Middle Class. *Independent.co.uk*.

Chapter 7
The Importance of Mentoring in the Development and Succession of Millennial Leaders

Kathryn Towe Littleton
Independent Researcher, USA

ABSTRACT

This chapter demonstrates that mentoring is an essential part of leadership development and succession planning when it comes to millennial leaders, because mentoring not only develops crucial skills and leadership capacity but also improves the organizational commitment and retention of millennials. The chapter begins by providing a survey of existing research into mentoring and leadership development, particularly through a transformational development lens, and outlining the findings pertaining to millennial retention and improved organizational commitment through mentoring. Next, it explores issues relevant to mentoring program development, such as millennial expectations of mentor qualities, the need to address diversity through mentoring, and the evolution of mentoring formats. Finally, the chapter provides recommendations for developing an optimal mentorship program and outlines possible directions for future research.

INTRODUCTION

Decades of research have shown that, like other leadership development approaches, mentoring helps to expand ascending leaders' capacity and skills. What is unique about mentoring is that it also improves the retention of millennials and enhances

DOI: 10.4018/978-1-6684-4711-6.ch007

their organizational commitment (Iverson, 2019). This is critical since millennials do not tend to stay with employers for as long as members of previous generations; instead, they are known for moving from job to job to advance their careers (LaBelle, 2018). Potential leaders cannot be part of a succession plan if they do not remain with a company. Mentoring is the ideal way to retain emerging leaders while also preparing them to take on senior roles within an organization (Iverson, 2019).

The objectives of this chapter are:

- To provide a comprehensive overview of research pertaining to millennials, mentoring, retention, and leadership development.
- To discuss several issues relevant to mentoring program development, including millennial expectations of mentors, the need to improve diversity through mentoring, and the evolution of mentoring formats.
- To provide recommendations for developing an optimal mentorship program.

BACKGROUND

Succession planning is a systematic process carried out by organizations to determine which individuals have the potential or the current ability to assume leadership positions when current leaders leave. It encompasses the identification, development, and training of workers so they will be ready for a smooth transition into the leadership of an organization (LaBelle, 2018). It is essential that there be individuals ready with the skills and knowledge required to take up the torch from departing leaders, especially in recent years with an increasing number of Baby Boomers retiring. In a 2021 survey of Americans over the age of 45, more than 75 percent indicated plans for early retirement (SOA Research Institute, 2021).

Although it is common to hire leaders from outside a company, research has shown that hiring from within is more effective. For example, in a meta-analysis of post-succession performance, Schepker et al. (2017) found that corporate sector CEOs hired from outside organizations have a longer-term failure rate seven times higher than CEOs promoted from within. The authors indicate this is often because CEOs who have been brought into a company unintentionally introduce change that clashes with an organization's existing culture.

HOW MENTORING HELPS DEVELOP TALENT

Using mentorship approaches in succession planning is an effective strategy for internal talent development and promotion (Cavanaugh, 2017). The term *mentor* has been used since ancient Greek times to describe an older adult with experience and expertise who helps a younger person learn to thrive (Kram, 1985). Levinson, Darrow, Klein, Levinson, and McKee (1978) are considered the first theorists in the field of mentoring relationships (Allen, Eby, Lentz, & Lima, 2004). Levinson et al.'s research concerning career development led the researchers to theorize that an individual with access to a mentor experienced career advantages because the mentor acted as an advisor, teacher, friend, and sponsor, thus helping the mentee develop their capabilities (Levinson et. al, 1978). Such career development effects have since been confirmed by a number of researchers (e.g. Blay et al., 2011).

Kram's (1985) seminal research established mentoring theory by postulating that two distinct types of support, career-related and psychosocial, pass from mentors to mentees. Career-development support includes providing challenging assignments; sponsoring, protecting, and coaching mentees; and ensuring mentees receive exposure to beneficial people and opportunities. By offering these types of support, mentors help mentees learn to be effective within an organization and obtain promotions (Allen, Eby, Lentz, & Lima, 2004). Psychosocial support involves the interpersonal functions of the relationship and relates to the mentor's role as a model, counselor, and friend. Through these functions, a mentor helps a mentee develop an increased sense of competence and confidence, a clearer identity, and greater interpersonal effectiveness on the job (Kram, 1985). Kram postulated that mentors who provided a larger number of the functions listed above had more beneficial relationships with mentees than those who provided a smaller number (Ragins & Cotton, 1999). Since millennials experienced helicopter parenting as children (Delorey, 2010) and tend to require ongoing feedback and support (Kilber, Barclay, & Ohmer, 2014), the concept of psychosocial support is an important one for understanding how mentoring meets the needs of millennial mentees.

FORMAL AND INFORMAL MENTORING

As interest in mentoring theory increased, formal mentor programs became more prevalent in the 1990s. The key distinction between formal and informal mentoring is how mentor-mentee relationships are developed and formed (Chao, 2009). Informal mentoring is often the result of a personal relationship, and a bond develops because of common goals, interests, and achievements (Kram & Isabella, 1985). Informal relationships tend to have a psychosocial focus achieved through a combination of counseling, friendship, acceptance, and role modeling (Siegel, Schulz & Landy, 2011).

Egan (1996) defined informal mentoring as relationships that occur over time without external intervention or planning. Guided external expectations do not exist, and the relationships emerge as a result of mutual initiation and ongoing connections rather than matching. Formal mentoring, on the other hand, is structured and includes several sequential procedures developed to foster meaningful relationships, facilitate expected actions of individuals engaged in mentoring, and assess the results of mentoring. The intention is to equip less experienced members of an organization with the skills and abilities to lead (Murray, 1991). Formal mentoring is most often instigated, planned, and facilitated by the organization. Expectations, meetings, goals, and discussion topics are established. Participants are paired carefully, and mentors often receive training in how to be supportive of the process.

Desimone et al. (2014) examined the benefits of mentoring, both formal and informal. They discovered that informal mentoring was more beneficial than formal mentoring on psychosocial dimensions, which led to a higher willingness to practice knowledge-sharing among employees, resulting in organizational retention of knowledge. Ghosh, Reio, and Haynes (2012) found that mentoring created perceived reciprocal support between mentors and mentees, which predisposed them to organizational citizenship behavior. In research that confirmed the necessity of non-formulaic approaches, Siu and Sivan (2011) reported that openness to an organic mentoring process resulted in the most beneficial mentor-mentee relationships.

Interviewees in the chapter author's doctoral research reflected the above findings. For example, Sally, an engineer who manages other engineers at a large manufacturer, described formal mentoring as stiff and unnatural at times:

In some ways, I thought it was maybe too... administrative. It wasn't very natural, if that makes sense. The company was trying to do the right thing. We still do have that program. There's value in it, but true mentoring, you can't be assigned, linked up with somebody on a spreadsheet. (Littleton, 2015, p. 96)

Mentees agreed that they preferred the organic feeling of informal mentorship and informal interactions as opposed to scheduled meetings. One participant said, "The informal mentors, it's just an organic relationship-driven or chemistry-driven relationship as opposed to, 'Here's our monthly lunch. What's the career advice that I'm supposed to get from this lunch?'" (Littleton, 2015, p. 128).

Another said, "When you sit down with somebody and you know that you have an hour to get all of their wisdom about their career and how to navigate a specific situation, it just really feels artificial" (Littleton, 2015, p. 129).

THE BENEFITS OF MENTORING

Whatever form it takes, mentoring has two benefits that are central to the current discussion: it helps emerging leaders develop the skills and knowledge to succeed in higher-level positions, and it increases organizational commitment so millennials are more likely to stay with the company. Since leaders must be retained before they can be developed and promoted, the discussion will begin there.

Mentoring and Retention

Das and Baruah (2013) described retention as a systematic effort by employers to create and encourage an environment that increases the likelihood that current employees will want to remain employed through policies and practices addressing the diverse needs of the employees. According to the Society for Human Resource Management (2017), the retention of skilled employees was a global concern even before the COVID-19 pandemic exacerbated labor shortages.

A number of researchers have found links between mentoring and retention (e.g., Race & Skees, 2010; Robinson & Reio, 2012). Craig et al. (2013) demonstrated that the more positively mentees felt about their mentoring experience, the less likely they were to report a desire to leave an organization. This is important because millennial workers have different needs from previous generations and are known for high turnover (Tews et al., 2015). A 2016 Gallup research study found that 21 percent of millennials had switched jobs in the previous year, and the same number expected to switch again within two to three years.

Millennials need to feel that an organization supports and meets their professional goals before committing to it, and LaBelle (2018) and noted it is common for them to find mentors who are willing and able to help them achieve their career goals and to seek external positions that provide them with lateral and upward professional growth if they do not find it in their workplace. Rather than being loyal to an organization, millennials proactively plan their careers by "moving from job to job in order to build skills and competencies to advance their career putting themselves on a fast track into management and leadership positions" (LaBelle, 2018, p. 5).

One way to retain millennials is to offer mentorship opportunities. The strong connection between mentoring and retention was demonstrated by a 2016 Deloitte survey, which found that millennials who anticipated staying with their current employer for more than five years were two times more likely to have a mentor.

A millennial interviewee in the author's doctoral research illustrates the sentiment behind this statistic. She said:

The relationship that I have with my mentor, from support, to challenging me, to asking me questions, to really helping pick me up when I'm down, and really helping push me to that next level, I think that that's a huge part of what keeps me where I am. I think that I've been in other positions where I haven't had that type or level of support, and that's caused me to kind of look around and go, 'Hey. That's something I need. That's what I want. Where else can I find it?' So, maybe that has to do with my previous transitions, but I couldn't be happier where I am now. (Littleton, 2015, p. 144)

In 2012, the researchers Ghosh, Reio, and Haynes demonstrated that mentees' levels of organizational commitment and organizational citizenship behavior (both related to retention) are higher than those of non-mentees. The researchers surveyed 264 young workers who were not being mentored and 160 young workers who were part of informal or formal mentoring relationships from three corporations in different industrial sectors in the U.S. The researchers found that mentored individuals demonstrated more organizational commitment and desire to engage in organizational citizenship behavior. That was because mentoring created perceived reciprocal support between mentors and mentees, which predisposed them to organizational citizenship behavior.

In 2013, Das and Baruah completed a review of all the academic literature at that point pertaining to employee retention. The researchers identified nine factors influencing employee retention, of which only two (compensation and job security) are not affected by mentoring. The other factors – reward and recognition, opportunity for growth, participation in decision-making, work-life balance, work environment, training and development, and leadership – all have some connection to the mentor-mentee relationship.

In that same year, the researchers Craig, Allen, Reid, Riemenschneider, and Armstrong surveyed mentored employees of an IT company and found that the more positively mentees felt about their mentoring experience, the less likely they were to report a desire to leave the organization. Employees responded to an online survey consisting of 145 questions assessing their feelings, such as, "To what extent do you have a mentor who has conveyed feelings of respect for you as an individual?" and assessing their turnover intention, such as, "It is likely you will be working for the state this time next year?" Craig and the others found that mentees with stronger positive feelings about their mentoring experience had less expectation of turnover (Craig et al., 2013).

Sharma and Rani (2017) also found a positive correlation between affective commitment to an organization and mentor engagement. In 2018, LaBelle noted, "Mentors help mentees set career goals and objectives and adjust career expectations to align with the organization and guide the mentee's career advancement. This often results in a close, professional relationship which fosters affective commitment from the mentee" (p. 5).

It is important to note that millennials move from job to job not only because of their attitudes about loyalty and commitment but also because, more than at any time in history, they are actively being recruited. Deal and Leveson (2016) obtained data from thousands of millennial workers and found that more than 70 percent had been contacted at least once in the previous six months about a job at another organization. Thirty percent had been contacted more than four times, and 16 percent had received 10 or more messages. The authors clarified, "These… aren't just calls. These conversations often include discussions about salary ranges and promotions, as well as learning and development opportunities at the new organization" (p. 30).

This means organizations must do a better job than ever at convincing employees that their career and personal lives will benefit from staying where they are. As more organizations understand this fact, the competition for the best employees will become even more fierce. Kaplan et al. (2018) asserted that "mentoring can provide those supportive structures that will increase millennial employees' willingness to stay" (p. 50).

A mentor who participated in the author's doctoral research described this kind of situation when he said:

I've even had that conversation with her: 'If you are offered another role where you think it's more in line with your long-term goals and it can offer you more money, you should definitely take it. Do not let me hold you back.' And she goes, 'You know what? You have never held me back. That's why I'm still here, because I always feel like every day is a challenge and that I'm going to get the most out of my career by being here with you and having those opportunities.' She has literally turned down roles that have been offered to her making double what she makes and she's said it's because she feels that she will learn more and she will have more opportunities for growth and more opportunities where she is at right now. (Littleton, 2015, p. 214)

Leadership Development Through Mentoring

Mentoring has been shown to contribute not only to retention but also to leadership development. For the purposes of this discussion, leadership development will be viewed through the lens of transformational development theory. This theory, introduced by Bass and Riggio in 2006, has the end goal of transforming followers into leaders. It does this through a competency-based approach with a focus on empowerment (Beiter, 2021). Mentoring helps to accomplish this through the career-related and psychosocial support it provides (Kram, 1985).

Millennials identify mentoring as a preferred source of professional growth (Iverson, 2019). In contrast, a 2018 study by Allio found that about half of leaders surveyed were disappointed and dissatisfied with leadership development experiences in the form of workshops and conferences. Researchers such as Short (2014) have identified mentoring as an optimal development strategy for emerging leaders as long as modern mentoring characteristics of immediacy, flexibility, mobility, innovation, and multigenerational, multi-disciplinary, holistic development are taken into consideration.

According to Beiter (2021), one of the greatest benefits of mentoring is the positive self-concept it can help to build and the empowerment that results. Such empowerment is "facilitated by a mentor who recognizes potential, encourages behavior, inspires, role models, and promotes opportunities" (p. 35). Hernandez et al. (2018) noted that through mentorship, millennials can learn to think flexibly and recognize the importance of looking for solutions beyond existing ground rules. They add, "such thinking, combined with the vigor and innovation of millennials, equates to the development of leaders optimally equipped to lead competitive firms" (p. 42).

Mentorship has also been credited with skill development in areas such as self-analysis, goal setting, self-development, networking, trust, priority setting, consistency, insight into others, communication, adaptability, reflection, and acceptance of critical feedback (Beiter, 2021). Using the transformational development approach, mentors are guided by leadership competencies and can ensure the feedback they provide is supportive and focuses on the specific skills required to enhance growth. In this way, high-potential millennial employees, with the help of mentors, can fill gaps in knowledge and skill and learn the optimal ways to navigate existing systems (Beiter 2021).

The target leadership competency most associated with succession planning is leading change, which specifically demonstrates innovative and strategic thinking, ambition, managing vision, and mission. Harrison (2015) says, "Overall, the research suggests that developing the leading change competency, when coupled with direct exposure to Baby Boomers, supports the successful transition of leadership between the generations" (p. 145).

As a mentee in the author's doctoral research said:

I absolutely agree with everyone that mentors are so essential. In my experience, I would not know, I would not be able to have developed a big picture view of my company, my work within the division, within the project, within a team, without talking to my mentor. Mentors, their experience allows us to step back and look at it from a holistic point of view. They can see things that for us mentees, because we simply don't have the experience, are nearly impossible for us to see. Mentors, they've been absolutely crucial for me. (Littleton, 2015, p. 149)

It is important to note that if succession is one of the main goals of mentorship, companies should not wait too long before engaging high-potential employees in a mentoring relationship. According to Zenger (2012), the average age at which individuals enter formal leadership programs is 42. Zenger notes that many companies waited too long to begin preparing members of Generation X for succession, resulting in a dearth of leaders ready to succeed retiring Baby Boomers. Because of this, Zenger predicted that millennials would take on leadership roles 5–10 years earlier than previous generations had.

Overall, mentoring helps to improve the efficacy of leadership transitions, enhancing organizational competitiveness. As Beiter (2021) said, "Organizations that utilize mentorship in succession planning are found to be effective, especially during times of leadership shortages where internal talent development, promotion, and dynamic leadership becomes even more critical" (p. 10).

Given the theoretical support for the importance of mentoring in the development and succession of millennial leaders, the next step is to determine what an organization's approach to mentoring should be. Different types of mentoring programs have been shown to have markedly different outcomes, so any organization looking to make strategic changes in this area would do well to consider issues relevant to mentoring program development, as outlined below.

ISSUES RELEVANT TO MENTORING PROGRAM DEVELOPMENT

As demonstrated above, mentoring is crucial for retaining millennial leaders and providing the career-related and psychosocial support necessary to ensure they gain the skills and knowledge necessary to take on more senior positions within an organization. With that in mind, the question becomes, how can a company optimize mentoring experiences to prepare the highest-potential millennial leaders for succession? This section explores the research around millennial expectations of mentors, the need to address inclusivity and diversity, and how mentoring has evolved through the years.

Millennial Expectations of Mentors

In order to develop an organizational approach to mentoring that will achieve the goal of preparing emerging millennial leaders to succeed in higher-level positions, it is necessary to understand what they expect from their mentors. Research indicates that millennial workers desire trust, connectedness, engagement, meaningful contribution, and space for growth in the workplace. They are looking for mentors who "can communicate transparently, genuinely, and effectively; demonstrate care, commitment, and individual methods; validate expectations and value with feedback; and participate in leadership by example" (Seheult, 2016, p. 28).

These assertions are supported by the chapter author's research, which found that what mentees were seeking, and found in informal mentorships, was the sense that someone else cared and wanted them to succeed. In the words of one millennial participant:

I think relatability is really the most important thing. I think, because those relationships are able to develop organically, that you are really able to buy in and understand that this wasn't something that anybody made them do. This is something that they're genuinely interested in because they are looking out for my best interests. (Littleton, 2015, p. 129)

This research concluded that millennials' priorities when it came to a mentoring relationship included personal connection, trust and openness frequent communication, flexibility, detailed ongoing feedback and recognition, advocacy, and providing opportunities (Littleton, 2015). Many of these priorities have to do with how available a mentor is and the amount of feedback they provide. Millennials are accustomed to consistent and constant feedback almost in real-time. They take issue with any model that does not allow for regular feedback (Koulopoulos & Keldsen, 2014).

Anne, the executive recruiter at a large retail lender who participated in an interview with the chapter author, described the necessity of openness for her millennial employees:

I feel like the people that we're hiring now, more Gen Ys, they want to feel like they have that open opportunity to go talk to their leader and they're more on the same playing field as opposed to, 'They're there behind that closed door; I can only talk to them when they want to talk to me.' (Littleton, 2015, p. 101)

Mentor Gail said she prefaces criticism by saying that mentees are the future of the large, traditional manufacturer where she works, and she wants to ensure the best possible future. She tries to show them what she is trying to accomplish when she corrects them or provides guidance by saying, "You guys need to understand that I am here to ensure your success and your future long after I'm gone." I think that again we have built that respect (Littleton, 2015, p. 104).

A focus group participant agreed that his mentors' trust in him was crucial to his career success:

I think the biggest thing that my mentors have done to really show they have faith in me is to really challenge me, constantly communicating with me, keeping that open line of communication with me, really keeping me accountable for those goals, and doing everything they can to challenging me and push me to maybe work a little bit harder. I've realized, 'Hey. This is someone that's really investing that time, and that energy, and that effort to see me develop,' and it's what really kind of pushes me, sometimes when things get rough, to really keep going. (Littleton, 2015, p. 133)

Another characteristic of highly effective mentoring relationships is that they make ample use of detailed ongoing feedback and recognition, because all of these are extremely important to millennial workers. According to Tulgan (2016), the more talented, skilled, and motivated millennials are, the more they want leaders and mentors "who know exactly who they are, help them succeed, and keep close track of their success" (p. 84).

During an interview with the chapter author, one millennial participant said he valued feedback from his mentor about how his actions could or would be interpreted by those in executive leadership positions in his company. He said:

The general skill and habit of trying to be self-aware and looking from an external perspective at how you're conducting yourself, how your work is, other things, because that can be really hard sometimes if there's difficult feedback to deal with or a difficult situation. (Littleton, 2015, p. 136)

Assistant Dean Jackie said sometimes her mentees need to be pushed to continue to improve and learn:

I think one of my strong suits has been being able to push people to that next level out of their comfort zone so they will have an opportunity to shine. If they fail on something, it's okay, get up and start moving, but also I believe that mentorship requires a lot, because if you're truly going to do it, you have to do it more than just name only. (Littleton, 2015, p. 113)

All of the above anecdotes connect to the traits that foster transformational development. According to Beiter (2021), "Empowerment is facilitated by a mentor who recognizes potential, encourages behavior, inspires, role models, and promotes opportunities" (p. 17).

It has been demonstrated that millennials "actively seek mentors and will look for new jobs if mentorship isn't available for career advancement" (Hernandez et al, 2018, p. 41). This generation's particular attitudes and values lead them to have high expectations for both meaningful, challenging work and for career advancement (Carter & Walker, 2018). As Tulgan (2016) noted:

Millennials, especially the most capable and ambitious among them, push hard for more significant roles with increased responsibilities at much earlier stages in their careers than new young workers of generations past. It's not just misplaced arrogance on their part, but rather a result of their natural adaptation to the information environment. The nature of professional learning today is a continuous just-in-time all-the-time endeavor. (p. 47)

This is good news for organizations that can harness the millennial approach to hasten their leadership development and, ultimately, readiness for succession. Mentors – at least, those with optimal attributes for working with millennials – can play a crucial role in this development. Organizations looking to develop millennials into leaders ready for succession would do well to keep in mind these high standards so they can identify and train mentors accordingly.

THE NEED TO ADDRESS DIVERSITY AND INCLUSIVITY THROUGH MENTORING

Given increasing understanding in the corporate world about the importance of inclusivity and diversity, it is crucial to provide insight into how mentoring specifically addresses the needs of women, people of color, and all underrepresented groups. Mentoring has been shown to be particularly effective in the development of leaders from underrepresented populations (Coe et al., 2020). Efficacy is highest when mentoring is pursued with intentionality; in other words, effective mentors "identify, improve and implement strategies and skills through a systematic approach to self-assessment and growth" (Broughton et al., 2019, p. 318). According to Coe et al. (2020), "though all leaders benefit from mentoring, underrepresented minorities and women need a team that can also help them navigate some of the unique challenges they face" (p. 108).

Studies have shown that mentorship improves retention, leadership development, and career path advancement for women (e.g. Hill & Wheat, 2017) and African-American men (Robinson & Reio, 2012). For both populations, mentoring can be an important way to break through the glass ceiling. However, at times, and when approached without a conscious focus on inclusivity, gender and race can impact the quality and efficacy of a mentoring relationship through barrier-inducing mentor and mentee-held stereotypes, attitudes, and perceptions about the other (Clutterbuck, 2002).

Women often face obstacles in networking and obtaining mentors, and sometimes they are hindered by 'benevolent sexism' in which mentors overhelp, underestimate, or otherwise treat women in patronizing ways that undermine their ability to advance in leadership positions (Hideg & Shen, 2019). As well, in a 2013 study by Meyer and Warner-Gordon, American mentees from racial or cultural minorities who were paired in a formal mentoring program with mentors from the racial and cultural majority had greater problems forming functional relationships that were personally and professionally helpful.

One participant in the author's doctoral study confirmed this tendency when she said:

I know that as a Latina, with a history of disenfranchisement especially, in a hierarchical very powerful institution within this country, trust is a huge issue, whether or not we are aware of it, whether or not we can be honest about it or say that it's very important. If you have that in a mentor, I think that has a huge impact in your ability to be confident in the work that you do and to be able to move within the structure of your company or your organization or the system that you want to work in, whatever impact you want to make. (Littleton, 2015, unpublished interview transcript)

Ho Sang (2022) confirmed that same-race mentoring can be beneficial, with mentees feeling that their racial affinity with their mentor created a safe space for them. They found that while cross-racial mentors tended to focus on providing professional support, mentors in same-race pairings also provided socio-emotional support to their mentees (Ho Sang, 2022).

According to Byars-Winston et al. (2019), while pairing mentees with mentors of the same race may be helpful, the relatively low number of racial and cultural minority members at higher organizational levels who are in a position to become mentors means it may not be feasible to expect them to mentor all newcomers who share their race. Zackery (2021) found that although having same-race mentors improved STEM mentees' self-efficacy, the same effect was found when they were paired with mentors of other races who were competent at handling diversity. This indicates that training mentors in diversity can alleviate some of the inequities that exist for minority mentees.

Relationships in which the mentor and mentee "differ on the basis of race, ethnicity, gender, sexual orientation, class, religion, disability, or other group memberships associated with power in organizations" (Ragins, 1999) are known as diversified mentoring relationships. Due to the lack of underrepresented individuals in higher positions, most millennials from underrepresented groups who have mentors experience this kind of relationship. Mentor training can mitigate the challenges posed by stereotypes and assumptions in diversified relationships by ensuring that those involved understand the nature of privilege (Clutterbuck, 2002) and by improving alignment of mentor and mentee expectations (Johnson et al., 2021).

According to Clutterbuck (2002):

One of the more difficult consciousness-raising tasks in diversified mentoring relationships is coming to terms with the nature of privilege. Privilege refers to the fact that some group memberships give individuals privileges and advantages that they may not ask for or even recognize, but certainly enjoy. There are multiple sources of privilege, based on race, ethnicity, gender, sexual orientation, class, age, religion, and other group memberships.... Since privilege is usually unacknowledged by its recipient, developing insights into the nature of privilege is one of the most daunting tasks faced by members of diversified mentoring relationships. (p. 37)

Training has been shown to result in long-term improvement in consistent, tailored mentoring that addresses diversity, equity, and inclusion (Johnson et al., 2021). In the best-case scenarios, mentorship can build leadership capacity among underrepresented groups, enhancing an organization's diversity by fostering positive relationships, increasing global awareness, and reducing anxiety and stress (Hamm, 2017). This is especially true when both mentors and mentees are trained to be aware of race, gender, and relationship dynamics and to articulate their needs clearly (Carter et al., 2020).

In 2021, Johnson et al. evaluated a program called "Mentoring the Mentors." The study's subjects had, between 2013 and 2020, attended a two-day training workshop designed to improve their competence in working with diverse mentees. They completed an online survey pertaining to the training and how it had affected their mentoring activities. Johnson et al. found that the training had had a lasting positive impact on 92 percent of participants, that 91percent felt they were now more effective mentors, and that 82 percent believed they had improved both their awareness of the need to address diversity equity and inclusion and their competence level in doing so via mentoring.

Any organization seeking to include a diverse workforce in its succession plans must include an awareness of diversity and inclusion in its mentor training if it is to harness the full potential of traditionally underrepresented groups.

THE EVOLUTION OF MENTORING FORMATS

"Mentor" is a derivative of the word "advise," which means to remember, recall, or counsel (Oxford English Dictionary, 1989). Existing literature regarding mentoring contains many definitions of the term. For example, Daloz (1986) described the role of mentors as assisting learners to navigate through unfamiliar situations by acting as environment interpreters. Vincent and Seymour (1995) defined mentors as individuals acting as teachers or coaches, helping others develop and reach their fullest potential by creating opportunities to learn.

More recently, Erdem and Aytemur (2008) used Levinson et al.'s (1978) definition of mentoring as a process in which senior, experienced organization members give guidance, share knowledge, and set up opportunities and support for the inexperienced, most often younger, members to assist with advancement. Erdem and Aytemur noted that according to Kram (1985), the mentoring relationship is expected to help mentees with both psychosocial and career development. Career development is supported and advanced through sponsorship, exposure to challenging assignments, and coaching, while the psychosocial function is achieved through friendship bonds, counseling, and confirmation. Erdem and Aytemur found that the mentor is an important role model of behavior and attitudes and that trust is essential in meeting mentor and protégé expectations and optimizing outcomes.

As mentioned previously, formal mentoring programs gained precedence in the 1990s. In many studies since then, both mentors and mentees have indicated a preference for informal mentoring. Perhaps as a result, in recent years, mentoring has taken on increasingly accommodating and accessible forms, incorporating practices that have been demonstrated to improve interpersonal and critical thinking skills while simultaneously enhancing knowledge transfer and employee engagement (Iverson, 2019). According to Short (2014), modern mentoring is characterized by flexibility, immediacy, mobility, innovation, multi-disciplinary approaches, and holistic development.

Another important focus of more recent mentoring approaches is the application of an intentional strategy. Intentionality, with its "identify, improve, and implement approach" (Broughton et al., 2019), helps to build mentors' cultural competency and interpersonal skills. Studies have shown that mentorship with a transformative leadership focus and a focus on intentionality results in the development of self-efficacy in emerging leaders (Cziraki et al., 2018).

In terms of format, mentoring has evolved "from strictly one-on-one matching and formal programs to various forms such as co-mentoring, reverse mentoring, group mentoring, and developmental networks" (Beiter, 2021). Instead of a model where one mentor functions as an expert focusing on one mentee's career performance and advancement, mentoring has developed an increasingly networked approach with an emphasis on cooperative learning and development through self-awareness (Kram & Higgins, 2009).

Co-mentoring is one modern form of mentoring. This collaborative model features a partnership that benefits both individuals involved, who are expected to both contribute to and gain from the relationship (Mullen, 2000). In this approach, responsibility for growth and learning are shared; however, interactions between participants follow the same format as traditional mentoring.

Another form of mentoring gaining prominence more recently is group mentoring, which can take place in person or online. The diversified and interactive learning made possible by such a format harnesses millennials' preference for working collaboratively. Jayadeva (2018) noted that "this approach has been found to be beneficial to both the emerging leader and the organization as there is usually less financial investment in group mentoring and increased flexibility with scheduling demands" (p. 31). Bittner (2019) recommends that organizations looking to use mentorship as a driver of leadership development and succession planning institute "a 'leadership cohort' in which new leaders can discuss ideas, action plans, or struggles, with the guidance and experience of a knowledgeable upper leadership team" (p. 55).

Like group mentoring, developmental networks allow emerging leaders to gain skills and knowledge from a wider variety of individuals. However, they provide an individualized, self-directed way for an emerging leader to support their career development needs as they arise (Short, 2014). To create a developmental network, an emerging leader identifies and connects with potential role models and mentors and develops a list of "experienced individuals who have interests and diversified qualifications to assist in growth and development" (Beiter, 2021, p. 32). Then, when appropriate and necessary, they access whichever individuals are most needed to contribute to their growth.

Termini et al. (2022) also discuss the benefits of diverse mentoring networks. They note that due to the diversification of the business landscape, one mentor alone may not be sufficient for helping to address the unique challenges potential leaders face. They say, "Diverse mentoring networks offer a more expansive and productive mechanism for mentees to grow" (p. 385). These researchers also discuss the value of virtual platforms for generating a collaborative network that transcends physical boundaries and is not affected by disruptions such as pandemics.

Given all this research, what is the best approach for an organization to take when designing or adapting its own mentoring programs to optimize its role in the succession of millennial leaders? Recommendations follow in the next section.

SOLUTIONS AND RECOMMENDATIONS

As demonstrated in the previous sections, mentoring is a critical component in any program hoping to achieve the successful identification, development, and preparation of ascending millennial leaders to move into the highest positions in their organizations. However, in the face of the ample research regarding mentoring approaches and outcomes, the question for leaders who want to implement such a program is how to do so most effectively.

Both mentors and mentees indicate a preference for informal mentoring. At the root of this preference is the sense that it involves a genuine, unforced relationship. Although formal mentoring programs tend to be structured to foster meaningful relationships and facilitate useful interactions, both mentors and mentees report being more attracted to the combination of counseling, friendship, acceptance, and role modeling that is common in informal mentoring, and this approach has been shown to be more effective for career and psychosocial development as well (Littleton, 2015).

The challenge for organizations wanting to capitalize on the superior results achieved through informal mentoring is that there is no guarantee workers left to their own devices will form mentoring relationships or that those mentor-mentee pairings will be fruitful. In fact, in the author's research, some mentees who said they were not fans of their organizations' formal mentoring programs said that they were nevertheless grateful the programs existed, because the organizations' obvious interest in mentoring and the process of meeting with an ill-fitting formal mentor gave them the experience and motivation to find themselves informal mentors (Littleton, 2015).

A successful organization cannot and will not take a passive, laissez-faire approach to mentoring, particularly given the urgency to find and develop leaders to replace retiring Baby Boomers. Leaders must ensure that effective mentoring is taking place. Among other things, they need to know that mentees are receiving appropriate messages and information and ensure that mentors are using intentional methods to build future leaders. This author recommends a formal approach to ensuring that a vibrant, robust informal mentoring network flourishes in organizations.

The term 'informal' does not imply a lack of intervention on the part of the company. Instead, an informal mentoring program requires a different kind of intervention. Rather than focusing on matching mentors with mentees and providing a framework for their interactions, as formal mentoring programs do, an organization must create a mentoring culture. This means encouraging an appreciation for ongoing feedback, expressing the expectation that employees will have at least one mentor, and training employees in the art of being both a mentor and a mentee.

A formal, organizational culture approach to informal mentoring suggests allowing mentor-mentee pairs and groups to form spontaneously, but within a culture that explicitly encourages mentoring and provides guidance to everyone involved. This recommendation is supported by Beiter (2021), who offered the following suggestion: "Consider creating the conditions for relationships and connections to develop with colleagues and subordinates. These conditions would include approachability/availability, shared experiences, and a willingness to challenge old ways and mindsets" (p. 46).

A formal, organizational culture approach to informal mentoring contains the following elements:

- An organization makes informal mentorship and ongoing feedback part of the culture. It is assumed that everyone in the organization will be involved as a mentor, mentee, or both. Mentor and mentee status will be fluid; anyone with a skill or knowledge to share can be a mentor in some way, and leaders will help individuals identify when they are ready to become full-scale, multifaceted mentors.

- Diverse and modern forms of mentorship are introduced during training and encouraged in the organization. Leaders create the conditions where informal mentoring, group mentoring, and developmental networks can flourish.
- New hires are trained in the art of being mentored. Millennials and other new employees learn about the benefits of mentoring, how to find available mentors, and how to develop the most beneficial relationships possible, with well-defined roles and effective communication. From the first day of employment, they will be directed to identify potential mentors. Part of this process involves being linked with interim mentors to help them find their feet until they identify their own mentors.
- At one time, succession and leadership development were limited to individuals in senior-level positions. However, research indicates that these strategies, including mentoring, are most effective when implemented at all levels of an organization (Beiter, 2021). This is because millennials are projected to assume leadership roles as much as 5-10 years earlier than previous generations (Zenger, 2012), so it is critical to provide broad experiences and skill development to high-potential employees as early as possible.
- Everyone with a certain amount of experience is treated as a potential mentor and receives extensive training. Training modules could include: a) the role of the mentor, b) organizational vision, message, or priorities, c) the needs of millennial workers, d) cultural and gender issues in mentoring, e) listening skills, f) providing feedback, g) providing context, h) an intentional approach to fostering social, emotional, and professional growth, and i) advocating for mentees and providing learning opportunities.
- Mentors are encouraged to have mentors so they can continue to learn and grow. These might be experienced colleagues, or mentors may benefit from 'reverse mentoring,' where they learn from young workers' expertise (for example, in new technologies).
- The organization puts formal mechanisms into place for assessing the mentoring program. Surveys, suggestion boxes, and focus groups can provide feedback about mentor and mentee experiences and how the program aligns with company culture, and metrics such as retention and job performance provide indicators of whether organizational goals are being met.

A mentor is not a mentee's parent or taskmaster or best friend, although certain aspects of the relationship may sometimes take on the characteristics of those roles. Without training and direction, mentors and mentees bring their unconscious expectations to the mentoring relationship. In the best situations, the expectations either align or are negotiated, with positive results. In the worst-case scenarios, misunderstandings, limited growth, disappointment, and, ultimately, turnover are the results.

Most companies with a mentoring program offer training for mentors, but training for mentees is much less common. However, this training has been shown to be very beneficial. Teaching new hires about the benefits of mentoring, how to find mentors, how to give and receive feedback, and how to develop beneficial relationships improves mentoring outcomes.

Organizations could go one step beyond mentee training by providing mentees with highly trained, welcoming 'interim mentors' to mentor new hires until they find their own best fit. Part of the training would then involve being assigned a short-term mentor until they move on to one or more mentors they have chosen independently. The short-term mentor would provide an introduction to the mentoring process and relationship without making mentees feel obliged to remain with the first person who mentored them.

This temporary formal structure would act like training wheels on a bicycle, easing mentees into the life of the company and reducing the probability of mentees blindly 'signing up' with any mentor who will have them, just so they do not remain unpaired. One mentee interviewed said, "This would be beneficial. You'd learn what questions you need to ask and what you need to stay with the mentor/mentee relationship" (Littleton, 2015).

With the above considerations in mind, it is possible to develop or adapt a mentorship program with the intent to strengthen succession planning to ensure millennial leaders gain the necessary skills and competencies while also enhancing their organizational commitment so they will be retained long enough to take the reins of an organization.

As Labelle (2018) said:

Fostering long-term commitment is a challenge for any organization. This could be achieved, and millennials' need for strong, close mentoring relationships met, if organizations adapt their succession planning program to include an individually customizable and flexible mentoring program that enables mentors to help mentees set career goals and adjust expectations while maintaining alignment with the organization's vision, mission, standards, and goals. (p. 95)

FUTURE RESEARCH DIRECTIONS

As noted earlier, mentoring has evolved dramatically over the decades. Research that continues to monitor and assess developments in the practical application of various types of mentoring would add to this body of knowledge.

As of yet, there has been no research to test the efficacy of the recommended formal approach to informal mentoring. Studies of the model as a whole, or specific subsections, such as the use of interim mentors to train mentees, would provide the data necessary to evaluate and fine-tune this model. Of particular interest would be an investigation of how well such a model meets the needs of emerging millennial leaders who belong to underrepresented groups.

Finally, while research regarding mentoring and millennials is extensive, the question of how the two can and should be combined to improve succession planning in organizations has been less studied. Considering the dire need for smooth and successful succession in organizations, and the likelihood that this need will likely persist for years to come, more research into this area would be helpful. For example, case studies of companies where mentoring enhanced the transition and comparisons of the ultimate success of mentored versus unmentored millennial leaders after succession would be excellent starting places.

CONCLUSION

With the retirement of the Baby Boomer generation, organizations face significant turnover in executive leadership. Considering the millennial tendency to move upward by changing companies and the recent increase in their mobility options, succession planning is more important than ever. Ascending leaders must develop the skills, experience, and institutional knowledge to ensure that companies continue to evolve and grow in positive ways, which is most likely to occur when organizations have targeted plans to achieve that leadership development, beginning early in employees' careers. Increasing diversity and ensuring that members of underrepresented groups have equal opportunities for career development will also enhance companies' future strength.

As demonstrated in this chapter, a comprehensive and effective succession plan must include modern forms of mentorship, which not only develop the skills and knowledge high performers will need to take on leadership roles but also serve to strengthen their organizational commitment, increasing the likelihood that they will remain with the company long enough to move into leadership roles. The recommendation is that organizations develop a formal approach to informal mentoring, including the development of a mentoring culture with an appreciation for feedback, the training of mentors and mentees, and an intentional, metric-driven approach to assessing program outcomes.

REFERENCES

Allen, T. D., Eby, L. T., Lentz, E., & Lima, L. (2004). Career benefits associated with mentoring for protégés. *The Journal of Applied Psychology*, *89*(1), 127–138. doi:10.1037/0021-9010.89.1.127 PMID:14769125

Allio, R. J. (2018). Barbara Kellerman: There's a better way to train leaders. *Strategy and Leadership*, *46*(6), 22–27. doi:10.1108/SL-09-2018-0083

Bass, B. M., & Riggio, R. E. (2006). *Transformational leadership* (2nd ed.). Lawrence Erlbaum Associates Publishers. doi:10.4324/9781410617095

Beiter, B. (2021). *The implications of modern mentorship in building self-efficacy and succession potential for millennial school leaders.* [Doctoral dissertation, Robert Morris University]. ProQuest Dissertations Publishing. https://www.proquest.com/openview/f392e8c1338d20817e08d3c24b9d38b3/1?pq-origsite=gscholar&cbl=18750&diss=y

Bittner, A. (2019). Mentoring millennials for nursing leadership. *Nursing*, *49*(10), 53–56. doi:10.1097/01.NURSE.0000580656.81188.ee PMID:31568084

Blay, N., Donoghue, J., Duffield, C. M., Moran, P., & Stasa, H. (2011). Factors impacting career progression for nurse executives. *Contemporary Nurse*, *38*(1), 45–56. https://www.ncbi.nlm.nih.gov/pubmed/21854237 PMID:21854237

Broughton, R. S., Plaisime, M. V., & Green, P. M. C. (2019). Mentorship: The necessity of intentionality. *The American Journal of Orthopsychiatry*, *89*(3), 317–320. doi:10.1037/ort0000412 PMID:31070416

Byars-Winston, A., Leverett, P., Benbow, R. J., Pfund, C., Thayer-Hart, N., & Branchaw, J. (2019). Race and ethnicity in biology research mentoring relationships. *Journal of Diversity in Higher Education*.

Carter, A. D., Sims, C., & de Peralta, A. M. (2020). Blazing the trail: A qualitative case study of mentoring in a gender equity leadership development program. *Journal of Business Diversity*, *20*(2), 35–49.

Carter, T. D., & Walker, W. D. (2018). Retaining, cultivating, and investing: Strategies for leading millennial managers. *Journal of Government Financial Management, 67*(2), 20–25.

Cavanaugh, J. C. (2017). Who will lead? the success of succession planning. *Journal of Management Policy and Practice, 18*(2), 22–27. http://www.na-businesspress.com/JMPP/CavanaughJC_Web18_2_.pdf

Chao, G. T. (2009). Formal mentoring: Lessons learned from past practice. *Professional Psychology, Research and Practice, 40*(3), 314–320. doi:10.1037/a0012658

Coe, C., Piggott, C., Davis, A., Hall, M. N., Goodell, K., Joo, P., & South-Paul, J. E. (2020). Leadership pathways in academic family medicine: Focus on underrepresented minorities and women. *Family Medicine, 52*(2), 104–111. doi:10.22454/FamMed.2020.545847 PMID:31940426

Craig, C. A., Allen, M. W., Reid, M. F., Riemenschneider, C. K., & Armstrong, D. J. (2013). The impact of career mentoring and psychosocial mentoring on affective organizational commitment, job involvement, and turnover intention. *Administration & Society, 45*(8), 949–973. doi:10.1177/0095399712451885

Cziraki, K., Read, E., & Spence Laschinger, H. K., & Wong, C. (2018). Nurses' leadership self-efficacy, motivation, and career aspirations. *Leadership in Health Services, 31*(1), 47-61.

Daloz, L. A. (1986). *Effective teaching and mentoring*. Jossey Bass.

Das, B. L., & Baruah, M. (2013). Employee retention: A review of the literature. *IOSR Journal of Business and Management, 14*(2), 8–16. doi:10.9790/487X-1420816

Deal, J. J., & Levenson, A. (2016). *What millennials want from work: How to maximize engagement in today's workforce*. McGraw Hill.

Delorey, R. (2010). Evidence-based Millennials. *Workplace Review, 7*(1), 37-46. http://library2.smu.ca/xmlui/bitstream/handle/01/24770/001_fulltextdec2010_000.pdf?sequence=1&isAllowed=y

Desimone, L. M., Hochbert, E. D., Porter, A. C., Polikoff, M. S., Schwartz, R., & Johnson, L. J. (2014). Formal and informal mentoring: Complementary, compensatory or consistent? *Journal of Teacher Education, 65*(2), 88–99. doi:10.1177/0022487113511643

Egan, K. S. (1996). Flexible mentoring: Adaptations in style for women's ways of knowing. *Journal of Business Communication, 33*(4), 401–425. doi:10.1177/002194369603300403

Erdem, F., & Aytemur, J. O. (2008). Mentoring: A relationship based on trust: Qualitative research. *Public Personnel Management, 37*(1), 55–66. doi:10.1177/009102600803700104

Gallup. (2016). *How millennials want to work and live.* Gallup. https://www.gallup.com/workplace/238073/millennials-work-live.aspx

Ghosh, R., Reio, T. G. Jr, & Haynes, R. K. (2012). Mentoring and organizational citizenship behavior: Estimating the mediating effects of organization-based self-esteem and affective commitment. *Human Resource Development Quarterly, 23*(1), 41–63. doi:10.1002/hrdq.21121

Hamm, L. (2017). Becoming a transformative vice-principal in culturally and linguistically rich diverse schools. *International Journal of Mentoring and Coaching in Education, 6*(2), 82–98. doi:10.1108/IJMCE-11-2016-0072

Hechl, C. (2017). Affective commitment to organizations: A comparative study of reverse mentoring versus traditional mentoring among millennials. *Binus Business Review, 8*(2), 157-165.

Hernandez, J. S., Poole, K. G. Jr, & Grys, T. E. (2018). Mentoring millennials for future leadership. *Physician Leadership Journal, 5*(3), 41.

Hideg, I., & Shen, W. (2019). Why still so few? A theoretical model of the role of benevolent sexism and career support in the continued underrepresentation of women in leadership positions. *Journal of Leadership & Organizational Studies, 26*(3), 287–303. doi:10.1177/1548051819849006

Hill, L. H., & Wheat, C. A. (2017). The influence of mentorship and role models on university women leaders' career paths to university presidency. *Qualitative Report, 22*(8), 2090–2111. doi:10.46743/2160-3715/2017.2437

Ho Sang, F. R. (2022). *Does race still matter? An exploration of race and mentoring relationships from the perspective of early career teachers of color and mentors.* [Doctoral dissertation, CUNY Hunter College]. Academicworks. https://academicworks.cuny.edu/hc_sas_etds/921

Iverson, A. (2019). General business: Developing and executing a corporate mentorship program. *Journal of Pension Benefits*, *27*(1), 51–53. https://pinnacle-plan.com/wp-content/uploads/2020/02/Amanda-Iverson-Article-Developing-and-Executing-a-Corporate-Mentorship-Program.pdf

Jayadeva, R. (2018). Mentoring millennials: Perceptions and analysis. *College and University*, *93*(2), 29–33.

Johnson, M. O., Fuchs, J. D., Sterling, L., Sauceda, J. A., Saag, M. S., Fernandez, A., Evans, C. H., & Gandhi, M. (2021). A mentor training workshop focused on fostering diversity engenders lasting impact on mentoring techniques: Results of a long-term evaluation. *Journal of Clinical and Translational Science*, *5*(1), e116. doi:10.1017/cts.2021.24 PMID:34221458

Kaplan, M., Lawson, K. A., & McCrady, V. (2018). The hero viewpoint and the perception of mentors: Why millennials need mentors and why they have problems finding them. *Academy of Business Research Journal*, *2*, 36–52.

Kilber, J., Barclay, A., & Ohmer, D. (2014). Seven tips for managing Generation Y. *Journal of Management Policy & Practice*, *15*(4), 50–91. http://www.na-businesspress.com/JMPP/BarclayA_Web15_4_.pdf

Koulopoulos, T., & Keldsen, D. (2014). *The Gen Z Effect: The six forces shaping the future of business*. Routledge.

Kram, K. E. (1985). *Mentoring at work: Developmental relationships in organizational life*. Scott Foresman.

Kram, K. E., & Higgins, M. C. (2009). A new mindset on mentoring: Creating developmental networks at work. *MIT Sloan Management Review*. https://provost.utsa.edu/mentoring/docs/Kram-Higgins.pdf

Kram, K. E., & Isabella, L. A. (1985). Mentoring alternatives: The role of peer relationships in career development. *Academy of Management Journal*, *28*(1), 110–132. doi:10.2307/256064

LaBelle, D. M. (2018). *Millennials' experiences with succession planning: A Basic Qualitative Study*. [Doctoral dissertation, Capella University]. Proquest Dissertations Publishing. https://www.proquest.com/openview/4a9552b8e83b7caa86ea01289b94ed97/1?pq-origsite=gscholar&cbl=18750

Littleton, K.T. (2015). *Mentoring Generation Y employees and retention in organizations: A phenomenological study*. [Unpublished doctoral dissertation, University of Phoenix].

Looseveld, L. M., Van Gerven, P. W. M., Driessen, E. W., Vanassche, E., & Artino, A. R. Jr. (2021). MERIT: A mentor reflection instrument for identifying the personal interpretative framework. *BMC Medical Education*, *21*(144), 144. https://bmcmededuc.biomedcentral.com/articles/10.1186/s12909-021-02579-x. doi:10.118612909-021-02579-x PMID:33663496

Meyer, M., & Warren-Gordon, K. (2013). Marginal Mentoring in the Contact Space: Diversified Mentoring Relationships at a Midsized Midwestern State University (MMSU). *Qualitative Report*, *18*(19), 1–18.

Mullen, C. A. (2000). Constructing co-mentoring partnerships: Walkways we must travel. *Theory into Practice*, *39*(1), 4–11. doi:10.120715430421tip3901_2

Murray, M. (1991). *Beyond the myths and magic of mentoring: How to facilitate an effective mentoring program*. Jossey-Bass.

Race, T., & Skees, J. (2010). Changing tides: Improving outcomes through mentorship on all levels of nursing. *Critical Care Nursing Quarterly*, *33*(2), 163–174. doi:10.1097/CNQ.0b013e3181d91475 PMID:20234205

Ragins, B. R., & Cotton, J. L. (1999). Mentor functions and outcomes: A comparison of men and women in formal and informal mentoring relationships. *The Journal of Applied Psychology*, *84*(4), 529–549. doi:10.1037/0021-9010.84.4.529 PMID:10504893

Robinson, D. M., & Reio, T. G. Jr. (2012). Benefits of mentoring African-American men. *Journal of Managerial Psychology*, *27*(4), 406–421. doi:10.1108/02683941211220207

Sathyakumar, J., & Ramakrishnan, M. (2013). Workplace expectations and organizational commitment of Generation Y: A case study at selective business schools. *TSM Business Review*, *1*(1), 1-13. http://www.tsm.ac.in/pdf/Samplepaper.pdf

Schepker, D. J., Kim, Y., Patel, P. C., Thatcher, S. M. B., & Campion, M. C. (2017). CEO succession, strategic change, and post-succession performance: A meta-analysis. *The Leadership Quarterly*, *28*(6), 701–720. doi:10.1016/j.leaqua.2017.03.001

Seheult, E. (2016). Generational mentorship: What millennial mentees want. *College and University*, *91*(3), 39–42.

Short, T. W. (2014). Workplace mentoring: An old idea with new meaning (part 2). *Development and Learning in Organizations*, *28*(2), 3–6. doi:10.1108/DLO-11-2013-0086

Siegel, P. H., Schultz, T., & Landy, S. (2011). Formal versus informal mentoring of MAS professionals. *Journal of Applied Business Research, 27*(2), 5–11. http://www.cluteinstitute.com/ojs/index.php/JABR/article/view/4135. doi:10.19030/jabr.v27i2.4135

Siu, G. P., & Sivan, A. (2011). Mentoring experiences of psychiatric nurses: From acquaintance to affirmation. *Nurse Education Today, 31*(8), 797–802. doi:10.1016/j.nedt.2010.11.014 PMID:21144626

Society for Human Resource Management. (2017). *Employee job satisfaction and engagement: The doors of opportunity are open.* SHRM. https://www.shrm.org/hr-today/trends-and-forecasting/research-and-surveys/Documents/2017-Employee-Job-Satisfaction-and-Engagement-Executive-Summary.pdf

SOA Research Institute. (2021). *Highlights of the 2021 retirement risk survey.* SOA Research Institute. https://www.soa.org/globalassets/assets/files/resources/research-report/2021/retirement-risk-survey-highlights.pdf

Termini, C. M., Hinton, A. O. Jr, Garza-Lopez, E., Koomoa, D. L., Davis, J. S., & Martinez-Montemayor, M. M. (2022). Building diverse mentoring networks that transcend boundaries in cancer research. *Trends in Cancer, 7*(5), 385–388. https://doi.10.1016/j.trecan.2021.01.001. doi:10.1016/j.trecan.2021.01.001 PMID:33563577

Vincent, A., & Seymour, J. (1995). Profile of women mentors: A national survey. *S.A.M. Advanced Management Journal, 60*, 4–10. https://www.freepatentsonline.com/article/SAM-Advanced-Management-Journal/17765188.html

Tews, M. J., Michel, J., Xu, S., & Drost, A. J. (2015). Workplace fun matters... but what else? *Employee Relations, 37*(2), 248–267. doi:10.1108/ER-10-2013-0152

Tulgan, B. (2016). *Not everyone gets a trophy: How to manage the millennials.* Wiley. doi:10.1002/9781119215073

Zackery, S. (2021). *Influence of STEM mentor race and cultural competency on racial and ethnic minority mentees.* [Masters thesis]. Oklahoma Baptist University. https://hdl.handle.net/11244/333649

Zenger, J. (2012, December 17). We wait too long to train our leaders [Blog post]. *Harvard Business Review*. https://hbr.org/2012/12/why-do-we-wait-so-long-to-trai/

ADDITIONAL READING

Deal, J., & Levenson, A. (2016). *What millennials want from work: How to maximize engagement in today's workforce*. McGraw-Hill.

Haynes, R. K., & Ghosh, R. (2008). Mentoring and succession management: An evaluative approach to the Strategic Collaboration Model. *Review of Business, 28*(2), 3–12. https://www.econbiz.de/Record/mentoring-and-succession-management-an-evaluative-approach-to-the-strategic-collaboration-model-haynes-ray/10009911726

Hobart, B., & Sendek, H. (2014). *Gen Y now: Millennials and the evolution of leadership* (2nd ed.). Wiley.

Johnson, W. B., & Ridley, C. R. (2018). *The elements of mentoring: 75 practices of master mentors* (3rd ed.). St. Martins.

Labin, J. (2017). *Mentoring programs that work*. ATD Press.

Lunsford, L. G. (2016). *A handbook for managing mentoring programs: Starting, supporting, and sustaining*. Routledge. doi:10.4324/9781315564760

McCann, J. (2012). Succession planning: Stewardship and mentoring. *Braille Forum, 51*, 23-25. https://acb.org/node/971

Morgan, J. (2014). *The future of work: Attract new talent, build better leaders, and create a competitive organization*. Wiley.

Okros, A. (2020). *Harnessing the potential of digital post-millennials in the future workplace*. Springer. doi:10.1007/978-3-030-25726-2

KEY TERMS AND DEFINITIONS

Career-Related Support: Assistance in matters such as company culture, work-related knowledge and skills, and career advancement opportunities.

Formal Mentoring: A structured approach to mentoring in which participants are matched based on specific criteria and then engage in prescribed activities designed with specific outcomes in mind.

Informal Mentoring: An approach to mentoring based on organic relationships without guided external expectations.

Organizational Commitment: A worker's involvement with and attachment to their organization.

Psychosocial Support: Assistance with social and emotional aspects of one's experience.

Retention: Ensuring that employees want to remain with their current company as opposed to leaving.

Succession Planning: A systematic process carried out by organizations to determine which individuals have the potential or the current ability to assume leadership positions when current leaders leave an organization.

Transformational Development Approach: A part of Transformational Leadership Theory, which has the end goal of transforming followers into leaders through a competency-based approach with a focus on empowerment.

Chapter 8
Educational Leadership:
Embracing the Benefits and the Challenges of the Millennial Leader in the Educational Organization

Thea Henderson Dirton
https://orcid.org/0000-0001-9856-1428
Independent Researcher, USA

ABSTRACT

Millennial leaders face many challenges when leading an organization. Their primary challenges involve their characteristics as a generational cohort and the benefits and challenges contained within them. Additional challenges that millennial leaders face while leading organizations are the interactions that they have with the other members of the organization from different generational cohorts. This chapter explores the benefits and challenges of millennial leadership, specifically in the educational setting, and presents rationales, examples, and solutions dealing with these challenges.

INTRODUCTION

Millennial Leaders face a complex dichotomy when leading organizations. Despite entering their leadership roles earlier than previous generations and having different values than the people they are leading, Millennial Leaders must still successfully lead their organizations. With the Baby Boomer generation population in the workforce decreasing and many of the Generation X population choosing to do things outside of the workforce, the Millennial population makes up the majority of the workforce

DOI: 10.4018/978-1-6684-4711-6.ch008

(McCleskey, 2018, p. 50). It is also for this reason that Millennials are becoming Leaders at a younger age than their counterparts.

Millennial Leaders are learning to navigate organizational logistics and leadership simultaneously and both come with challenges and opportunities. Michael Fullan, an expert in the field of education and leadership, calls this type of leader a "Lead Learner" because they must "be apprentices and experts at the same" (Fullan, 2022). This chapter will explore the differences between Millennial leaders and leaders from other generations in the educational setting, highlights their strengths and weaknesses, and provides insights and tools for the staff members that work with them.

HISTORICAL BACKGROUND

Millennials are categorized as people who were born between the years of 1982 to 2000 (Carter, 2016). At the writing of this book chapter, the oldest Millennials are forty years old while younger Millennials are twenty-two years old. The researcher finds it important to note that while the people who were born between the years of 1982 to 2000 are all considered Millennials with similar characteristics, there are notable differences between Millennials who were born at the beginning of the time period and those that were born at the end of the time period. An example of this is that older Millennials are generally children of Baby Boomers and younger Millennials are children of Generation Xers (Carter, 2016). Even this singular difference significantly modifies the characteristics between the two subgroups. Due to the sometimes vast differences between these two subgroups, the researcher will discuss only the characteristics that both older Millennials and younger Millennials share.

Although this book chapter will focus on the Millennial Leader, many comparisons will be drawn between the Millennial Leader and members of other generations, specifically Baby Boomers and Generation X. The Baby Boomer generation consists of people that were born between the years of 1946 to 1964 and the Generation X generation consists of people that were born between 1965 to 1981. At the writing of this book chapter, Baby Boomers range in age from fifty-eight to seventy-six and Generation Xers range in age from forty-one to fifty-seven. The ages and the years in which the members of a different generation were born is important because each generation has various characteristics that are specific to them.

Carter (2016) refers to this as Generational Identity Theory. In his discussion of this theory, Carter states that "members of a generational cohort or people born between a select range of calendar years will experience historic events and develop a set of cultural norms at common relative ages, thereby influencing the cohort's collective perceptions of society and history" (p. 9). Members of the various generations experienced different events as they were growing up and learning to interact in society and this affected the way that they viewed society and the way that they participated in it. For example, a person who grew up during civil unrest, such as Baby Boomers or Generation Z, behaves differently than a person who grew up in the period after it as in the case of Generation X (Grotkamp et al., 2020).

Baby Boomers, who were born during the years of 1946-1964 and came of age during many of society's most important movements, experienced the aftermath of war, the birth of Civil Rights, and the tremendous growth of society in many different areas. After World War II, many factors led to the substantial growth of the middle class. Baby Boomers grew up during this time period and witnessed their parents who suffered through the Great Depression and World War II begin to thrive, thus cementing the idea of the American Dream (Carter, 2016). During this time, the economic growth experienced led to an increase in birth rates, which is why the Baby Boomer generation is larger than Generation X (Carter, 2016). However, this economic growth was not experienced by everyone in the entire generation equally; African-Americans were being discriminated against, which led to the birth of the Civil Rights Movement (Carter, 2016). Often referred to as the "greatest generation", Baby boomers experienced first-hand many of the events that shaped society as a whole and it is evident in how they interact in the World.

Generation Xers, who were born from 1965 to 1981, were born during a time of cable tv, video games, microwaves, and other technological advances (Carter, 2016). This led the members of this generation to have immediate access to things like news from around the country and food. The "instantaneous response and fulfillment" (Carter, 2016, p. 19) that Generation Xers experienced growing up, along with witnessing foreign and local conflicts such as Operation Desert Storm, the Los Angeles Riots, and an increasing divorce rate, made them skeptical and cynical (Carter, 2016). This skepticism and cynicism led to Generation Xers not being dedicated to their employer and an "overdeveloped sense of individualism" (Pardekooper, 2019, p. 29).

Millennials are those who were born between 1982 to 2000. These years fluctuate and some sources list the Millennial generation starting as early as 1980 (Carter, 2016; Grotkamp et al., 2022). One of the most discussed characteristics of Millennials is their proficiency with technology and its effect on their lives, but there are other characteristics that set them apart from the previous generations. The prevalence of technology in Millennials' lives is all-encompassing; they were born during a time in which "cell phones, personal computers, and ATMs [are] commonplace" (Carter, 2016, p. 21) which means that most members of the generation use social media or other technology-based devices to connect with friends and family, to be informed about societal issues, and to research various topics. Millennials also grew up during a time there were many positive and negative societal changes and events that molded their lives. During their formative years, there was an increase in immigration and many Millennials are the children of immigrants making Millennials the "most racially diverse generation in the nation's history" (Carter, 2016, p. 22), and the first African-American president was elected. During the Millennial's childhood, there were also school shootings and the September 11th terrorist attack, which impacted the way that Millennials were raised and how they interact in society (Carter, 2016).

Each of the generations mentioned above have defining characteristics based on the years in which they were born and the environmental phenomena that occurred during that time period. Whether it was war or an infusion of technology, it had an effect on the people that lived through it. It affects the way that they interact with their peers and the generations before them, both personally and professionally. Throughout this chapter, the researcher will specifically discuss the characteristics of the Millennial Leader and how their characteristics differ from the generations that came before them.

METHODOLOGY

To explore the differences between leaders from different areas, in particular how the Millennial leader differs from leaders from other generations the researcher observed various leaders in the educational setting. The researcher also interviewed their staff members and researched the topic. The questions and research centered on the various characteristics of Millennial leaders and their similarities and differences from members of other generations. Discussions with staff members that work in Millennial Leaders' buildings and the Baby Boomers' buildings, observations, and research yielded many qualitative data points. The questions included effectiveness questions such as "What makes your leader effective?" and "What drives your leader's decision-making?" and the follow-up question of "Is that effective in the educational organization?". The researcher also encouraged staff members at her current school to discuss the similarities between their current Millennial leader and their past Baby Boomer principal.

Generational Clash

Pardekooper (2019) refers to the combination of different generations in an organization as a "generational clash" (p. 29). In this clash, Baby Boomers, who have the confidence of living through war, and Generation Xers, who had to be independent at an early age due to their working parents, are often in opposition with Millennials, who value personal relationships and thrive in spaces that have "a preference for highly social and connected interactions in the work-place" (McCleskey, 2018, p. 51). The characteristics and values of each generation formed by the time and environments in which they were raised oftentimes lead to "a great deal of misunderstanding from all parties" (Pardekooper, 2019, p. 28). These misunderstandings have the opportunity to decrease an organization's productivity and success. However, with Millennial Leaders at the helm of these organizations, due to their value of collaboration and shared leadership, a decrease in misunderstandings and an increase in partnerships and teamwork is possible if members of the organizations that Millennials work and lead in embrace their benefits and challenges and provide opportunities for growth in these areas.

"Generational diversity is the new normal in most organizations" (McCleskey, 2018, p. 50), but none more so than in an educational organization. The most recent data shows that the average age of teachers in the United States is 42.4; 15.0% are less than thirty years old, 56.9% are thirty to forty-nine years old, 11.6% are fifty to fifty-four years old, and 16.5% are fifty-five or older (National, 2018). Not only are there several generations represented by the educators in an educational organization, but there is also an additional generation of students that have their own characteristics, values, and needs. Arguably, it is the needs of this generation, Generation Z, that is the most important in an educational organization because their education is the very reason for the organization, however, the needs of the teachers must be met as well in order for the organization to be successful. Although the leader is ultimately in charge of making the policies and procedures in the educational organization, it is up to the educators and staff to implement the policies and procedures. The students must abide by the policies and procedures and subsequently provide the output necessary to show the organization's success. Because each stakeholder in the educational organization is essential to its success if the needs of either one of these stakeholders are not met the organization will not be successful.

In an educational organization, the combination of the various generations and the characteristics and values that they hold would require any Leader to employ a specific set of skills in order to provide an opportunity for all involved to teach and learn. The Millennial Leader is optimal for this task because they have "an increased awareness of the needs of individualistic workers (McCleskey, 2018, p. 50) and they also value the opinions and viewpoints of those that they lead. McClesky (2018) states "utilizing a focused effort, taking advantage of member expertise, and engaging in collaboration, knowledge sharing, and joint decision-making, teams make more effective use of Leader capabilities and problem-solving (p. 51)", these are all Millennial ways of leading that if honed will lead the organization to success.

In this chapter, the researcher will discuss the unique challenges and benefits of Millennial leadership and the impact that they have in an organization, with a specific focus on the educational organization.

BENEFITS OF MILLENNIAL LEADERSHIP

Millennials have very distinct characteristics due to their upbringing and the environment they grew up in; they have different characteristics from the generations that came before them and even those that are coming after them. In researching the Millennial generation, it is evident that there are "differences between generations and that generational membership is crucial to an individual's identity due to the unique social and historic influences experienced by a generation. (Grotkamp et al., 2020, p. 59). These differences are evident in many ways throughout an organization. The differences affect how they communicate with their peers and supervisors, the level of collaboration they use in making decisions and reaching goals, and how they help move the organization forward. These differences, in the context of today's society, are beneficial. They not only help drive the Millennial's personal mission, but also help drive the mission of the organization. This portion of the chapter will discuss the benefits of Millennial leadership. Characteristics such as perseverance, embracing change, and the desire to provide a better future for themselves and the stakeholders in their organization provide opportunities for the Millennial Leader to create lasting change in their lives and the lives of all stakeholders in the organization.

Data-Driven Decision Making

Although Millennial Leaders are known for their proficiency in the areas of technology and creativity, there are many additional benefits to having a Millennial Leader at the helm of an organization, particularly an educational organization. Millennial Leaders are problem-solvers and critical thinkers that use data to guide their decisions which is a best practice in educational leadership. Data-driven decision-making is a characteristic of other generations as well; however, Millennial Leaders take the use of data to extreme levels, using extensive data and data tools, such as pivot tables and linear regression graphs to diagnose problems and determine the effectiveness of policies, programs, and people. This is important in an educational setting because there are many different strategies and programs that are touted as effective, however, Leaders need strategic ways of determining which one is most effective in their school.

The Millennial Leader uses data on a daily basis in the researcher's educational organization. There are programs and strategies suggested at the school, district, and state levels, and as an educational best practice, our current leadership team uses data from many different sources to determine which one is best for our students. The researcher is in a unique situation of experiencing a Leader from the Baby Boomer generation and a Leader from the Millennial generation. The previous principal, a Baby Boomer, implemented programs of his choosing, sometimes based on what worked for him in a previous school or what "felt right". This is in stark contrast to our current Millennial Leader, who uses data and the opinion of the school leadership team almost exclusively.

When surveyed teachers who work in schools led by a Millennial Leader indicated that being data-driven was one of their most effective characteristics. Out of the ten teachers surveyed, seven of them listed data-driven as their top effective characteristic. One teacher in particular stated that being data-driven was the number one reason for their principal's success. In another school, one Millennial leader starts each meeting with a piece of relevant data and this makes her staff value and focus on the different data points.

There is a vast difference in how members from the different generations use data to drive the programs and strategies implemented in the organization. The Millennial Leader uses continuous cycles of action research to collect qualitative and quantitative data to determine which programs and strategies are most effective. The action research process is beneficial to the organization because using data to drive decisions is a research-based strategy that has been proven to provide effective solutions.

Perseverance

Perseverance is a trait that Leaders from all generations share. Leaders from the Baby Boomer generation and Generation X experienced situations in the World and in their personal lives that required them to overcome adversity and persevere in order to be successful. Surviving war and high unemployment rates tested the resolve of earlier generations which subsequently increased their level of perseverance (Pardekooper, 2019). Millennials also have a high level of perseverance; however, they differ from the older generations in that they have access to information like no other generations. This means that when faced with an issue, the Millennial Leader, unlike previous generations, has an unlimited amount of knowledge at their fingertips (Pardekooper, 2019). Armed with this knowledge, along with an unwavering sense of confidence, the Millennial Leader forges ahead, unsure of the specific outcome or the tools that they will need, but confident that they will be successful (Pardekooper, 2019). This blind perseverance goes above and beyond the previous generations because the Millennial may not know precisely how they are going to reach his or her goal, but they do not doubt that they can and will reach it, thus taking perseverance to a higher level.

The Millennial's high level of perseverance holds in the researcher's educational organization. The Millennial Leader uses the practice of data-driven action research to solve any problems that arise. He uses continuous cycles of collecting data, which includes qualitative and quantitative data points, researching strategies and solutions, and implementation of the strategies and solutions to solve problems. If the data is not up to the expectations of the principal or his supervisors, then he begins the process again. This cyclical process takes a large amount of perseverance and is challenging to the non-Millennial stakeholders in the organization who do not understand the processes that Millennial Leaders engage in to make decisions. Starting the process of decision-making with a discovery mindset and using technology and those around them to create a continuous stream of information are various ways Millennial Leaders in an educational setting increase their capacity to lead (Grotkamp et al., 2020). This practice allows them to persevere in the face of generational misunderstandings, lack of leadership experiences, and the high expectations that they have of themselves and that others have of them.

Embraces Change

Along with their ability to persevere, the Millennial Leader's ability to embrace change is also beneficial to the organizations that they lead. Specifically, in educational organizations, the ability to not only embrace change, but in many cases to also seek it out allows for practices to be examined and modified or replaced if needed. Pardekooper (2019) states that while the rest of the World is resistant to change, Millennials look at change as an "opportunity to learn…[t]hey want to learn how to make an impact on the world and they are willing to do what they have to" (p. 52) in order to do this. The Millennial Leader uses many possible processes to evaluate current processes and find solutions, including the action research process discussed in the previous chapter. The Millennial Leader's solutions change in a way that integrates their own ideas with the ideas that they're able to pull together with the group and then move forward on to that basis The Millennial Leader uses those processes because he or she "expects a continuous exchange of information, regular performance evaluations, a supportive environment, and organizational transparency" (Grotkamp et al., 2020, p. 62) and use this information to create change.

In the researchers' organization, the current Millennial Leader is open to change in any area. At the suggestion of teachers, students, parents, his supervisor, qualitative data, or quantitative data, the Millennial Leader would begin to analyze the processes that make up that area. Though at times this is a daunting challenge for the Millennial Leader and the leadership team, the Leader's Shared leadership style, transparency, and consistent and constant communication distributes the work evenly and creates an environment in which it is possible for the work to be accomplished. Though initiated by the Millennial Leader, the change that he wants to happen in the organization, which is only possible through implementing and evaluating solutions, requires the help of the entire leadership team.

Under the previous Baby Boomer Leader, policies and procedures were not changed unless deemed absolutely necessary, which was usually after several complaints or an incident. When the Leader decided a change was needed, there was not a consistent process and the Leader made the majority of the decisions with little input from the stakeholders in the organization. When the Leader decided on the course of action that he was going to take he would then communicate the decided upon solution. On a few occasions, there would be a cursory leadership meeting so that the leadership team members could offer any suggestions that they had; however, during these meetings it often felt as though the Baby Boomer Leader already knew the solution to the problem and that the meeting was superficial.

Desires to Provide a Better Future for Everyone

The Millennial Leader's propensity for change is fueled by his/her desire to provide a better future for themselves and for the stakeholders in their organization. When choosing an organization to become involved in, Millennials "value companies that positively impact society and reflect their own core values" (Grotkamp et al., 2020, p. 62). They choose to work in companies that they value because working in companies and organizations that align with their values motivates them to be successful (Grotkamp et al., 2020). Millennials become personally invested and involved with these companies and organizations and are "willing to invest their time when day-to-day tasks are connected to bigger issues impacting their lives (Grotkamp et al., 2020, p. 62)". If Millennials are not personally invested in the companies in which they work, their desire for autonomy and their tendency to get bored with mundane tasks causes them to move from job to job without loyalty to a specific company (Grotkamp et al., 2020).

The alignment of their personal values with the organization in which they work and eventually lead motivates the Millennial Leader to "want to… make an impact on the world and they are willing to do what they have to" (Pardekooper, 2019, p. 52). Millennial Leaders want to make a difference in their organizations and the World around them, so they embrace change and work systematically toward finding solutions that will make the World a better place. Organizations recognize that "[m] illennials are described as the key generation to drive change towards a better future in a world confronted with diverse economic, political, and environmental challenges (Grotkamp et al., 2020, p. 58) and are trying to "win and keep Millennial Leaders to guide their business into the future" (Grotkamp et al., 2020, p. 70).

Members of the Baby Boomer generation also believe in making a difference in the communities around them, though this is not necessarily through the organizations in which they work. Throughout history, Baby Boomers have stepped up wherever they were needed "because it was their responsibility, it was their purpose in life, [and] it was their pleasure to answer the call to change the world" (Pardekooper, 2019, p. 49). After World War II ended, Baby Boomers used newly available resources to attend college and start professional careers (Carter, 2020). Most were not working to change the World, they were working to improve their lives and the lives of their families; the expansion of the middle class during this time is evidence that this was achieved (Carter, 2020).

In the educational setting, the Millennial Leaders' desire to improve the lives of the stakeholders in their organization is characterized by their focus on the needs of the whole child, not just the child's academic needs. While leading an educational organization, the Millennial Leader's goal is to provide students with opportunities that will not only help them grow academically, but will also help them to grow socially and emotionally. One of the major strategies that Millennial Leaders use to provide opportunities for students to do this is incorporating research-based SEL Programs that focus on helping students acknowledge and solve issues related to their social and emotional habits. This also extends to the other stakeholders within the organization; Millennial Leaders want all of the stakeholders to learn and grow. Ways that Millennial Leaders provide opportunities for staff to do this is to promote activities that encourage "highly social and connected interactions in the workplace" (McKlesky, 2018, p. 51) and by "redefin[ing] the relationship between supervisor and employee" (McKlesky, 2018, p. 51).

Under the researcher's current Millennial principal, the educational organization has focused on meeting as many of the students' academic, social, and emotional needs as possible. Through federal, state, district, and school programs, students are able to form bonds with community members and teachers, receive mentorship opportunities, learn life and leadership skills, see a nurse practitioner for any medical needs, see a mental health specialist, identify interventions that are specific to them, and receive financial help. Our principal, like most other Millennial Leaders, is trauma-informed and incorporates trauma-informed practices into all areas of the school. Practices such as Conscious Discipline and Capturing Kids Hearts focus on creating relationships and providing reflection time for teachers and students so that students can acquire any skills that they may be missing. The school has also intentionally made space for students to practice mindfulness by including a mindfulness room and having schoolwide mindful moments at the beginning and end of the day. The focus on growth in all areas also extends to faculty and staff; teachers have mentors, access to free counseling, donated food and treats, and other appreciation gifts that are meant to provide professional and emotional support.

Millennial Leaders have other characteristics that benefit an organization such as their global thinking, their belief in leading using a followers' mindset, and their desire to enter leadership at a young age (Pardekooper, 2019). These characteristics, which differ from Leaders of other generations, allow Millennial Leaders to provide space for change and growth for all of the stakeholders in the organization. It allows the Leader to use the organization "to drive change towards a better future in a world confronted with diverse economic, political, and environmental challenges" (Grotkamp et al., 2020, p. 58). Leaders from earlier generations who do not value these ways of thinking limit the productivity of their organization and its ability to create global change by not fully exploring these ways of thinking.

CHALLENGES OF MILLENNIAL LEADERSHIP

Due to societal norms, lived experiences, and organizational expectations, Millennial Leaders have many characteristics that are optimal for leading in today's global society. However, these same norms, experiences, and expectations have also caused Millennial Leaders to develop characteristics and engage in situations that cause challenges in their organizations. These challenges are unique and specific to Millennial Leaders because of their values and beliefs. These challenges are also unique to Millennial Leaders because of the generational disconnect that is present between themselves and the people that they work with (Pardekooper, 2019). Challenges that Millennial Leaders face in their organizations are their lack of leadership experience when entering leadership roles, their lack of sense of urgency, their need for non-traditional professional development, and the issues that arise when they work with members of different generations.

Lack of Experience

As discussed earlier, Millennials are entering leadership at a younger age. Harrison (2015) states that "[a]dult Millennials, approximately age eighteen through thirty-four, have surpassed Generation X in the workforce and will be needed to fill the leadership gaps" (p. 11). The absence of members of Generation X and the retirement of members of the Baby Boomer generation in the workforce means that members of the Millennial generation have to fill in the voids left in leadership roles. This is a challenge because, as Harrison (2015) states, traditionally "most individuals enter formal leadership programs at age 42" (p.13). When entering these leadership programs, these individuals are able to rely on both professional and personal experiences to guide them in their leadership journey. However, due to employee voids in organizations, Millennials are being forced or choosing to take leadership roles without the benefit of experiences that a member of the Baby Boomer or Generation X generations might have.

This lack of experience might also exacerbate the "generational clash" between Leaders and subordinates in an organization. Members from older generations may challenge the Millennial Leader's authority more frequently and may be directly and indirectly insubordinate. When a Leader is perceived as incompetent due to any issue, such as a lack of experience, some members of the organization may purposefully or inadvertently question their decisions which could lead to the decisions being overridden. This dissension in the organization is toxic to the environment in the organization.

This lack of experience also impedes the Millennial Leader's decision-making ability. Professionally, entering leadership positions at an early age limits the experiences that the Millennial Leader has working in the lower levels of the organization. This means that they may not have become knowledgeable about the intricacies of the organization and what is needed in order for it to be successful. The Millennial Leader's personal life experiences somewhat mirror this. Grotkamp et al. (2020) state that the Millennial's "parents often took on the task of making important decisions for their children. Hence, they often did not learn to evaluate situations by themselves" (p. 61). Millennials were not able to experience decision-making and risk-taking as children in their personal lives and this adds to the challenges that they experience in their professional lives.

In order to overcome this challenge, the Millennial Leader should rely on their positive characteristics, including but not limited to having "a continuous exchange of information, regular performance evaluations, a supportive environment, and organizational transparency" (Grotkamp et al., 2020, p. 61). These characteristics are what make the Millennial Leader successful at using a shared leadership style. Shared leadership, otherwise known as collaborative leadership, co-leadership, collective leadership, or distributive leadership, is characterized by the Leader engaging in a team approach to all areas involving leadership (McCleskey, 2018). When a Leader with limited leadership experience practices Shared leadership, the leadership team's experiences, ideas, and opinions ensure that any issue that could arise because of a lack of experience is neutralized (McCleskey, 2018).

The shared leadership style also highlights the role of collaboration in the educational organization. The Association for Supervision and Curriculum Development (ASCD), a leader in the field of educational leadership facilitates a principal leadership course that contains many elements of shared leadership. In the framework for their Principal Leadership Development Program, they teach that an effective leader "Articulates, communicates, and leads the collaborative implementation and ongoing revision of the school's mission and vision" and that a leader "Promotes the collaborative creation, monitoring, and refinement of short- and long-term school improvement plans" (ASCD, 2015).

In the researcher's educational organization, the Millennial Leader intentionally shares the leadership responsibility with many different groups. The first level of leadership is the core leadership team which consists of the three grade-level administrators and the school-based instructional coaches. The second level of the leadership team is the core team and the guidance counselors and the district-based coaches. Another level of the leadership team includes both mandated and voluntary teachers, which consists of the department chairs and any other teachers who would like to volunteer. In his research on Shared leadership, McCleskey (2018) found that Shared leadership provided organizations with the opportunity to come together for a shared goal and use the expertise of other members within the organization to solve problems. In the researcher's organization, this holds. Shared leadership allows for joint problem solving, which leads to more effective and efficient solutions. The principal's lack of experience is bolstered by the other leadership team members and the organization is not negatively affected by it.

Lack of Urgency

Another challenge that Millennial Leaders face is their lack of urgency. There are many characteristics of Millennials that combine to lessen their sense of urgency. One is the desire to have a work-life balance and another is the fact that some Millennials do not tend to stay at their jobs very long (McCleskey, 2018; Harrison, 2015). Millennials value the time they spend outside of work and do not feel that their professional life should overshadow this. This desire for work-life balance is in contrast to the Baby Boomer generation that "equates success with work and personal sacrifice" (Harrison, 2015, p. 12). When the tendency to not stay at a job very long is added to this, it results in the Millennial's lack of urgency.

As discussed earlier in the chapter, Millennials desire to find jobs that provide them with autonomy and the opportunity to make a difference in the World. If this is not the case, Millennials will not stay at a company long because they are "highly energetic, skillful, and always looking for new challenges" (Grotkamp et al., 2020, p. 64). If they are not given the autonomy to work the way that they prefer, given the opportunity to grow through professional development and mentorship, and given the opportunity to utilize their skills, Millennials will not be loyal to the company (Grotkamp et al., 2020). For these reasons, Millennials are said to "display lower levels of loyalty than other generations" (Grotkamp et al., 2020, p. 64). The lack of personal investment by Millennials leads to a lack of urgency in the organization.

A lack of urgency is a challenge to Millennial Leaders because within an organization, there are many times when an immediate decision has to be made or when, regardless of the Shared leadership model, the ultimate decision must rest the

Leader. If the Leader lacks the ability to evaluate immediate problems and prefers to make decisions as a team rather than individually, their productivity and goal achievement could be hampered negatively affecting the organization.

In the researcher's educational organization, our Millennial Leader's lack of urgency has at times been detrimental to the success of the organization. There have been instances in which the Millennial Leader's indecisiveness or lack of action, even after hearing the opinions of the different levels of the leadership team, has caused a situation to escalate or unravel. There have also been times in which the Millennial Leader has not taken any action when action was required. This hesitancy to act is in stark contrast to our previous principal, who, as a member of the Baby Boomer generation, had a definitive answer and took action almost immediately. It always felt as if he was operating under a sense of urgency and whether the decisions that he made were based on his past experiences or his personal beliefs, he was always ready to answer any question or solve any issue that arose, this included overriding decisions that were previously made that he could have agreed or disagreed with.

Although a lack of urgency is a challenge that Millennial Leaders face, Grotkamp et al. (2020) note that Millennial Leaders are overachievers and thrive when they know what is expected of them. These characteristics can offset the lack of urgency that Millennials experience because if they know the expectations required of them they will work tirelessly toward meeting them (Grotkamp et al., 2020). Another positive characteristic of Millennial Leaders that offsets the challenge of their lack of urgency is that they build strong relationships with their supervisors and they value feedback (Grotkamp et al., 2020). Pardekooper (2019) states that Millennial always perform at a high level when the "expectations were tied to clear vision and objectives" (p. 57). If supervised effectively and provided feedback on their job performance, the Millennial Leader will be productive in the organization and effectively drive both their goals and the goals of their organization forward.

Need for Non-Traditional Professional Development

Professional Development is another area that is a challenge for Millennial Leaders. Millennial Leaders require new and innovative professional development programs due to their age and characteristics. Because Millennials are entering leadership roles at an earlier age, many are not benefitting from the traditional leadership programs. As stated earlier, Harrison (2015) states that most aspiring leaders enter leadership programs at a later age. This means that because aspiring Millennial Leaders are entering leadership at an earlier age, "many companies might have waited too long to implement programs that prepare [them]" (Harrison, 2015, p. 13). The lack of effective leadership programs is a larger issue because Millennials also lack leadership experience.

When Millennial Leaders do have access to professional development, it may not be effective because their leaders, members of the Baby boomer and Generation X generations, "lack a clear understanding of the unique perspective held by the Millennial Leaders moving up in their organizations and do not know how best to develop needed competencies among Millennial Leaders" (Harrison, 2015, p. 14). Harrison (2015) goes on to say that "[w]ithout this understanding, managers might not always select the best [professional development] program approaches." (p. 13). Grotkamp et al. (2020) states that Millennial Leaders prefer to learn "based on an interactive and comparatively unstructured, learning-by-doing approach" (p. 60), they also go on to say that the Millennial Leader's "preferred personal development process starts with discovery and only secondly moves on to learning about techniques and applying a more rigid structural approach" (Grotkamp et al., 2020, p. 60). Because Millennial Leaders have different needs than previous generations, the people who lead them must develop programs that appeal to their needs and characteristics.

One potential solution to the challenge of implementing non-traditional professional development for Millennial Leaders is implementing a mentorship program in which Millennials learn from their predecessors. However, due to the aforementioned "generational clash" and the misunderstandings that are created by the phenomenon, members of previous generations are hesitant to reach out to Millennials and Millennials are hesitant to reach out to members of previous generations. Pardekooper (2019) states that the differences and consequential misunderstandings "causes Millennials to avoid seeking out mentors and they miss out on learning the valuable skills they need" (p. 26).

In lieu of finding and being supported by a mentor, Millennial Leaders who wish to go into leadership are drawn to their supervisors (Grotenkamp et al., 2020). So instead of seeking out a peer to mentor them, Millennials seek out a trusted supervisor to provide feedback, advice, and suggestions that help them be successful. The intentional pairing of a Millennial Leader with a supervisor in his or her field to act as a mentor and provide professional development would satisfy the Millennial's need for non-traditional professional development and guiding feedback.

In the researcher's educational setting, the Millennial Principal thrives when he feels supported by his supervisors. Due to our status as a Title 1 school, the leadership team meets monthly with district office personnel. During these meetings, we receive feedback on various processes and situations going on within the school. Our Millennial Principal thrives at these meetings when he knows what is expected of him and is able to prepare, he flounders when unexpected items arise or when specific action steps are not given. These meetings are also beneficial to our Millennial Leader because he does not interact with other principals in the district because the majority of them are from different generations than he is. He also meets with his supervisor on a regular basis outside of these meetings for feedback, information, and encouragement. As one of the Instructional Leaders in the school, being a part of these meetings are beneficial because they help to inform the researcher's practice as she is working with other stakeholders around the school. It helps the researcher understand the benefit of clear and consistent feedback and helps her incorporate it into her practice.

Another potential solution to the need for non-traditional professional development is using Individualized Professional Development as a means to grow professionally and meet his growth targets. Individualized Professional Development (IPD) is a professional development plan implemented in the researcher's educational organization that has been successful with Millennial learners as well as staff members from the other generations. The researcher, along with members of the leadership team, created the IPD and its components to address the unavailability of effective professional development. In Individualized Professional Development, the Leader, teacher, or student creates a problem of practice based on the needs of the people that he/she is leading and researches that area. This method is effective because it allows participants to identify their own area of need and work on that area. Along with identifying the problem and researching reasons for the problem, the participant also finds solutions to the problem and then implements these possible solutions. The final component to the IPD is the participant reflecting on the effectiveness of the implementation of the solution and sharing his/her learning with supervisors and peers in the educational organization. This process of action research as a means of professional development is effective for Millennials because it helps them develop professionally while allowing for their preferences of working independently, completing tasks that they choose, and following a clear, researched path to improvement (Grotkamp et al., 2020). Our principal, along with the rest of our staff, engages in IPD monthly and it has improved their educational practice.

ISSUES THAT ARISE WHEN NAVIGATING OTHER GENERATIONS

At various points throughout this chapter, the differences between Millennials and other generations have been highlighted. These differences, which were created by a combination of parental involvement and changes in societal norms, cause Millennials to interact differently with the people in their organizations. Millennial Leaders are often misunderstood by members of other generations so they prefer non-face-to-face communication and to work independently on projects (Grotkamp et al., 2020). Millennial Leaders form close relationships with supervisors and other authority figures, but they do not seek out mentors among their peers because they "feel devalued by the frustration previous generations have of them" (Pardekooper, 2019, p. 26).

Members of the other generations, specifically the Generation X and Baby Boomer generations, are complicit in the misconceptions that they have about Millennials. Instead of trying to understand the values of Millennials and the reasonings behind them, most members of the older generations do not try to understand Millennials and instead write off these differences as trivial, but detrimental to society (Pardekooper, 2019). The feeling that the upcoming generation will ruin the progress that the previous generation has made is common and has been expressed by the most recent generations (Pardekooper, 2019). However, when dealing with Millennials, little effort is made by the previous generations to understand their characteristics and how they help further society instead of hurting it. Pardekooker (2019) writes about this in The Millennial Leader, he states "[o]ne of the complaints about Millennials I hear all the time is they are cocky and unteachable. When I hear this, what most people are really referring to is the tendency Millennials have to act as though they know everything and do not need anyone else's help. When a Millennial hears this, it can be quite offensive because it could not be further from the truth." (p. 52). This is an example of a misconception of Millennials that could be rectified by members of all of the generations talking openly and honestly with each other.

Another layer of generational navigation appears in the educational organization. In an educational organization, not only is the Millennial Leader responsible for managing teachers spanning all generations from Millennials to Baby Boomers, but they also are responsible for educating the students from Generation Z. This means that the Millennial Principal has to lead professionals and students with vastly different characteristics, values, and ideas of educational best practices from their own, with limited experience, ineffective professional development, and a lack of peer mentorship. This leadership dichotomy causes conflicts when determining the importance of various programs, disciplinary actions regarding students, and allocating funds. The various generations found in educational organizations value different things, so they place different levels of importance on various programs, student issues, and funding needs.

The Millennial Principal's main goal centers on the whole child, specifically the students' academic, social, and emotional needs. The Millennial Principal values the students' social and emotional needs and realizes the effect that they have on the students' academic needs. They use this comprehensive focus to navigate their interactions with the members of Generation Z. The Millennial Principal is cognizant of Generation Z's needs and balances their social-emotional needs with their academic needs. This is similar to how Millennials live their lives in general and how they interact with the various generations in the non-educational work environment; they believe in balance and in using leadership to create change in the World (McCleskey, 2018). Millennials are also "described as the key generation to drive change towards a better future in a world confronted with diverse economic, political, and environmental challenges" (Grotkamp et al., 2020, p. 2). In order for Millennials, especially those that work in the educational system, to effect this change, they must not only focus on the academic skills that the future generation needs to be successful in today's global society, but they must also focus on the soft skills that students need make the World a better place for themselves, previous generations, and future generations.

Along with the strategies mentioned above that meet the majority of the needs of students, such as practicing mindfulness, the researcher's educational organization also focuses on goal setting, building relationships with students, and providing services such as mental health counseling. These focuses help the students prepare for the global society in which they live and it also provides opportunities for the older generations to get to know and understand the younger generation.

CONCLUSION

The Millennial Leader is faced with a challenging task while leading in today's global society. They are leading people from two to four different generations that may misunderstand or misinterpret their characteristics, think that they are more experienced than them, and have different values, characteristics, and processes from them. The benefits and the challenges of the Millennial Leader combine to make a thoughtful, driven leader that thrives off of feedback and implements different types of leadership strategies in order to lead (McCleskey, 2018). Millennial Leaders are natural-born problem solvers that can persevere through any situation and use change to make the World a better place, however without clear expectations and the autonomy to follow these expectations as they see fit, they will not be successful (Grotkamp et al., 2020).

The Millennial Leader is driven to be successful more than any of the other generations before them or after them. They are not driven by blind loyalty like Baby Boomers or a strong sense of cynical individualism like Generation Xers; they are driven by their mission to effect change on societal systems for the greater good (Pardekooper, 2019). The Millennial Leader's mission to change the world for the better is what motivates them to work within their organizations and "organizations are eager to utilize the unique characteristics of [Millennials] to increase the efficiency and effectiveness…to improve company performance" (Grotkamp et al., 2020). In today's global society, it is important that the Millennial Leader and the organizations they lead capitalize on their benefits and find solutions to their challenges to work with the other generations so the organization can be successful.

REFERENCES

ASCD. (2015) *Leadership Matters Building Principals' Capacity with the ASCD Principal Leadership Development Framework.* ASCD. https://files.ascd.org/staticfiles/ascd/pdf/siteASCD/publications/leadership-matters-whitepaper.pdf

Carter, F. (2016). *Generation X and Millennial Generation Assistant Principals' Perceptions of the Challenges and Rewards of the Principalship*. Virginia Polytechnic Institute and State University.

Fullan, M. (2022). *Michael Fullan on Leading Change in a New Era*. Victorian Academy of Teaching and Leadership. https://www.academy.vic.gov.au/learning-resources/michael-fullan-leading-change-new-era

Grotkamp, L., Schaumann, J. M., & Riehm, P. (2020). Millennial Leaders' Display Of Generational Cohort Stereotypes: A Qualitative Research Approach. *Journal of leadership in Organizations, 2*(2).

Harrison, A. E. (2015). *Millennial leadership development: Building competencies with best practices* [Doctoral dissertation, University of Maryland University College].

McCleskey, J. A. (2018). Millennial leadership expectations, shared leadership, and the future of organizations. *J Manage Sci Bus Intell, 3*(2), 50–52.

National Center for Education Statistics (2018). Average and median age of public school teachers and percentage distribution of teachers by age category, sex, and state: 2017-2018. *National Teacher and Principal Survey.* NCES.

Pardekooper, B. (2019). *Millennial leadership: Equipping Generations to Influence a New Millennium.* Author Academy Elite.

Chapter 9
Leadership Qualities of Successful Millennial Leaders in Developmental Agenda in Africa

Ranson Sifiso Gwala
https://orcid.org/0000-0002-1545-2259
University of KwaZulu-Natal, South Africa

ABSTRACT

Leadership is the glue that bridges good ideas to action. Leadership is the ability to influence people to follow, and then bring about fundamental changes in society. Scholars have widely postulated different kinds of leadership styles. With the changing technological environment and millennials, these studies are further extrapolated to what skills should millennial leaders possess in this digital age. The study adopted exploratory direction using a desktop review of literature. The study revealed five themes that millennial leaders must exhibit. The study identified visionary, crisis, innovation, and adaptability leadership; inclusive, empathetic, integrity and accountability leadership; resilience, perseverance, cultural appreciation, and contextual understanding; it also viewed youth, women empowerment, environmental stewardship, and long-term thinking as another group of though leadership that millennial leaders ought to advance. Lastly, the ability of millennial leaders to communicate, educate and share knowledge is critical in ringing and growing new leaders through education.

DOI: 10.4018/978-1-6684-4711-6.ch009

INTRODUCTION

Africa remains the most underdeveloped continent in the world. It is however a continent with some of the world riches that reside under the earth. It is also a mecca for the world tourists as it contains the world greatest game reserves, showing a variety of fauna and flora. Africa still lags behind many continents, long after colonisation ended. Some of the African countries are still riddled by wars and plunder of economic resources. Africa, today, is still plagued by aid, which continues to put Africa in shackles of poverty, war, poverty and under-development. The former colonisers still see Africa as their lands where they collect their labour and raw materials for their own economic development. The colonial links are still laid bare and are a burden of retrogression. Africa remain a dumping site of "cheap products", which undermine the productive forces of the African continue to grow its productive power and ability to grow its own local production and markets. Any cheap imports which destroy local production are not good for any country. Whilst the fourth industrial revolution continues the fifth industrial revolution has also been introduced to harmonise human-machine cooperation is central to the Fifth Industrial Revolution (5IR), with a particular emphasis on the welfare of the many stakeholders (i.e., society, companies, employees, customers) (Noble et al., 2022), and leadership remains a crucial element of development.

The Background

South Africa was, in 1994, the last country to be free when it went through its first democratic elections. To many Africans, this was the end of the chapter and the beginning of a free Africa (Everatt & Ebrahim, 2020; Mlambo & Adetiba, 2020). In 1963, the Organisation of African Unity (OAU), now the African Union (AU) was formed. It sought to build a united Africa, which has been elusive even since Dr Kwame Nkrumah stood on the podium to lay a manifesto of a truly independent Africa (Duignan & Jackson, 2022; Roberts, 2022). There has been a lot of predecessors who have come to elucidate his vision and though, but it has been elusive for many African leaders to understand.

The Literature Review

Successful millennial leaders in the developmental agenda in Africa possess a range of leadership qualities that contribute to their effectiveness and impact. Here are some key qualities that are commonly found in these leaders. Successful millennial leaders in Africa have a clear and inspiring vision for the future of their country or region. They are able to articulate their vision and communicate it effectively to others, inspiring them to work towards a common goal. Millennial leaders are known for their innovative thinking and ability to adapt to rapidly changing environments. They embrace new technologies and approaches to problem-solving, leveraging them to drive positive change and development. These leaders understand the importance of collaboration and partnership in achieving developmental goals. They actively seek out opportunities to work with diverse stakeholders, including governments, NGOs, businesses, and local communities, to create shared solutions. Millennial leaders in Africa prioritize inclusivity and diversity in their leadership approach. They value different perspectives and actively seek to understand the needs and challenges of marginalized groups. They strive to create an environment where everyone feels valued and empowered to contribute. Developmental agendas often face numerous challenges and setbacks. Successful millennial leaders demonstrate resilience in the face of adversity. They learn from failures, adapt their strategies, and persevere in their pursuit of positive change. These leaders prioritize integrity, ethical behaviour, and accountability in their actions. They lead by example, promoting transparency and fairness in their decision-making processes.

Millennial leaders have grown up in the digital age and are comfortable using technology to their advantage. They leverage digital tools and platforms to connect with stakeholders, gather data, and drive innovation in their developmental initiatives. Successful millennial leaders have a strong commitment to personal and professional growth. They are avid learners, continuously seeking new knowledge and skills to enhance their leadership capabilities. Millennial leaders in Africa are driven by a deep passion for their work and a strong sense of purpose. They are committed to making a positive impact and are motivated by the desire to create a better future for their communities and nations.

Definition of Leadership

Aggarwal, (2022); Yukl, (2006); Yukl & Gardiner (2020) defines leadership as "*the process of influencing others to understand and agree about what needs to be done and how to do it, and the process of facilitating individual and collective efforts to accomplish shared objectives*" whilst(Northouse, 2021)defines leadership as "a process whereby an individual influences a group of individuals to achieve a common goal."

The definitions of leadership as outlined suggest that there are central components to the phenomenon of leadership. There are as follows:

Figure 1. A representation of characteristics of the process of leadership

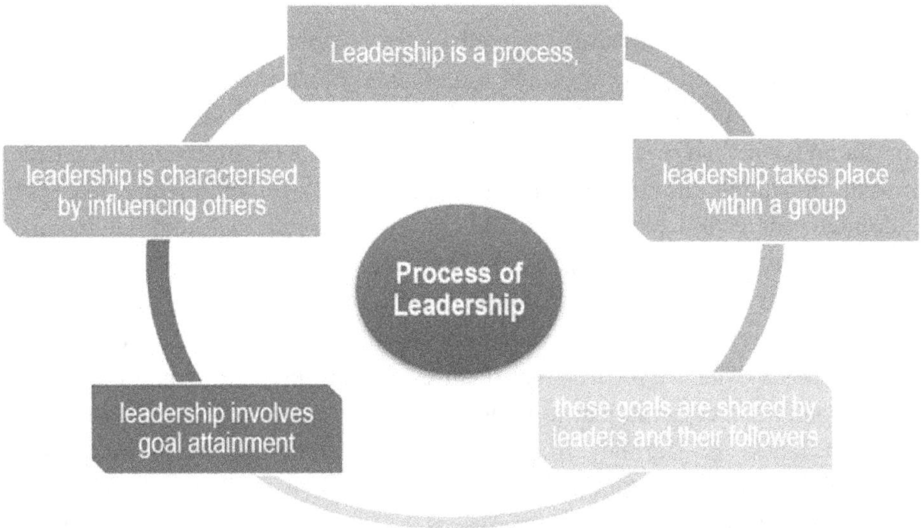

The above definition of leadership negates the theory of trait as major part of leadership theory. Defining leadership as a process means that leadership is an interaction between the leader and a follower, one of give and take and such can easily be characterised as a transaction (Yukl, 2023). In such an interaction comes influence by either the leader or the follower negatively or positively. The definition emphasizes the point that leadership is at least an interaction between two parties, that may be individuals or a group, it is not one directional, it is interactive, the leader affects the follower and the follower reciprocates. Leadership is about a process of influencing a peer, a subordinate, a group to achieve a goal or certain goals (Sudrajat et al., 2023). There is a transaction that is taking place and a leader's task is the ability not to just sell the idea but to ensure that it is sold and properly executed.

Leadership is a process by which a person influences others to accomplish an objective and directs the organization in a way that makes it more cohesive and coherent. This definition is similar to (Alkaabi et al., 2022; Jacob et al., 2022) definition. Leadership is a process whereby an individual influences a group of individuals to achieve a common goal. On the other hand, effective leadership has been described, according to the literature, to be delocalized in the school, in a place where a group of people come together to achieve a certain goal. The easier definition of leadership is the ability to influence other to follow you. Some have said that if you don't have followers you are not a leader. Leadership is about influence and the extension of such an influence so that the followers are able to articulate the vision and stay motivated to achieve such goals.

Process and Environment of Leadership

The leader must therefore be able to mediate the competing interests and resources in order to make them work together to produce the required results (Althnayan et al., 2022; Karimi et al., 2023). Leadership involves guiding individuals toward a common vision, fostering collaboration, and creating an environment that nurtures growth, innovation, and ethical behaviour. The process and environment of leadership encompass the actions, behaviours, and context through which individuals guide, inspire, and influence others to achieve common goals (Zen et al., 2023). Leadership involves more than just holding a position of authority; it entails inspiring and motivating individuals to work together effectively toward a shared vision Effective leadership is a dynamic process that requires adaptability, strong communication, motivation, and a commitment to building a positive and inclusive organizational culture (Ganske & Carbon, 2023). Overall leadership generally involves the following four pillars, which are planning; organising; motivation, and control. Whilst leadership is a process which involves the following players, leader; follower, and the environment.

Figure 2. Diagram representing the definition of leadership

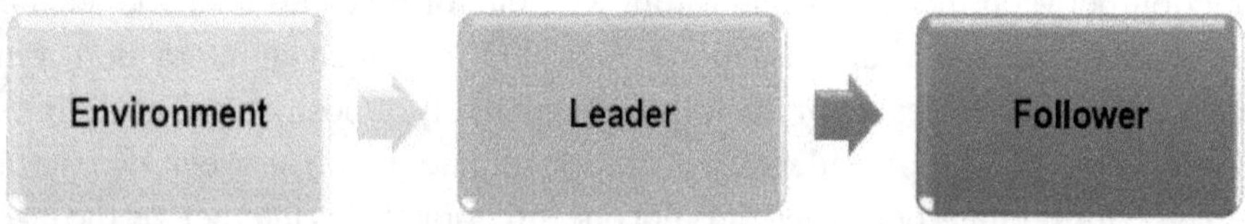

Power Approach to Leadership

Power in leadership is very crucial. Its application by those who in the position of influence also needs to be critically understood as it has both positive and negative impacts if applied wrongly (Bastardoz & Day, 2022). A leader must not rely on the position they hold but must extend themselves to understand that the people they are dealing with are also leaders in their own rights and understand what is at play. Good leaders lead by influence and such is more important that leading by transaction (Baig et al., 2021). It creates a situation where leaders understand and are in a position to take organisations from where they are to greater heights. It is such power that must be protected from abuse. It must be used to advance the strategic objective of the entity. The studies in the field of leadership has shown that leadership is not simple as many would think. The following is a list of all abbreviated leadership theories.

Table 1. Theories of leadership as adapted from Malos, 2012

No.	Theory/ Model	Primary Theme	Pioneers
	Trait	Personality Characteristics	Carlyle, Cowley, Gayton
	Behavioural	Leader actions and behaviour	Blacke; Mouton; Lewin; Tannenbaun; Schmidt
	Contingency	Style depends on situation	Fiedler; Morgan; Hersey & Blanchard
	Power and Influence	Leveraging power to accomplish goals or tasks	French & Raven
	Charismatic	Inspirational and motivational	Weber
	Ethical	Value based approach	Brown; Trevino; Bandura
	Authentic	Integrity and transparency	Avolio
	Transactional	Compliance through rewards and punishment	Weber; Bass
	Transformational	Inspire followers to change expectations	Burns; Bass
	Servant	Enriching the lives of the individuals	Liden; Greenleaf
	Systems Thinking	Study systems and systems thinking	Bertalaffy; Kast & Rosensweig

Adapted from (Malos, 2012)

There are leaders who would use their power and position to coheres their subordinates to do what they want. Holbrook and Holbrook (2021) reiterates that the first three forms of power are known as formal power, (coercive, reward and legitimate power) and the latter (referent and expert power) are known as personal power. The formal power is given to one through their positions whilst the personal power is created by the individual through their skills, experience and knowledge.

THEORIES OF LEADERSHIP

Leadership has been part of human development for centuries. The building of great empires like Kingdom of Pharaohs and the establishment of the Roman Empire applied the very principles of leadership that today, still raise so much interest. The research of leadership theories has been classified into the five approaches of trait, behaviour, power-influence, situational and integrative, which are further conceptualised as intra-individual, dyadic, group and organisational processes. Competencies have emerged strongly under the study of management, it is now moving closer to the study of leadership their dominance and influence in both leadership and leadership development should give new pause for concern and reflection. The Art of War by Sun Tsu has also been quoted o many times in dealing with strategy which is closely linked to leadership. The following are theories that have been studied and have evolved over time.

Great Man Theory (1840 Onwards)

Great Man Theory (GMT) is the genesis of leadership studies in the leadership literature derives(Bass, 1990). The Great Men theory is derived from practical experience and study of leaders who came and made a difference. It was believed that these leaders were great by design. They were born leaders, unfortunately some of these leaders when they are told and praised how great they are they tend to behave in a manner unbecoming of great leaders. They tend to believe that they are irreplaceable. Great Man Theory has some similarities to the Trait Theory, whilst some argue that it is derived from Trait theory, where leaders are born and look, act, and lead by preset, often genetic, fundamentals. This can be derived from kings and great church leaders who came forward and produced traits that made many believe that they could not be great as those leaders. concluded that traits of great leaders are intelligence, masculinity, adjustment, dominance, extroversion and conservatism (Northhouse, 2013; Northouse, 2021). Early research on leadership often emphasized that leaders inherited certain characteristics or traits(Bass, 1990).

Trait Theory (1910-1948)

Trait theory of leadership thrives on the assumption that extraordinary personal attributes, abilities, skills, and physical characteristics are distinct features of leadership (Khan, 2021). This assertion says that leaders are born into leadership. Trait theory is also referred to as Great Man Theory as leadership was believed to be the playground and the arena of males.

A leader has trails and values that he or she envisages and encompasses in his/her leadership. When we think of Nelson Mandela we remember a leader who was inclusive and accommodative of different views. When he negotiated the settlement in the early nineties between the then state President de Klerk, he was firm yet accommodating to the views that they had. The leadership of Margaret Thatcher, who was also known as the Iron Lady was firm, she wanted to get everything that she wanted. The room for negotiation and compromise when negotiating with her was very small. She led when women leaders were far and few in between but she proved that leadership was never a preserve of men. Drucker (1998) characterises Margaret Thatcher as having exhibited personal traits such as aggressiveness, self-confidence, dominance, ambition and strong moral belief of how things should be. One would say she was inflexible, she knew what she wanted and she went for it. Many regard her leadership as one of the greatest that Europe ever had. Leadership does not happen in a vacuum. Northhouse, (2013); Northhouse, (2021) agrees that there are five major traits of leadership, these are intelligence; self-confidence; determination; integrity and sociability.

Behaviourist Theory (1950-1970)

The behavioural theory to leadership continues from the earlier theories, namely the traits and great man theory is based on the thinking that specific behaviours differentiate leaders from non-leaders (Dinibutun, 2020). This theory is firmly rooted in the notion that leaders are born and not made. Whilst others argue strongly that leadership behaviours can be taught. (Senge, 1990) argues strongly that the primary task of leaders is the facilitation of learning, hence the creation of a learning organisation. Leaders must be able to make a compelling case for the need to change or their constituents must be willing to accept the current situation no matter how dire or bad it is. The paradigm-shift in many leaders who want to push for learning organisations believe that leaderships must be nurtured and developed through the acquisition of desirable leadership skills (Rupčić, 2020). Leaders fail or succeed based on their behaviour and the behavioural those who follow them. Relationships are based on give and take, reciprocity. The themes that dominate behavioural approach of leadership are relationships; task orientation; achievement; consideration and participation (Korkmaz et al., 2022).

Situational Contingency Theory (1967-1990)

Contingency theory is a leader-match theory, which means that it tries to match a leader to an appropriate situation. This form of leadership is concerned with the styles and situations. The situational variables in the contingency are, leader-member relations, task structure and position power (Omazić et al., 2023). Situational leadership points out that leadership composes of a directive and supportive dimension and that it is crucial that each must be applied appropriately in a given situation. The main theory that is characterized by situational leadership is the Hersey-Blanchard Situational Theory. (Blanchard et al., 1985) using the four tasks of management define the four leadership styles. Leadership is a process where an individual influences a group of people to achieve a common goal. The key here is achieving a common goal. The leader must be able to define the goal so that the followers are able to understand and take it as their own. The work of a leader involves influencing and without influence there is no leadership (Alblooshi et al., 2021).

Figure 3. Situation leadership theory

No	Theory/ Model	Primary Theme	Pioneers
1.	Trait	Personality Characteristics	Carlyle, Cowley, Gayton
2.	Behavioural	Leader actions and behaviour	Blacke; Mouton; Lewin; Tannenbaun; Schmidt
3.	Contingency	Style depends on situation	Fiedler; Morgan; Hersey & Blanchard
4.	Power and Influence	Leveraging power to accomplish goals or tasks	French & Raven
5.	Charismatic	Inspirational and motivational	Weber
6.	Ethical	Value based approach	Brown; Trevino; Bandura
7.	Authentic	Integrity and transparency	Avolio
8.	Transactional	Compliance through rewards and punishment	Weber; Bass
9.	Transformational	Inspire followers to change expectations	Burns; Bass
10.	Servant	Enriching the lives of the individuals	Liden; Greenleaf
11.	Systems Thinking	Study systems and systems thinking	Bertalaffy; Kast & Rosensweig

Adapted from (Malos, 2012)

Transformational Theory (1985-2010)

Transformational Leadership has been popular since the early 1990s and is part of the so called new paradigm. Northhouse, (2013); Northhouse, (2021) defines, transactional leadership is the process whereby a leader engages with others and creates a connection that raises the level of motivation and morality in both the leader and the follower. This type of a leader is concerned with the growth and potential of the follower and the leader has the interests of the follower at heart. They want to see the follower reach their potential and succeed. The leaders like Mahatma Gandhi, Nelson Mandela, are but a few of such examples who were able to raise the bar and the hopes of the followers and in the process they were changed themselves. The term transformational leadership is closely associated with charismatic leaders. Leaders who are able to use their charm and presence to influence others are able to get a lot done without saying much. Their presence alone exudes authority and power. It is enough to get the job done. Many of the charismatic leaders' rise is their character and charisma and unfortunately their downfall is also of the same reason (Poddar, 2023). Innovation is regarded as one of the most important determinants of performance, (Adegoke et al., 2012). Leadership style has also been recognised as one of the most important factors influencing the relationship between innovation and organisational behavioural performance, because leaders have the authority to set specific goals and encourage innovative initiatives from subordinates. The common themes that emerge about transformational leadership are influence; charisma, motivation, inspiration and intellectually stimulating.

Transactional Theory (1985-2010)

Bass (1999) defines transactional leadership as an exchange relationship between a leader and a follower. This may take many forms though as it assumes that leadership does not happen in a vacuum but takes place in a given situation and at a given time. The leaders use the so called carrot stick model to entice their followers to perform in order to achieve certain desired outcomes by promising them certain rewards and benefits (Phyu, 2023). The effectiveness of the leader in this situation to lead the followers is based on such an enticing relationship. This leadership model may work in situations where there is less competition and pressure. In an agile environment where competition is rife and less and less rewards can be given, this model tends to fail or is less effective. This model works where there is a close relationship between the leader and the follower and such a relationship is based on the leader knowing the follower well (Ahmad et al., 2021). There should be short term and long term goals which all need different forms of enticement. The problem sometimes is when the form of carrot is not what the follower needs motivation would no longer exist.

Charismatic Leadership

The word or the term charisma, is derived from the Greek word meaning, "gifts of grace". It was used in the Christian faith to denote God's gift to certain people to perform great deeds, to make prophecies, or to heal the sick (Kravis, 2021). This clearly could only be done by a few gifted individuals who had such gifts. Charisma by its definition creates a special relationship between the leader and the followers(Weber, 1986). There is a leader and follower relationship which inspires the follower to aspire to the leader's charm and charisma. The follower follows the leader based on a hunch, faith and trust in him/her. The leader's power is personal and due to his/her "extraordinary qualities" (Dladla, 2020). There is a concerted view in research that the result of charismatic leadership is increased motivation and greater performance on the part of the followers. The charismatic form of leadership is thus closely linked to transformational leadership. Charismatic leadership arouses the emotional side of a follower which makes the follower go an extra mile in the execution of their duties as they see the mission and vision clearly in their heads.

Figure 4. Factors that affect leadership in the charismatic leadership theory

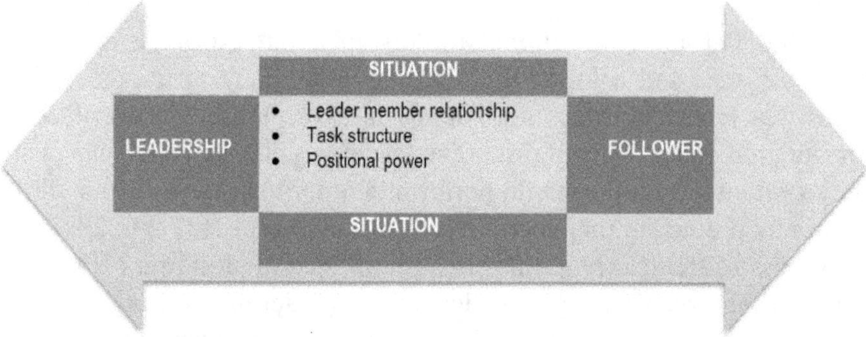

They don't need to be followed in what they do. It is like they represent a part of the leader that resides in them all the time. They defend the leader as much as they defend the vision. Charismatic leadership theory, identifies that the leader traits, behaviours, influence, and situational factors combine to seduce the follower to be receptive to the leader's suggestions. Charisma has been found to be a key variable in the prediction of performance in organisations which operate in environments of significant uncertainty. Men, L. R., Qin, Y. S., & Mitson, R. (2021) argues that charisma is important at the top executive level as charismatic leaders are able to use their charisma to address environmental issues which at times are left unattended as the boards and leaders jostle for positions and profits. (Klein & House, 1995) conclude that participation in a charismatic relationship has a potential to inspire a subordinate or a follower to new goals, new aims and objectives, new values, and new levels of performance. This clearly shows that when a subordinate or a follower is properly engaged, they reciprocate through motivation which leads to performance.

Participative Leadership

According to (Bell et al., 2018) when a leader involves and consults with their subordinates to resolve an issue and decide the corrective action, it is referred to as participative leadership and is also referred to as shared influence or joint decision-making . Participatory Leadership is defined as the unity of taking decision by a leader and subordinates (Khassawneh & Elrehail, 2022). This matter is also regarded as relatively same of participation level in decision making in an organization (Bell et al., 2014; Bell et al., 2018) The leadership with participatory style, has important task to motivate subordinates, growing up self-esteem, providing sense of subordinates "Psychological Ownership", and reduce helplessness sense. The involvement of subordinates in achieving organizational goals will increase if there is ownership feeling from subordinates in meaning believe that they are really accepted by leaders as important human assets. Since 1980 various scholars have studied the concept of participative leadership. Researchers argue that due to the complex changing environment previous styles of leadership seem to hinder organizational performance hence there is a need for new leadership styles based on participative principles to be able to cope with the rapid rate of changes in order to have effective leadership the leader should influence/ inspire people toward group goals through individual motivation rather than coercion. Participative leadership style focuses on the intrinsic motivation of followers (Gwala, 2022). Participation can contribute to intrinsic motivation by enriching subordinates' jobs through autonomy, variety and empowerment. Leadership is at the core of public administration' s concern with the relationship between administrative structures and democracy (de Geus et al., 2020). The most recent wave of scholarly interest in leadership can be traced to the early 1990s, when it took on a new character, given role redefinitions for public managers in a changing environment. The conceptual shift implied a rethinking of the public manager as an active creator of public value, that is, *a leader* with discretion, advancing, shaping and directing—with conviction—a complex agenda of policy. Reform movements challenging the neo-Weberian paradigm—from the New Public Management in the late 1980s to the recent New Public Governance—offer different visions of leadership. These are associated with debate around how much and under what circumstances "administrative leaders" should be neutral or entrepreneurial, conservators or innovators, and recently, facilitators of democratic, inclusive, and participatory processes. Participative leadership increases the feeling of ownership of goals among subordinates, in the sense of believing that they are truly accepted by their leaders as important human assets in the organisation (Ince, 2023). They also give autonomy to organisational members and developing their abilities to achieve long-term organizational goals. Thus, they communicate a vision and empower subordinates to achieve it. Participative leaders manage shared values and vision.

THE RESEARCH METHODOLOGY

The research shall utilise desktop review of literature. Secondary data from a variety of sources (websites, journals, books, and other e-content) are used in this study to accomplish the aforementioned objectives. This will mainly be using Google Scholar, Web of Science, Scopus, etc. as the source of peer-reviewed articles databases capturing the leadership theories, millennial leadership as well as identify qualities that are exhibited by successful developmental leadership in Africa. The analysis of the literature using keywords that are directly related to the chapter's goals and subject. The goal of the literature review is to observe and comprehend the richness of the data to identify themes and sub-themes.

DISCUSSION

There are five emerging themes that have been observed. These topics may help African leaders in several societal areas by enhancing their social and economic circumstances (Grybauskas et al., 2022). It is noteworthy, nonetheless, that political leadership has a bigger role in preventing injustice and fostering an atmosphere where society may succeed (Dimitriou, 2022). These are:

- Visionary leadership, crisis, leadership and adaptability.
- Inclusive, empathetic integrity and accountability leadership.
- Resilience, perseverance, cultural appreciation and contextual understanding.
- Youth and women empowerment, environmental stewardship, holistic and long-term thinking.
- Communication skills education and knowledge sharing propensity.

Visionary Leadership, Crisis Leadership, Innovation, and Adaptability

African democracies are infant, emerging from the bondage of capitalist led colonialism (Zakharov et al., 2023). African leadership today is still entangled in western interests which undermine African independence (Mabula, 2022). However, new leaders are emerging from the African continent, these are millennial leaders in business, politics, education, economics, agriculture and many other sectors. The visionary leadership of Kwame Nkrumah, Kenneth Kaunda, Nelson Mandela, have seen the formation and the reshaping of the Organisation of African Unity to the African Union. Interference in African politics have derailed many dreams to dreams deferred. Crises are unanticipated, unforeseen, highly visible, disruptive occurrences that have both immediate and long-term effects on an organisation (Marshall, 2023). They often have a direct effect on the performance of the company and may have negative effects, hence crisis leadership is necessary (Brem et al., 2020; Nguyen et al., 2022). African millennial leaders are essential to promoting the continent's development agenda. As the younger generation assumes leadership roles, they bring special traits and viewpoints that support Africa's development and change (Davids et al., 2021). The millennial leaders of Africa demonstrate visionary leadership, with a distinct and motivating vision for the future of both their nations and the continent as a whole. They are dedicated to promoting positive change and sustainable development, setting bold objectives and inspiring people to contribute to achieving them (Ojo, 2021). African millennial leaders are renowned for their creative thinking and capacity to quickly adjust to new situations. They welcome new technologies and creative methods to problem-solving and use them to successfully address developmental challenges.

INCLUSIVE, EMPATHETIC INTEGRITY, AND ACCOUNTABILITY LEADERSHIP

It is crucial for principals to be able to adapt and evolve when tackling issues in a constantly shifting and complicated external environment (Schiffling et al., 2022). When these difficulties manifest as adaptive issues or difficulties demanding that leaders and their followers utilise creative ways to problem-solving rather than tried-and-true technical fixes (Santra & Alat, 2022; Shukla et al., 2022). African millennial leaders should and some have prioritized inclusivity and empathy in their leadership approach. They should value diverse perspectives and understand the importance of involving all stakeholders (Gwala & Mashau, 2023), including marginalized communities, in decision-making processes to ensure that development benefits reach everyone (Madden & Rood, 2023). Young leaders are now using innovation and accountability in business and in education to show that change comes from all sectors of society not just politics. These leaders recognize the power of collaboration and actively seek partnerships with governments, NGOs, businesses, and international organizations. They understand that addressing complex developmental challenges requires collective efforts and global cooperation (Ansell et al., 2022). Organisations like Gift of the Givers is a uniquely South African organisations providing leadership in aid and rescue all over the world. Their characterise inclusivity, adaptation, empathy and inclusivity in their actions (Gwagwa et al., 2022). African millennial leaders uphold high standards of integrity and accountability in their actions and decision-making, that is why a number of them hold politicians to account. They are transparent in their leadership, foster trust among their constituents, and take responsibility for the outcomes of their initiatives. While taking into account the cultural circumstances of historically marginalised groups, such as those in Africa, the new African networked relational approaches promoted by Ubuntu may be utilised to establish frameworks for the implementation of universal ideals like justice and solidarity (Lastikova, 2023; Mhlambi & Tiribelli, 2023). Ubuntu can serve as a foundation for inclusive discourse and something that Africa can export to international fora by outlining how the benefits of AI may be shared. It is not just a foundation for communities.

Resilience and Perseverance, Cultural Appreciation, and Contextual Understanding

Millennial leaders in Africa value their cultural heritage and appreciate the diversity of the continent. They recognize the importance of understanding the local context and tailor their developmental strategies accordingly to meet the unique needs of their communities (Jones, 2021). African youth and women continue to make meaningful changes in their daily lives by ensuring that the innovate and persevere. Many people in Africa live side by side with people of diverse cultures, this allows them to understand, learn and adapt (Hill et al., 2020; Mhongera & Lombard, 2020). The African millennial leaders demonstrate resilience in the face of obstacles and setbacks. They learn from failures, adapt their strategies, and persevere in their pursuit of sustainable development despite the challenges they encounter (Kurniadi et al., 2023; Yu et al., 2022). When African nations took over from their colonisers, many things were not going well. Many resources had been stolen. The social order was in turmoil, and there was a high degree of mistrust among the populace. Despite living in such dreadful social and economic situations, the people persevered despite the difficulties (Carter & Cordero, 2022; Okwuwada, 2023). For many people, their cultural practises served as their sole source of enjoyment. Dances from their communities that were performed in shanties and hostels maintained their tenacity. The social structure demonstrated that leadership is effective everywhere, even in the most challenging social and economic environments (Samuelson, 2021). The story of the kidnapping of nearly 270 Nigerian girls outraged the entire globe, yet the state was powerless to stop it. Those girls undoubtedly experienced severe trauma and torture, yet they still managed to bounce back (Denckla et al., 2020; Henderson & Rhodes, 2022). Older adults typically serve as the leaders of political parties worldwide. Young people are rising through the ranks and pushing for major changes (House, 2023). As a result of constitutional court rulings supporting equality and human rights, several laws have been amended or are currently being amended (Valenti, 2021). Politicians have been compelled to reform by the courts' tenacious leadership in preserving the constitution (Le Roux & Davis, 2019).

Youth and Women Empowerment, Environmental Stewardship Holistic, and Long-Term Thinking

These leaders are often advocates for youth and women empowerment. They recognize the potential of young people and women in driving change and actively promote their inclusion in leadership roles and decision-making processes African millennial leaders prioritize environmental sustainability and recognize the importance of balancing economic development with environmental protection (Genon, 2023). They embrace green technologies and sustainable practices to address environmental challenges. These leaders adopt a holistic and long-term perspective in their developmental agendas. They recognize that sustainable development requires addressing social, economic, and environmental dimensions simultaneously and plan for the future well-being of generations to come. Empowering youth and women is crucial for the sustainable development of Africa. By investing in education, skills training, and equal opportunities, young people and women can actively participate in the economic, social, and political spheres (Tursunova et al., 2022). Empowering youth and women leads to increased innovation, productivity, and inclusive growth, driving the continent towards a more prosperous future (Nwakanma, 2021).

Environmental stewardship is essential to protect Africa's natural resources and ecosystems. Sustainable practices, such as promoting renewable energy, responsible agriculture, and conservation efforts, safeguard the environment for future generations. By prioritizing environmental sustainability, Africa can mitigate the impacts of climate change, preserve biodiversity, and create green job opportunities. Holistic and long-term thinking is essential in developing Africa sustainably. This approach involves considering interconnected issues, such as education, health, poverty alleviation, and environmental protection, when formulating policies and initiatives. A long-term perspective ensures that decisions made today contribute to a resilient and prosperous Africa for future generations. By promoting youth and women's empowerment and environmental stewardship with a holistic and long-term vision, Africa can build a more equitable, prosperous, and sustainable future for all its citizens.

Communication Skills Education and Knowledge-Sharing

Millennial leaders in Africa value education and knowledge-sharing as essential tools for development. They promote educational opportunities, encourage research and innovation, and actively share best practices and lessons learned across the continent. African millennial leaders excel in communication, utilizing various channels to engage with their constituents and the global community. They leverage social media and digital platforms to share their vision, garner support, and raise awareness about developmental issues. Communication skills education and knowledge-sharing play a vital role in the developmental agenda of Africa. Effective communication and knowledge-sharing are essential for fostering social, economic, and technological advancements in the continent. Communication skills education equips individuals with the ability to express themselves clearly and persuasively. By enhancing literacy, language proficiency, and public speaking abilities, people can actively participate in decision-making processes, advocate for their rights, and contribute to community development. Empowered communities can collaboratively address local challenges and drive inclusive development.

Promoting knowledge-sharing in education systems facilitates the dissemination of information, experiences, and best practices. Access to quality education and information empowers students to develop critical thinking, problem-solving, and research skills, preparing them for productive roles in society (Çebi & Reisoğlu, 2022). By encouraging a culture of knowledge-sharing among educators, students, and researchers, African countries can foster innovation and lifelong learning. Effective communication and knowledge-sharing are essential for fostering innovation and entrepreneurship in Africa. By sharing research findings, best practices, and success stories, aspiring entrepreneurs can learn from each other and create transformative solutions to local challenges. Additionally, strong communication skills enable entrepreneurs to pitch their ideas, attract investments, and market their products effectively. Transparent and effective communication is vital for promoting good governance and accountability (Sifiso & Pfano, 2022). By encouraging open dialogue and public participation, citizens can engage with policymakers and hold governments accountable for their actions. Transparent dissemination of information and data fosters trust between governments and citizens, enhancing development initiatives' success. Effective communication is critical in healthcare to disseminate information about disease prevention, treatment, and health promotion. Knowledge-sharing among healthcare professionals improves medical practices and fosters cross-border collaborations to combat infectious diseases and public health challenges. Knowledge-sharing about sustainable practices, climate change, and environmental conservation can inspire communities to adopt eco-friendly initiatives. By sharing successful conservation efforts and promoting sustainable lifestyles, Africa can work towards achieving environmental goals and preserving its rich biodiversity for future generations.

The rapid growth of digital technology has transformed communication and knowledge-sharing opportunities in Africa (Ziegler, 2022). Digital platforms provide access to information, education, and resources even in remote areas. Leveraging technology enables cross-border collaborations, facilitates e-learning, and enhances the exchange of knowledge and expertise. Effective communication and knowledge-sharing are vital for addressing socioeconomic inequalities in Africa. By bridging the digital divide and promoting inclusive access to information, marginalized communities can benefit from development initiatives and actively participate in decision-making processes (Kolotouchkina et al., 2023). Communication skills education and knowledge-sharing are integral components of Africa's developmental agenda. By empowering individuals and communities, fostering innovation, promoting accountability, and leveraging technology, African countries can create a vibrant and sustainable future for their citizens. Encouraging open communication and fostering a culture of knowledge-sharing contribute to the continent's progress and inclusive development.

IMPLICATIONS ON AFRICA'S DEVELOPMENTAL AGENDA

Leadership must embrace a quicker and more flexible decision-making process. The imaginative and adaptive character of millennial leaders enables them to make choices more swiftly and efficiently, facilitating speedier progress toward developmental goals. This is a quality that these leaders must discourage. Successful millennial leaders' leadership traits have significant significance for Africa's development goal. Their boldness, creativity, diversity, and resiliency help to advance the cause, promote sustainable growth, and create a more just and prosperous continent. Africa's transformational and sustainable development journey depends on embracing and supporting the leadership of millennials.

Leaders should put more of an emphasis on innovation and technology given their technological aptitude. To improve development results, the millennial leaders place a high priority on integrating cutting-edge solutions and digital technology. The focus millennial leaders place on inclusion and empathy guarantees that development projects prioritise the needs of marginalised populations and address socioeconomic inequality in order to build the leaders of the future.

Through collaboration and partnership, strengthened regional and international collaborations, will prove very critical (Gwala, R.S. & Mashau, P., 2023). The millennial leaders should foster stronger relationships with other African countries and international organizations, leading to enhanced regional and global cooperation for development. The ethical and visionary approach of millennial leaders drives a focus on sustainable development that leaves a positive and lasting impact on Africa's future.

CONCLUSION

The likes of Motsepe from South Africa and Dangote from Nigeria are a glimmer of hope of what Africa can be (Falola, 2022). In conclusion, the leadership qualities of successful millennial leaders play a pivotal role in shaping Africa's developmental agenda. As a generation known for its vision, innovation, adaptability, and collaboration, millennial leaders bring a fresh and dynamic approach to addressing the continent's developmental challenges. Their emphasis on inclusivity, empathy, and ethical behaviour ensures that development initiatives prioritize the needs of marginalized communities and foster a more equitable society.

The tech-savvy nature of millennial leaders enables them to harness the power of digital tools and technologies, driving innovation and efficiency in developmental endeavours. Their resilience and perseverance in the face of obstacles lead to continuous learning and adaptation, promoting long-term sustainability and impactful outcomes. Furthermore, the passionate drive and strong sense of purpose exhibited by millennial leaders fuel their commitment to creating a positive and lasting impact on their communities and nations. They actively seek regional and international collaborations, fostering stronger relationships and partnerships that contribute to enhanced regional cooperation and global development efforts. The implications of these leadership qualities are far-reaching, resulting in faster and more agile decision-making, increased focus on innovation and technology, and strengthened efforts towards inclusive and sustainable development. By embracing the leadership of successful millennial leaders, Africa can accelerate its progress, address developmental challenges effectively, and forge a path towards a more prosperous and equitable future.

However, it is essential to recognize that while millennial leaders bring unique strengths to the table, a successful developmental agenda in Africa requires a multi-generational approach. Collaboration between millennial leaders and experienced leaders from previous generations can foster mentorship, knowledge-sharing, and the blending of diverse perspectives for a comprehensive and effective development strategy. The leadership qualities of successful millennial leaders hold great promise for Africa's developmental agenda. By empowering and supporting these leaders, Africa can harness their vision, innovation, and passion to create a brighter future for the continent, characterized by sustainable and inclusive growth, and improved quality of life for all its citizens.

REFERENCES

Adegoke, O., Walimba, F. O., & Myers, A. (2012). Innovation Strategy, Human Resource policy and firm's revenue growth: The roles of envoronmental uncertaintly and inovation perfomance. *A Journal of Decision Sciences Institute, 43*(2), 273-301.

Aggarwal, J. (2022). Yukl, GA, & Gardner, WL (2020). Leadership in Organizations. Pearson Education, Inc. *Journal of Leadership Studies, 16*(3), 57–60. doi:10.1002/jls.21826

Ahmad, M. G., Klotz, A. C., & Bolino, M. C. (2021). Can good followers create unethical leaders? How follower citizenship leads to leader moral licensing and unethical behavior. *The Journal of Applied Psychology, 106*(9), 1374–1390. doi:10.1037/apl0000839 PMID:32955268

Alblooshi, M., Shamsuzzaman, M., & Haridy, S. (2021). The relationship between leadership styles and organisational innovation: A systematic literature review and narrative synthesis. *European Journal of Innovation Management, 24*(2), 338–370. doi:10.1108/EJIM-11-2019-0339

Alkaabi, M., Kudus, N., & Ab Rahman, Z. (2022). A Literature Review on the Impact of Work Environment, Leadership Styles and Resilience on Job Performance in UAE. *Journal of Pharmaceutical Negative Results*, 2332–2341. doi:10.47750/pnr.2022.13.S06.304

Althnayan, S., Alarifi, A., Bajaba, S., & Alsabban, A. (2022). Linking environmental transformational leadership, environmental organizational citizenship behavior, and organizational sustainability performance: A moderated mediation model. *Sustainability (Basel), 14*(14), 8779. doi:10.3390u14148779

Ansell, C., Sørensen, E., & Torfing, J. (2022). *Co-creation for sustainability: The UN SDGs and the power of local partnerships*. Emerald Publishing. doi:10.1108/9781800437982

Baig, S. A., Iqbal, S., Abrar, M., Baig, I. A., Amjad, F., Zia-ur-Rehman, M., & Awan, M. U. (2021). Impact of leadership styles on employees' performance with moderating role of positive psychological capital. *Total Quality Management & Business Excellence, 32*(9-10), 1085–1105. doi:10.1080/14783363.2019.1665011

Bass, B. M. (1990). *Bass and Stioghills's Handbook of Leadership: Theory, reaserch and managerial applications*. Free Press.

Bass, B. M. (1999). Two Decades of Research and Development in TRansformational Leadership. *European Journal of Work and Organizational Psychology, 8*(1), 9–32. doi:10.1080/135943299398410

Bastardoz, N., & Day, D. V. (2022). *Integrating leadership and power: a micro process model. Leadership: Leaders, Folowers, Contexts*. Information Age Publishing.

Bell, C., Chan, M., & Nel, P. (2014). The Impact of Participative and Directive Leadership on Organisational Culture: An Organisational Development Perspective *Mediterranean Journal of Social Sciences. Mediterranean Journal of Social Sciences, 5*(23), 1970–1985. doi:10.5901/mjss.2014.v5n23p1970

Bell, C., Dodd, N., & Mjoli, T. (2018). The effect of participative and directive leadership on team effectiveness among administrative employees in a South African Tertiary Institution. *The Social Science Journal, 55*, 81–91.

Blanchard, K., Zigarmi, P., & Zigarmi, D. (1985). *Leadrship and the one munite Manager: Increasing effectiveness Through Sitiuational Leadership*. William Morrow.

Brem, A., Nylund, P., & Viardot, E. (2020). The impact of the 2008 financial crisis on innovation: A dominant design perspective. *Journal of Business Research, 110*, 360–369. doi:10.1016/j.jbusres.2020.01.048

Carter, E. D., & Cordero, M. L. (2022). Salir Adelante: Social capital and resilience during the Covid-19 pandemic in Argentina. *Health & Place, 77*, 102870. doi:10.1016/j.healthplace.2022.102870 PMID:35933852

Çebi, A., & Reisoğlu, İ. (2022). Defining "digitally competent teacher": An examination of pre-service teachers' metaphor. *Journal of Digital Learning in Teacher Education, 38*(4), 185–198. doi:10.1080/21532974.2022.2098210

Davids, I., Appiah, K., Davids, G., & Ofori, F. N. K. (2021). The effectiveness of transformational leadership: a qualitative-based study on millennial perceptions in South Africa. *Archives of Business Research.*

de Geus, C. J., Ingrams, A., Tummers, L., & Pandey, S. K. (2020). Organizational citizenship behavior in the public sector: A systematic literature review and future research agenda. *Public Administration Review, 80*(2), 259–270. doi:10.1111/puar.13141

Denckla, C. A., Cicchetti, D., Kubzansky, L. D., Seedat, S., Teicher, M. H., Williams, D. R., & Koenen, K. C. (2020). Psychological resilience: An update on definitions, a critical appraisal, and research recommendations. *European Journal of Psychotraumatology, 11*(1), 1822064. doi:10.1080/20008198.2020.1822064 PMID:33244362

Dimitriou, C. K. (2022). The critical role that national culture and ethical leadership play in fostering employee commitment to service quality in the hotel industry. *Research in Hospitality Management, 12*(3), 255–271. doi:10.1080/22243534.2022.2133770

Dinibutun, S. R. (2020). Leadership: A comprehensive review of literature, research and theoretical framework. *Research and Theoretical Framework.*

Dladla, T. (2020). *Exploring ethical leadership practices in challenging township school contexts: a multiple case study*

Drucker, P. F. (1998). *The coming of a new organisation*. Harvard Business Review, January -February.

Duignan, P., & Jackson, R. H. (2022). *Politics and government in African states: 1960-1985*. Taylor & Francis. doi:10.4324/9781003312130

Everatt, D., & Ebrahim, Z. (2020). Urban policy in South Africa. *Developing national urban policies: Ways forward to green and smart cities*, 281-298.

Falola, T. (2022). Global African Business Leaders. The Palgrave Handbook of Africa and the Changing Global Order, 1099-1115. Palgrave.

Ganske, P., & Carbon, C.-C. (2023). Successful clusters through successful communication: Why clusters should be managed by Place Leaders. *Frontiers in Communication*, *8*, 1194103. doi:10.3389/fcomm.2023.1194103

Genon, L. J. D. (2023). 9 Toward 2030. *Sustainable Development Goal 16 and the Global Governance of Violence: Critical Reflections on the Uncertain Future of Peace*.

Grybauskas, A., Stefanini, A., & Ghobakhloo, M. (2022). Social sustainability in the age of digitalization: A systematic literature Review on the social implications of industry 4.0. *Technology in Society*, *70*, 101997. doi:10.1016/j.techsoc.2022.101997

Gwagwa, A., Kazim, E., & Hilliard, A. (2022). The role of the African value of Ubuntu in global AI inclusion discourse: A normative ethics perspective. *Patterns (New York, N.Y.)*, *3*(4), 100462. doi:10.1016/j.patter.2022.100462 PMID:35465235

Gwala, R. S. (2022). A framework for corporate governance and organisational performance in the Fourth Industrial Revolution (Doctoral dissertation).

Gwala, R. S., & Mashau, P. (2023). Tracing the Evolution of Agency Theory in Corporate Governance. In *Governance as a Catalyst for Public Sector Sustainability* (pp. 260–285). IGI Global.

Henderson, A. C., & Rhodes, S. M. (2022). "Got sold a dream and it turned into a nightmare": The victim-offender overlap in commercial sexual exploitation. *Journal of Human Trafficking*, *8*(1), 33–48. doi:10.1080/23322705.2021.2019530

Hill, R., Walsh, F. J., Davies, J., Sparrow, A., Mooney, M., Council, C. L., Wise, R. M., & Tengö, M. (2020). Knowledge co-production for Indigenous adaptation pathways: Transform post-colonial articulation complexes to empower local decision-making. *Global Environmental Change*, *65*, 102161. doi:10.1016/j.gloenvcha.2020.102161

Holbrook, R. L., & Holbrook, A. R. (2021). For Such a Time as This: Helping Students Understand Power and Authority by Examining National Events from Spring 2020. *Christian Business Academy Review, 16*.

House, F. (2023). *Freedom in the World 2022: The Annual Survey of Political Rights and Civil Liberties*. Rowman & Littlefield.

Ince, F. (2023). Transformational Leadership in a Diverse and Inclusive Organizational Culture. Handbook of Research on Promoting an Inclusive Organizational Culture for Entrepreneurial Sustainability, 188-201.

Jacob, M. U., Chukwuemaka, O., & Nkatomba, E. N. (2022). Political Leadership and Socio-economic Development of Rivers State. *Central Asian Journal of Social Sciences and History*, *3*(4), 29–45.

Jones, J. T. (2021). *An Illumination of the Road to Resilience for Black Millennial Teachers as a Means of Addressing the Black Teacher Shortage*. Liberty University.

Karimi, S., Ahmadi Malek, F., Yaghoubi Farani, A., & Liobikienė, G. (2023). The role of transformational leadership in developing innovative work behaviors: The mediating role of employees' psychological capital. *Sustainability (Basel)*, *15*(2), 1267. doi:10.3390u15021267

Khan, M. R. (2021). A critical analysis of Elon Musk's leadership in Tesla motors. *Journal of Global Entrepreneurship Research*, *11*(1), 213–222. doi:10.100740497-021-00284-z

Khassawneh, O., & Elrehail, H. (2022). The effect of participative leadership style on employees' performance: The contingent role of institutional theory. *Administrative Sciences*, *12*(4), 195. doi:10.3390/admsci12040195

Klein, K. J., & House, R. J. (1995). On Fire: Charismatic Leadership and Levels of Analysis. *The Leadership Quarterly*, *6*(2), 183–198. doi:10.1016/1048-9843(95)90034-9

Kolotouchkina, O., Viñarás-Abad, M., & Mañas-Viniegra, L. (2023). Digital Ageism: Emerging Challenges and Best Practices of Age-Friendly Digital Urban Governance. *Media and Communication*, *11*(3), 6–17. doi:10.17645/mac.v11i3.6711

Korkmaz, A. V., Van Engen, M. L., Knappert, L., & Schalk, R. (2022). About and beyond leading uniqueness and belongingness: A systematic review of inclusive leadership research. *Human Resource Management Review*, *32*(4), 100894. doi:10.1016/j.hrmr.2022.100894

Kravis, N. (2021). Charisma. *The Psychoanalytic Quarterly*, *90*(4), 523–554. doi:10.1080/00332828.2021.1983332 PMID:35312425

Kurniadi, K., Meiliyandrie, L., & Rahmah, R. (2023). *Digital Mapping of Resilience and Academic Skills in the Perspective of Society 5.0 for Higher Education Level Students*. Qeios. doi:10.32388/FO9ZQO

Lastikova, M. (2023). *Context-Specific Peace Education Initiatives within local communities in Western Cape*. Lessons from Ubuntu.

Le Roux, M., & Davis, D. (2019). *Lawfare: Judging Politics in South Africa*. Jonathan Ball Publishers.

Mabula, D. (2022). *Implementing the new partnership for Africa's development (NEPAD): challenges and prospects*. North-West University.

Madden, M., & Rood, E. (2023). *Gen Z in the Room: Making Public Media by and with Youth for the Future*. Joan Ganz Cooney Center at Sesame Workshop.

Malos, R. (2012). *The most important leadership theories.*

Marshall, M. (2023). Prepared for a crisis and the unexpected: Managing everyday eventualities through food storage practices. *Food, Culture, & Society*, *26*(2), 305–326. doi:10.1080/15528014.2021.1967643

Men, L. R., Qin, Y. S., & Mitson, R. (2021). Engaging startup employees via charismatic leadership communication: The importance of communicating "vision, passion, and care". *International Journal of Business Communication*, 23294884211020488.

Mhlambi, S., & Tiribelli, S. (2023). Decolonizing AI ethics: Relational autonomy as a means to counter AI Harms. *Topoi*, *42*(3), 1–14. doi:10.100711245-022-09874-2

Mhongera, P. B., & Lombard, A. (2020). Pathways of resilience for children facing socio-economic adversities: Experiences from Future Families' OVC programmes in South Africa. *Children and Youth Services Review*, *108*, 104657. doi:10.1016/j.childyouth.2019.104657

Mlambo, D. N., & Adetiba, T. C. (2020). Post-1994 South Africa's peacekeeping and military intervention in Southern Africa, reference from the Democratic Republic of Congo (DRC) and Lesotho. *Journal of Public Affairs*, *20*(1), e1984. doi:10.1002/pa.1984

Nguyen, T.-M., Malik, A., & Budhwar, P. (2022). Knowledge hiding in organizational crisis: The moderating role of leadership. *Journal of Business Research*, *139*, 161–172. https://www.ncbi.nlm.nih.gov/pmc/articles/PMC8516615/pdf/main.pdf. doi:10.1016/j.jbusres.2021.09.026 PMID:34667337

Noble, S. M., Mende, M., Grewal, D., & Parasuraman, A. (2022). The Fifth Industrial Revolution: How Harmonious Human–Machine Collaboration is Triggering a Retail and Service [R]evolution.[[DOI:]. *Journal of Retailing*, *98*(2), 199–208. doi:10.1016/j.jretai.2022.04.003

Northhouse, P. G. (2013). *Leadership: Theory and Practice*. Sage Publications, Inc.

Northouse, P. G. (2021). *Leadership: Theory and practice*. Sage publications.

Nwakanma, A. P. (2021). women, entrepreneurship, and economic development in Africa. In The Palgrave Handbook of African Women's Studies (pp. 1583-1599). Springer.

Ojo, A. (2021). *Social Revolutions and Governance Aspirations of African Millennials: Emerging from the Political Shadows of Strongmen*. Springer Nature.

Okwuwada, N. (2023). *The modern day consequences, causes, and nature of kidnapping, terrorism, banditry, and violent crime in Nigeria: A comprehensive analysis*.

Omazić, M. A., Labaš, D., & Uroić, P. (2023). *Contingency Theory*.

Phyu, S. O. (2023). *Leadership Styles, Job Satisfaction, and Employee Performance of Glory Farmer Development Bank*. MERAL Portal.

Poddar, A. (2023). *A comparative analysis of charismatic leadership between Donald Trump and Narendra Modi during the Covid crisis*. Sistema de Bibliotecas FGV.

Roberts, G. (2022). *Revolutionary State-making in Dar Es Salaam: African Liberation and the Global Cold War, 1961-1974*. Cambridge University Press.

Rupčić, N. (2020). Learning organisation as technology for the socio-economic paradigm implementation. *International Journal of Agile Systems and Management*, *13*(2), 182–212. doi:10.1504/IJASM.2020.107899

Samuelson, M. (2021). *Claiming the city in South African literature*. Taylor & Francis. doi:10.4324/9781003174189

Santra, S., & Alat, P. (2022). Adaptive leadership of doctors during COVID-19. *Leadership in Health Services*, *35*(2), 246–266. doi:10.1108/LHS-08-2021-0073 PMID:34882361

Schiffling, S., Hannibal, C., Tickle, M., & Fan, Y. (2022). The implications of complexity for humanitarian logistics: A complex adaptive systems perspective. *Annals of Operations Research*, *319*(1), 1379–1410. doi:10.100710479-020-03658-w

Senge, P. M. (1990). *The Fifth Discipline: The Art & Practice of the Learning Organisation*. Currency and DoubleDay.

Shukla, B., Sufi, T., Joshi, M., & Sujatha, R. (2022). Leadership challenges for Indian hospitality industry during COVID-19 pandemic. *Journal of Hospitality and Tourism Insights*.

Sifiso, G., & Pfano, M. (2022). Corporate governance and organisational performance in Africa: A systematic literature review. *African Journal of Business Management, 16*(10), 210–223.

Sudrajat, D., Siswondo, S., Harsono, Y., & Fajarianto, O. (2023). THE INFLUENCE OF LEADERSHIP STYLE AND WORK DISCIPLINE ON EMPLOYEE PERFORMANCE. *International Journal of Economics* [IJEBAR]. *Business and Accounting Research, 7*(2), 641–648.

Tursunova, D. T., Abobakirova, O. N., Buzrukova, D. M., Mahmudova, O. T., Ubaydullayeva, Z. H., & Kholmatova, N. N. (2022). Principal Principles And Important Factors Of Student Women's Social Activity. *Journal of Positive School Psychology*.

Valenti, A. (2021). LGBT employment rights in an evolving legal landscape: The impact of the Supreme Court's decision in Bostock v. Clayton County, Georgia. *Employee Responsibilities and Rights Journal, 33*(1), 3–23. doi:10.100710672-020-09359-7

Weber, M. (1986). Världsreligonernas ekonomiska etik (The economic ethics of the world religions). *Ratio*.

Yu, M., Wen, J., Smith, S. M., & Stokes, P. (2022). Building-up resilience and being effective leaders in the workplace: A systematic review and synthesis model. *Leadership and Organization Development Journal, 43*(7), 1098–1117. doi:10.1108/LODJ-09-2021-0437

Yukl, G. (2006). *Leadership in organizations*. Pearson-Prentice Hall.

Yukl, G. (2023). Effective Use of Power and Influence Tactics in Organizations. Principles of Organizational Behavior: The Handbook of Evidence-Based Management, 311.

Yukl, G., & Gardner, W. (2020). *Leadership in organizations (Global)*. Pearson Education Limited.

Zakharov, N., Tate, S. A., Law, I., & Bernardino-Costa, J. (2023). South Africa and the Struggle for Racial Equality: Debating Deracialization, Non-racialism, Decolonization, and Africanization. In Futures of Anti-Racism: Paradoxes of Deracialization in Brazil, South Africa, Sweden, and the UK (pp. 15-67). Springer.

Zen, A., Yanti, S., Hutomo, M. R., Kraugusteeliana, K., & Arisutama, H. Y. (2023). The Role of Leadership in Managing Organisational Culture Change in the Context of Information Technology Implementation. *Jurnal Minfo Polgan*, *12*(1), 1247–1255. doi:10.33395/jmp.v12i1.12697

Ziegler, M. G. (2022). *Web 2.0 and knowledge sharing. A literature review*. AI, Computer Science and Robotics Technology. doi:10.5772/acrt.03

Chapter 10
Antecedents and Outcomes of Positive Social Psychology on Millennial Leader Behavior:
A Review of Literature

Nandini M.H.
REVA Business School, REVA University, India

Shakti Chaturvedi
https://orcid.org/0000-0001-5680-4727
REVA Business School, REVA University, India

ABSTRACT

This chapter will systematically review the effects of positive social psychology interventions applied through organizational context on the wellbeing and performance of millennial leaders. This literature study envelopes the independent variables, dependent variables, outcomes, the contexts of positive social psychology, and types of studies performed on positive social psychology systems concerning the millennial leaders in the organizations. Consequent evaluations of these learnings have uncovered that the positive social psychology intrusions appear to be a promising instrument for improving millennial leaders' performance and wellbeing. However, research investigating happiness in the workplace among a sample of millennial leaders has been minimal to none. Thus, it is essential to explore the motivation for millennial leaders and how it contributes to their happiness. Repercussions of these findings for both theory and practice and recommendations for further research in positive social psychology interventions within institutions are being discussed.

DOI: 10.4018/978-1-6684-4711-6.ch010

INTRODUCTION

In the modern era, people worldwide have been watching the ascent of positive social psychology, which is well-defined to be practiced, and the science of enhancing welfare (Lomas et.al., 2015). In earlier days, Psychology skills, its learning, and implementation of positive social psychology stood assumed as unfavorable as per our society and the organizations, but in recent days significance of Psychology has progressed from not just concentrating on the negative aspects of humans but also the positive and constructive aspects of Human, society, and organizations (Schneider et.al.,2005). Positive social psychology research highlights the need to investigate the processes and circumstances that may lead to beneficial outcomes (Abbasi et al., 2020). Work environment characteristics, which influence intellectual development, play an influential role in improving the impact of HPWS on results instead of concentrating on flaws and glitches. Positive social Psychology is defined as positive intellectual strength and optimum modification to living. Compared to clinical psychology or abnormal psychology, we may consider social psychology the most balanced term for the study of individual nature (Schneider et.al., 2005). Positive employee behavior similarly recognizes several positive theories learned during years like positive reinforcement, positive affectivity (PA), procedural justice, dedication and work satisfaction, citizenship behavior and prosocial, core self-evaluations, and many more. In lieu, positive psychology combined with social psychology is currently applicable to the workplace as Positive social psychology (Youssef & Luthans, 2007). Several psychologists have recently started exploring the link between human wellbeing and social psychology concepts. It's understood from the latest research that positive social psychology is the concoction of positive thinking in addition to social psychology (Schneider et.al.,2005). The combination of social psychology and positive psychology will assist in attaining the improved social consciousness, sense of maturity, fulfillment, discipline, and positivity in work and personnel life. (Schneider et.al., 2005). Mihaly Csikszentmihalyi and Martin Seligman are critical specialists in the discipline of positive social psychology. Also, they defend that PSP would help achieve efficient mediations and technical insight to establish flourishing in organizations, people, families, and societies.

PSP is usually referred to have three different levels which are (Group level, society level, and individual level). Martin Seligman coined a PERMA model to determine well and characterize welfare; PERMA has the five components of wellbeing: Positive feelings, Engagement, Relationship, Meaning, Accomplishments (Seligman & Csikszentmihalyi, 2000).

American psychology experts have recently dedicated their millennial problem to new science and the innovation of affirmative psychology, positive personality, and positive organizations (Seligman & Csikszentmihalyi, 2000). Early personifications of human psychology did not have sufficient empirical data; hence some directions encouraged selfishness, egoism, narcissism, and self-centeredness (Seligman & Csikszentmihalyi, 2000).

An initial revolutionary illustration is World Health, which is a Meta-Hypothetica Abstract Chart considered aimed at Applied Positive social Psychology definition of health which says, "a state of complete physical, mental and social well-being, and not merely the absence of disease and infirmity." (Lomas et al., 2015). Namely, the corporate culture is considered a series of communal rules, influencing the behavior of millennial workers in the organization. It is to be understood that all these ideals, norms, and opinions are established in various ways, such as the traditions and practices followed in the organization, form of communications and the languages used, legends, myths, and the stories that are stated and repeated and conclusively the signs or symbols found inside the firm (Andriopoulos, 2001).

This chapter reevaluates the works of academics in positive social psychology. We will provide more information concerning Positive social psychology throughout this document in detail. The main objective of this document is to explain and help millennials and organizations to understand social cognitive evolutions and help them be successful in their work-life balance and perform better (Schneider et.al., 2005). To uncover/comprehend basic models of relations among the three ideas – Positive social psychology, antecedent terms, and conditions that will lead to Positive social psychology and millennial leader behavior. Research further aims to chart above which the behavior effects were associated with PSP. In the present study, although the authors considered identical antecedents/predictors as previous models did, the proposed model is different as in this model, the millennial employee behavior efficacy was taken as the outcome variable and positive social psychology as an intervening variable.

DEFINING POSITIVE SOCIAL PSYCHOLOGY

Around 16 years after the Martin Seligman utilized his 1998 APA presidential speech before inaugurating a brand-new zone of positive social psychology (PSP). Since then, PSP has bloomed and attracted various students, well-established intellectuals, finance, and interest from multiple sources inside and outside academic and research institutions (Lomas et al., 2015). Comparatively, we have more knowledge today than before on why and how people have different personalities, behavior, depression, anxiety, and other forms of positive and negative mental health. In addition, this paper helps us fill the gap overlooked towards the positive side of human nature (Schneider et.al., 2005). Positive social psychology or well-being is an optimal adaptation for life and positive psychological health. We can quote many examples for the same, while the highly studied of these are feeling of contentment and happiness with excellence in life (Abbasi et al., 2020).

Also, through various research, it is understood that mentally empowered millennial leaders feel greater self-efficacy in performing, have satisfactory job sovereignty, and their conduct gives a positive shift in the companies (Meyers et.al.,2013; Luthans et.al., 2010) defined Positive social psychology as research and application of positively developed strength of human potential and the psychological magnitudes that can be created, restrained, and efficiently administered for the performance development in present companies. PSP is defined as positive psychological coaching, which is strength-centered or constructive coaching. It's also found that positive millennial leaders in an organization will appropriately behave and adapt to programs and changes initiated by the management, which can bring success to the organization. Many experimental data have supported that PSP influences organizational behaviors and outcomes (Youssef & Luthans, 2007). To achieve this positivity in humans, which is reflected through knowledge, skills, and attitudes, it must be firstly identified, developed, and managed for improved performance in organizations which is essential (Atatsi et al., 2019)

DEFINING MILLENNIAL LEADERS

Millennials, otherwise familiar as Gen Y or also Generation Y, constitute the generational group that follows Generation X, then is preceded by Generation Z. Constant theme is that millennials tend to be more entitled than earlier generations. Millennials have "overstated self-esteem, impractical and extravagant prospects about key jobs, rewards, and promotions. Also, the overall shortage of tolerance and commitment to work over the discreet elements of the job (Brant & Castro, 2019). This generation is also known as a "Wired Generation" who wants to be constantly linked to digital assets, and they feel highly comfortable in a digital environment (Arora & Dhole, 2019). It's additionally found that Millennials have different positive characteristics such as team working, motivated to make an influence on their organizations, which are open to favor and are good at communicating with their leaders. They are comfortable using communications technology (Myers & Sadaghiani, 2010). Millennials are usually multitaskers and optic learners; they quickly get bored of old traditions and work environments (Holliday & Li, 2004). Recently, the "Net Generation," "Generation Me," or "Millennials" are suggested to fit the idea that these individuals focus more on their work and personal life balance than the goals and objectives of the organization. Millennials have a right, in serious need of regular feedback and compliments, attracted in the direction of technological learning, and just how having brief attention areas suitable for multi-tasking (Jauregui, Watsjold, Welsh, Ilgen, & Robins, 2020). Usually, conventional social structures that earlier generations followed are either taken for granted or often mistaken or overlooked by Millennials. They comply with authority but do not necessarily understand the significance of a social hierarchy that earlier generations acknowledge (Langan, 2012). They are also the more stressed generation and struggling for work-life balance (Sneha, Chaturvedi and Pasipanodya, 2022).

METHODOLOGY

This literature review utilizes a systemic system to select, identify, and censoriously assess the available research to discover a response to the well-defined research problem. A systematic analysis of literature was carried out to determine how we could conceptualize Positive Social Psychology (PSP), frame a definition, PSP model, and explain the components involved in such an approach. We have applied the "Preferred Reporting Items for Systematic Reviews and Meta-Analyses (PRISMA)" reporting standards for this methodical review. Guidelines of PRISMA offer a widely accepted data-centered specification of elements, which improves precision, transparency, and reliability.

Based on the guidelines, we conducted a thorough, methodical literature study between May and September 2021 at the bibliographical databases such as ScienceDirect, Emerald, Wiley, SAGE, Scopus, Taylor and Francis, Google Scholar, and APA PsycInfo. In these databases, we used almost ten primary search items such as "positive social psychology," "Employee Behavior," "Psychology based HRM," "Positive management," "Positive Behavior and organization success," "Positive personality development," "social psychology and employee behavior," "employee wellbeing," "Industrial psychology," and "Millennial leader Behavior." Firstly, these fundamental look for the items have been used, and secondly, in the later examination, databases that have been challenged using a combination of every primary phrase by secondary Phrase "process, model, theory, OR program" (E.g., "positive social psychology" AND "process, model, theory, OR program"). Utilizing these search phrases, 70 papers were identified from 2017 to 2020.

For the research papers to qualify for inclusion in the Paper, several exclusion and inclusion standards have been set before the start of the Paper. Involved research papers should:

- Be peer-reviewed with a strong emphasis on theory or model formation.
- The study must be focused on positive social psychology.

- The study should be explicitly allied with the theoretical emphasis of positive social psychology and can originate from any area (e.g., IT business, hospitals, or institutes).

In disparity, we omitted: (1) non-English formats; (2) non-peer studied articles and books (3) unpublished doctoral theses and masters; (4) conference proceedings and textbooks; (5) any other publication by a non-focus on positive social psychology besides (6) articles which are only focused on outcomes rather than process.

Conceptual Development and Review

This part aims to determine the foundation for the theoretic expansion of the conceptual prototype and to unambiguously resolve the 'why' factor for conducting a study on this subject and similarly discovering and integrating crucial variables of the research. The review process explicitly fulfills the objectives by intensely evaluating the existing literature by keeping the purposes of this study in mind. Briefly, Positive Social Psychology is well-defined as the application and analysis of individual powers which are constructively adapted and inner psychological strengths which can be advanced, quantifiable, and efficiently adapted for performance and behavior enhancement at work. It focuses on behavior, hopefulness, psychological capital, effectiveness, and flexibility (Lomas, 2015). In addition, Social cognitive theory advocates that personality is something one learns from the environment and people. Researcher Walter Mischel established an approach in which he argues that humans are social creatures who possess the skills and the ability to consciously discover and adapt what is excellent in the environment and avoid bad things (Nuckcheddy, 2018). Positive social psychology is critical to bring Organizational shifts, which has growing pressure on corporate leaders, which play a significant role in influencing organizational transformation. American Management Association surveys have demonstrated that leadership was the most critical factor in successful modification, followed by business values and communication (Yue et al., 2019). According to Social interchange, it refers to the fact that relationships and positive behaviors are instigated when one person or team does anything for the benefit of others. Trust is essential in the positive social psychology process and a prerequisite for continuing the relationship (Lujun Su et.al., 2019). Positive social psychology is also majorly related to the technology sector these days that has increased exponentially over the past few decades. Though modern technology can be considered significant stressors in the workplace for millennial leaders, accredited to producing enormously negative job-related consequences linked to damage of employee relations and impact their behavior, instigating extreme insecurity at the job, and creating ambiguity about the future (Justin et.al., 2019). Considering today's work-life balance issues, millennial leaders should not just be able to endure the typical stresses at the workplace; they should also be able to cope with regularly changing market conditions and technology. In companies with high levels of employee empowerment and companies that implement a positive social psychology work environment, millennial leaders will believe in their abilities, strengths, and organization and can operate independently. In these organizations, conditions which evoke a feeling of helplessness are finite (Caniëls et al., 2016).

The Models and Propositions

At the outset, Positive social psychology and work cultures in an Indian organization were explained by (Bhatia & Priya, 2018); they elucidated that cultural change in a knowledgeable economy emphasizes management and senior-level managers to form a positive and precise culture in organizations for it to become an outstanding and effective organization. Later, theories about the notion of culture, such as solid representations or "economics as a culture," were progressively employed to discover precisely how the worldwide attitudes concerning economic procedures were enforced and how they managed to form the lives of organizations and millennial leaders. A discourse of generating such culture is focused on utilizing a "combination of rules" and the techniques of behavior that allow "self-realizing capabilities of individuals to become arrayed" with the organization (Bhatia & Priya, 2018; Du Gay & Pryke, 2002)

Another Positive social and psychological approach, fundamental to several psychological theories (Potgieter & Snyman, 2018; Jordan & Troth, 2011), claimed that millennial leaders with a high emotional quotient tend to stay in jobs because they can adjust to the workplace differences. They are more inclined to administer their emotions, thus increasing career satisfaction associated with performance, positive behavior, and retention. There are few studies on the human and psychological dimensions linked to this change and its impact on employee behavior, employee well-being, work systems, and organization success (Ghislieri et.al., 2018). Also, the existing literature on Positive social psychology concentrates mainly on innovation and technology, disruption, application fields, challenges, and new opportunities.

Yet added element of theorizing on Positive social psychology and employee behavior focused on behavioral approach which stipulates that everyone can find evidence in their own lives which controversies their own intellectual biases when they learn how to find them. This requires Newtonian skill to see beyond apple trees and imply a presence of gravitation. Administrators, managers, and supervisors must practice questioning 'Why did this happen?' instead of only 'who did this? Similarly, a leader must think: 'would others commit the same mistakes if they were in my position?' 'What things could improve a work environment if I gave awareness for this mistake?' Slowly, these issues will change the concept to the one which promotes a culture of adopting and not simply penalizing (Han et.al., 2017).

Another characteristic of current research has been using process patterns like which developed in fatigue and stress research. These models start with work features that can impact welfare (e.g., adverse features such as career difficulties; constructive elements such as controller and sustenance), consequences (well-being results such as nervous and unhappiness, musculoskeletal illnesses and diseases instigated or made worse by exertion; nonattendance; mishaps; presenteeism and presentation effectiveness) and assessments (e.g., apparent tension; employment fulfillment). Apart from the job-related factors, it is essential to gauge personal qualities (e.g., healthy lifestyle and positive behavior). It is also necessary to evaluate lives outside of the job (Smith & Smith, 2017).

Among all the antecedents, management styles or leadership styles ought to be viewed as significant determinants of millennial employee behavior since leaders generally substantially impact their underlings (Wu et.al., 2017). Even though many studies demonstrated a connection between innovation and HRM (Nehles et.al., 2017) by former influence and affecting millennial leaders' behaviors, knowledge, and attitudes, they have all linked HRM to innovation at the organizational level. Nevertheless, employee innovatory behavior is fundamental to the creative ability of organizations such as millennial leaders can be seen as a cornerstone of any innovation. Despite the reputation, millennial leader behavior, information regarding and how it could be affected are split and contrary. Effective participatory management, and HR interference, involve the millennial leaders in the decision process, which improves positive social psychology which they use in added discussions to comply with business objectives (Abbasi et.al., 2020). It provides a more consistent image of the link between HRM and employee positive, innovative behavior.

Subsequent research (Lujun Su et.al., 2019) propose that positive social psychology influences administrative identification, which is significant for the listed reasons: 1) organizational identification gives a feeling and sense of belief for millennial leaders to understand their personality and their position in the world, 2) it satisfies the crucial need of humans which is to get an identity in society and be the portion of the more significant assembly and 3) it is also allied with various consequences which are very significant for organizations. For instance, great heights of organization identity positively affected employee loyalty and cooperative behaviors. Organizational identity signifies employee and organization bonding. Henceforth, it is examined as a significant aspect of present learning. Their theory essentially differentiates among two groups of member relations: outgroup and ingroup millennial leaders. The ingroup includes millennial leaders who have strong ties with their supervisors. They are categorized based on their loyalty, support, and mutual trust. Conversely, the outgroups include millennial leaders who have less bonding with their supervisors.

Emotion and behavior exchange are relatively limited, formal, and promised (Schuh et al., 2021; Graen & Uhl-Bien, 1995).

In the subsequent section, we have described our proposals concerning the antecedents of employee behavior by considering Leader Behavior, job design, organization socialization, Advancement opportunities, work environment, innovation support, Technology adaptation, and work-life balance. We have also elaborated the role of positive social psychology as a possible antecedent of positive social psychology. Subsequently, we dive into the potential effects of Positive social psychology.

Figure 1. Antecedents of positive social psychology

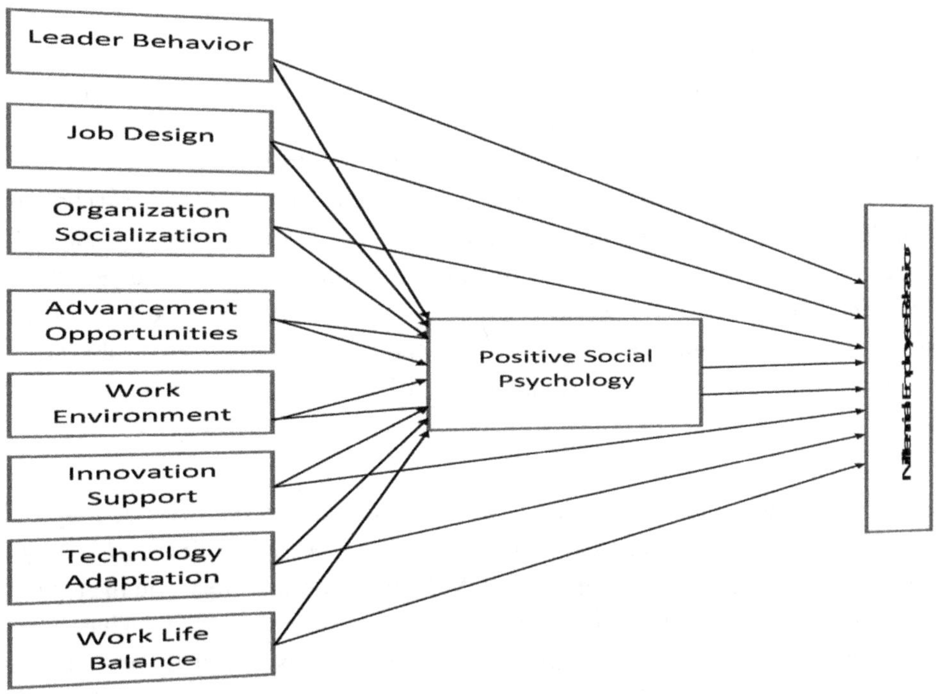

Antecedents of Positive Social Psychology

Leader Behavior

Researchers in Positive social psychology has extensively investigated the connection between Leader behavior and positive social psychology. Similarly, cross-sectional and longitudinal studies suggest a strong relationship between the two terms. Social exchange theory states that solid leader and employee relations elasticities added strength and confidence to members' expression. This behavior favors workforces to give back the support and admiration of their leaders. The current study suggests that millennial leaders believe their executives comprehend their desires and recognize their emotions in high- worth regards. Therefore, in exchange, millennial leaders are more willing to put more extraordinary efforts by identifying prevailing difficulties or prospects they see within the organization and notifying leaders about the conducts to represent optimistic changes (Carnevale et.al., 2017). Conferring to (Roeck & Farooq, 2017), the moral leader is categorized by profound anxiety in how their decisions can disturb others' wellbeing. Therefore, moral frontrunners seem to concern a lot about superior decent about their millennial leaders, society, and organization instead of their own personnel life and interests. Ethical leaders' concern for others' wellbeing is copied by followers, encouraging them to care for their colleagues and entities by executing additional organization citizenship behavior (Gao & Wei He, 2017).

Another theory suggests that millennial leaders display a higher level of job commitment once their social-psychological demands go satisfied by the support of their direct managers (Dhar, 2017). experimentally proves that encouraging leadership is the influential forecaster of positive social psychology. Positive social psychology can also result in the desired specific results such as positive wellbeing (Hmieleski & Carr, 2007; Avey et al., 2010) and occupational commitment (Chaturvedi, Rizvi and Pasipanodya, 2019). Scientists suggest that workers react positively to supervisors' behavior, mainly employee orientated. Leaders' pro-employee actions also affect workers' turn-over objectives (Haque et al., 2019).

Job Design

Following various theories and research, Millennial leaders enjoy technology and then navigate to the net as a trusted and comfortable source (Holliday & Li, 2004). Hiring and retention tactics that target Millennial leaders are recommended to associate themselves with the notion that these people focused further on their work and personal life than the objectives of their establishment (Jauregui, Watsjold, Welsh, Ilgen, & Robins, 2020). A more successful way to reach these Millennials is not only to provide them with how to perform with the technology in a reference communication, but it also provides them with why. Instead of imposing conduct, preparation must be based on the concept to gratify their necessity for a superior overall considerate and the necessity for the education, keeping in mind that the Millennial leader in the office needs to check and looks forward to a specified level of independence (Langan, 2012).

However, few young job-seekers choose challenging positions despite social working conditions or are slightly more fascinated by business standards than CSR programs (Klimkiewicz & Oltra, 2017). A full explanation that considers individual capabilities required in performing job roles and the vitality in a job as a substitute for the tilted emphasis on definite jobs and projects essential in fixed occupations is endorsed in a period of teamwork and job rotation (Atatsi et.al., 2019). Millennials are also called a generation by a high degree of privilege. Millennial leaders are expected to take excellent positions and reach high livelihood standards. Subsequently, millennials are among the highly educated group, raising their aspirations when entering the workforce.

Furthermore, millennials frequently have multiple liabilities and face a significantly higher price of living compared to earlier peers at their age. In brief, weak job prospects and challenging economic conditions mean that many millennial leaders have already begun with a noticeably different disadvantage than previous generations. These common conditions lead to millennials feeling deprived and not receiving what they consider worthy or waiting for, and, therefore, their unfulfilled hopes are often seen as entitled (Brant & Castro, 2019). In India, a few firms consider the attrition rate, and the expense related to them remain so elevated that they can ignore the advantages of smaller salary costs. It is simply that the drop-out people are not staying sufficiently to train or gain work skills. Thus, it is becoming essential that we understand the high expectations of workers and work out job designs and policies that are towards them for making a Gen Y worker more robust to jobs (Arora and Dhole, 2019).

Organizational Socialization

Important aspect of human resources management is to facilitate of entry and alignment of organizational new joiners. New entrants experience uncertainty concerning their respective roles, completing work, relations with colleagues and their status within a different workgroup. Millennials usually have got significant relations as well as spend very a smaller amount of time alone. Additional interactivity coupled with a superior satisfaction from the personal relationships will be linked to a higher social well-being. Organizational socialization is also a major mechanism where corporate culture is broadcast and is maintained. Investigations have indicated that newly recruited individuals, at the time they join in the organization, they seem to be thrilled with a new organization and the job, but they possess feelings of ambiguity and anxiety. In this condition, organization must exercise two things, initially, they must try to minimize the state of anxiety of the new millennial leaders by encouraging them, furthermore, they must shape culture of enthusiasm access which eventually help them engage through the working atmosphere (Kerdpitak & Jermsittiparsert, 2020). Timing is valuable while onboarding new recruits. Sooner the new workers can integrate into a new work environment and start to contribute effectively, the faster the organization will bounce back from its return of investments in attracting new recruits.

Official guidelines, unofficial standards, and procedures. This helps is enhancing positive work environment, social psychology, and positive well-being in an organization.

Advancement Opportunities

Millennials, like other leaders, are similarly led by the opportunity to broaden their skills. The Deloitte (2016) study revealed that, following a paycheck and other economic advantages, developing opportunities have been a primary inspiration; Traditional societal structures that earlier generations took for granted are frequently misinterpreted, otherwise neglected by the millennium (Langan, 2012). Millennials have different expectations of their leaders than earlier generations; among other things, a better job and family life balance enough attention and acknowledgment makes more sense to function and training and opportunities for (Brant & Castro, 2019). Indian Millennial workforce is thought to be the most challenging population by impressive expectations from employment conditions from the perspective of superior quality, on-site aid, and amenities at this norm for the job and personal life. The present age group of Indian teenagers is technically savvy, enterprising, aspirational, confident, and willing to walk the extra mile to accomplish their dreams or objectives (Arora and Dhole, 2019).

Additionally, several Millennials have been using this period of fewer jobs for additional job finding, like on the assumption placements, which provide prospects to experiment in different career choices. A unique way for many Millennials who have not been led by pressure to provide support to themselves or family is treating the first few years above their university graduation as a moment to expand their training with an advanced degree (Myers & Sadaghiani, 2010). However, further years of research, the shortage of quantifiable yields in the shape of employment prospects could make higher education irrelevant for social wellbeing. Likewise, the time frame of millennials is lesser; they will want to accomplish all over a snappier period; thus, advancement opportunities in jobs help millennials achieve positive wellbeing. (Damodar Suar et al., 2019).

Work Environment

The social workplace atmosphere debates interactions in the job settings. This includes communicative designs the connection between the supervisor and subordinates. This also consists of the relationship between colleagues, the willingness of other people to support, and teamwork (Arora & Dhole, 2019). The present generation has stumbled upon a solid and significant pattern for modifying the world and workplaces. Indian Millennial workers are the highly challenging population who has high expectations from the working conditions and the perspective of improved on-site support facilities and standards for the job and personal life balance. Their selection of enterprise hinges on the learning opportunities, excellence of living, and colleagues. Millennials have multiple aspirations, including the prospects for job diversity, individual development, fascinating and agile job environments, and utilization of technologies (Brant & Castro, 2019). the millennial leaders feel steady characteristics of the working atmosphere as individual experiences. Such incidents can yield positively or negatively common emotional conditions within workers. For the occasion, while the millennial leaders acknowledge that their firm is honest, they are likely to experience increased professional satisfaction and emotional engagement, which increases the probability that the millennial leaders would respond in nature along with the behavior chosen by the company (Jackson et.al., 2012). Offering millennial leaders with honest and inspiring surroundings could have positive results in socially responsible behaviors and job satisfaction. By assisting with the employee decision-making, a chance to think, and self-development, establishments can either directly or indirectly encourage nationality conduct and an increase in job satisfaction (Singh & Singh, 2018; Nuckheddy, 2018).

Employee Innovation Support

Today, innovation is essential in empowering organizations to adapt to immediate economic modifications and achieve practical benefits. Research indicates that the invention is suitable for the accomplishment of organizations because organizations are then able to meet the challenges more rapidly improve new product development and market prospects (Nehles et.al., 2017). High-performance exertion systems with employee innovation support have a strong positive influence on the individual and the structural results like invention, inspiration, application, human investment, career, and wellbeing in the organization, as well as flexible labor plans, work sovereignty, personality-effectiveness, Labor resources, natural, societal, or emotional assistance in the job productivity and reduces adverse consequences (Abbasi et.al., 2020). Additionally, it is not unbelievable that the diverse essentials of inventiveness and modernization have dissimilar backgrounds; it may not be astonishing if knowledge production remained maximum closely connected to the behavior characteristic of frankness, that impression elevation was utmost meticulously connected to socialness (Hughes et.al., 2018) High millennial privilege is likely to have cross-over-degree impacts, positively affecting unit-level results like unit ingenuity and unit efficiency (Brant & Castro, 2019). New York journalist and writer of numerous bestsellers, including "Outliers: The Story of Success," revealed what will the millennial point of view bring into American society and organizations. Gladwell adds that the most innovative companies now comprehend the dynamism of networks and the classified concepts; as an instance, Apple company used both principles to construct the world's most successful company in the world, he told. Beneath their lead, Steve Jobs, the firm imbued transparency and the elasticity for hierarchies to attain incredible innovations and spectacular profits. Gladwell advises employers to mimic Apple's approach to blend the very best networking and hierarchy patterns (Arora & Dhole, 2019). Transformative executives create confidence, dignity, and mutual regard from employees and are constantly being combined for a positive employee attitude and behavior in the workplace (Yue et.al., 2019).

Technology Adaptation

Positive monitoring is an essential component of companies' psychologically healthy job environment (Gilbreath, 2004). Psychological and social assistance at the workplace improves workers' participation (Chan et al., 2008). It's been discovered that the organizational and communal such as (apparent managerial rapport, team collaboration, and individual organization fit) and functional subsystems such as (administrative work characteristics, knowledge and technology provision, and transparent executive backing) have a substantial influence on employee's performance and behaviors. Millennials are more inclined to remain when there's a favorable technological working environment and vice-versa (Kundu & Lata, 2017).

Work Life Balance

Founded on reviews of existing literature, in which many research declares that millennials "want it all" and "want it now" in the form of "good salaries and benefits, quick progression, job, and personal life balance, exciting and challenging job" (p. 282). Few of those aspirations might be translated into positive findings within the unit level (Brant & Castro, 2019). Positive organizational or social psychology has emerged as one of the top strategies to help workers significantly reduce stress and restore control of their job and personal life balance (Justin et.al., 2019, Srivastava and Chaturvedi, 2014). Employee welfare is related to numerous performance measurement systems, including efficiency, worker attrition, work fulfillment, stress, and job-personnel life balance. Additionally, it's not only concerning a worker's general welfare and satisfaction with life, but it also influences healthcare nationwide (Tuzovic & Kabadayi, 2020). Researchers also showed that work aspects such as incentives, management style, job opportunities, education and development of the skill, physical work conditions, and the work and personal life balance have an indirect impact on retention (Kundu & Lata, 2017). Work-life equilibrium contributes to a healthy, joyful, and most successful living. This has always been of great interest for people who wish to have a good quality of work and personal life balance and eventually the excellent quality of their lives (Soomro et.al., 2017). Therefore, many studies suggest that adapting positive social psychology practices in organizations and creating a favorable environment generates confidence in millennial leaders, reduces stress, and helps work–life balance.

Consequences of Positive Social Psychology on Behavior

This section aims to help broaden your understanding of the scope of positive social psychology that goes beyond the subject of optimism. At the beginning of the paper, we have suggested that many theories and concepts explored in areas of positive social psychology originated from social psychology (Schneider et.al., 2005). A profound sense of identity augments the millennial leaders' sense of selection after doing the job through its organization. Studies prove that the psychological condition of being endowed leads to the desired behavior in millennial leaders. As a constructive consequence, millennial work behavior and knowledge-sharing behavior are also enhanced (Abbasi et.al., 2020; Chaturvedi & Tushar, 2021). Subsequently, the work environment and the organizational trust have a direct and statistically meaningful relationship to employee wellbeing and employee environment-friendly behavior (Lujun Su et.al., 2019). Meanwhile, a limited number of studies that measured negative welfare describe that there are differentiated relationships among leadership behaviors and intermediaries for positive wellbeing and negative wellbeing. They discovered that the consequences have been larger for social-cognitive than a relational path forecasting detrimental wellbeing, although they have been similar for hedonistic wellbeing (Inceoglua et.al.,2018). Likewise, additional research about the work environment and organizational culture recommends that the work environment and organization practices inspire millennial leaders to implement socially responsible behaviors, besides this empowers them to conduct in the manner which replicates the organization culture, accordingly leading millennial, millennial leaders to develop commitment and 'live the brand' (Gilani, 2017). Weak administrative support has been associated with prevention behavior and anger in millennial leaders. Employers' insufficient emotional support and inadequate compensation, workforce opinions not reaching the managers, and the poor feeling of 'group spirit' have been identified as the risk factors associated with mental illness (Brooks et al., 2017). Motivational processes have gotten the greatest attention at the individual, team, and organizational levels. Both (Amabile's, 1996) effective componential theories of originality and pioneering innovation paper point to internal encouragement as a key factor of workplace creation, innovation, as well as positive behavior amongst millennial leaders. Actual inspiration results are from the individual's interest, commitment, gratification, or a positive task associated with the work dedication (Hughes et.al., 2018). Social identity besides social support is concerned,

Directly or indirectly, in the varied collection of study subjects, comprising imprint administration, interactive relations, companion selection, intergroup and intragroup procedures, the understanding than the appearance of feeling, gender discrepancies in conduct, and also the creation and preservation of societal status. Documents covered in this literature review are testimony to the fundamental importance of the social image for these and other societal–emotional methods (Rodriguez et.al., 2011). In the mentioned papers, most researchers mention that positive social-psychological training involves "recognition, application, optimization, combined with the advancement of strengths and an individual resources." As an example, (Kauffman, 2006) explained constructive social-emotional training and practice as follows: "It emphasizes on serving millennial leaders to practice their present strengths to recognize the idea of whatever they want and they can convert it into reality by concentrating on vision, strengths, and dreams."

Given the above discussion, it is possible to conclude that positive social psychology operates as a tool for motivating millennial leaders and achieving positive workplace behaviors. Like improved productivity and job satisfaction (Zaman, Ansari and Chaturvedi, 2021), and decreased truancy, attrition, and workplace disputes. The researchers collectively describe positive workplace behaviors as millennial employee behavior effectiveness. Current analysis suggested that Positive social psychology has a substantial positive influence on millennial employee behavior efficacy. Subsequently, recent research has reflected the outcome of positive social psychology on organizational output, absenteeism, job satisfaction, workplace disputes, turnover, and isolation. Thus, the authors in this review mainly have endeavored to assemble the presently disseminated outcomes through positive social psychology below the shared title of millennial employee behavior effectiveness.

DISCUSSION

The literature review has demonstrated the significance and unquestionably the assurance of impending happiness and positivity through the positive social psychology within different social and cultural spheres, beginning with an ecosystem to the microsystem. There is an expanding awareness that happiness and positivity are not just a topic of a worker's inclinations or psychological characteristics but are primarily established throughout the cultural and social aspects at various scaling levels (Lomas, 2015). Evidence about this subject is added as an outline by positive social psychologists. The psychology department emphasizes positive behavior, attitude, health, and performance, which is described as the ideal adaption for living conditions and favorable emotional suitability. The close link between positive psychology and social psychology, scientific studies, patterns, and the theory in organizational positive social psychology has significantly contributed to a direction of sensitivity of positive thinking, wellbeing, and behaviors. This includes Leader Behavior, Advancement opportunities, technology adaptation, work environment, work-life balance, Innovation support, organization socialization, and job design. Though several of their theoretical ideas studied following our article shared over the exercise of works, we think that the vital part for future studies is to improve understanding of the interaction amongst these concepts in positive social psychology and practice perspective (Bozer & Jones, 2018). Our assessment has shown that the Leader Behavior, Advancement opportunities, technology adaptation, work environment, work-life balance, Innovation sustenance, organization socialization, and work characteristics have been a dynamic and budding area of research that has formed numerous exhilarating and fascinating consequences. A distinct theory with anecdotal evidence shows that leadership is a critical variable that can improve or suppress workplace positivity, improved performance, and innovation (Hughes et.al., 2018). Privilege is a critical problem that almost all organizations visage, boosted by a highly empowered millennial team.

With the ongoing influx of millennials hooked on to employment, organizations still must experience the overall effect of "Me Generation. Thus, knowing millennial privilege is crucial for HRM. With an existing condition of understanding, HRM now lacks adequate information to deal with the consequences of people, organizations, groups, and society.Investigators must contest the traditional wisdom of just contemplating a privilege to be a constant characteristic, concentrating solely on entitled persons, and seeing the negative aspects of benefit (Brant & Castro, 2019).. Outcomes of factorial analysis have underlined millennials' prevailing prospects, which indicate that the expectations are different. The inference will be a self-assured relation developed over job life balance and enhanced worker satisfaction from dream boss who commiserates with the workforce requirements and fulfillment. This increase in contentment would be helpful for organizations and the individual wellbeing of workers. The experimental improvement proves that employers who are thinking about those factors for the planning of worker involvement the driver may have better withholding and improved engagement and workers' participation (Arora & Dhole, 2019).

The study reviews indicate that wellbeing is associated with a large variety of clinically essential phenomena, involving psychopathology (especially depression), universal personality traits, positive public relations, and physical wellbeing (especially sleep and anxiety).

It is becoming increasingly recognized that prospearity is not just a matter of personal human choices or psychological characteristics but is comprehensively determined through social and cultural elements on many different levels of magnitude. Our paper has shown values and, in fact, the need to get close to prosperity at several sociocultural levels, from micro-systems to ecosystems. Such as, from within an employed viewpoint, our combined prosperity will be strengthened to the extent to which we can form our social-cultural environment to better contribute to that purpose. Suggested 'positive social psychology' – in which this document has sought to introduce and summarize – we hope it will be beneficial as we move forward in helping achieve this objective (Lomas, 2015).

Strengths, Limitations, and Future Research Directions

Indeed, it has been a massive task for investigators to demonstrate the experimental connections in-between performance, behavior, and positive employee characteristics. These discoveries are formidable, showing how to study outcomes and organizational performance or behavior may also be beneficial in giving evidence and directing supervisors about their ideas and behaviors in administering personnel in the present labor force. Finally, the study outcomes, exceptional hypotheses, and backgrounds will generate viable, valuable benefits for developing companies. The Meta- typecasts are reputation and fit in, Confront and respect, Admiration and disregard, Ego-management, Dishonor, and humiliation. All the preceding conditions summarize a widespread interest in societal living: the concern for our view in the sight of everyone else. Contributions made to this topic gave a brand-new illumination as to how and when fear for societal perspective impacts feelings with social, within the group, and between groups associations.

Additionally, this exclusive edition has discovere`11qqd connections amongst regions of study that would not necessarily be effortlessly linked to everyone devoid of an appropriate context. As A Result, public view functions as a consolidative outline of study embedded in various hypothetical and theoretical practices. We expect this combination of documents with diverse techniques and hypothetical proclivities will rejuvenate curiosity in shared vision as a typical theory in a positive social mindset (Mosquera et.al., 2011). The very kind of an individual's impact on prospects is crucial to the descriptions of positivity and negativity. The study suggests that individuals who possess positive consequence probabilities experience positive health in various territories of their lifetime; there are advantages of feeling optimistic instead of negative (Schneider et.al., 2005).

cording to whatever we know so far, we can conclude that positive social psychology contributions appear to be a valuable method for businesses that complements benefit exceptionally in the aspect of increased worker welfare. Likewise, we discovered that enhancement in optimistic variables is more likely to be vital in developing positive behavior, employee welfare, and organizational performance with positive social psychology involvement (Meyers et.al., 2013).

The Constraints notwithstanding, the intuitions that have been created are theoretically of great real-world importance for researchers and doctors as the results specify that Positive social psychology is not just an intellectual perception or a pointer of inactive approaches. Instead, it is a fundamental idea that can transform into constructive job behavior.

Figure 2. Antecedents of positive social psychology

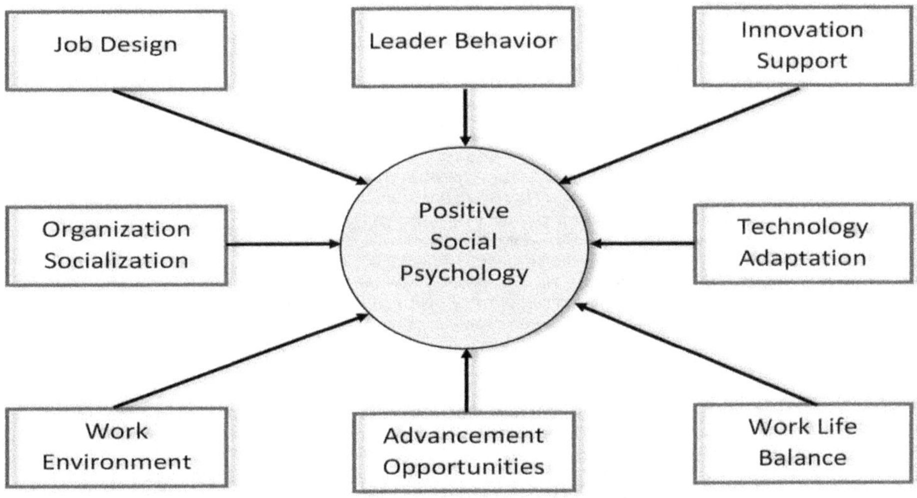

Table 1. Abstract of the recognized research variables – definitions and supporting literature sources

Variable	Definition	Sources
Leader Behavior	Leader Behavior is just about how to distribute control and power to make decisions. Inspirational leader supports members to resolve issues at their own rather than recommending solutions, inspires the millennial leaders to make use of their talents and to come forward with fresh ideas, provides prospects to acquire different competences and build their own right. Positive leader empowers the millennial leaders to enhance the agility, productivity, and innovation of an establishment.	Akdol, B., & Arikboga, F. S. (2015). The Effects of Leader Behavior on Job Satisfaction: A Research on Technology Fast50 Turkey Companies. Procedia – Social sciences and Behavioral Sciences, 195, 278-282, 282.
Job Design	Job design refers to the subject matter and association of individuals work assignments, behaviors, relations, and duties. When job is designed in such a way that it has inspiring attributes like job sovereignty and social assistance, in addition to inspirational amounts of job demand, several favorable personal and administrative outcomes occur. A huge amount of research indicates that job design influences the work-related stress, work satisfaction, effectiveness, truancy, mishaps, group creativity, business economic revenue, and more.	Parker, S. K., Van den Broeck, A., & Holman, D. (2017). *Work Design Influences: A Synthesis of Multilevel Factors that Affect the Design of Jobs.* Academy of Management Annals, 11(1), 267–308.

continued on following page

Table 1. Continued

Variable	Definition	Sources
Organizational Socialization	Organization Socializing is a process in which brand new or already existing workers slip into a brand-new function or the system in a positive manner. Administrative socialization remains a crucial human resource function which will have the consequences for people, group, and organizations. This is the primary tool through which millennial leaders grow to be modified and absorbed into groups, as well as it additionally has impacts on the professional accomplishment of individuals and the efficiency of businesses.	Saks, A. M., & Gruman, J. A. (2018). *Socialization resources theory and newcomers' work engagement.*Career development International, 23(1), 12–32.
Advancement Opportunities	Career advancement opportunities theory is broadly specified as a sequence of job experience which is aimed at the individual and organizational objectives either in keeping with his or her command or in accordance with the control of other people. The typical structures of this conceptualization are that the workforces consume an extended-period perception, enlarge outside present fulfilment and member performance, not proceeding the objective feature equally on the particular features of the occupation, nonetheless marginally observing by the side of job efficiency as the accomplishment of common agreement or vigorous positions.	Napitupulu, S., Haryono, T., Laksmi Riani, A., Sawitri, H. S. R., & Harsono, M. (2017). *The impact of career development on employee performance: an empirical study of the public sector in Indonesia.* International Review of Public Administration, 22(3), 276–299.
Work Environment	The work environment will be able to link the collective relation within the workplace in addition keep a relationship between the teammate, administrator, as well as the organization. A contented, cheerful, and diligent worker is the most asset of any establishment. Effective outcomes & efficiency for any organization remains hinge on the amount of contentment of workers and the working atmosphere are one of the most important factors affecting the happiness & inspiration intensity of workers. Effective human resource management and to preserve the excellent work atmosphere or culture impacts not just the performance of worker & society but also influences the economic expansion.	Thusyanthini Nadarasa, Ravivathani Thuraisingam (2012) *The influence of principal leadership styles on schoolteachers job satisfaction-study of secondary school in Jaffna District*, International Journal of Scientific and Research Publications, Volume 2, Issue 2, February 2012, ISSN 2250-3153
Innovation Support	Innovations and entrepreneurship are crucial drivers causing the competitive edge of businesses. Worker specific creative conduct establishes a micro-foundation of organizational creativity and entrepreneurship. Innovative conduct contains multiple aspects that evolve as time goes on. Creativity remains additionally communal in nature, such as when some millennial leaders innovate and get appreciated, others must be motivated and persuaded about the worth of the concept or their assistance will have to be prepared to execute innovative concepts.	Lukes, M., & Stephan, U. (2017). Measuring employee innovation. International Journal of Entrepreneurial Behavior & Research, 23(1), 136–158. doi:10.1108/ijebr-11-2015-0262
Technology adaptation	Three biggest drivers renovating work environments these days consist of technological development, globalized world, and a multi-generational staff. Globalized and the multigenerational staff have had a substantial impact on the evolving composition of the staff, although technology remains the deciding factor which generates the most drastic and swift changes. Such As the expenditure of technological equipment declines and technological innovation continues to rise, evolving technologies have been influencing the world we're living in and changing our life at an extraordinary rate. Advances in technology are altering our working environment and guiding us to reassess the skills needed to be successful in the twenty-first-century work environment.	Lewis, K. (2020). *Technology in the Workplace: Redefining Skills for the 21st Century.* The Midwest Quarterly, 61(3), vol. 61, no. 3, 2020, p. 348+. Gale Academic OneFile.
Work life Balance	Work-life balance" is a reference to the relationship between the work and personal life characteristics of persons. In which to achieve satisfying work life balance has typically been interpreted as limiting one hand (usually work), get more time on other. Relationships between the work and life initially became a focal point of interest because the increasing numbers of females were looking for a paid job outside of the household, since the second world war. Ever since the 1970s onwards, the emphasis on employed moms extended to integrate work-life balance between the dual career couples while the primary focus remained for women in the couples bargaining work and caring for children.	Kelliher, C., Richardson, J., & Boiarintseva, G. (2018). *All of work? All of life? Reconceptualising work-life balance for the 21st century.* Human Resource Management Journal. doi:10.1111/1748-8583.12215

REFERENCES

Abbasi, S. G., Shabbir, M. S., Abbas, M., & Tahir, M. S. (2020). HPWS and knowledge sharing behavior: The role of psychological empowerment and organizational identification in public sector banks. *Journal of Public Affairs, 2512*. Advance online publication. doi:10.1002/pa.2512

Albrecht, S. L., & Marty, A. (2017). Personality, self-efficacy and job resources and their associations with employee engagement, affective commitment and turnover intentions. *International Journal of Human Resource Management*. doi:10.1080/09585192.2017.1362660

Amabile, T. M. (1996). *Creativity and innovation in organizations* (Vol. 5). Harvard Business School.

Andriopoulos, C. (2001). Determinants of organisational creativity: A literature review. *Management Decision, 39*(10), 834–841. doi:10.1108/00251740110402328

Arora, N., & Dhole, V. (2019). Generation Y: Perspective, engagement, expectations, preferences, and satisfactions from workplace; a study conducted in Indian context, Benchmarking. *Benchmarking, 26*(5), 1378–1404. Advance online publication. doi:10.1108/BIJ-05-2018-0132

Ashveen, N. (2018). The Effect of Personality on Motivation and Organisational Behaviour. *Psychol Behav Sci Int J., 9*(2), 555760. doi:10.19080/PBSIJ.2018.09.555760

Bhatia, S., & Priya, K. R. (2018). Decolonizing culture: Euro-American psychology and the shaping of neoliberal selves in India. *Theory & Psychology, 28*(5), 645–668. doi:10.1177/0959354318791315

Bhatia, S., & Priya, K. R. (2018). Decolonizing culture: Euro-American psychology and the shaping of neoliberal selves in India. *Theory & Psychology, 28*(5), 645–668. doi:10.1177/0959354318791315

Bos-Nehles, A., Renkema, M., & Janssen, M. (2017). HRM and innovative work behaviour: A systematic literature review. *Personnel Review, 46*(7), 1228–1253. doi:10.1108/PR-09-2016-0257

Bozer, G., & Jones, R. J. (2018). Understanding the factors that determine workplace coaching effectiveness: A systematic literature review. *European Journal of Work and Organizational Psychology, 27*(3), 342–361. doi:10.1080/1359432X.2018.1446946

Brant, K. K., & Castro, S. L. (2019). You can't ignore millennials: Needed changes and a new way forward in entitlement research. *Human Resource Management Journal, 29*(4), 1–12. doi:10.1111/1748-8583.12262

Caniëls, M., Neghina, C., & Schaetsaert, N. (2016). Ambidexterity of employees: The role of empowerment and knowledge sharing. *Journal of Knowledge Management*. doi:10.1108/JKM-10-2016-0440

Carnevale, J. B., Huang, L., Crede, M., Harms, P., & Uhl-Bien, M. (2017). Leading to Stimulate Employees' Ideas: A Quantitative Review of Leader-Member Exchange, Employee Voice, Creativity, and Innovative Behavior. *Applied Psychology*, *66*(4), 517–552. doi:10.1111/apps.12102

Chaturvedi, S., Rizvi, I. A., & Pasipanodya, E. T. (2019). How Can Leaders Make Their Followers to Commit to the Organization? the Importance of Influence Tactics. *Global Business Review*, *20*(6), 1462–1474. doi:10.1177/0972150919846963

Chaturvedi, S., & Singh, T. (2021). "Knowledge management initiatives for tackling the COVID-19 pandemic in", Metamorphosis. *Journal of Management Research*, *20*(1), 25–34. 10.1177%2F09726225211023677

Csikszentmihalyi, M., & Seligman, M. (2000). Positive psychology. *The American Psychologist*, *55*(1), 5–14. doi:10.1037/0003-066X.55.1.5 PMID:11392865

Darvishmotevali, M., Arasli, H., & Kilic, H. (2017). Effect of job insecurity on frontline employee's performance: Looking through the lens of psychological strains and leverages. *International Journal of Contemporary Hospitality Management*, *29*(6), 1724–1744. doi:10.1108/IJCHM-12-2015-0683

De Roeck, K., & Farooq, O. (2017). Corporate Social Responsibility and Ethical Leadership: Investigating Their Interactive Effect on Employees' Socially Responsible Behaviors. *Journal of Business Ethics*. Advance online publication. doi:10.100710551-017-3656-6

Erin, M. (2012). Relationships of leader reward behavior with employee behavior. *Leadership and Organization Development Journal*, *33*(7), 646–661. doi:10.1108/01437731211265232

Gao, Y., & He, W. (2017). Corporate social responsibility and employee organizational citizenship behavior: The pivotal roles of ethical leadership and organizational justice. *Management Decision*, *55*(2), 294–309. doi:10.1108/MD-05-2016-0284

Ghislieri, C., Molino, M., & Cortese, C. G. (2018). Work and Organizational Psychology Looks at the Fourth Industrial Revolution: How to Support Workers and Organizations? *Frontiers in Psychology*, *9*, 2365. doi:10.3389/fpsyg.2018.02365 PMID:30546335

Ghosh, K., & Sahney, S. (2011). Impact of organizational sociotechnical system on managerial retention: A general linear modeling approach. *Journal of Modelling in Management*, *6*(1), 33–59. doi:10.1108/17465661111112494

Gilani, H. (2017). University of Brighton, UK*Lucy Cunningham, University of Brighton, UK, Employer branding and its influence on employee retention: A literature review. *The Marketing Review, 17* (2), pp.239-256 doi:10.1362/1469347 17X14909733966209

Gilbreath, B., & Benson, P. G. (2004). The contribution of supervisor behaviour to employee psychological well-being. *Work & Stress, 18*(3), 255-266.

Graen, G. B., & Uhl-Bien, M. (1995). Relationship-based approach to leadership: Development of leader-member exchange (LMX) theory of leadership over 25 years: Applying a multi-level multi-domain perspective. *The Leadership Quarterly*, *6*(2), 219–247. doi:10.1016/1048-9843(95)90036-5

Han, J., LaMarra, D., & Vapiwala, N. (2017). Applying lessons from social psychology to transform the culture of error disclosure. *Medical Education*, *51*(10), 996–1001. doi:10.1111/medu.13345 PMID:28523743

Haque, A., Fernando, M., & Caputi, P. (2019). The relationship between responsible leadership and organisational commitment and the mediating effect of employee turnover intentions: An empirical study with Australian employees. *Journal of Business Ethics*, *156*(3), 759–774. doi:10.100710551-017-3575-6

Hmieleski, K. M., & Carr, J. C. (2007). The relationship between entrepreneur psychological capital and well-being. *Frontiers of Entrepreneurship Research.*

Holliday, W., & Li, Q. (2004). Understanding the millennials: Updating our knowledge about students. *RSR. Reference Services Review*, *32*(4), 356–366. doi:10.1108/00907320410569707

Hughes, D. Allan Leeb, Amy Wei Tianc, Alex Newmand, Alison Le good. (2018). *The Leadership Quarterly*. Advance online publication. doi:10.1016/j.leaqua.2018.03.001

Inceoglu, I., Thomas, G., Chu, C., Plans, D., & Gerbasi, A. (2018). Leadership behavior and employee well-being: An integrated review and a future research agenda. *The Leadership Quarterly, 29*(1), 179-202. doi:10.1016/j.leaqua.2017.12.006

Inceoglu, I., Thomas, G., Chu, C., Plans, D., & Gerbasi, A. (2018). Leadership behavior and employee well-being: An integrated review and a future research agenda. *The Leadership Quarterly*, *29*(1), 179–202. doi:10.1016/j.leaqua.2017.12.006

Jason Han, L. P., & Snyman, A. M. (2018). Personal factors in talent retention in the South African banking industry. *Journal of Psychology in Africa*, *28*(6), 455–461. doi:10.1080/14330237.2018.1544393

Jauregui, J., Watsjold, B., Welsh, L., Ilgen, J. S., & Robins, L. (2020). Generational 'othering': The myth of the Millennial learner. *Medical Education*, *54*(1), 60–65. doi:10.1111/medu.13795 PMID:31515842

Joo, B.-K., & Jo, S. J. (2017). The effects of perceived authentic leadership and core self-evaluations on organizational citizenship behavior: The role of psychological empowerment as a partial mediator. *Leadership and Organization Development Journal*, *38*(3), 463–481. doi:10.1108/LODJ-11-2015-0254

Kauffman, C. (2006). Positive psychology: The science at the heart of coaching. *Evidence based coaching handbook: Putting best practices to work for your clients*. Springer.

Kerdpitak, C., & Jermsittiparsert, K. (2020). The Impact of Human Resource Management Practices on Competitive Advantage: Mediating Role of Employee Engagement in Thailand. *Systematic Reviews in Pharmacy*, *11*, 443–452. doi:10.5530rp.2020.1.56

Khoreva, V., & Wechtler, H. (2018). HR practices and employee performance: The mediating role of well-being. *Employee Relations*, *40*(2), 227–243. doi:10.1108/ER-08-2017-0191

Klimkiewicz, K., & Oltra, V. (2017). Does CSR Enhance Employer Attractiveness? The Role of Millennial Job Seekers' Attitudes. *Corporate Social Responsibility and Environmental Management*, *24*(5), 449–463. doi:10.1002/csr.1419

Kundu, S. C., & Lata, K. (2017). Effects of supportive work environment on employee retention: Mediating role of organizational engagement. *The International Journal of Organizational Analysis*, *25*(4), 703–722. doi:10.1108/IJOA-12-2016-1100

Langan, K. (2012). Training Millennials: A practical and theoretical approach. *RSR. Reference Services Review*, *40*(1), 24–48. doi:10.1108/00907321211203612

Li, J., Bonn, M. A., & Ye, B. H. (2019). Hotel employee's artificial intelligence and robotics awareness and its impact on turnover intention: The moderating roles of perceived organizational support and competitive psychological climate. *Tourism Management*, *73*, 172–181. doi:10.1016/j.tourman.2019.02.006

Lomas, T. (2015). Positive social psychology: A multilevel inquiry into sociocultural well-being initiatives. *Psychology, Public Policy, and Law*, *21*(3), 338–347. doi:10.1037/law0000051

Lomas, T., Hefferon, K., & Ivtzan, I. (2015). The LIFE model: A meta-theoretical conceptual map for applied positive psychology. *Journal of Happiness Studies*, *16*(5), 1347–1364. doi:10.100710902-014-9563-y

Lomas, T., Ivtzan, I., & Fu, C. H. (2015). A systematic review of the neurophysiology of mindfulness on EEG oscillations. *Neuroscience and Biobehavioral Reviews*, *57*, 401–410. doi:10.1016/j.neubiorev.2015.09.018 PMID:26441373

Luthans, F., Avey, J. B., Avolio, B. J., & Peterson, S. J. (2010). The development and resulting performance impact of positive psychological capital. *Human Resource Development Quarterly*, *21*(1), 41–67. doi:10.1002/hrdq.20034

Meyers, M. C., van Woerkom, M., & Bakker, A. B. (2013). The added value of the positive: A literature review of positive psychology interventions in organizations. *European Journal of Work and Organizational Psychology*, *22*(5), 618–632. doi:10.1080/1359432X.2012.694689

Moyson, S., Raaphorst, N., Groeneveld, S., & Van de Walle, S. (2017). Organizational Socialization in Public Administration Research: A Systematic Review and Directions for Future Research. *American Review of Public Administration*, *48*(6), 610–627. doi:10.1177/0275074017696160

Myers, K. K., & Sadaghiani, K. (2010). Millennials in the Workplace: A Communication Perspective on Millennials' Organizational Relationships and Performance. *Journal of Business and Psychology*, *25*(2), 225–238. doi:10.100710869-010-9172-7 PMID:20502509

Ng, K. Y., Ang, S., & Chan, K. Y. (2008). Personality and leader effectiveness: A moderated mediation model of leadership self-efficacy, job demands, and job autonomy. *The Journal of Applied Psychology*, *93*(4), 733–743. doi:10.1037/0021-9010.93.4.733 PMID:18642980

Nuckcheddy, A. (2018). The effect of personality on motivation and organisational behaviour. *Psychology and Behavioral Science International Journal*, *9*(2), 1–5. doi:10.19080/PBSIJ.2018.09.555760

Park, J. G., Kim, J. S., Yoon, S. W., & Joo, B. K. (2017). The effects of empowering leadership on psychological well-being and job engagement: The mediating role of psychological capital. *Leadership and Organization Development Journal*.

Rodriguez Mosquera, P. M., Uskul, A. K., & Cross, S. E. (2011). The centrality of social image in social psychology. *European Journal of Social Psychology*, *41*(4), 403–410. doi:10.1002/ejsp.820

Saks, A. M., & Gruman, J. A. (2018). Socialization resources theory and newcomers' work engagement: A new pathway to newcomer socialization. *Career Development International*, *23*(1), 12–32. doi:10.1108/CDI-12-2016-0214

Schneider, F. W., Gruman, J. A., & Coutts, L. M. (2005). Defining the field of applied social psychology. *Applied social psychology: Understanding and addressing social and practical problems*, 1-18.

Schuh, S. C., Cai, Y., Kaluza, A. J., Steffens, N. K., David, E. M., & Haslam, S. A. (2021). Do leaders condone unethical pro-organizational employee behaviors? The complex interplay between leader organizational identification and moral disengagement. *Human Resource Management*, *60*(6), 969–989. doi:10.1002/hrm.22060

Shreya, G. R. D. (2017). Employee service innovative behavior: The roles of Leader-Member Exchange (LMX),work engagement, and job autonomy. *International Journal of Manpower*, *38*(2).

Singh, S. K., & Singh, A. P. (2018). Interplay of organizational justice, psychological empowerment, organizational citizenship behavior, and job satisfaction in the context of circular economy. *Management Decision*. doi:10.1108/MD-09-2018-0966

Smith, A., & Smith, H. (2017). An International Survey of the Wellbeing of Employees in the Business Process Outsourcing Industry. *Psychology (Irvine, Calif.)*, *8*(1), 160–167. doi:10.4236/psych.2017.81010

Soomro, A. A., Breitenecker, R. J., & Syed, A. M. S. (2017). *Relation of work-life balance, work-family conflict, and family-work conflict with the employee performance-moderating role of job satisfaction*. South Asian Journal of Business Studies. doi:10.1108/SAJBS-02-2017-0018

Srivastava, A. K., & Chaturvedi, S. (2014). Negative Job Experiences and Employees Job Attitudes and Health in High-Performance Work Organizations. *Metamorphosis*, *13*(2), 22–28. doi:10.1177/0972622520140205

Su, L., & Swanson, S. (2019). Perceived corporate social responsibility's impact on the well-being and supportive green behaviors of hotel employees: The mediating role of the employee-corporate relationship. *Tourism Management, 72*, 437-450. doi:10.1016/j.tourman.2019.01.009

Suar, D., Jha, A. K., Das, S. S., & Alat, P. (2019). The structure and predictors of subjective well-being among millennials in India. *Cogent Psychology*, *6*(1), 1584083. doi:10.1080/23311908.2019.1584083

Tang, G., Yu, B., Cooke, F. L., & Chen, Y. (2017). High-performance work system and employee creativity: The roles of perceived organisational support and devolved management. *Personnel Review*, *46*(7), 1318–1334. doi:10.1108/PR-09-2016-0235

Tuzovic, S., & Kabadayi, S. (2018). The influence of social distancing on employee well-being: A conceptual framework and research agenda. *Journal of Service Management*, *32*(2), 145–160. doi:10.1108/JOSM-05-2020-0140

Van Zyl, L. E., Roll, L. C., Stander, M. W., & Richter, S. (2020). Positive Psychological Coaching Definition and Models: A Systematic Literature Review. *Frontiers in Psychology*, *11*, 793. doi:10.3389/fpsyg.2020.00793 PMID:32435218

Wei-Li, Y.-C. L. (2017). Empowering group leaders encourages knowledge sharing: Integrating the social exchange theory and positive organizational behavior perspective. *Journal of Knowledge Management*, *21*(2), 474–491. doi:10.1108/JKM-08-2016-0318

Wu, W.-L., & Lee, Y.-C. (2017). Empowering group leaders encourages knowledge sharing: Integrating the social exchange theory and positive organizational behavior perspective. *Journal of Knowledge Management*, *21*(2), 474–491. doi:10.1108/JKM-08-2016-0318

Youssef, C. M., & Luthans, F. (2007). Positive organizational behavior in the workplace: The impact of hope, optimism, and resilience. *Journal of Management*, *33*(5), 774–800. doi:10.1177/0149206307305562

Zaman, S., Ansari, A. H., & Chaturvedi, S. (2021). Work-life enablers for job satisfaction in healthcare: Moderating role of organization type. *Industrial and Commercial Training*. doi:10.1108/ICT-05-2020-0060

Chapter 11
Navigating the New Frontier:
Analysing the Leadership Qualities of Successful Millennial Business Leaders in the Digital Age

Bhavna Taneja
https://orcid.org/0000-0002-5447-7758
Amity University, Ranchi, India

ABSTRACT

The rise of the millennial generation in leadership positions has redefined traditional notions of leadership in today's rapidly changing global landscape. This chapter explores and analyzes the distinct leadership qualities that characterize successful millennial business leaders. By examining the unique attributes and skills that set them apart, the author seeks to shed light on how millennial business leaders are transforming organizational dynamics, fostering innovation, and driving positive change across industries. Through a comprehensive review of the literature and case studies, this chapter presents valuable insights into the leadership traits that enable millennial business leaders to thrive in their roles and impact their organizations and society.

INTRODUCTION

The Millennial generation, born between the early 1980s and mid-1990s, is making a significant impact on the global workforce, with many assuming leadership positions in various sectors. As this cohort takes the reins of organizations, it is essential

DOI: 10.4018/978-1-6684-4711-6.ch011

to understand the distinctive leadership qualities that contribute to their success. In the rapidly evolving landscape of today's global society, the emergence of the Millennial generation as a dominant force in the workforce has led to a paradigm shift in leadership styles and expectations.

The Millennial Business leader operates in a world vastly different from that of their predecessors. Their formative years were shaped by technological advancements and a burgeoning global interconnectedness, which fostered a unique set of skills and traits. Moreover, the Millennial generation grew up in an era marked by economic turbulence, political instability, and environmental concerns, all of which have had a profound impact on their values and priorities as leaders.

In this research, the authors explore the interplay between the Millennial Business leader's adaptability and open-mindedness, their inclination towards collaboration and inclusivity, and their preference for work-life balance and social consciousness. We examine how these traits contribute to reshaping organizational structures and engender a more agile and socially responsible approach to leadership. Understanding the Millennial Business leader is crucial as they navigate complex challenges and capitalize on opportunities in the fast-paced, interconnected global landscape.

Furthermore, the paper examines the challenges faced by Millennial Business leaders as they transition into key roles, including scepticism from older generations, navigating the intricacies of cross-generational collaboration, and balancing technological advancements with human-centric leadership. These challenges not only affect the individual Millennial Business leader but also have broader implications for the organizations they lead and the communities they serve.

Understanding the characteristics of the Millennial Business leader is essential for creating a sustainable and thriving global society. By harnessing their unique skill set, values, and approach to leadership, organizations can foster environments that encourage innovation, diversity, and meaningful social impact. As the authors explores the dynamics of Millennial leadership, they lay the foundation for future research and practical recommendations to support and cultivate effective leadership in an increasingly interconnected and dynamic world.

- Objectives:
    - To identify and analyse the unique leadership qualities exhibited by successful Millennial Business leaders.
    - To explore how these leadership qualities have influenced organizational outcomes and fostered positive change.
    - To offer practical implications for organizations seeking to develop and nurture Millennial Business leaders.

The Rise of the Millennial Leader

The demographic shift in leadership is a significant phenomenon that has been unfolding over the past decade, with Millennials increasingly taking on leadership roles in organizations worldwide. Born between the early 1980s and mid-1990s, Millennials are now entering their late 20s to mid-30s, making them eligible for leadership positions as more experienced leaders from previous generations retire.

Generational Characteristics of Millennials

Understanding the generational characteristics of Millennials helps shed light on their impact as leaders. Millennials are often characterized as tech-savvy, adaptable, collaborative, purpose-driven, and eager to make a positive impact on society. They value work-life balance, seek opportunities for professional development, and prefer a flexible and inclusive work environment.

- **Leadership Aspirations of Millennials:** Research has shown that Millennials aspire to leadership positions and are eager to take on managerial roles early in their careers. Unlike previous generations, Millennials prioritize leadership roles not only for financial gain but also for the opportunity to create a meaningful impact and drive positive change within their organizations.
- **Advancement Opportunities and Career Progression:** As the Baby Boomer and Generation X leaders retire, Millennials are presented with increased advancement opportunities and career progression. Organizations are recognizing the value of promoting young talent and leveraging the unique perspectives and skills that Millennials bring to leadership roles.
- **Impact of Technology and Digitalization:** Millennials have grown up in a digitally connected world, and their familiarity with technology has contributed to their rapid rise in leadership positions. Their proficiency with digital tools and social media enables them to navigate the fast-paced, technology-driven business landscape more effectively.
- **Shift in Leadership Styles:** The rise of Millennials in leadership positions in business, is accompanied by a shift in leadership styles. Millennials tend to exhibit more collaborative and inclusive leadership styles, fostering a flatter organizational structure and promoting cross-functional collaboration. They prioritize open communication, transparency, and feedback to create a more engaging and empowering work environment.
- **Focus on Diversity and Inclusion:** Millennial leaders are more conscious of diversity and inclusion in the workplace. They actively seek to create a

diverse workforce, recognizing the importance of different perspectives in driving innovation and problem-solving.

- **Balancing Traditional and Modern Approaches:** While Millennials bring fresh perspectives and innovative approaches to leadership, they also recognize the value of learning from experienced leaders. Successful Millennial leaders strike a balance between traditional leadership wisdom and modern techniques to achieve organizational goals.
- **Addressing Complex Challenges:** As Millennials step into leadership roles, they are faced with addressing complex challenges such as globalization, technological disruptions, and changing consumer preferences. Their ability to adapt to these challenges and capitalize on emerging opportunities is crucial for organizational success.

The demographic shift in leadership, with an increasing representation of Millennials in leadership positions, is transforming the way organizations operate and respond to the evolving business landscape. The distinctive characteristics of Millennials, combined with their tech-savviness, purpose-driven mindset, and collaborative leadership style, contribute to their effectiveness as leaders. As they continue to rise through the ranks, Millennials will shape the future of work, driving innovation, embracing diversity, and championing positive change within organizations. Understanding and embracing the leadership potential of Millennials is vital for business organizations seeking to remain agile and competitive in today's global society.

The socio-cultural context in which Millennials were raised has had a profound impact on shaping their values, beliefs, and approach to leadership. Born between the early 1980s and mid-1990s, Millennials experienced a unique set of social, economic, and technological influences during their formative years. Some key factors that have influenced Millennials' upbringing and subsequently shaped their leadership approach include:

- **Technological Revolution:** Millennials are often referred to as "digital natives" because they grew up during a time of rapid technological advancements. The proliferation of computers, the internet, and mobile devices profoundly influenced their communication, learning, and social interactions. This exposure to technology has made Millennials more tech-savvy and open to adopting innovative solutions in their leadership roles.
- **Globalization and Cultural Diversity:** Millennials were raised in an increasingly interconnected and diverse world. They have experienced globalization and cultural diversity through increased international travel, immigration, and exposure to global media. This exposure has instilled a

sense of openness, empathy, and appreciation for different cultures, which often translates into their approach to inclusive leadership.

- **Helicopter Parenting and Supportive Upbringing:** Many Millennials experienced "helicopter parenting," characterized by close parental involvement and support. Their parents often emphasized the importance of self-esteem and personal growth. As a result, Millennials tend to value feedback, seek continuous learning, and place importance on personal development and well-being, all of which influence their leadership style.
- **Focus on Work-Life Balance:** Millennials observed their parents struggling with work-life balance and often prioritize it in their own lives. This emphasis on maintaining a healthy balance between work and personal life influences their leadership approach, as they seek to create supportive and flexible work environments for their teams.
- **Social Activism and Civic Engagement:** Growing up in a time of significant social and environmental challenges, Millennials developed a strong sense of social responsibility and environmental consciousness. They tend to be purpose-driven leaders, seeking to make a positive impact on their organizations and society at large.
- **Education and Focus on Collaboration:** Millennials experienced an education system that increasingly emphasized collaboration, teamwork, and project-based learning. This cooperative learning environment fosters their inclination towards collaborative leadership styles, valuing diverse perspectives and teamwork.
- **Experience of Economic Recession:** Many Millennials entered the workforce during the global economic recession of the late 2000s and early 2010s. This experience shaped their attitudes towards job security, career stability, and financial planning. As leaders, they may prioritize employee well-being, professional development, and job satisfaction.
- **Instant Gratification and Entrepreneurship:** With the advent of social media and technology, Millennials have been exposed to instant gratification and a culture that celebrates entrepreneurship and innovation. This exposure has made them more risk-tolerant and entrepreneurial in their leadership approach, seeking creative solutions and taking calculated risks.

The socio-cultural context in which Millennials were raised has significantly influenced their values, beliefs, and approach to leadership. Their exposure to technology, globalization, supportive upbringing, focus on work-life balance, social activism, collaborative education, and experience of economic recession have collectively shaped their leadership style. Millennials tend to be purpose-driven, innovative, collaborative, and inclusive leaders who prioritize employee well-being and strive to make a positive impact on their organizations and society. Understanding the socio-cultural context that has shaped Millennial leaders is crucial for organizations seeking to effectively engage, develop, and leverage this generation's unique leadership qualities.

Leadership Theories and Styles

Various leadership theories and styles have been proposed over the years, each offering different perspectives on effective leadership. When examining the leadership qualities displayed by successful Millennial leaders, certain theories and styles align more closely with their approach to leadership. Given below are some leadership theories and styles that resonate well with the leadership qualities of successful Millennial Business leaders:

- **Transformational Leadership:** Transformational leadership is a popular theory that emphasizes inspiring and motivating followers to achieve extraordinary outcomes. Successful Millennial leaders often display transformational qualities, such as vision, charisma, and the ability to empower and develop their teams. They focus on shared values, encourage creativity, and foster a culture of continuous learning and growth. Transformational leadership aligns with the purpose-driven and collaborative nature of Millennial leaders.
- **Servant Leadership:** Servant leadership centres on serving others and focusing on the well-being of team members. Millennials tend to prioritize empathy, inclusivity, and a sense of purpose, making servant leadership a natural fit for their approach. Successful Millennial leaders often display humility, active listening, and a willingness to support the growth and development of their employees.
- **Authentic Leadership:** Authentic leadership emphasizes leaders' genuine and transparent behaviour. Millennials value authenticity and are more likely to connect with leaders who are open, honest, and true to their values. Successful Millennial leaders often exhibit authenticity by being true to themselves, acknowledging their strengths and weaknesses, and building trust with their teams.
- **Democratic Leadership:** Democratic leadership involves involving team members in decision-making and valuing their input. Millennials tend to favour collaboration and inclusivity, making democratic leadership appealing to their leadership style. Successful Millennial leaders often seek input from their teams and foster an environment where diverse perspectives are considered.

- **Laissez-Faire Leadership:** Laissez-Faire leadership allows employees considerable autonomy in decision-making and task completion. While this style may not align with every Millennial leader, those in tech-savvy and innovative fields often embrace it. In such settings, Millennial leaders trust their team members' expertise and provide them with the freedom to explore new ideas and approaches.
- **Situational Leadership:** Situational leadership theory suggests that leadership styles should adapt to the readiness and development level of followers. Millennial leaders often emphasize personalized leadership, recognizing that different team members may require varying levels of guidance and support. They are flexible in their approach, providing direction when needed and stepping back when team members can take the lead.

Successful Millennial leaders tend to exhibit leadership qualities that align with transformational leadership, servant leadership, authentic leadership, democratic leadership, and situational leadership. These theories and styles resonate with the purpose-driven, collaborative, and inclusive nature of Millennial leaders. While not every Millennial leader adheres strictly to a single leadership theory, they often integrate aspects from various styles to create their unique leadership approach. Understanding these theories can help organizations better support and develop the leadership potential of their Millennial employees, fostering a new generation of effective and impactful leaders.

LITERATURE REVIEW

This section will present a comprehensive review of relevant literature on leadership theories, styles, and models, as well as existing research on the leadership qualities of millennial Business leaders. It will highlight the differences between millennial leaders and previous generations of leaders, drawing upon studies that have explored the impact of the digital age on leadership practices.

Qualities Needed in a Leader

Adaptability and Flexibility

Adaptability and flexibility are multidimensional leadership qualities that involve the ability to respond, adjust, and thrive in dynamic and unpredictable environments. According to researchers like Dinh et al. (2014), these qualities enable leaders to make agile decisions, change course when necessary, and capitalize on emerging opportunities. As organizations face constant change and disruption, leaders who exhibit adaptability and flexibility are better equipped to lead their teams through uncertain times. Researchers have highlighted the Millennial generations adaptability and flexibility as notable leadership qualities, according to a study by Wong and Gardener (2017).

Several researchers have identified adaptability as a critical competency for effective leadership. In their study, DeRue and Ashford (2010) emphasize that adaptive leaders can navigate complex situations and quickly learn from their experiences. They exhibit a willingness to experiment, embrace new ideas, and adjust their strategies based on feedback, which contributes to enhanced organizational resilience and performance.

Researchers like Vasilopoulos et al. (2020) emphasize the importance of developing adaptability and flexibility in leaders. They argue that leadership development programs should incorporate strategies to cultivate these qualities, such as exposure to diverse experiences, coaching, and feedback. By enhancing these skills, leaders can effectively handle unforeseen challenges and lead their teams to achieve sustained success.

Flexibility in decision-making is an essential aspect of leadership adaptability. According to research by Simsek and Heavey (2011), flexible leaders are open to considering alternative viewpoints and are willing to revise their decisions based on changing circumstances. This quality enhances the leader's ability to make sound judgments, particularly in unpredictable environments where rigid decision-making approaches may prove ineffective.

Leaders who demonstrate adaptability and flexibility are better equipped to lead their teams through organizational change. Research by Yukl and Lepsinger (2004) highlights that these leaders exhibit a positive attitude towards change, communicate effectively during transitions, and facilitate a smooth adaptation process among their team members. Their capacity to navigate change fosters employee trust and engagement, ultimately driving successful organizational transformations.

In an increasingly interconnected global world, cross-cultural adaptability has emerged as a crucial aspect of leadership effectiveness. Research by Gregersen et al. (2013) indicates that leaders who demonstrate the ability to adapt to different cultural contexts foster inclusive and collaborative environments. Cross-culturally adaptable leaders are better equipped to manage diverse teams, engage with international stakeholders, and lead successful global initiatives.

Tech-Savviness and Digital Fluency

In the digital age, leadership qualities such as tech-savviness and digital fluency have become essential for leaders to navigate the complexities of modern organizations and industries. By examining the impact of tech-savviness and digital fluency in effective leadership on decision-making, innovation, and organizational performance, the author aims to gain valuable insights into how these qualities contribute to the success of leaders in a technology-driven world.

Tech-savviness and digital fluency refer to a leader's proficiency in using technology and their understanding of digital tools and platforms. Research by Alsop (2016) emphasises that growing up in the digital era has provided millennials with natural affinity for technology. Researchers like Weill and Woerner (2013) stress the importance of these qualities in modern Business leadership, as they enable leaders to harness technology for strategic decision-making, data analysis, and effective communication.

Leaders with tech-savviness and digital fluency are more likely to drive innovation within their organizations. A study by Choi and Eboch (2018) highlights that digitally fluent leaders can identify and implement technological advancements, enabling their teams to adapt quickly to changing market conditions and emerging opportunities.

Digital fluency enhances a leader's ability to communicate and collaborate with their team members effectively. Research by Carmeli et al. (2013) suggests that tech-savvy leaders can leverage various digital communication channels, fostering seamless information flow and fostering a culture of open dialogue and idea-sharing.

In the era of big data, digital fluency empowers Business leaders to harness information and analytics for making informed decisions. According to research by Cao et al. (2019), leaders who possess data fluency can extract valuable insights from vast datasets, leading to more accurate and data-driven decision-making.

Tech-savvy leaders can bridge the generational gap within their organizations. A study by Raines and Twenge (2018) suggests that leaders who embrace technology can effectively manage and motivate diverse generations in the workforce, creating a cohesive and collaborative work environment.

Tech-savvy leaders are more likely to be continuous learners, staying up to date with the latest technological trends. Research by Lee and Wong (2018) emphasizes that these leaders actively seek opportunities to learn and adapt, making them better equipped to lead their organizations through digital transformation and disruptive innovations.

The literature on the leadership qualities of tech-savviness and digital fluency highlights their critical role in modern leadership. Leaders who possess these qualities can drive innovation, make informed decisions based on data insights, enhance communication and collaboration, and effectively manage diverse teams. In the ever-evolving digital landscape, tech-savviness and digital fluency are no longer optional but essential attributes for Business leaders to succeed in their roles. Organizations that recognize and nurture these qualities in their leaders are more likely to thrive in a technology-driven world, embracing change, and capitalizing on the opportunities presented by emerging technologies.

Embracing Diversity and Inclusion

Embracing diversity and inclusion has become a crucial aspect of effective leadership and organizational success. By examining the impact of inclusive leadership on team dynamics, innovation, and overall organizational performance, the author aims to understand how embracing diversity can create a more inclusive and productive work environment.

Diversity refers to the variety of differences among individuals in terms of race, ethnicity, gender, age, religion, sexual orientation, and other characteristics. Inclusion, on the other hand, focuses on creating an environment where all individuals feel valued, respected, and empowered to contribute their unique perspectives and talents. Cox and Blake (1991) emphasize that embracing diversity and fostering inclusion is critical for enhancing employee engagement, creativity, and organizational adaptability. A Study by Deloitte (2020) found that millennial leaders prioritise creating inclusive work environments that embrace diversity of thought, backgrounds, and experiences.

Research by Carmeli and Josman (2016) reveals that inclusive leadership positively impacts team dynamics. Leaders who promote diversity and inclusion are more likely to create a psychologically safe environment where team members feel comfortable expressing their ideas and challenging the status quo. These fosters open communication, collaboration, and higher levels of trust among team members, leading to improved team performance.

Diversity and inclusion have been linked to increased innovation and creativity within organizations. A study by Bell et al. (2018) demonstrates that diverse teams with inclusive leadership are more adept at generating novel ideas and solutions. The diverse perspectives and experiences of team members stimulate creativity, leading to a competitive advantage in today's fast-paced and dynamic business landscape.

Research by Ferdman and Deane (2014) indicates that organizations that prioritize diversity and inclusion experience higher levels of employee engagement and overall well-being. Inclusive leaders create a sense of belonging and psychological safety, which fosters greater job satisfaction and reduced turnover rates. Moreover, employees in inclusive workplaces are more likely to experience lower stress levels and higher work-life satisfaction.

Leaders who embrace diversity and inclusion actively advocate for fairness and equality within their organizations. A study by Shore et al. (2011) highlights that inclusive leaders implement policies and practices that promote equal opportunities and ensure that all employees are treated with dignity and respect, regardless of their backgrounds. This commitment to fairness and equality enhances employee morale and commitment to the organization.

Diverse and inclusive organizations are often perceived as more attractive by potential employees and customers. A research study by Hewlett et al. (2013) shows that companies with inclusive leadership are more likely to attract top talent and enjoy greater customer loyalty. In turn, this positive reputation contributes to higher organizational performance and sustainable growth.

The literature on embracing diversity and inclusion underscores its importance in contemporary leadership practices. Inclusive leaders cultivate a diverse and respectful work environment, driving team dynamics, fostering innovation, and enhancing employee engagement and well-being. Organizations that actively promote diversity and inclusion not only create a positive workplace culture but also gain a competitive advantage by leveraging the diverse perspectives and talents of their workforce. Embracing diversity and inclusion is no longer merely a moral imperative but a strategic approach to achieving organizational success in today's diverse and interconnected global landscape.

Purpose-Driven Leadership

Purpose-driven leadership is a leadership style that centres on a clear sense of mission, vision, and values, with a focus on making a positive impact beyond mere financial success. This literature review explores the significance of purpose-driven leadership in contemporary organizations.

Purpose-driven leadership is characterized by leaders who are deeply committed to a higher purpose beyond profits, aligning their organization's mission with societal or environmental goals. Steger et al. (2018) argue that purpose-driven leaders foster a sense of meaningfulness and fulfilment among employees, inspiring them to work towards a shared purpose. According to a study by PwC 2016, millennials seek leadership roles that align with their personal values and offer opportunities to make a positive impact on society.

Research by Bailey and Madden (2017) suggests that purpose-driven leadership plays a crucial role in motivating employees. When leaders articulate a compelling purpose that resonates with employees' values, it fosters a sense of connection and commitment to the organization's mission. Purpose-driven leaders create a positive work environment, where employees feel a sense of meaning and are more engaged in their work.

Purpose-driven leaders prioritize ethical considerations and long-term sustainability over short-term gains. A study by Maak and Pless (2009) highlights that leaders who operate from a clear sense of purpose are more likely to make ethical decisions, prioritize stakeholder interests, and contribute positively to society.

Purpose-driven leadership is a catalyst for shaping a strong organizational culture. The work of Serrat (2017) suggests that purpose-driven leaders instil a shared sense of purpose and values within the organization, creating a unifying force that aligns employees' efforts towards common goals. This sense of purpose strengthens teamwork and fosters a positive and cohesive organizational culture.

Research by Russo and Schoemaker (2019) demonstrates that purpose-driven leaders inspire innovation and creativity within their organizations. By encouraging employees to connect their work with the organization's purpose, leaders stimulate a sense of ownership and autonomy, leading to more innovative ideas and problem-solving approaches.

Purpose-driven leadership enhances relations with various stakeholders, including employees, customers, investors, and the community. A study by Mackey and Sisodia (2014) indicates that organizations led by purpose-driven leaders build strong relationships based on trust and mutual respect, which contributes to long-term sustainability and stakeholder loyalty.

The literature on purpose-driven leadership highlights its profound impact on employee motivation, ethical decision-making, organizational culture, innovation, and stakeholder relations. Purpose-driven Business leaders inspire their teams to go beyond conventional measures of success and focus on making a positive impact on society and the world. Organizations led by purpose-driven Business leaders are more likely to attract and retain top talent, foster a culture of trust and innovation, and achieve sustainable long-term success. As organizations face ever-increasing challenges and societal demands, purpose-driven leadership emerges as a vital approach to addressing complex issues and creating a meaningful and prosperous future for all stakeholders involved.

Collaborative Leadership Style

Collaborative leadership is a leadership style that emphasizes cooperation, teamwork, and shared decision-making. This literature review explores the significance of collaborative leadership in Business organizational contexts. By examining the impact of collaborative leadership on team effectiveness, organizational performance, and employee satisfaction, we aim to gain insights into how this leadership approach fosters a culture of collaboration and drives success in diverse settings.

Collaborative leadership involves leaders who actively seek input and involvement from team members in decision-making processes. According to Uhl-Bien and Arena (2018), collaborative leaders promote open communication, value diverse perspectives, and encourage cooperation to achieve common goals. Research by Clavelle et al. (2019) suggests that millennials prefer working in teams and value collective decision-making process the foster a collaborative and inclusive work environment where ideas are shared openly, and diverse perspectives are respected leading to increased creativity and engagement.

Research by Ancona et al. (2016) highlights that collaborative leadership positively affects team effectiveness. When leaders foster a collaborative culture, team members feel empowered and engaged, leading to higher levels of creativity, problem-solving, and collective performance.

Collaborative leadership plays a critical role in fostering innovation within organizations. A study by West and Sacramento (2012) suggests that leaders who encourage collaboration among employees create an environment where diverse ideas are exchanged and explored. This fosters a culture of continuous improvement and innovation.

Collaborative leadership contributes to higher employee satisfaction and retention. Research by Guillaume et al. (2019) shows that collaborative leaders actively involve employees in decision-making, leading to a greater sense of ownership and commitment to the organization. This, in turn, reduces turnover rates and enhances overall employee well-being.

Collaborative leadership is associated with building trust and positive relationships among team members. A study by Reeves et al. (2017) indicates that leaders who practice collaboration are perceived as approachable and supportive, leading to stronger interpersonal connections and improved cooperation among team members.

Collaborative leadership contributes to the development of learning organizations. Research by Schein (2016) suggests that leaders who value collaboration create an environment that encourages continuous learning and adaptation. This supports the organization's ability to navigate change and stay agile in dynamic markets.

Cross-Functional Collaboration

Cross-functional collaboration is a strategic approach that involves individuals from different departments or disciplines working together to achieve common organizational goals. According to O'Neill and Xiao (2017), cross-functional collaboration is essential for breaking down silos, sharing knowledge, and aligning diverse skills towards achieving collective business objectives.

Research by Ancona and Bresman (2007) highlights that cross-functional collaboration is positively linked to innovation and creativity. When employees from different areas collaborate, they bring together unique insights and diverse perspectives, fostering creativity and generating novel ideas.

Cross-functional collaboration enhances problem-solving capabilities within organizations. A study by Ibarra (2010) indicates that diverse teams formed through cross-functional collaboration are better equipped to analyze complex problems from multiple angles, leading to more effective decision-making.

Cross-functional collaboration contributes to improved organizational performance and efficiency. Research by Martins and Terblanche (2003) shows that when different departments collaborate seamlessly, information flows more smoothly, and processes become more streamlined, leading to enhanced productivity and overall performance.

Cross-functional collaboration positively impacts employee engagement and satisfaction. A study by Edmondson and McManus (2007) reveals that when employees work collaboratively across departments, they experience a greater sense of connection, pride, and engagement with their work, leading to higher job satisfaction.

Cross-functional collaboration creates a culture of continuous learning and knowledge sharing. Research by Leonard-Barton (1995) suggests that when individuals interact with colleagues from different backgrounds, they gain new insights and skills, leading to personal and professional development.

Cross-functional collaboration helps organizations overcome challenges effectively. A study by Heijstra and de Vries (2017) indicates that this collaborative approach allows organizations to leverage diverse expertise and resources to address complex problems that require input from multiple perspectives.

The literature on cross-functional collaboration highlights its significance in driving innovation, problem-solving, organizational performance, employee engagement, and learning within organizations. By breaking down departmental barriers, cross-functional collaboration enables organizations to harness the collective knowledge and skills of their workforce, leading to enhanced creativity, improved decision-making, and overall efficiency. This collaborative approach fosters a culture of cooperation and mutual respect among employees, contributing to higher employee satisfaction and retention. As organizations continue to face dynamic and complex challenges, cross-functional collaboration emerges as a critical factor in building agile, adaptable, and successful organizations in today's competitive business landscape.

Work-Life Balance and Employee Well-Being

Work-life balance refers to the equilibrium between an individual's professional responsibilities and personal life. This literature review explores the importance of work-life balance in promoting employee well-being and overall organizational performance. By examining the impact of work-life balance on employee health, job satisfaction, productivity, and retention, we aim to understand how organizations can foster a supportive work environment that prioritizes employee well-being.

Work-life balance is crucial for maintaining the physical, emotional, and mental well-being of employees. Greenhaus and Allen (2011) define work-life balance as the extent to which individuals can effectively manage their work-related demands and personal life commitments, without one negatively impacting the other. Research by Hira and Ghani 2(019) indicates that millennials prioritise their own wellbeing and the wellbeing of their team members.

Research by Hill et al. (2010) suggests that employees with better work-life balance experience improved mental health, reduced stress, and a lower risk of burnout. Organizations that prioritize work-life balance contribute to healthier and more motivated employees.

Work-life balance is linked to higher job satisfaction and organizational commitment. A study by Kalliath and Brough (2008) reveals that employees who perceive their organization as supportive of work-life balance are more likely to be satisfied with their jobs and remain committed to the organization.

Work-life balance positively influences employee productivity and performance. Research by Lockwood (2003) demonstrates that when employees have adequate time and resources to manage their personal and family obligations, they are more focused and engaged during work hours, leading to higher productivity levels.

Work-life balance initiatives play a significant role in reducing turnover rates and improving employee retention. A study by Thompson et al. (2016) indicates that organizations that offer flexible work arrangements and support work-life balance are more likely to retain their top talent.

Work-life balance practices contribute to enhanced employee engagement and commitment to the organization. A research study by Casper et al. (2007) suggests that employees who feel supported in managing their work and personal life are more likely to be engaged in their roles and feel a stronger sense of loyalty to the organization.

Work-life balance initiatives influence the overall organizational culture. A study by Allen et al. (2013) shows that organizations that value work-life balance create a positive and inclusive culture, leading to higher employee morale and a more supportive work environment.

The literature on work-life balance and employee well-being highlights its critical role in promoting employee health, job satisfaction, productivity, and retention. Organizations that prioritize work-life balance initiatives create a positive and supportive work environment, resulting in healthier and more engaged employees. The benefits of work-life balance extend beyond the individual level, as organizations experience higher productivity, reduced turnover, and a positive organizational culture. As the modern business workplace continues to evolve, recognizing the importance of work-life balance and implementing strategies to support employees' well-being becomes essential for building successful, resilient, and sustainable organizations.

CASE STUDIES OF SUCCESSFUL MILLENNIAL BUSINESS LEADERS

Case Study 1: Mark Zuckerberg—Co-Founder and CEO of Facebook

Mark Zuckerberg, born in 1984, is a prominent example of a successful millennial business leader. In 2004, while still a student at Harvard University, Zuckerberg co-founded Facebook, a social networking platform that has since grown into one of the largest and most influential companies in the world. As CEO of Facebook, Zuckerberg has demonstrated various leadership qualities that have contributed to the company's success.

Leadership Qualities

- **Visionary Leadership:** Visionary Leadership: Zuckerberg's vision for Facebook was to create a platform that connects people globally and facilitates meaningful interactions. His unwavering focus on this vision has guided the company's growth and development over the years.
- **Adaptability and Innovation:** Zuckerberg has shown adaptability in responding to changing market trends and technological advancements. Facebook has constantly evolved its features and services to meet user demands and stay ahead of the competition.
- **Purpose-Driven Leadership:** Zuckerberg has emphasized Facebook's mission of bringing the world closer together. He has prioritized social impact and philanthropy through initiatives like the Chan Zuckerberg Initiative, focusing on education, health, and other social challenges.

Case Study 2: Bhavish Aggarwal—Co-Founder and CEO of Ola

Background and career journey: Bhavish Aggarwal is the co-founder and CEO of Ola, India's leading ride-hailing platform. He started his entrepreneurial journey in 2010 when he co-founded Ola Cabs (now known as Ola). Aggarwal holds a bachelor's degree in computer science and engineering from the Indian Institute of Technology (IIT) Bombay. His passion for transforming the transportation industry in India led him to create Ola, which has become one of the most successful startups in the country.

Leadership Qualities Exhibited

Aggarwal has demonstrated several key leadership qualities throughout his career. He possesses a strong vision and the ability to inspire and motivate his team. His strategic thinking and problem-solving skills have enabled him to navigate through complex challenges in the highly competitive ride-hailing industry. Aggarwal also exhibits excellent communication skills, fostering transparency and trust within the organization.

- **Innovative strategies employed:** Aggarwal has employed various innovative strategies to drive Ola's growth and transformation. One of his notable strategies is the focus on customer-centricity. Ola has consistently introduced new features and services to enhance the user experience, such as in-app payments, ride-sharing options, and the integration of electric vehicles into their fleet. Aggarwal has also prioritized building strategic partnerships with automobile manufacturers, fleet owners, and government entities to expand Ola's reach and offerings.
- **Impact on organizational growth and transformation:** Under Aggarwal's leadership, Ola has witnessed significant growth and transformation. The company has expanded its operations across multiple cities in India and expanded internationally to countries like Australia, New Zealand, and the United Kingdom. Aggarwal's innovative strategies have helped Ola become a market leader in India's ride-hailing industry. Additionally, Ola's emphasis on sustainable transportation through initiatives like Ola Electric has contributed to the company's positive impact on the environment.

Aggarwal's leadership and innovative approach have not only propelled Ola's growth but have also revolutionized the transportation industry in India. By analysing his leadership qualities, strategies, and the impact on organizational growth, researchers can gain valuable insights into the success of millennial leaders in the Indian business landscape.

Case Study 3: Whitney Wolfe Herd—Founder and CEO of Bumble

Whitney Wolfe Herd, born in 1989, is a successful millennial Business leader known for her role in co-founding Tinder and later founding Bumble, a popular dating app with a unique focus on women's empowerment. Herd's leadership style has been instrumental in the success of Bumble.

Leadership Qualities

- **Empowerment and Inclusivity:** Herd's leadership philosophy centres on empowering women in both the workplace and the dating sphere. Bumble's unique feature, where women make the first move, reflects her commitment to gender equality and inclusivity.
- **Innovation and Disruption:** Herd's approach to dating app design disrupted the industry norms. By challenging traditional gender dynamics in online dating, she created a platform that resonates with modern values and preferences.
- **Authenticity and Transparency:** Herd's leadership is characterized by authenticity and transparency. She has openly shared her experiences as a woman in the tech industry, inspiring others to overcome challenges and pursue their ambitions.

Case Study 4: Vijay Shekhar Sharma—Founder and CEO of Paytm

Background and career journey: Vijay Shekhar Sharma is the founder and CEO of Paytm, India's leading digital payments and financial services platform. Born in Aligarh, Uttar Pradesh, Sharma displayed entrepreneurial spirit from a young age. He pursued a degree in engineering and later worked for various technology companies before venturing into entrepreneurship. In 2010, he founded Paytm with the aim of revolutionizing digital payments in India.

Leadership Qualities Exhibited

Sharma exhibits several key leadership qualities that have contributed to his success. He possesses a strong vision for transforming the financial services landscape in India. He is known for his relentless drive and determination, which has enabled him to overcome challenges and build a successful business. Sharma also demonstrates excellent communication skills and the ability to inspire and motivate his team.

- **Innovative strategies employed:** Sharma has implemented several innovative strategies to propel the growth of Paytm. One of the key strategies was focusing on mobile payments and creating a user-friendly digital wallet app. Paytm's user-friendly interface and seamless payment experience revolutionized the way Indians transact digitally. Additionally,

Sharma expanded Paytm's offerings beyond payments to include services such as e-commerce, wealth management, and digital banking, catering to the evolving needs of Indian consumers.

- **Impact on organizational growth and transformation:** Under Sharma's leadership, Paytm has experienced exceptional growth and transformation. The company has become synonymous with digital payments in India, catering to millions of users and partnering with numerous merchants across the country. Paytm's innovative strategies and emphasis on financial inclusion have played a significant role in transforming India's digital payments landscape. The company's success has also spurred the adoption of digital payments, driving India's transition toward a cashless economy.

Sharma's leadership, innovative strategies, and the resulting impact on organizational growth make him a compelling case study for understanding the leadership qualities of successful millennial business leaders in India. Analysing his journey and the transformative impact of Paytm can provide valuable insights into the role of technology, innovation, and entrepreneurial mindset in shaping the digital ecosystem of a country.

Case Study 5: Brian Chesky—Co-Founder and CEO of Airbnb

Born in 1981, Brian Chesky is a millennial Business leader who co-founded Airbnb in 2008. Under his leadership, Airbnb revolutionized the travel and hospitality industry by connecting travellers with unique accommodation options worldwide.

Leadership Qualities

- **Customer-Centric Approach:** Chesky's leadership is deeply rooted in understanding and meeting the needs of Airbnb's customers. He prioritizes feedback and constantly seeks ways to improve the user experience.
- **Resilience and Adaptability:** Chesky's ability to navigate challenges and adapt to changing market dynamics has been crucial in Airbnb's growth. He has successfully led the company through various regulatory and economic hurdles.
- **Purpose-Driven Innovation:** Chesky's vision for Airbnb goes beyond providing lodging; he envisions a world where people can belong anywhere. This purpose-driven approach has guided Airbnb's expansion and its commitment to diversity and inclusion.

Case Study 6: Ritesh Agarwal—Founder and CEO of OYO Rooms

Background and career journey: Ritesh Agarwal is the founder and CEO of OYO Rooms, a hospitality chain that offers affordable accommodations. He started his entrepreneurial journey at a young age and founded OYO Rooms in 2013 when he was only 19 years old. Agarwal dropped out of college to focus on building his business. His ambition and entrepreneurial spirit led him to create a disruptive model in the hospitality industry.

Leadership Qualities Exhibited

- **Agarwal possesses several noteworthy leadership qualities:** He demonstrates a strong vision and determination to disrupt the traditional hospitality sector in India. Agarwal is known for his innovative thinking and willingness to take risks. He also exhibits excellent strategic planning and execution skills, allowing him to steer OYO Rooms through rapid growth and expansion.
- **Innovative strategies employed:** Agarwal has implemented innovative strategies to drive the growth and success of OYO Rooms. One of his key strategies was transforming budget hotels into standardized, affordable accommodations by partnering with independent hoteliers. Agarwal leveraged technology to create a seamless booking experience for customers and streamlined operations for hotel partners. Additionally, he focused on delivering a consistent guest experience through quality control and training programs.
- **Impact on organizational growth and transformation:** Under Agarwal's leadership, OYO Rooms has achieved remarkable growth and transformation. The company expanded rapidly, not only within India but also internationally, establishing a presence in several countries. Agarwal's innovative strategies and emphasis on technology disrupted the hospitality industry, providing a platform for small hotel owners to access a larger customer base. OYO Rooms' success has had a profound impact on the Indian hospitality sector, transforming the way people experience budget accommodations.

Agarwal's leadership qualities, innovative strategies, and the resulting impact on organizational growth and transformation make him an excellent case study for understanding the leadership qualities of successful Indian millennial business leaders. Analysing his journey and achievements can provide valuable insights into the entrepreneurial mindset and strategies employed by millennial leaders in the Indian business landscape.

The case studies of Mark Zuckerberg, Bhavish Aggarwal, Whitney Wolfe Herd, Vijay Shekhar Sharma, and Brian Chesky, Ritesh Agarwal exemplify the leadership qualities of successful millennial leaders. These leaders have demonstrated visionary thinking, adaptability, innovation, and purpose-driven leadership. Their approaches to leadership have not only led to the success of their respective companies but also influenced industries and society at large. As the millennial generation continues to make significant contributions to the business world, studying their leadership styles can offer valuable insights for future leaders and organizations.

Implications for Organizations

Cultivating and supporting the development of millennial leaders is essential for organizations to remain competitive in today's dynamic business landscape. To effectively nurture millennial leadership, organizations should consider implementing the following practical recommendations:

- **Create a Leadership Development Program:** Establish a structured leadership development program specifically designed for millennials. This program should offer a blend of formal training, mentorship opportunities, coaching, and on-the-job experiences to help millennials build essential leadership skills and gain practical knowledge.
- **Emphasize Purpose and Meaning:** Millennials are driven by a sense of purpose and a desire to make a positive impact. Organizations should articulate a clear and compelling vision that aligns with their values and social impact goals. Encourage millennial leaders to connect with the organization's purpose and integrate it into their decision-making and leadership approach.
- **Foster a Culture of Learning and Growth:** Create a culture that promotes continuous learning and growth. Offer learning opportunities such as workshops, seminars, online courses, and access to relevant industry resources. Encourage millennial leaders to invest time in their personal and professional development.
- **Provide Opportunities for Cross-Functional Collaboration:** Encourage cross-functional collaboration to enable millennial leaders to work with diverse teams and gain exposure to different areas of the organization. Cross-functional projects help foster collaboration, problem-solving skills, and a broader understanding of the organization's operations.

- **Offer Flexible Work Arrangements:** Recognize the importance of work-life balance for millennial leaders. Provide flexible work arrangements, such as remote work options and flexible hours, to accommodate personal commitments and promote employee well-being.
- **Promote Diversity and Inclusion:** Embrace diversity and inclusion at all levels of the organization. Encourage millennial leaders to actively seek diverse perspectives and create inclusive environments that foster creativity and innovation.
- **Encourage Innovation and Risk-Taking:** Support millennial leaders in taking calculated risks and experimenting with new ideas. Foster a culture where failure is viewed as an opportunity for learning and growth, encouraging innovation and creativity.
- **Recognize and Celebrate Achievements:** Regularly recognize and celebrate the achievements of millennial leaders. Publicly acknowledge their contributions and efforts, which reinforces a positive and motivating work environment.
- **Provide Regular Feedback and Growth Opportunities:** Offer regular feedback and performance evaluations to millennial leaders. Provide opportunities for them to reflect on their progress and areas for improvement and support their growth through constructive feedback and coaching.
- **Enable Access to Technology and Digital Tools:** Millennial leaders are often tech-savvy and embrace digital tools for efficiency and collaboration. Ensure that they have access to the latest technology and resources to enhance their leadership capabilities.

By implementing these practical recommendations, organizations can effectively cultivate and support the development of millennial leaders. Providing a nurturing environment that aligns with millennials' values and aspirations will not only help organizations attract and retain top talent but also foster a generation of forward-thinking and impactful leaders who can drive the organization's success in the future.

Challenges Faced by Millennial Leaders in Transitioning to Key Roles

This paper examines the challenges faced by Millennial leaders as they transition into key roles, including scepticism from older generations, navigating the intricacies of cross-generational collaboration, and balancing technological advancements with human-centric leadership. These challenges not only affect the individual Millennial Business leader but also have broader implications for the organizations they lead and the communities they serve.

- **Scepticism from Older Generations:** Millennial leaders often encounter scepticism and resistance from older generations who may question their experience, skills, and ability to lead effectively. Overcoming this scepticism requires building trust through consistent performance, open communication, and demonstrating the value of their unique perspectives and approaches.
- **Navigating Cross-Generational Collaboration:** As Millennial leaders assume key roles; they often find themselves leading teams comprising members from different generations, including generation X and baby boomers. Navigating cross-generational collaboration can be challenging, as each generation may have different work styles, communication preferences, and expectations. Building strong relationships, fostering understanding, and adapting leadership approaches to accommodate diverse generational needs are essential for effective collaboration.
- **Balancing Technological Advancements and Human-Centric Leadership:** Millennial leaders are often hailed as digital natives, familiar with the latest technologies. However, striking a balance between leveraging technology and maintaining a human-centric leadership approach is crucial. Over-reliance on technology without considering human aspects such as empathy, effective communication, and building relationships can hinder leadership effectiveness.
- **Overcoming Perceived Entitlement:** Millennial leaders are sometimes stereotyped as entitled and lacking in work ethic due to generational generalizations. Overcoming these perceptions requires dispelling misconceptions through hard work, dedication, and consistently delivering results. Demonstrating a strong work ethic, resilience, and a willingness to go the extra mile can help Millennial leaders overcome such biases.
- **Managing Impatience for Rapid Progress:** Millennial leaders often possess a desire for rapid progress and change, driven by their ambition and familiarity with the fast-paced digital age. However, managing expectations and balancing long-term strategic goals with short-term milestones is essential. Millennial Business leaders need to demonstrate patience, strategic thinking, and the ability to align their ambitions with the realities of the business environment.

By acknowledging and actively addressing these challenges, Millennial Business leaders can navigate the transition into key roles more effectively. Their ability to build bridges with older generations, foster cross-generational collaboration, maintain a human-centric approach, dispel entitlement stereotypes, and manage expectations contributes to their growth and success as leaders.

CONCLUSION

In conclusion, understanding the considerations and characteristics of the Millennial Business leader is essential for creating a sustainable and thriving global society. By harnessing their unique skill set, values, and approach to leadership, organizations can foster environments that encourage innovation, diversity, and meaningful social impact. As we explore the dynamics of Millennial Business leadership, we lay the foundation for future research and practical recommendations to support and cultivate effective leadership in an increasingly interconnected and dynamic world.

FUTURE RESEARCH

Further research is needed to explore the long-term impact of these qualities on organizational performance and the effectiveness of Millennial Business leaders in different contexts.

REFERENCES

Allen, T. D., Eby, L. T., Poteet, M. L., Lentz, E., & Lima, L. (2013). Career benefits associated with mentoring for protégés: A meta-analysis. *The Journal of Applied Psychology*, *98*(3), 533–562.

Alsop, R. (2016). *The 2020 workplace: How innovative companies attract, develop, and keep tomorrow's employees today*. Jossey-Bass.

Ancona, D., Malone, T. W., Orlikowski, W. J., & Senge, P. M. (2016). In praise of the incomplete leader. *Harvard Business Review*, *94*(2), 92–100. PMID:17345683

Bailey, C., & Madden, A. (2017). What makes millennials different? A new review. *Journal of Management Development*, *36*(1), 95–111.

Bell, B. S., Kanar, A. M., & Kozlowski, S. W. J. (2018). Current perspectives on millennial leadership. *Industrial and Organizational Psychology: Perspectives on Science and Practice*, *11*(4), 412–424.

Cao, Q., Gedajlovic, E. R., & Zhang, H. (2019). When and how does entrepreneurial orientation influence the growth of family firms? *Entrepreneurship Theory and Practice*, *43*(1), 146–173.

Carmeli, A., & Josman, Z. E. (2016). When leadership powers team performance: The moderating role of individual-level and team-level power. *The Leadership Quarterly*, *27*(2), 312–326.

Carmeli, A., Meitar, R., & Weisberg, J. (2013). Self-leadership skills and innovative behavior at work. *International Journal of Manpower*, *34*(2), 122–135.

Casper, W. J., Eby, L. T., Bordeaux, C., Lockwood, A., & Lambert, D. (2007). A review of research methods in IO/OB work-family research. *The Journal of Applied Psychology*, *92*(1), 28–43. doi:10.1037/0021-9010.92.1.28 PMID:17227149

Choi, S. L., & Eboch, K. (2018). Transformational leadership, empowerment, and organizational commitment: Evidence from Korean organizations. *Journal of World Business*, *53*(4), 493–503.

Clavelle, J. T., Drenkard, K., Tullai-McGuinness, S., Fitzpatrick, J. J., & Galloway, S. (2019). Authentic leadership, empowerment and nurse-assessed adverse patient outcomes. *Journal of Nursing Management*, *27*(7), 1457–1465.

Cox, T., & Blake, S. (1991). Managing cultural diversity: Implications for organizational competitiveness. *The Academy of Management Perspectives*, *5*(3), 45–56. doi:10.5465/ame.1991.4274465

Deloitte. (2020). *The millennial survey 2020: Reshaping the workplace*. Deloitte Development LLC.

DeRue, D. S., & Ashford, S. J. (2010). Who will lead and who will follow? A social process of leadership identity construction in organizations. *Academy of Management Review*, *35*(4), 627–647.

Dinh, J. E., Lord, R. G., Gardner, W. L., Meuser, J. D., Liden, R. C., & Hu, J. (2014). Leadership theory and research in the new millennium: Current theoretical trends and changing perspectives. *The Leadership Quarterly*, *25*(1), 36–62. doi:10.1016/j.leaqua.2013.11.005

Ferdman, B. M., & Deane, B. R. (2014). *Diversity at work: The practice of inclusion*. John Wiley & Sons.

Greenhaus, J. H., & Allen, T. D. (2011). Work-family balance: A review and extension of the literature. In J. C. Quick & L. E. Tetrick (Eds.), *Handbook of occupational health psychology* (2nd ed., pp. 165–183). American Psychological Association.

Gregersen, H. B., Morrison, A. J., & Black, J. S. (2013). Developing leaders for the global frontier. *Organizational Dynamics*, *42*(1), 12–25.

Guillaume, Y. R., Dawson, J. F., Otaye-Ebede, L., Woods, S. A., & West, M. A. (2019). Harnessing demographic differences in organizations: What moderates the effects of workplace diversity? *Journal of Organizational Behavior*, *40*(3), 276–303. PMID:28239234

Hewlett, S. A., Sherbin, L., & Sumberg, K. (2013). How Gen Y & Boomers will reshape your agenda. *Harvard Business Review*, *91*(7/8), 71–76. PMID:19630257

Hill, R., Stahl, G., & Cooke, F. (2010). The human resource management profession: A comprehensive review. *Journal of Management Studies*, *47*(3), 534–557.

Hira, A., & Ghani, U. (2019). Generational differences and employee well-being: The moderating role of work–family interface. *Journal of Business Ethics*, *158*(4), 1009–1026.

Kalliath, T., & Brough, P. (2008). Work-life balance: A review of the meaning of the balance construct. *Journal of Management & Organization*, *14*(3), 323–327. doi:10.5172/jmo.837.14.3.323

Lee, A., & Wong, S. (2018). Understanding work-life balance and well-being outcomes: The role of work-life interference and facilitation. *Journal of Happiness Studies*, *19*(7), 2101–2124.

Lockwood, N. R. (2003). Workplace diversity: Leveraging the power of difference for competitive advantage. *HRMagazine*, *48*(6), 1–14.

Maak, T., & Pless, N. M. (2009). Business leaders as citizens of the world. *Advances in Global Leadership*, *5*, 225–256.

Mackey, A., & Sisodia, R. S. (2014). *Conscious capitalism: Liberating the heroic spirit of business*. Harvard Business Review Press.

PwC. (2016). *The millennial mind: How millennial preferences will shape the economy*. PwC Consumer Intelligence Series.

Raines, C., & Twenge, J. (2018). *Managing Millennials: How to bridge the generation gap*. American Management Association.

Reeves, M., Levin, S., & Ueda, D. (2017). *The longevity dividend: Work in an era of 100-year lives*. Harvard Business Review Press.

Russo, R., & Schoemaker, P. (2019). *Winning with uncertainty: Modern leadership lessons from history's great strategic thinkers*. Oxford University Press.

Schein, E. H. (2016). *Organizational culture and leadership* (5th ed.). Wiley.

Serrat, O. (2017). Building a learning organization. In *Knowledge solutions: Tools, methods, and approaches to drive organizational performance* (2nd ed., pp. 79–86). Springer.

Shore, L. M., Randel, A. E., Chung, B. G., Dean, M. A., Ehrhart, K. H., & Singh, G. (2011). Inclusion and diversity in work groups: A review and model for future research. *Journal of Management, 37*(4), 1262–1289. doi:10.1177/0149206310385943

Simsek, Z., & Heavey, C. (2011). The mediating role of knowledge-based capital for corporate entrepreneurship and radical innovation in large, diversified firms. *Strategic Entrepreneurship Journal, 5*(4), 317–337.

Steger, M. F., Dik, B. J., & Duffy, R. D. (2018). Measuring meaningful work: The work and meaning inventory (WAMI). *Journal of Career Assessment, 26*(3), 514–527.

Thompson, L. F., Cramton, C. D., & O'Connor, K. M. (2016). Subgroups of newcomers and socialization outcomes: How organizations can leverage informal groups. *Academy of Management Journal, 59*(3), 802–822.

Uhl-Bien, M., & Arena, M. (2018). Leadership for organizational adaptability: A theoretical synthesis and integrative framework. *The Leadership Quarterly, 29*(1), 89–104. doi:10.1016/j.leaqua.2017.12.009

Vasilopoulos, N. L., Ng, K. Y., Xanthopoulou, D., Chasiotis, A., van der Heijden, B. I., & de Witte, H. (2020). Work-related needs and job crafting: A longitudinal study among employees in Greece. *European Journal of Work and Organizational Psychology, 29*(4), 569–582.

Weill, P., & Woerner, S. (2013). Thriving on digital ecosystems. *MIT Sloan Management Review, 55*(1), 27–34.

West, M., & Sacramento, C. A. (2012). Creativity and innovation implementation in work groups: The paradoxical role of demands. *Journal of Organizational Behavior, 33*(6), 704–724.

Wong, C. S., & Gardiner, E. (2017). Leadership and creativity: A meta-analytic review. *Psychological Bulletin, 143*(4), 367–409.

Yukl, G., & Lepsinger, R. (2004). *Flexible leadership: Creating value by balancing multiple challenges and choices*. Jossey-Bass.

Compilation of References

Abbasi, S. G., Shabbir, M. S., Abbas, M., & Tahir, M. S. (2020). HPWS and knowledge sharing behavior: The role of psychological empowerment and organizational identification in public sector banks. *Journal of Public Affairs, 2512*. Advance online publication. doi:10.1002/pa.2512

Abu Bakar, H., & Connaughton, S. L. (2022). Ethical leadership, perceived leader–member ethical communication and organizational citizenship behavior: Development and validation of a multilevel model. *Leadership and Organization Development Journal, 43*(1), 96–110. doi:10.1108/LODJ-07-2021-0356

Adams, K. (2021). *The audacity: When Black women decide for themselves*. FaithandLeadership.com

Adegoke, O., Walimba, F. O., & Myers, A. (2012). Innovation Strategy, Human Resource policy and firm's revenue growth: The roles of envoronmental uncertaintly and inovation perfomance. *A Journal of Decision Sciences Institute, 43*(2), 273-301.

Aggarwal, J. (2022). Yukl, GA, & Gardner, WL (2020). Leadership in Organizations. Pearson Education, Inc. *Journal of Leadership Studies, 16*(3), 57–60. doi:10.1002/jls.21826

Ahmad, M. G., Klotz, A. C., & Bolino, M. C. (2021). Can good followers create unethical leaders? How follower citizenship leads to leader moral licensing and unethical behavior. *The Journal of Applied Psychology, 106*(9), 1374–1390. doi:10.1037/apl0000839 PMID:32955268

Ajayi-Hackworth, F, (2021). A Point of View: You Don't Sound Black. *TheInclusionSolution.Me.*

Alblooshi, M., Shamsuzzaman, M., & Haridy, S. (2021). The relationship between leadership styles and organisational innovation: A systematic literature review and narrative synthesis. *European Journal of Innovation Management, 24*(2), 338–370. doi:10.1108/EJIM-11-2019-0339

Albrecht, S. L., & Marty, A. (2017). Personality, self-efficacy and job resources and their associations with employee engagement, affective commitment and turnover intentions. *International Journal of Human Resource Management*. doi:10.1080/09585192.2017.1362660

Alesso-Bendisch, F. (2020). Millennials want a healthy work-life balance. here's what bosses can do. *Forbes*. https://www.forbes.com/sites/ellevate/2020/07/23/millennials-want-a-healthy-work-life-balance-heres-what-bosses-can-do/?sh=7d37e6127614

Alkaabi, M., Kudus, N., & Ab Rahman, Z. (2022). A Literature Review on the Impact of Work Environment, Leadership Styles and Resilience on Job Performance in UAE. *Journal of Pharmaceutical Negative Results*, 2332–2341. doi:10.47750/pnr.2022.13.S06.304

Allen, T. D., Eby, L. T., Lentz, E., & Lima, L. (2004). Career benefits associated with mentoring for protégés. *The Journal of Applied Psychology*, *89*(1), 127–138. doi:10.1037/0021-9010.89.1.127 PMID:14769125

Allen, T. D., Eby, L. T., Poteet, M. L., Lentz, E., & Lima, L. (2013). Career benefits associated with mentoring for protégés: A meta-analysis. *The Journal of Applied Psychology*, *98*(3), 533–562.

Allio, R. (2007). Bad leaders: How they get that way and what to do about them. *Strategy and Leadership*, *35*(3), 12–17. doi:10.1108/10878570710745785

Allio, R. J. (2018). Barbara Kellerman: There's a better way to train leaders. *Strategy and Leadership*, *46*(6), 22–27. doi:10.1108/SL-09-2018-0083

Alsop, R. (2008). *The trophy kids grow up: How the millennial generation is shaking up the workplace*. Jossey-Bass.

Alsop, R. (2016). *The 2020 workplace: How innovative companies attract, develop, and keep tomorrow's employees today*. Jossey-Bass.

Alter, C. (2020, January 23). How millennial leaders will change America. *Time*. https://time.com/5770140/millennials-change-american-politics/

Althnayan, S., Alarifi, A., Bajaba, S., & Alsabban, A. (2022). Linking environmental transformational leadership, environmental organizational citizenship behavior, and organizational sustainability performance: A moderated mediation model. *Sustainability (Basel)*, *14*(14), 8779. doi:10.3390u14148779

Amabile, T. M. (1996). *Creativity and innovation in organizations* (Vol. 5). Harvard Business School.

Ancona, D., Malone, T. W., Orlikowski, W. J., & Senge, P. M. (2016). In praise of the incomplete leader. *Harvard Business Review*, *94*(2), 92–100. PMID:17345683

Andriopoulos, C. (2001). Determinants of organisational creativity: A literature review. *Management Decision*, *39*(10), 834–841. doi:10.1108/00251740110402328

Ansell, C., Sørensen, E., & Torfing, J. (2022). *Co-creation for sustainability: The UN SDGs and the power of local partnerships*. Emerald Publishing. doi:10.1108/9781800437982

Arnold, J., & Kowalski-Braun, M. (2011). The journey to an inaugural chief diversity officer: Preparation, implementation and beyond. *Innovative Higher Education*, *37*(1), 27–36. doi:10.100710755-011-9185-9

Arora, N., & Dhole, V. (2019). Generation Y: Perspective, engagement, expectations, preferences, and satisfactions from workplace; a study conducted in Indian context, Benchmarking. *Benchmarking, 26*(5), 1378–1404. Advance online publication. doi:10.1108/BIJ-05-2018-0132

Arsenault, P. M. (2004). Validating generational differences: A legitimate diversity and leadership issue. *Leadership and Organization Development Journal, 25*(1/2), 124–141. doi:10.1108/01437730410521813

Asante, M. K. (1998). The African American as African. *Diogenes, 46*(184), 39–50. doi:10.1177/039219219804618405

ASCD. (2015) *Leadership Matters Building Principals' Capacity with the ASCD Principal Leadership Development Framework*. ASCD. https://files.ascd.org/staticfiles/ascd/pdf/siteASCD/publications/leadership-matters-whitepaper.pdf

Ashford, S. J., & Sitkin, S. B. (2019). From problems to progress: A dialogue on prevailing issues in leadership research. *The Leadership Quarterly, 30*(4), 454–460. doi:10.1016/j.leaqua.2019.01.003

Ashveen, N. (2018). The Effect of Personality on Motivation and Organisational Behaviour. *Psychol Behav Sci Int J., 9*(2), 555760. doi:10.19080/PBSIJ.2018.09.555760

Avdeeff, M. Mangaoang, A., Fogarty Woehrel, M., Viñuela, E., Tinsley, O.N., Kooijman, J., & Iddon, M. (2020). Beyoncé: At Work, On Screen, and Online. Bloomington: Indiana University Press.

Baig, S. A., Iqbal, S., Abrar, M., Baig, I. A., Amjad, F., Zia-ur-Rehman, M., & Awan, M. U. (2021). Impact of leadership styles on employees' performance with moderating role of positive psychological capital. *Total Quality Management & Business Excellence, 32*(9-10), 1085–1105. doi:10.1080/14783363.2019.1665011

Bailey, C., & Madden, A. (2017). What makes millennials different? A new review. *Journal of Management Development, 36*(1), 95–111.

Baldonado, A., & Spangenburg, J. (2009). Leadership and the future: Gen Y workers and two-factor theory. *The Journal of American Academy of Business, Cambridge, 15*(1), 99–103.

Banks, L. (2019). *Emerging Scholars, Transforming the future. 2019 Annual Report*. The Leadership Alliance.

Baporikar, N. (2021). Human Resource Management for Managing Cultural Diversity. In I. Management Association (Ed.), Research Anthology on Empowering Marginalized Communities and Mitigating Racism and Discrimination (pp. 976-1004). IGI Global. doi:10.4018/978-1-7998-8547-4.ch046

Baporikar, N. (Ed.). (2018). *Global Practices in Knowledge Management for Societal and Organizational Development*. IGI Global. doi:10.4018/978-1-5225-3009-1

Baporikar, N. (Ed.). (2023). *Leadership and Governance for Sustainability*. IGI Global. doi:10.4018/978-1-6684-9711-1

Barkley, R. A. (2022). Parents as Shepherds, Not Engineers, Journal. *The ADHD Report, 30*(8), 11–14. doi:10.1521/adhd.2022.30.8.11

Bass, B. M. (1990). *Bass and Stioghills's Handbook of Leadership: Theory, reaserch and managerial applications*. Free Press.

Bass, B. M. (1999). Two Decades of Research and Development in TRansformational Leadership. *European Journal of Work and Organizational Psychology, 8*(1), 9–32. doi:10.1080/135943299398410

Bass, B. M., & Riggio, R. E. (2006). *Transformational leadership* (2nd ed.). Lawrence Erlbaum Associates Publishers. doi:10.4324/9781410617095

Bastardoz, N., & Day, D. V. (2022). *Integrating leadership and power: a micro process model. Leadership: Leaders, Folowers, Contexts*. Information Age Publishing.

Battle, M. (2021). *How Tutu's Spirituality Incorporated Christian Mysticism with the African Notion of Interdependency*. Religion News Service.

Beckwith, A. (2018). C.S.Peirce and Adduction Inference. Johnson County Community College Honors Journal, 10(1).

Beiter, B. (2021). *The implications of modern mentorship in building self-efficacy and succession potential for millennial school leaders*. [Doctoral dissertation, Robert Morris University]. ProQuest Dissertations Publishing. https://www.proquest.com/openview/f392e8c1338d20817e08d3c24b9d38b3/1?pq-origsite=gscholar&cbl=18750&diss=y

Bellamy, W. (2019). *Monumental: it was never about a statue*. BlackGold Publishing.

Bell, B. S., Kanar, A. M., & Kozlowski, S. W. J. (2018). Current perspectives on millennial leadership. *Industrial and Organizational Psychology: Perspectives on Science and Practice, 11*(4), 412–424.

Bell, C., Chan, M., & Nel, P. (2014). The Impact of Participative and Directive Leadership on Organisational Culture: An Organisational Development Perspective *Mediterranean Journal of Social Sciences. Mediterranean Journal of Social Sciences, 5*(23), 1970–1985. doi:10.5901/mjss.2014.v5n23p1970

Bell, C., Dodd, N., & Mjoli, T. (2018). The effect of participative and directive leadership on team effectiveness among administrative employees in a South African Tertiary Institution. *The Social Science Journal, 55*, 81–91.

Bell, E. (2008). Exploring employee perception of the work environment along generational lines. *Performance Improvement, 47*(9), 35–45. doi:10.1002/pfi.20032

Bencie, L., & Khadim, B. (2022, October 7). Imposter syndrome causes a decline in leadership. *IACSP Journal*. https://iacspjournal.com/uncategorized/imposter-syndrome-causes-a-decline-in-leadership/

Berge, Z. L., & Berge, M. B. (2019). The economic ABCs of educating and training generations X, Y, and Z. *Performance Improvement*, *58*(5), 44–53. doi:10.1002/pfi.21864

Bhatia, S., & Priya, K. R. (2018). Decolonizing culture: Euro-American psychology and the shaping of neoliberal selves in India. *Theory & Psychology*, *28*(5), 645–668. doi:10.1177/0959354318791315

Bialik, K., & Fry, R. (2019). *Millennial life: How young adulthood today compares with prior generations*. Pew Research Center's Social & Demographic Trends Project. https://www.pewresearch.org/social-trends/2019/02/14/millennial-life-how-young-adulthood-today-compares-with-prior-generations-2/

Bialystok, E., Majumder, S., & Martin, M. M. (2003, March). there a bilingual advantage? *Applied Psycholinguistics*, *24*(1), 27–44. doi:10.1017/S014271640300002X

Bittner, A. (2019). Mentoring millennials for nursing leadership. *Nursing*, *49*(10), 53–56. doi:10.1097/01.NURSE.0000580656.81188.ee PMID:31568084

Blanchard, K., Zigarmi, P., & Zigarmi, D. (1985). *Leadrship and the one munite Manager: Increasing effectiveness Through Sitiuational Leadership*. William Morrow.

Blay, N., Donoghue, J., Duffield, C. M., Moran, P., & Stasa, H. (2011). Factors impacting career progression for nurse executives. *Contemporary Nurse*, *38*(1), 45–56. https://www.ncbi.nlm.nih.gov/pubmed/21854237 PMID:21854237

Bolman, L. G., & Deal, T. E. (2003). *Reframing organizations: Artistry, choice, and leadership* (3rd ed.). Jossey-Bass.

Bolman, L. G., & Deal, T. E. (2003). *Reframing organizations: Artistry, choice, and leadership (Jossey-Bass Higher and adult education series)*. Jossey Bass Inc.

Bordas, J. (2012). *Salsa, soul, and spirit: Leadership for a multicultural age* (2nd ed.). Berrett-Koehler.

Bos-Nehles, A., Renkema, M., & Janssen, M. (2017). HRM and innovative work behaviour: A systematic literature review. *Personnel Review*, *46*(7), 1228–1253. doi:10.1108/PR-09-2016-0257

Bozer, G., & Jones, R. J. (2018). Understanding the factors that determine workplace coaching effectiveness: A systematic literature review. *European Journal of Work and Organizational Psychology*, *27*(3), 342–361. doi:10.1080/1359432X.2018.1446946

Brabaw, K. (2021, November 2). FYI: Perfectionism is definitely a type of impostor syndrome. *Women's Health*. https://www.womenshealthmag.com/health/a27018815/what-is-impostor-syndrome/?utm_source=google&utm_medium=cpc&utm_campaign=arb_ga_whm_md_pmx_us_urlx&gclid=Cj0KCQjw0oyYBhDGARIsAMZEuMvzIBPlhWwLT7thnmgg1ff4iBA-CCKR5-dnq16um9Z0trSo59nVe3caAtBQEALw_wcB

Brant, K. K., & Castro, S. L. (2019). You can't ignore millennials: Needed changes and a new way forward in entitlement research. *Human Resource Management Journal*, *29*(4), 1–12. doi:10.1111/1748-8583.12262

Brem, A., Nylund, P., & Viardot, E. (2020). The impact of the 2008 financial crisis on innovation: A dominant design perspective. *Journal of Business Research, 110*, 360–369. doi:10.1016/j.jbusres.2020.01.048

Broughton, R. S., Plaisime, M. V., & Green, P. M. C. (2019). Mentorship: The necessity of intentionality. *The American Journal of Orthopsychiatry, 89*(3), 317–320. doi:10.1037/ort0000412 PMID:31070416

Brown, M. C. II. (2013). The declining significance of historically Black colleges and universities: Relevance, reputation, and reality in Obamamerica. *The Journal of Negro Education, 82*(1), 3–19. doi:10.7709/jnegroeducation.82.1.0003

Brown, T. (2021). *Feeding the Soul (Because It's My Business)*. Finding Our Way to Joy, Love, and Freedom.

Brozek, C. (2020, May 5). *Five ways to make your thought leadership content stand out when the whole world is turning to digital*. Forrester. https://www.forrester.com/blogs/how-to-create-great-b2b-marketing-thought-leadership-content/

Burns, J. M. (1978). *Leadership*. Harper & Row.

Burstein, D. D. (2013). *Fast Future: How the millennial generation is shaping our world*. Beacon Press.

Byars-Winston, A., Leverett, P., Benbow, R. J., Pfund, C., Thayer-Hart, N., & Branchaw, J. (2019). Race and ethnicity in biology research mentoring relationships. *Journal of Diversity in Higher Education*.

Campbell, S. (2015). *5 Ways, Criticism and Rejection Builds your Capacity to Succeed*. Entrepreneur.com

Caniëls, M., Neghina, C., & Schaetsaert, N. (2016). Ambidexterity of employees: The role of empowerment and knowledge sharing. *Journal of Knowledge Management*. doi:10.1108/JKM-10-2016-0440

Cao, Q., Gedajlovic, E. R., & Zhang, H. (2019). When and how does entrepreneurial orientation influence the growth of family firms? *Entrepreneurship Theory and Practice, 43*(1), 146–173.

Carey, H. (2016). *Ubuntu: My life in other people*. Matador.

Carmeli, A., & Josman, Z. E. (2016). When leadership powers team performance: The moderating role of individual-level and team-level power. *The Leadership Quarterly, 27*(2), 312–326.

Carmeli, A., Meitar, R., & Weisberg, J. (2013). Self-leadership skills and innovative behavior at work. *International Journal of Manpower, 34*(2), 122–135.

Carnevale, J. B., Huang, L., Crede, M., Harms, P., & Uhl-Bien, M. (2017). Leading to Stimulate Employees' Ideas: A Quantitative Review of Leader-Member Exchange, Employee Voice, Creativity, and Innovative Behavior. *Applied Psychology, 66*(4), 517–552. doi:10.1111/apps.12102

Carter, C. M. (2019, January 13). Why so many millennials experience impostor syndrome. *Forbes*. https://www.forbes.com/sites/christinecarter/2016/11/01/why-so-many-millennials-experience-imposter-syndrome/?sh=11f1a17d6aeb

Carter, A. D., Sims, C., & de Peralta, A. M. (2020). Blazing the trail: A qualitative case study of mentoring in a gender equity leadership development program. *Journal of Business Diversity*, *20*(2), 35–49.

Carter, E. D., & Cordero, M. L. (2022). Salir Adelante: Social capital and resilience during the Covid-19 pandemic in Argentina. *Health & Place*, *77*, 102870. doi:10.1016/j.healthplace.2022.102870 PMID:35933852

Carter, F. (2016). *Generation X and Millennial Generation Assistant Principals' Perceptions of the Challenges and Rewards of the Principalship*. Virginia Polytechnic Institute and State University.

Carter, T. D., & Walker, W. D. (2018). Retaining, cultivating, and investing: Strategies for leading millennial managers. *Journal of Government Financial Management*, *67*(2), 20–25.

Casper, W. J., Eby, L. T., Bordeaux, C., Lockwood, A., & Lambert, D. (2007). A review of research methods in IO/OB work-family research. *The Journal of Applied Psychology*, *92*(1), 28–43. doi:10.1037/0021-9010.92.1.28 PMID:17227149

Cavanaugh, J. C. (2017). Who will lead? the success of succession planning. *Journal of Management Policy and Practice*, *18*(2), 22–27. http://www.na-businesspress.com/JMPP/CavanaughJC_Web18_2_.pdf

Çebi, A., & Reisoğlu, İ. (2022). Defining "digitally competent teacher": An examination of pre-service teachers' metaphor. *Journal of Digital Learning in Teacher Education*, *38*(4), 185–198. doi:10.1080/21532974.2022.2098210

Chao, G. T. (2009). Formal mentoring: Lessons learned from past practice. *Professional Psychology, Research and Practice*, *40*(3), 314–320. doi:10.1037/a0012658

Chaturvedi, S., Rizvi, I. A., & Pasipanodya, E. T. (2019). How Can Leaders Make Their Followers to Commit to the Organization? the Importance of Influence Tactics. *Global Business Review*, *20*(6), 1462–1474. doi:10.1177/0972150919846963

Chaturvedi, S., & Singh, T. (2021). "Knowledge management initiatives for tackling the COVID-19 pandemic in", Metamorphosis. *Journal of Management Research*, *20*(1), 25–34. 10.1177%2F09726225211023677

Cheng, M. (2022, April 14). 8 characteristics of Millennials That Support Sustainable Development Goals (sdgs). *Forbes*. https://www.forbes.com/sites/margueritacheng/2019/06/19/8-characteristics-of-millennials-that-support-sustainable-development-goals-sdgs/?sh=7f99a0b029b7

Chicca, J., & Shellenbarger, T. (2018). Connecting with generation Z: Approaches in nursing education. *Teaching and Learning in Nursing*, *13*(3), 180–184. doi:10.1016/j.teln.2018.03.008

Chigangaidze, R. K. (2021). Utilising Ubuntu in social work practice: Ubuntu in the eyes of the multimodal approach. *Journal of Social Work Practice*. doi:10.1080/02650533.2021.1981276

Chillakuri, B. (2020). Understanding Generation Z expectations for effective onboarding. Journal of Organizational Change Management, *33*(7), 1277-1296.

Chillakuri, B., & Mahanandia, R. (2018). Generation Z entering the workforce: The need for sustainable strategies in maximizing their talent. *Human Resource Management International Digest*, *26*(4), 34–38. doi:10.1108/HRMID-01-2018-0006

Choi, S. L., & Eboch, K. (2018). Transformational leadership, empowerment, and organizational commitment: Evidence from Korean organizations. *Journal of World Business*, *53*(4), 493–503.

Chua, A. (2011). *Battle Hymn of the Tiger Mother*. Bloomsbury Publishing PLC.

Clance, P., & Imes, S. A. (1978). The impostor phenomenon in high achieving women: Dynamics and therapeutic intervention. *Psychotherapy: Theory, Research and Practice, 15*, 241-247.

Clavelle, J. T., Drenkard, K., Tullai-McGuinness, S., Fitzpatrick, J. J., & Galloway, S. (2019). Authentic leadership, empowerment and nurse-assessed adverse patient outcomes. *Journal of Nursing Management*, *27*(7), 1457–1465.

Claytor, P., & Pittman, C. (2020). *Black Privilege: Modern Middle-Class Blacks with Credentials and Cash to Spend*. Stanford University Press. www.sup.org/books/title/?id=25892 doi:10.1515/9781503613188

Coe, C., Piggott, C., Davis, A., Hall, M. N., Goodell, K., Joo, P., & South-Paul, J. E. (2020). Leadership pathways in academic family medicine: Focus on underrepresented minorities and women. *Family Medicine*, *52*(2), 104–111. doi:10.22454/FamMed.2020.545847 PMID:31940426

Cox, K., & Tamir, C. (2022). *Race is Central to Identity for Back Americans and Affects How They Connect With Each Other.* PewResearch.

Cox, T., & Blake, S. (1991). Managing cultural diversity: Implications for organizational competitiveness. *The Academy of Management Perspectives*, *5*(3), 45–56. doi:10.5465/ame.1991.4274465

Craig, C. A., Allen, M. W., Reid, M. F., Riemenschneider, C. K., & Armstrong, D. J. (2013). The impact of career mentoring and psychosocial mentoring on affective organizational commitment, job involvement, and turnover intention. *Administration & Society*, *45*(8), 949–973. doi:10.1177/0095399712451885

Creswell, J. W., & Creswell, J. D. (2017). *Research design: Qualitative, quantitative, and mixed methods approaches*. Sage publications.

Crumbley, J. L., III. (2021). *Millennial Leadership: A Phenomenological Assessment into the Preparedness of the Millennial Leader* [Doctoral dissertation, Northcentral University].

Crumpacker, M., & Crumpacker, J. (2007). Succession planning and generational stereotypes: Should HR consider age-based values and attitudes a relevant factor or a passing fad? *Public Personnel Management, 36*(4), 349–369. doi:10.1177/009102600703600405

Csikszentmihalyi, M., & Seligman, M. (2000). Positive psychology. *The American Psychologist, 55*(1), 5–14. doi:10.1037/0003-066X.55.1.5 PMID:11392865

Cziraki, K., Read, E., & Spence Laschinger, H. K., & Wong, C. (2018). Nurses' leadership self-efficacy, motivation, and career aspirations. *Leadership in Health Services, 31*(1), 47-61.

Dahl, M. (2013, February 8). *Millennials are the most stressed-out generation, new survey finds.* NBCNews.com. https://www.nbcnews.com/health/health-news/millennials-are-most-stressed-out-generation-new-survey-finds-flna1b8296642

Daloz, L. A. (1986). *Effective teaching and mentoring.* Jossey Bass.

Darby, J. (2020). *Black Millennials: Identity, Ambition, and Activism.* Lexington Books.

Darity, W. A., Mullen, A. K., & Mullen, A. K. (Andrea K. (2020). From here to equality: reparations for Black Americans in the twenty-first century. The University of North Carolina Press.

Darvishmotevali, M., Arasli, H., & Kilic, H. (2017). Effect of job insecurity on frontline employee's performance: Looking through the lens of psychological strains and leverages. *International Journal of Contemporary Hospitality Management, 29*(6), 1724–1744. doi:10.1108/IJCHM-12-2015-0683

Das, B. L., & Baruah, M. (2013). Employee retention: A review of the literature. *IOSR Journal of Business and Management, 14*(2), 8–16. doi:10.9790/487X-1420816

Davids, I., Appiah, K., Davids, G., & Ofori, F. N. K. (2021). The effectiveness of transformational leadership: a qualitative-based study on millennial perceptions in South Africa. *Archives of Business Research.*

Davis, S. & Gopal, T. (2022). Serena Williams became the greatest tennis player of all-time even as she endured racist and sexist attacks in the media. *Insider.com.*

De Bruyn, S. (2017). *An Afrocentric Inquiry on Lived Experiences of Ubuntu Among Isizulu-Speaking Persons From Different Geographic Areas, South Africa.* School of Applied Human Sciences at the University of KwaZulu- Natal.

de Geus, C. J., Ingrams, A., Tummers, L., & Pandey, S. K. (2020). Organizational citizenship behavior in the public sector: A systematic literature review and future research agenda. *Public Administration Review, 80*(2), 259–270. doi:10.1111/puar.13141

De Roeck, K., & Farooq, O. (2017). Corporate Social Responsibility and Ethical Leadership: Investigating Their Interactive Effect on Employees' Socially Responsible Behaviors. *Journal of Business Ethics.* Advance online publication. doi:10.100710551-017-3656-6

Deal, J. J., & Levenson, A. (2016). *What millennials want from work: How to maximize engagement in today's workforce.* McGraw Hill.

Deloitte. (2020). *The millennial survey 2020: Reshaping the workplace*. Deloitte Development LLC.

Delorey, R. (2010). Evidence-based Millennials. *Workplace Review*, *7*(1), 37-46. http://library2.smu.ca/xmlui/bitstream/handle/01/24770/001_fulltextdec2010_000.pdf?sequence=1&isAllowed=y

Denckla, C. A., Cicchetti, D., Kubzansky, L. D., Seedat, S., Teicher, M. H., Williams, D. R., & Koenen, K. C. (2020). Psychological resilience: An update on definitions, a critical appraisal, and research recommendations. *European Journal of Psychotraumatology*, *11*(1), 1822064. doi:10.1080/20008198.2020.1822064 PMID:33244362

DeRue, D. S., & Ashford, S. J. (2010). Who will lead and who will follow? A social process of leadership identity construction in organizations. *Academy of Management Review*, *35*(4), 627–647.

Descartes, R. (1637). *Discourse on the Method of Rightly Conducting the Reason, and Seeking*. Truth in the Sciences.

Desimone, L. M., Hochbert, E. D., Porter, A. C., Polikoff, M. S., Schwartz, R., & Johnson, L. J. (2014). Formal and informal mentoring: Complementary, compensatory or consistent? *Journal of Teacher Education*, *65*(2), 88–99. doi:10.1177/0022487113511643

DeVaney, S. (2015). Understanding the millennial generation. *Journal of Financial Service Professionals*, *69*(6), 11–14.

Dimitriou, C. K. (2022). The critical role that national culture and ethical leadership play in fostering employee commitment to service quality in the hotel industry. *Research in Hospitality Management*, *12*(3), 255–271. doi:10.1080/22243534.2022.2133770

Dimock, M. (2019). *Defining generations: Where millennials end and generation Z begins*. Pew Research Center. https://www.pewresearch.org/fact-tank/2019/01/17/where-millennials-end-and-generation-z-begins/

Dinh, J. E., Lord, R. G., Gardner, W. L., Meuser, J. D., Liden, R. C., & Hu, J. (2014). Leadership theory and research in the new millennium: Current theoretical trends and changing perspectives. *The Leadership Quarterly*, *25*(1), 36–62. doi:10.1016/j.leaqua.2013.11.005

Dinibutun, S. R. (2020). Leadership: A comprehensive review of literature, research and theoretical framework. *Research and Theoretical Framework*.

Dladla, T. (2020). *Exploring ethical leadership practices in challenging township school contexts: a multiple case study*

Donahue, J. (2021, November 30). *How to better lead millennials in 2021*. Jenn Donahue. https://www.jenndonahue.com/news-and-views/how-to-better-lead-millennials-in-2021

Douglas, T.-R. M. O., & Little, M. (2017). Voice From the Field. *The Journal of Negro Education*, *86*(3), 381–391. doi:10.7709/jnegroeducation.86.3.0381

Drucker, P. F. (1998). *The coming of a new organisation*. Harvard Business Review, January -February.

DuBrin, A. J. (1995). *Leadership: Research findings, practice, skills*. Houghton Mifflin.

Duignan, P., & Jackson, R. H. (2022). *Politics and government in African states: 1960-1985*. Taylor & Francis. doi:10.4324/9781003312130

Dulin, L. (2008). Leadership preferences of a generation Y cohort: A mixed-methods investigation. *Journal of Leadership Studies*, *2*(1), 43–59. doi:10.1002/jls.20045

Easton, C., & Steyn, R. (2023). Millennial leaders and leadership styles displayed in the workplace. *South African Journal of Business Management*, *54*(1), a3139. doi:10.4102ajbm.v54i1.3139

Egan, K. S. (1996). Flexible mentoring: Adaptations in style for women's ways of knowing. *Journal of Business Communication*, *33*(4), 401–425. doi:10.1177/002194369603300403

Elam, C., Stratton, T., & Gibson, D. (2007). Welcoming a new generation to college: The millennial students. *Journal of College Admission*, *195*, 20–25.

Ellis, A. (n.d.). *What Jay-Z's 4:44 Means for Black Millennial Leaders*. Aerialellis. https://aerialellis.wordpress.com/tag/black-millennial-leaders/

Erdem, F., & Aytemur, J. O. (2008). Mentoring: A relationship based on trust: Qualitative research. *Public Personnel Management*, *37*(1), 55–66. doi:10.1177/009102600803700104

Erin, M. (2012). Relationships of leader reward behavior with employee behavior. *Leadership and Organization Development Journal*, *33*(7), 646–661. doi:10.1108/01437731211265232

Everatt, D., & Ebrahim, Z. (2020). Urban policy in South Africa. *Developing national urban policies: Ways forward to green and smart cities*, 281-298.

Falola, T. (2022). Global African Business Leaders. The Palgrave Handbook of Africa and the Changing Global Order, 1099-1115. Palgrave.

Fasanella, K. (2019). Serena Williams Shares the History of Hair Braiding in a Touching Photo with her Daughter. *Allure.com*.

Ferdman, B. M., & Deane, B. R. (2014). *Diversity at work: The practice of inclusion*. John Wiley & Sons.

Ferlazzo, L. (2019). *When People Say They Don't See Race 'I Ask Them if They Don't See Me'*. EducatonWeek.org.

Ferrari, J. R. (2005). Impostor Tendencies and Academic Dishonesty: Do They Cheat Their Way to Success? *Social Behavior and Personality*, *33*(1), 11–17. https://doi-org.vsu.idm.oclc.org/10.2224/sbp.2005.33.1.11. doi:10.2224bp.2005.33.1.11

France, D., Leahy, M., & Parsons, M. (2009). Attracting, developing, and retaining talent. *Research Technology Management*, *52*(6), 33–44. doi:10.1080/08956308.2009.11657598

Fries, K. (2018). 7 Ways millennials are changing traditional leadership. *Forbes*. https://www.forbes.com/sites/kimberlyfries/2018/01/18/7-ways-millennials-are-changing-traditional-leadership/

Fries, K. (2018, January 31). 7 Ways Millennials Are Changing Traditional Leadership. *Forbes*. https://www.forbes.com/sites/kimberlyfries/2018/01/18/7-ways-millennials-are-changing-traditional-leadership/?sh=217d541d7dae

Fry, R. (2018). *Millennials are the largest generation in the U.S. labor force. Fact Tank: News in the Numbers*. Pew Research Center. Available: https://www.pewresearch.org/fact-tank/2018/04/11/millennials-largest-generation-us-labor-force

Fry, R., & Parker, K. (2018). *Early benchmark Shows 'Post-Millennials' on Track to be Most Diverse, Best-Educated Generation Yet*. Pew Research Center.

Fullan, M. (2022). *Michael Fullan on Leading Change in a New Era*. Victorian Academy of Teaching and Leadership. https://www.academy.vic.gov.au/learning-resources/michael-fullan-leading-change-new-era

Gabriel, A. G. & Alvarez, J. (2020). How Do Millennial Managers Lead Older Employees? *The Philippine Workplace Experience*. SAGE. journals.sagepub.com/home/sgo doi:10.1177/2158244020914651

Gale, F. S. (2015). Forget millennials: Are you ready for gen Z? *Chief Learning Officer*, *14*(7), 38–48.

Gallup. (2016). *How millennials want to work and live*. Gallup. https://www.gallup.com/workplace/238073/millennials-work-live.aspx

Ganske, P., & Carbon, C.-C. (2023). Successful clusters through successful communication: Why clusters should be managed by Place Leaders. *Frontiers in Communication*, *8*, 1194103. doi:10.3389/fcomm.2023.1194103

Gao, Y., & He, W. (2017). Corporate social responsibility and employee organizational citizenship behavior: The pivotal roles of ethical leadership and organizational justice. *Management Decision*, *55*(2), 294–309. doi:10.1108/MD-05-2016-0284

Gardner, J. W. (1990). *On leadership*. The Free Press.

Garmon, C. W., & Mgijima, M. (2012). *Using Ubuntu: A New Research Trend for Developing Effective Communication across Cultural Barriers*. Communication Faculty Publication. https://digitalcommons.wku.edu/comm_fac_pub/1

Garnand, I. (2021). *How Transitional, Restorative, and Transformative Justice Will Address Racial Injustice*. [University Honors Theses, U.C. Law].

Gassam, A. (2021). Understanding the White Gaze and How it Impacts Your Workplace. *Forbes.com*.

Genon, L. J. D. (2023). 9 Toward 2030. *Sustainable Development Goal 16 and the Global Governance of Violence: Critical Reflections on the Uncertain Future of Peace*.

Ghislieri, C., Molino, M., & Cortese, C. G. (2018). Work and Organizational Psychology Looks at the Fourth Industrial Revolution: How to Support Workers and Organizations? *Frontiers in Psychology*, *9*, 2365. doi:10.3389/fpsyg.2018.02365 PMID:30546335

Ghosh, K., & Sahney, S. (2011). Impact of organizational sociotechnical system on managerial retention: A general linear modeling approach. *Journal of Modelling in Management*, *6*(1), 33–59. doi:10.1108/17465661111112494

Ghosh, R., Reio, T. G. Jr, & Haynes, R. K. (2012). Mentoring and organizational citizenship behavior: Estimating the mediating effects of organization-based self-esteem and affective commitment. *Human Resource Development Quarterly*, *23*(1), 41–63. doi:10.1002/hrdq.21121

Gibson, D. E. (2003). Developing the professional self-concept: Role model construals in early, middle, and late career stages. *Organization Science*, *14*(5), 591–610. doi:10.1287/orsc.14.5.591.16767

Gilani, H. (2017). University of Brighton, UK*Lucy Cunningham, University of Brighton, UK, Employer branding and its influence on employee retention: A literature review. *The Marketing Review, 17* (2), pp.239-256 doi:10.1362/146934717X14909733966209

Gilbreath, B., & Benson, P. G. (2004). The contribution of supervisor behaviour to employee psychological well-being. *Work & Stress, 18*(3), 255-266.

Giovanni, N. (1968). Dreams. Black Feeling, Black Talk, Black Judgment. HarperCollins Publishers.

Gouldner, K. (2016). Millennial mindset: How to attract millennials to an aging industry. *GEN*, *75*(66), 65.

Grace, C. & Rosenberg, S. (2016). Nielsen Report, Young, Connected, and Black. *African American Consumer Report.*

Graen, G. B., & Uhl-Bien, M. (1995). Relationship-based approach to leadership: Development of leader-member exchange (LMX) theory of leadership over 25 years: Applying a multi-level multi-domain perspective. *The Leadership Quarterly*, *6*(2), 219–247. doi:10.1016/1048-9843(95)90036-5

Graham, T. M., Coleman, C., & Coleman, J. (2021). Teachable moments and strategies for first-time leaders. In M. Guah (Ed.), *Handbook of research on innate leadership characteristics and examinations of successful first-time leaders* (pp. 1–15). IGI Global. doi:10.4018/978-1-7998-7592-5.ch001

Graves, L. (2020). *Black Millennial Movement Seeks to Offer Different Perspective Among Black Leaders.* KATU (Channel 2).

Green, D. (2007). Leading a postmodern workforce. *Academy of Strategic Management Journal*, *6*, 15–26.

Green, D. (2008). Value transformation in 21st century organizations. *Journal of Organizational Culture. Communication and Conflict*, *12*(2), 95–102.

Greenhaus, J. H., & Allen, T. D. (2011). Work-family balance: A review and extension of the literature. In J. C. Quick & L. E. Tetrick (Eds.), *Handbook of occupational health psychology* (2nd ed., pp. 165–183). American Psychological Association.

Gregersen, H. B., Morrison, A. J., & Black, J. S. (2013). Developing leaders for the global frontier. *Organizational Dynamics*, *42*(1), 12–25.

Gregory, S. (2021). Motherhood Could Have Cost Olympian Allyson Felix. She Wouldn't let it. *Time.com*.

Grotkamp, L., Schaumann, J. M., & Riehm, P. (2020). Millennial Leaders' Display Of Generational Cohort Stereotypes: A Qualitative Research Approach. *Journal of leadership in Organizations*, *2*(2).

Grow, J. M., & Yang, S. (2018). Generation-Z enters the advertising workplace: Expectations through a gendered lens. *Journal of Advertising Education*, *22*(1), 7–22. doi:10.1177/1098048218768595

Grybauskas, A., Stefanini, A., & Ghobakhloo, M. (2022). Social sustainability in the age of digitalization: A systematic literature Review on the social implications of industry 4.0. *Technology in Society*, *70*, 101997. doi:10.1016/j.techsoc.2022.101997

Guillaume, Y. R., Dawson, J. F., Otaye-Ebede, L., Woods, S. A., & West, M. A. (2019). Harnessing demographic differences in organizations: What moderates the effects of workplace diversity? *Journal of Organizational Behavior*, *40*(3), 276–303. PMID:28239234

Gupta, T. (2018). Changing the face of instructional practice with twitter: generation-Z perspectives. In *Communicating Chemistry through Social Media* (pp. 151–172). American Chemical Society. doi:10.1021/bk-2018-1274.ch009

Gwagwa, A., Kazim, E., & Hilliard, A. (2022). The role of the African value of Ubuntu in global AI inclusion discourse: A normative ethics perspective. *Patterns (New York, N.Y.)*, *3*(4), 100462. doi:10.1016/j.patter.2022.100462 PMID:35465235

Gwala, R. S. (2022). A framework for corporate governance and organisational performance in the Fourth Industrial Revolution (Doctoral dissertation).

Gwala, R. S., & Mashau, P. (2023). Tracing the Evolution of Agency Theory in Corporate Governance. In *Governance as a Catalyst for Public Sector Sustainability* (pp. 260–285). IGI Global.

Hackman, M., & Johnson, C. (2009). *Leadership: A communication perspective* (5th ed.). Waveland Press.

Hamm, L. (2017). Becoming a transformative vice-principal in culturally and linguistically rich diverse schools. *International Journal of Mentoring and Coaching in Education*, *6*(2), 82–98. doi:10.1108/IJMCE-11-2016-0072

Han, J., LaMarra, D., & Vapiwala, N. (2017). Applying lessons from social psychology to transform the culture of error disclosure. *Medical Education*, *51*(10), 996–1001. doi:10.1111/medu.13345 PMID:28523743

Hanks, T. L. (2008). The Ubuntu Paradigm: Psychology's Next Force? *Journal of Humanistic Psychology*, *48*(1), 116–135. doi:10.1177/0022167807303004

Hannon, K. (2018). Black Women Entrepreneurs; The Good and Not-so-Good News. *Forbes.*

Haque, A., Fernando, M., & Caputi, P. (2019). The relationship between responsible leadership and organisational commitment and the mediating effect of employee turnover intentions: An empirical study with Australian employees. *Journal of Business Ethics*, *156*(3), 759–774. doi:10.100710551-017-3575-6

Hardy, J. (2020). *Symone Sanders viewed as millennial force for candidates*. TheGrio. https://thegrio.com/2020/02/04/symone-sanders-viewed-as-millennial-force-for-candidates/

Harrison, A. E. (2015). *Millennial leadership development: Building competencies with best practices* [Doctoral dissertation, University of Maryland University College].

Haserot, P. (2007). Generational transformation, leadership, development, and much more. *Of Counsel, 26*(7), 5-9.

Hawkins-Moore, V. (2022). *Ubuntu Epistemology, Sankofa Scale, Africana Womanism, and African American Male Theory in Leadership: African American Mentoring*. IGI Global.

Haynie, D. (2016). Millennial Leaders Around the World. *U.S. News*. https://www.usnews.com/news/best-countries/slideshows/10-millennial-leaders-around-the-globe

Hechl, C. (2017). Affective commitment to organizations: A comparative study of reverse mentoring versus traditional mentoring among millennials. *Binus Business Review, 8*(2), 157-165.

Henderson, A. C., & Rhodes, S. M. (2022). "Got sold a dream and it turned into a nightmare": The victim-offender overlap in commercial sexual exploitation. *Journal of Human Trafficking*, *8*(1), 33–48. doi:10.1080/23322705.2021.2019530

Hernandez, J. S., Poole, K. G. Jr, & Grys, T. E. (2018). Mentoring millennials for future leadership. *Physician Leadership Journal*, *5*(3), 41.

Hewlett, S. A., Sherbin, L., & Sumberg, K. (2013). How Gen Y & Boomers will reshape your agenda. *Harvard Business Review*, *91*(7/8), 71–76. PMID:19630257

Hicks, R., & Hicks, K. (1999). *Boomers, Xers, and other strangers*. Tyndale House.

Hideg, I., & Shen, W. (2019). Why still so few? A theoretical model of the role of benevolent sexism and career support in the continued underrepresentation of women in leadership positions. *Journal of Leadership & Organizational Studies*, *26*(3), 287–303. doi:10.1177/1548051819849006

Hill-Collins, P. Black Women and Motherhood. In *Black Feminist Thought*. Routledge.

Hill, L. H., & Wheat, C. A. (2017). The influence of mentorship and role models on university women leaders' career paths to university presidency. *Qualitative Report*, *22*(8), 2090–2111. doi:10.46743/2160-3715/2017.2437

Hill, R., Stahl, G., & Cooke, F. (2010). The human resource management profession: A comprehensive review. *Journal of Management Studies*, *47*(3), 534–557.

Hill, R., Walsh, F. J., Davies, J., Sparrow, A., Mooney, M., Council, C. L., Wise, R. M., & Tengö, M. (2020). Knowledge co-production for Indigenous adaptation pathways: Transform post-colonial articulation complexes to empower local decision-making. *Global Environmental Change*, *65*, 102161. doi:10.1016/j.gloenvcha.2020.102161

Hira, A., & Ghani, U. (2019). Generational differences and employee well-being: The moderating role of work–family interface. *Journal of Business Ethics*, *158*(4), 1009–1026.

Hmieleski, K. M., & Carr, J. C. (2007). The relationship between entrepreneur psychological capital and well-being. *Frontiers of Entrepreneurship Research.*

Ho Sang, F. R. (2022). *Does race still matter? An exploration of race and mentoring relationships from the perspective of early career teachers of color and mentors.* [Doctoral dissertation, CUNY Hunter College]. Academicworks. https://academicworks.cuny.edu/hc_sas_etds/921

Holbrook, R. L., & Holbrook, A. R. (2021). For Such a Time as This: Helping Students Understand Power and Authority by Examining National Events from Spring 2020. *Christian Business Academy Review, 16.*

Holliday, W., & Li, Q. (2004). Understanding the millennials: Updating our knowledge about students. *RSR. Reference Services Review*, *32*(4), 356–366. doi:10.1108/00907320410569707

House, F. (2023). *Freedom in the World 2022: The Annual Survey of Political Rights and Civil Liberties*. Rowman & Littlefield.

Howe, N., & Strauss, W. (2003). *5 characteristics of millennials*. Michigan Scouting. https://michiganscouting.org/wp-content/uploads/2017/11/Five-Characteristics-of-Millennials.pdf

Howe, N., & Strauss, W. (2000). *Millennials rising: The next great generation*. Random House.

Hughes, D. Allan Leeb, Amy Wei Tianc, Alex Newmand, Alison Le good. (2018). *The Leadership Quarterly*. Advance online publication. doi:10.1016/j.leaqua.2018.03.001

Ince, F. (2023). Transformational Leadership in a Diverse and Inclusive Organizational Culture. Handbook of Research on Promoting an Inclusive Organizational Culture for Entrepreneurial Sustainability, 188-201.

Inceoglu, I., Thomas, G., Chu, C., Plans, D., & Gerbasi, A. (2018). Leadership behavior and employee well-being: An integrated review and a future research agenda. *The Leadership Quarterly*, *29*(1), 179-202. doi:10.1016/j.leaqua.2017.12.006

Iruka, I. U. (2013). The Black family: Re-imagining family support and engagement. In *Being Black is not a risk factor: A strengths-based look at the state of the Black child* (pp. 18–23). National Black Child Development Institute.

Iverson, A. (2019). General business: Developing and executing a corporate mentorship program. *Journal of Pension Benefits, 27*(1), 51–53. https://pinnacle-plan.com/wp-content/uploads/2020/02/Amanda-Iverson-Article-Developing-and-Executing-a-Corporate-Mentorship-Program.pdf

Jacob, M. U., Chukwuemaka, O., & Nkatomba, E. N. (2022). Political Leadership and Socio-economic Development of Rivers State. *Central Asian Journal of Social Sciences and History, 3*(4), 29–45.

Jacobs, T., & Jaques, E. (1987). Leadership in complex systems. In J. Zeider (Ed.), *Human productivity enhancement: Organizations, personnel, and decision making* (Vol. 2, pp. 7–65). Praeger.

Jameson, R. (2013). Amos Wilson: Toward a Liberation Psychology. *The Journal of Pan African Studies, 6*(2).

Jason Han, L. P., & Snyman, A. M. (2018). Personal factors in talent retention in the South African banking industry. *Journal of Psychology in Africa, 28*(6), 455–461. doi:10.1080/14330237.2018.1544393

Jauregui, J., Watsjold, B., Welsh, L., Ilgen, J. S., & Robins, L. (2020). Generational 'othering': The myth of the Millennial learner. *Medical Education, 54*(1), 60–65. doi:10.1111/medu.13795 PMID:31515842

Jayadeva, R. (2018). Mentoring millennials: Perceptions and analysis. *College and University, 93*(2), 29–33.

Jefferies, F. L., & Hunte, T. L. (2003). Generations and motivation: A connection worth making. *Journal of Behavioral and Applied Management, 6*(1), 37–70.

Johnson, J. A., & Lopes, J. (2008). The intergenerational workforce, revisited. *Organization Development Journal, 26*(1), 31–36.

Johnson, M. O., Fuchs, J. D., Sterling, L., Sauceda, J. A., Saag, M. S., Fernandez, A., Evans, C. H., & Gandhi, M. (2021). A mentor training workshop focused on fostering diversity engenders lasting impact on mentoring techniques: Results of a long-term evaluation. *Journal of Clinical and Translational Science, 5*(1), e116. doi:10.1017/cts.2021.24 PMID:34221458

Johny, R. M. (2022, April 8). *BuzzFix: Is impostor syndrome special to millennials or are we all just human?* News18. https://www.news18.com/news/buzz/buzzfix-is-impostor-syndrome-special-to-millennials-gen-z-or-are-we-all-just-human-4952846.html

Jones, J. T. (2021). *An Illumination of the Road to Resilience for Black Millennial Teachers as a Means of Addressing the Black Teacher Shortage*. Liberty University.

Joo, B.-K., & Jo, S. J. (2017). The effects of perceived authentic leadership and core self-evaluations on organizational citizenship behavior: The role of psychological empowerment as a partial mediator. *Leadership and Organization Development Journal, 38*(3), 463–481. doi:10.1108/LODJ-11-2015-0254

Jubenville, C. B. (2016). Colin Kaepernick and millennials. *The Washington Times*. https://www.washingtontimes.com/news/2016/sep/8/colin-kaepernick-and-millennials/

Kalliath, T., & Brough, P. (2008). Work-life balance: A review of the meaning of the balance construct. *Journal of Management & Organization*, *14*(3), 323–327. doi:10.5172/jmo.837.14.3.323

Kananen, J. (2020). Why Did Beyonce Create Alter-Ego Sasha Fierce? *Showbiz Cheatsheet*. https://www.cheatsheet.com/entertainment/why-did-beyonce-create-alter-ego-Sasha-fierce.html/

Kapitan, T. (1992). Peirce and the Autonomy of Abductive Reasoning. *Erkenntnis (1975-)*, *37*(1), 1–26. https://www.jstor.org/stable/20012421

Kaplan, M., Lawson, K. A., & McCrady, V. (2018). The hero viewpoint and the perception of mentors: Why millennials need mentors and why they have problems finding them. *Academy of Business Research Journal*, *2*, 36–52.

Karima, S., Uusiautti, S., & Määttä, K. (2022). Defining the core of successful millennial leadership. *European Journal of Workplace Innovation*, *7*(1), 109–131. doi:10.46364/ejwi.v7i1.917

Karimi, S., Ahmadi Malek, F., Yaghoubi Farani, A., & Liobikienė, G. (2023). The role of transformational leadership in developing innovative work behaviors: The mediating role of employees' psychological capital. *Sustainability (Basel)*, *15*(2), 1267. doi:10.3390u15021267

Kauffman, C. (2006). Positive psychology: The science at the heart of coaching. *Evidence based coaching handbook: Putting best practices to work for your clients*. Springer.

Kerdpitak, C., & Jermsittiparsert, K. (2020). The Impact of Human Resource Management Practices on Competitive Advantage: Mediating Role of Employee Engagement in Thailand. *Systematic Reviews in Pharmacy*, *11*, 443–452. doi:10.5530rp.2020.1.56

Khan, M. R. (2021). A critical analysis of Elon Musk's leadership in Tesla motors. *Journal of Global Entrepreneurship Research*, *11*(1), 213–222. doi:10.100740497-021-00284-z

Khassawneh, O., & Elrehail, H. (2022). The effect of participative leadership style on employees' performance: The contingent role of institutional theory. *Administrative Sciences*, *12*(4), 195. doi:10.3390/admsci12040195

Khoreva, V., & Wechtler, H. (2018). HR practices and employee performance: The mediating role of well-being. *Employee Relations*, *40*(2), 227–243. doi:10.1108/ER-08-2017-0191

Kilber, J., Barclay, A., & Ohmer, D. (2014). Seven tips for managing Generation Y. *Journal of Management Policy & Practice*, *15*(4), 50–91. http://www.na-businesspress.com/JMPP/BarclayA_Web15_4_.pdf

King, R., & Kuschminder, K. (Eds.). (2022). *Handbook of Return Migration*. Edward Elgar Publishing. DOI., doi:10.4337/9781839100055

Kiunguyu, K. (2020). *Ghana's Year of Return Campaign Dramatically Boosts the Country's Destination Profile*. ThisIsAfrica.me

Klein, K. J., & House, R. J. (1995). On Fire: Charismatic Leadership and Levels of Analysis. *The Leadership Quarterly*, *6*(2), 183–198. doi:10.1016/1048-9843(95)90034-9

Klimkiewicz, K., & Oltra, V. (2017). Does CSR Enhance Employer Attractiveness? The Role of Millennial Job Seekers' Attitudes. *Corporate Social Responsibility and Environmental Management*, *24*(5), 449–463. doi:10.1002/csr.1419

Kolotouchkina, O., Viñarás-Abad, M., & Mañas-Viniegra, L. (2023). Digital Ageism: Emerging Challenges and Best Practices of Age-Friendly Digital Urban Governance. *Media and Communication*, *11*(3), 6–17. doi:10.17645/mac.v11i3.6711

Korkmaz, A. V., Van Engen, M. L., Knappert, L., & Schalk, R. (2022). About and beyond leading uniqueness and belongingness: A systematic review of inclusive leadership research. *Human Resource Management Review*, *32*(4), 100894. doi:10.1016/j.hrmr.2022.100894

Koulopoulos, T., & Keldsen, D. (2014). *The Gen Z Effect: The six forces shaping the future of business*. Routledge.

Kouzes, J. M., & Posner, B. Z. (2007). *The leadership challenge* (4th ed.). Jossey-Bass.

Kram, K. E., & Higgins, M. C. (2009). A new mindset on mentoring: Creating developmental networks at work. *MIT Sloan Management Review*. https://provost.utsa.edu/mentoring/docs/Kram-Higgins.pdf

Kram, K. E. (1985). *Mentoring at work: Developmental relationships in organizational life*. Scott Foresman.

Kram, K. E., & Isabella, L. A. (1985). Mentoring alternatives: The role of peer relationships in career development. *Academy of Management Journal*, *28*(1), 110–132. doi:10.2307/256064

Kravis, N. (2021). Charisma. *The Psychoanalytic Quarterly*, *90*(4), 523–554. doi:10.1080/00332828.2021.1983332 PMID:35312425

Kruglanski, A., Pierro, A., & Higgins, E. (2007). Regulatory mode and preferred leadership styles: How fit increases job satisfaction. *Basic and Applied Social Psychology*, *29*(2), 137–149. doi:10.1080/01973530701331700

Kundu, S. C., & Lata, K. (2017). Effects of supportive work environment on employee retention: Mediating role of organizational engagement. *The International Journal of Organizational Analysis*, *25*(4), 703–722. doi:10.1108/IJOA-12-2016-1100

Kunjufu, J. (2005). *Keeping black boys out of special education*. African American Images.

Kurniadi, K., Meiliyandrie, L., & Rahmah, R. (2023). *Digital Mapping of Resilience and Academic Skills in the Perspective of Society 5.0 for Higher Education Level Students*. Qeios. doi:10.32388/FO9ZQO

Kyles, D. (2005). Managing your multigenerational workforce. *Strategic Finance*, *87*(6), 52–55.

LaBelle, D. M. (2018). *Millennials' experiences with succession planning: A Basic Qualitative Study.* [Doctoral dissertation, Capella University]. Proquest Dissertations Publishing. https://www.proquest.com/openview/4a9552b8e83b7caa86ea01289b94ed97/1?pq-origsite=gscholar&cbl=18750

Lancaster, L., & Stillman, D. (2002). *When generations collide: Who they are. Why they clash. How to solve the generational puzzle at work.* Harper Collins.

Langan, K. (2012). Training Millennials: A practical and theoretical approach. *RSR. Reference Services Review, 40*(1), 24–48. doi:10.1108/00907321211203612

Lanier, K. (2017). 5 Things HR professionals need to know about generation Z: Thought leaders share their views on the HR profession and its direction for the future. *Strategic HR Review, 16*(6), 288–290. doi:10.1108/SHR-08-2017-0051

Lastikova, M. (2023). *Context-Specific Peace Education Initiatives within local communities in Western Cape.* Lessons from Ubuntu.

Lazányi, K., & Bilan, Y. (2017). Generetion Z on the labourmarket - do they TrustOthers within TheirWorkplace? *Polish Journal of Management Studies, 16*(1), 78–93. doi:10.17512/pjms.2017.16.1.07

Le Roux, M., & Davis, D. (2019). *Lawfare: Judging Politics in South Africa.* Jonathan Ball Publishers.

Lebowitz, S. (2016, January 12). Men are suffering from a psychological phenomenon that can undermine their success, but they're too ashamed to talk about it. *Business Insider.* https://www.businessinsider.com/men-suffer-from-impostor-syndrome-2016-1

Lee, A., & Wong, S. (2018). Understanding work-life balance and well-being outcomes: The role of work-life interference and facilitation. *Journal of Happiness Studies, 19*(7), 2101–2124.

Legg, D. (2020, June 16). How long should you wait to switch positions within a company after you start? *The Washington Post.* https://jobs.washingtonpost.com/article/how-long-should-you-wait-to-switch-positions-within-a-company-after-you-start/

Leon, R. A. (2014). The chief diversity officer: An examination of CDO models and strategies. *Journal of Diversity in Higher Education, 7*(2), 77–91. doi:10.1037/a0035586

Li, J., Bonn, M. A., & Ye, B. H. (2019). Hotel employee's artificial intelligence and robotics awareness and its impact on turnover intention: The moderating roles of perceived organizational support and competitive psychological climate. *Tourism Management, 73*, 172–181. doi:10.1016/j.tourman.2019.02.006

Lipkin, N. A., & Perrymore, A. J. (2009). *Y in the workplace: Managing the "me first" generation.* The Career Press.

Littleton, K.T. (2015). *Mentoring Generation Y employees and retention in organizations: A phenomenological study.* [Unpublished doctoral dissertation, University of Phoenix].

Llopis, G. (2022). 5 powerful things happen when a leader is transparent. *Forbes*. https://www.forbes.com/sites/glennllopis/2012/09/10/5-powerful-things-happen-when-a-leader-is-transparent/?sh=3efd86f84a3a

Lockhat, P.R. (2018). What Serena Williams's scary childbirth story says about medical treatment Of Black women. *Vox.com*.

Lockwood, N. R. (2003). Workplace diversity: Leveraging the power of difference for competitive advantage. *HRMagazine*, *48*(6), 1–14.

Lomas, T. (2015). Positive social psychology: A multilevel inquiry into sociocultural well-being initiatives. *Psychology, Public Policy, and Law*, *21*(3), 338–347. doi:10.1037/law0000051

Lomas, T., Hefferon, K., & Ivtzan, I. (2015). The LIFE model: A meta-theoretical conceptual map for applied positive psychology. *Journal of Happiness Studies*, *16*(5), 1347–1364. doi:10.100710902-014-9563-y

Lomas, T., Ivtzan, I., & Fu, C. H. (2015). A systematic review of the neurophysiology of mindfulness on EEG oscillations. *Neuroscience and Biobehavioral Reviews*, *57*, 401–410. doi:10.1016/j.neubiorev.2015.09.018 PMID:26441373

Looseveld, L. M., Van Gerven, P. W. M., Driessen, E. W., Vanassche, E., & Artino, A. R. Jr. (2021). MERIT: A mentor reflection instrument for identifying the personal interpretative framework. *BMC Medical Education*, *21*(144), 144. https://bmcmededuc.biomedcentral.com/articles/10.1186/s12909-021-02579-x. doi:10.118612909-021-02579-x PMID:33663496

Loughlin, C., & Barling, J. (2001). Young workers' work values, attitudes, and behaviors. *Journal of Occupational and Organizational Psychology*, *74*(4), 543–559. doi:10.1348/096317901167514

Lowe, D., Levitt, K., & Wilson, T. (2008). Solutions for retaining generation Y employees in the workplace. *Business Renaissance Quarterly*, *3*(3), 43–57.

Luthans, F., Avey, J. B., Avolio, B. J., & Peterson, S. J. (2010). The development and resulting performance impact of positive psychological capital. *Human Resource Development Quarterly*, *21*(1), 41–67. doi:10.1002/hrdq.20034

Ma, J. (2017, January 12). 25 famous women on impostor syndrome and self-doubt. *The Cut*. https://www.thecut.com/2017/01/25-famous-women-on-impostor-syndrome-and-self-doubt.html

Maak, T., & Pless, N. M. (2009). Business leaders as citizens of the world. *Advances in Global Leadership*, *5*, 225–256.

Mabula, D. (2022). *Implementing the new partnership for Africa's development (NEPAD): challenges and prospects*. North-West University.

Mackey, A., & Sisodia, R. S. (2014). *Conscious capitalism: Liberating the heroic spirit of business*. Harvard Business Review Press.

Madden, M., & Rood, E. (2023). *Gen Z in the Room: Making Public Media by and with Youth for the Future.* Joan Ganz Cooney Center at Sesame Workshop.

Maftei, A., Dumitriu, A., & Holman, A. (2021). "They will discover I'm a fraud!" the impostor syndrome among psychology students. *Studia Psychologica, 63*(4), 337–351. doi:10.31577p.2021.04.831

Malos, R. (2012). *The most important leadership theories.*

Marshall, M. (2023). Prepared for a crisis and the unexpected: Managing everyday eventualities through food storage practices. *Food, Culture, & Society, 26*(2), 305–326. doi:10.1080/15528014.2021.1967643

Martin, A. (2006). The demise of the heroic leader. *Leader to Leader, 42*, 55–56.

Martin, C., & Tulgan, B. (2001). *Managing generation Y: Global citizens born in the late seventies and early eighties.* HRD Press.

Martin, D. R., Winchatz, M. R., Knight, K., & Burrows, L. (2023). Managing Workplace Boredom: Employee Coping Strategies, Supervisor Communication, and Job Satisfaction. *Journal of Leadership & Organizational Studies, 30*(3), 314–326. doi:10.1177/15480518231168209

Matsumoto, S. (2020). Black Millennial Movement Seeks to Empower Young Leaders. *OBP In The News.* https://www.opb.org/article/2020/08/26/black-millennial-movement-seeks-to-empower-young-leaders/

Maxwell, J. C. (2005). *The 360 degree leader: Developing your influence from anywhere in the organization.* Thomas Nelson Inc.

McAllum, K. (2016). Managing Imposter Syndrome among the "Trophy kids": Creating teaching practices that develop independence in millennial students. *Communication Education, 65*(3), 363–365. doi:10.1080/03634523.2016.1177848

McCleskey, J. A. (2018). Millennial leadership expectations, shared leadership, and the future of organizations. *J Manage Sci Bus Intell, 3*(2), 50–52.

McGhee, H. (2021). *The Sum of Us: What Racism Costs Everyone and How We Can Proser.* One World Publishing.

McKenzie, L. M. (2017). *The Stereotypes and Biases that Plague Millennial leaders: Best Practices and Strategies for Job Promotion.* [Thesis, Pepperdine University].

McLoyd, V. C., Hardaway, C., & Jocson, J. (2019). *African American Parenting from: Handbook of Parenting, Volume 4: Social Conditions and Applied Parenting.* Routledge. https://www.routledgehandbooks.com/doi/10.4324/9780429398995-3

Men, L. R., Qin, Y. S., & Mitson, R. (2021). Engaging startup employees via charismatic leadership communication: The importance of communicating "vision, passion, and care". *International Journal of Business Communication*, •••, 23294884211020488.

Metz, T. (2019). *The African Ethic of Ubuntu.* 1000-Word Philosophy. An Introductory Anthology.

Meyer, M., & Warren-Gordon, K. (2013). Marginal Mentoring in the Contact Space: Diversified Mentoring Relationships at a Midsized Midwestern State University (MMSU). *Qualitative Report, 18*(19), 1–18.

Meyers, M. C., van Woerkom, M., & Bakker, A. B. (2013). The added value of the positive: A literature review of positive psychology interventions in organizations. *European Journal of Work and Organizational Psychology, 22*(5), 618–632. doi:10.1080/1359432X.2012.694689

Mhlambi, S., & Tiribelli, S. (2023). Decolonizing AI ethics: Relational autonomy as a means to counter AI Harms. *Topoi, 42*(3), 1–14. doi:10.100711245-022-09874-2

Mhongera, P. B., & Lombard, A. (2020). Pathways of resilience for children facing socio-economic adversities: Experiences from Future Families' OVC programmes in South Africa. *Children and Youth Services Review, 108*, 104657. doi:10.1016/j.childyouth.2019.104657

Miller, J. (2018). *The Secret to a Good Meeting: The Meeting before the Meeting.* TheLadders.com

Mlambo, D. N., & Adetiba, T. C. (2020). Post-1994 South Africa's peacekeeping and military intervention in Southern Africa, reference from the Democratic Republic of Congo (DRC) and Lesotho. *Journal of Public Affairs, 20*(1), e1984. doi:10.1002/pa.1984

Montanez, R. (2020). 5 Strategies for Engaging a Workforce Inclusive of Millennial Talent. *Forbes.com.*

Morales, S. (2017). *Re-defining Counterspaces: New Directions and Implications for Research and Praxis. Issue No.8.* Center for Critical Race Studies.

Morreale, S. P., & Staley, C. M. (2016). Millennials, teaching and learning, and the elephant in the college classroom. *Communication Education, 65*(3), 370–373. doi:10.1080/03634523.2016.1177842

Morrisette, S., & Schraeder, M. (2010). Leadership development approaches. *Journal for Quality and Participation, 32*(4), 32–34.

Moyson, S., Raaphorst, N., Groeneveld, S., & Van de Walle, S. (2017). Organizational Socialization in Public Administration Research: A Systematic Review and Directions for Future Research. *American Review of Public Administration, 48*(6), 610–627. doi:10.1177/0275074017696160

Mugumbate, J., & Nyanguru, A. (2013). Exploring African Philosophy: The Value of Ubuntu in Social Work. *African Journal of Social Work, 3*(1).

Mullen, C. A. (2000). Constructing co-mentoring partnerships: Walkways we must travel. *Theory into Practice, 39*(1), 4–11. doi:10.120715430421tip3901_2

Munley, A. E. (2011). Culture differences in leadership. *The IUP Journal of Soft Skills, 5*(1).

Murray, M. (1991). *Beyond the myths and magic of mentoring: How to facilitate an effective mentoring program.* Jossey-Bass.

Myers, K. K., & Sadaghiani, K. (2010). Millennials in the Workplace: A Communication Perspective on Millennials' Organizational Relationships and Performance. *Journal of Business and Psychology, 25*(2), 225–238. doi:10.100710869-010-9172-7 PMID:20502509

National Center for Education Statistics (2018). Average and median age of public school teachers and percentage distribution of teachers by age category, sex, and state: 2017-2018. *National Teacher and Principal Survey.* NCES.

Ng, K. Y., Ang, S., & Chan, K. Y. (2008). Personality and leader effectiveness: A moderated mediation model of leadership self-efficacy, job demands, and job autonomy. *The Journal of Applied Psychology, 93*(4), 733–743. doi:10.1037/0021-9010.93.4.733 PMID:18642980

Nguyen, T.-M., Malik, A., & Budhwar, P. (2022). Knowledge hiding in organizational crisis: The moderating role of leadership. *Journal of Business Research, 139*, 161–172. https://www.ncbi.nlm.nih.gov/pmc/articles/PMC8516615/pdf/main.pdf. doi:10.1016/j.jbusres.2021.09.026 PMID:34667337

Niemann, Y. F. (2016). The Social Ecology of Tokenism in higher education. *Peace Review, 28*(4), 451–458. doi:10.1080/10402659.2016.1237098

Noble, S. M., Mende, M., Grewal, D., & Parasuraman, A. (2022). The Fifth Industrial Revolution: How Harmonious Human–Machine Collaboration is Triggering a Retail and Service [R]evolution. [[DOI:]. *Journal of Retailing, 98*(2), 199–208. doi:10.1016/j.jretai.2022.04.003

Northhouse, P. G. (2013). *Leadership: Theory and Practice*. Sage Publications, Inc.

Northouse, P. (2010). *Leadership theory and practice* (5th ed.). Sage.

Northouse, P. G. (2021). *Leadership: Theory and practice*. Sage publications.

Nwakanma, A. P. (2021). women, entrepreneurship, and economic development in Africa. In The Palgrave Handbook of African Women's Studies (pp. 1583-1599). Springer.

Nyerere, J. K. (1974). From Uhuru to Ujamaa. *Africa Today, 21*(3), 3–8. https://www.jstor.org/stable/4185420

Ojo, A. (2021). *Social Revolutions and Governance Aspirations of African Millennials: Emerging from the Political Shadows of Strongmen*. Springer Nature.

Okwuwada, N. (2023). *The modern day consequences, causes, and nature of kidnapping, terrorism, banditry, and violent crime in Nigeria: A comprehensive analysis.*

Olson, M. E. (2009). The "Millennials": First year in practice. *Nursing Outlook, 57*(1), 10-17.

Omazić, M. A., Labaš, D., & Uroić, P. (2023). *Contingency Theory.*

Ong, L. (2022, June 6). Dealing with imposter syndrome at work: A Millennial's two cents. *Calm Collective Asia Blog*. https://www.blog.calmcollective.asia/blog/dealing-with-imposter-syndrome-at-work-a-millennials-two-cents

Pardekooper, B. (2019). *Millennial leadership: Equipping Generations to Influence a New Millennium*. Author Academy Elite.

Park, J. G., Kim, J. S., Yoon, S. W., & Joo, B. K. (2017). The effects of empowering leadership on psychological well-being and job engagement: The mediating role of psychological capital. *Leadership and Organization Development Journal*.

Pegram, B., & Bonner, F. (2021). Code-Stitching to Code Stitching: Theorizing an Alternative Framework. *Diverse Issues in Higher Education*.

Pennamon, T. (2017). The Emergence of the Community College Chief Diversity Officer. *Diverse Issues in Higher Education*, 17–19.

Phyu, S. O. (2023). *Leadership Styles, Job Satisfaction, and Employee Performance of Glory Farmer Development Bank*. MERAL Portal.

Piktialis, D. (2007). Adaptations to an aging workforce: Innovative responses by the corporate sector. *Generations (San Francisco, Calif.)*, *31*(1), 76–82.

Pilcher, J. (1994). Mannheim's sociology of generations: An undervalued legacy. *The British Journal of Sociology*, *45*(3), 481–494. doi:10.2307/591659

Poddar, A. (2023). *A comparative analysis of charismatic leadership between Donald Trump and Narendra Modi during the Covid crisis*. Sistema de Bibliotecas FGV.

Pogored. (2022, April 4). *What's imposter syndrome and how to overcome it*. Cleveland Clinic. https://health.clevelandclinic.org/a-psychologist-explains-how-to-deal-with-imposter-syndrome/

Post, J. (2022) What Does Modern Leadership Really Mean? *Business.com*.

Post, J. (2022). Millennials and modern leadership styles. *business.com*. https://www.business.com/articles/leadership-styles-millennials/

Puiu, S. (2017). Generation Z — an educational and managerial perspective. *Young Economists Journal/Revista Tinerilor Economisti*, *14*(29), 62-72.

PwC. (2016). *The millennial mind: How millennial preferences will shape the economy*. PwC Consumer Intelligence Series.

Quaye, S., Karikari, S., Allen, C., Okello, W., & Carter, K. (2019). Strategies for Practicing Self-Care from Racial Battle Fatigue. *JCSCORE*, *5*(2), 94–131. doi:10.15763/issn.2642-2387.2019.5.2.94-131

Race, T., & Skees, J. (2010). Changing tides: Improving outcomes through mentorship on all levels of nursing. *Critical Care Nursing Quarterly*, *33*(2), 163–174. doi:10.1097/CNQ.0b013e3181d91475 PMID:20234205

Ragins, B. R., & Cotton, J. L. (1999). Mentor functions and outcomes: A comparison of men and women in formal and informal mentoring relationships. *The Journal of Applied Psychology*, *84*(4), 529–549. doi:10.1037/0021-9010.84.4.529 PMID:10504893

Raines, C., & Twenge, J. (2018). *Managing Millennials: How to bridge the generation gap.* American Management Association.

Reeves, M., Levin, S., & Ueda, D. (2017). *The longevity dividend: Work in an era of 100-year lives.* Harvard Business Review Press.

Roberts, G. (2022). *Revolutionary State-making in Dar Es Salaam: African Liberation and the Global Cold War, 1961-1974.* Cambridge University Press.

Robertson, S. (2018). Generation Z characteristics & traits that explain the way they learn. *JKCP.* https://info.jkcp.com/blog/generation-z-characteristics

Robinson, C. K. (2017). In the Trump Era, Black Women Must be Allowed to Lead. *PeoplesWorld.org*

Robinson, C. (2021). *How this Millennial Democracy Director Influences the Political Landscape, Especially for Black Women. Forbes.com.* ForbesWomen.

Robinson, D. M., & Reio, T. G. Jr. (2012). Benefits of mentoring African-American men. *Journal of Managerial Psychology, 27*(4), 406–421. doi:10.1108/02683941211220207

Rodriguez Mosquera, P. M., Uskul, A. K., & Cross, S. E. (2011). The centrality of social image in social psychology. *European Journal of Social Psychology, 41*(4), 403–410. doi:10.1002/ejsp.820

Rogers, C. R. (1963). Toward a Science of the Person. *Journal of Humanistic Psychology, 3*(2), 72–92. doi:10.1177/002216786300300208

Rupčić, N. (2020). Learning organisation as technology for the socio-economic paradigm implementation. *International Journal of Agile Systems and Management, 13*(2), 182–212. doi:10.1504/IJASM.2020.107899

Russo, R., & Schoemaker, P. (2019). *Winning with uncertainty: Modern leadership lessons from history's great strategic thinkers.* Oxford University Press.

Saks, A. M., & Gruman, J. A. (2018). Socialization resources theory and newcomers' work engagement: A new pathway to newcomer socialization. *Career Development International, 23*(1), 12–32. doi:10.1108/CDI-12-2016-0214

Salahuddin, M. (2010). Generational differences impact on leadership style and organizational success. *Journal of Diversity Management, 5*(2), 1–6. doi:10.19030/jdm.v5i2.805

Samuelson, M. (2021). *Claiming the city in South African literature.* Taylor & Francis. doi:10.4324/9781003174189

Santra, S., & Alat, P. (2022). Adaptive leadership of doctors during COVID-19. *Leadership in Health Services, 35*(2), 246–266. doi:10.1108/LHS-08-2021-0073 PMID:34882361

Sathyakumar, J., & Ramakrishnan, M. (2013). Workplace expectations and organizational commitment of Generation Y: A case study at selective business schools. *TSM Business Review, 1*(1), 1-13. http://www.tsm.ac.in/pdf/Samplepaper.pdf

Sauce, B. & Matzel, L. (2017). *Inductive Reasoning*. Springer. . doi:10.1007/978-3-319-47829-6_1045-1

Schein, E. H. (2016). *Organizational culture and leadership* (5th ed.). Wiley.

Schepker, D. J., Kim, Y., Patel, P. C., Thatcher, S. M. B., & Campion, M. C. (2017). CEO succession, strategic change, and post-succession performance: A meta-analysis. *The Leadership Quarterly*, *28*(6), 701–720. doi:10.1016/j.leaqua.2017.03.001

Schiffling, S., Hannibal, C., Tickle, M., & Fan, Y. (2022). The implications of complexity for humanitarian logistics: A complex adaptive systems perspective. *Annals of Operations Research*, *319*(1), 1379–1410. doi:10.100710479-020-03658-w

Schneider, F. W., Gruman, J. A., & Coutts, L. M. (2005). Defining the field of applied social psychology. *Applied social psychology: Understanding and addressing social and practical problems*, 1-18.

Schuh, S. C., Cai, Y., Kaluza, A. J., Steffens, N. K., David, E. M., & Haslam, S. A. (2021). Do leaders condone unethical pro-organizational employee behaviors? The complex interplay between leader organizational identification and moral disengagement. *Human Resource Management*, *60*(6), 969–989. doi:10.1002/hrm.22060

Seheult, E. (2016). Generational mentorship: What millennial mentees want. *College and University*, *91*(3), 39–42.

Senge, P. (2000). The leadership of profound change. *SPC Ink*, 1-3.

Senge, P. M. (1990). *The Fifth Discipline: The Art & Practice of the Learning Organisation*. Currency and DoubleDay.

Senge, P. M. (2017). The leaders' new work: Building learning organizations. In *Leadership perspectives* (pp. 51–67). Routledge. doi:10.4324/9781315250601-6

Serrat, O. (2017). Building a learning organization. In *Knowledge solutions: Tools, methods, and approaches to drive organizational performance* (2nd ed., pp. 79–86). Springer.

Sessa, V. I., Kabacoff, R. I., Deal, J., & Brown, H. (2007). Generational differences in leader values and leadership behaviors. *The Psychologist Manager Journal*, *10*(1), 47–74. doi:10.1080/10887150709336612

Sharma, D. (2019). *How to recruit, incentivize and retain millennials*. SAGE/Response Business Books.

Shore, L. M., Randel, A. E., Chung, B. G., Dean, M. A., Ehrhart, K. H., & Singh, G. (2011). Inclusion and diversity in work groups: A review and model for future research. *Journal of Management*, *37*(4), 1262–1289. doi:10.1177/0149206310385943

Short, T. W. (2014). Workplace mentoring: An old idea with new meaning (part 2). *Development and Learning in Organizations*, *28*(2), 3–6. doi:10.1108/DLO-11-2013-0086

Shreya, G. R. D. (2017). Employee service innovative behavior: The roles of Leader-Member Exchange (LMX), work engagement, and job autonomy. *International Journal of Manpower*, *38*(2).

Shukla, B., Sufi, T., Joshi, M., & Sujatha, R. (2022). Leadership challenges for Indian hospitality industry during COVID-19 pandemic. *Journal of Hospitality and Tourism Insights*.

Siegel, P. H., Schultz, T., & Landy, S. (2011). Formal versus informal mentoring of MAS professionals. *Journal of Applied Business Research*, *27*(2), 5–11. http://www.cluteinstitute.com/ojs/index.php/JABR/article/view/4135. doi:10.19030/jabr.v27i2.4135

Sifiso, G., & Pfano, M. (2022). Corporate governance and organisational performance in Africa: A systematic literature review. *African Journal of Business Management*, *16*(10), 210–223.

Simmonds-Jordan, N. A., & Mills, B. (2021, October 14). Why a black chief diversity officer is not the answer when it comes to inclusion. *C Level Magazine*. http://c-levelmagazine.com/why-a-black-chief-diversity-officer-is-not-the-answer-when-it-comes-to-inclusion

Simsek, Z., & Heavey, C. (2011). The mediating role of knowledge-based capital for corporate entrepreneurship and radical innovation in large, diversified firms. *Strategic Entrepreneurship Journal*, *5*(4), 317–337.

Singh, S. K., & Singh, A. P. (2018). Interplay of organizational justice, psychological empowerment, organizational citizenship behavior, and job satisfaction in the context of circular economy. *Management Decision*. doi:10.1108/MD-09-2018-0966

Singh, V., Vinnicombe, S., & James, K. (2006). Constructing a professional identity: How young female managers use role model. *Women in Management Review*, *26*(1), 67–81. doi:10.1108/09649420610643420

Siu, G. P., & Sivan, A. (2011). Mentoring experiences of psychiatric nurses: From acquaintance to affirmation. *Nurse Education Today*, *31*(8), 797–802. doi:10.1016/j.nedt.2010.11.014 PMID:21144626

Smith, S. (2020). Why Radical Self-Care Cannot Wait: Strategies for Black Women Leaders Now. *Urban Education Journal UPENN Graduate School of Education, 18*(1).

Smith, A., & Smith, H. (2017). An International Survey of the Wellbeing of Employees in the Business Process Outsourcing Industry. *Psychology (Irvine, Calif.)*, *8*(1), 160–167. doi:10.4236/psych.2017.81010

SOA Research Institute. (2021). *Highlights of the 2021 retirement risk survey*. SOA Research Institute. https://www.soa.org/globalassets/assets/files/resources/research-report/2021/retirement-risk-survey-highlights.pdf

Society for Human Resource Management. (2017). *Employee job satisfaction and engagement: The doors of opportunity are open*. SHRM. https://www.shrm.org/hr-today/trends-and-forecasting/research-and-surveys/Documents/2017-Employee-Job-Satisfaction-and-Engagement-Executive-Summary.pdf

Solomon, M. (2017). *5 characteristics of Millennials - Michigan Scouting*. Michigan Scouting. https://michiganscouting.org/wp-content/uploads/2017/11/Five-Characteristics-of-Millennials.pdf

Soomro, A. A., Breitenecker, R. J., & Syed, A. M. S. (2017). *Relation of work-life balance, work-family conflict, and family-work conflict with the employee performance-moderating role of job satisfaction*. South Asian Journal of Business Studies. doi:10.1108/SAJBS-02-2017-0018

Soussi, N. (n.d.). *4 Skills millennials bring to leadership positions*. Simon Sinek. https://simonsinek.com/discover/4-skills-millennials-bring-to-leadership-positions/

Srivastava, A. K., & Chaturvedi, S. (2014). Negative Job Experiences and Employees Job Attitudes and Health in High-Performance Work Organizations. *Metamorphosis*, *13*(2), 22–28. doi:10.1177/0972622520140205

Starcher, R. L. (2012). How Higher Education in the U.S. Can Inform Missions' Diversification Efforts. *Mission Studies: Journal of the International Association for Mission Studies*, *29*(2), 201–212. doi:10.1163/15733831-12341237

Steger, M. F., Dik, B. J., & Duffy, R. D. (2018). Measuring meaningful work: The work and meaning inventory (WAMI). *Journal of Career Assessment*, *26*(3), 514–527.

Stewart, T. J. (2019). "Where We Are, Resistance Lives": Black Women, Social Media, and Everyday Resistance in Higher Education. [JCSCORE]. *Journal Committed to Social Change on Race and Ethnicity*, *5*(2), 3–32. https://www.jstor.org/stable/48645354. doi:10.15763/issn.2642-2387.2019.5.2.1-31

Stop telling women they have imposter syndrome. Harvard Business Review. (2022, August 4). Retrieved August 27, 2022, from https://hbr.org/2021/02/stop-telling-women-they-have-imposter-syndrome#:~:text=Imposter%20syndrome%20is%20loosely%20defined,they're%20deserving%20of%20accolades

Strauss, W., & Howe, N. (1991). *Generations: The history of America's future, 1584 to2069*. William Morrow.

Stroshine, M. S., & Brandl, S. G. (2011). Race, gender, and tokenism in policing. *Police Quarterly*, *14*(4), 344–365. doi:10.1177/1098611111423738

Su, L., & Swanson, S. (2019). Perceived corporate social responsibility's impact on the well-being and supportive green behaviors of hotel employees: The mediating role of the employee-corporate relationship. *Tourism Management, 72*, 437-450. doi:10.1016/j.tourman.2019.01.009

Suar, D., Jha, A. K., Das, S. S., & Alat, P. (2019). The structure and predictors of subjective well-being among millennials in India. *Cogent Psychology*, *6*(1), 1584083. doi:10.1080/23311908.2019.1584083

Sudrajat, D., Siswondo, S., Harsono, Y., & Fajarianto, O. (2023). THE INFLUENCE OF LEADERSHIP STYLE AND WORK DISCIPLINE ON EMPLOYEE PERFORMANCE. *International Journal of Economics* [IJEBAR]. *Business and Accounting Research*, *7*(2), 641–648.

Sumanth, J. J., Černe, M., Hannah, S. T., & Škerlavaj, M. (2023). Fueling the Creative Spark: How Authentic Leadership and LMX Foster Employees' Proactive Orientation and Creativity. *Journal of Leadership & Organizational Studies, 30*(3), 356–374. doi:10.1177/15480518231180064

Suyanto, U.Y., Mu'ah, M., Purwanti, I.S., & Sayyid, M. (2019). Transformational Leadership: Millennial Leadership Style. In *Industry 4.0.*

Swanson, D. M. (2007). Ubuntu: An African contribution to (re)search for/with a "humble Togetherness". *Journal of Contemporary Issues in Education.*

T&T Loop News. (2021). CNN Anchor with Trini Roots Listed Among Times Emerging leaders. *T & T Loop News.* https://tt.loopnews.com/content/cnn-anchor-trini-roots-listed-among-times-emerging-leaders

Tang, G., Yu, B., Cooke, F. L., & Chen, Y. (2017). High-performance work system and employee creativity: The roles of perceived organisational support and devolved management. *Personnel Review, 46*(7), 1318–1334. doi:10.1108/PR-09-2016-0235

Tanner, L. (2010). Who are the Millennials? Defence Research and Development Canada Ottawa (Ontario) Centre for Operational Research and Analysis.

Tapscott, D. (2009). *Grown up digital: How the net generation is changing your world.* McGraw-Hill.

Tavernaro-Haidarian, L. (2018). Deliberative epistemology: Towards an ubuntu-based Epistemology that accounts for a priori knowledge and objective truth. *South African Journal of Philosophy, 37(*2). doi:10.1080/025801362018.1470374

Team, T. K. (2017, March 30). Real stories: Imposter Syndrome. *Medium.* https://medium.com/kip-blog/real-stories-imposter-syndrome-15bce02a5c1e

Tensley, B. (2021). *Analysis: How 'the kaepernick effect' has propelled a new generation of athletes to take a stand against racial injustice.* CNN. https://www.cnn.com/2021/10/28/politics/the-kaepernick-effect-race-deconstructed-newsletter/index.html

Termini, C. M., Hinton, A. O. Jr, Garza-Lopez, E., Koomoa, D. L., Davis, J. S., & Martinez-Montemayor, M. M. (2022). Building diverse mentoring networks that transcend boundaries in cancer research. *Trends in Cancer, 7*(5), 385–388. https://doi.10.1016/j.trecan.2021.01.001. doi:10.1016/j.trecan.2021.01.001 PMID:33563577

Tews, M. J., Michel, J., Xu, S., & Drost, A. J. (2015). Workplace fun matters... but what else? *Employee Relations, 37*(2), 248–267. doi:10.1108/ER-10-2013-0152

The Institute of Politics at Harvard University. (n.d.). *Symone Sanders.* Harvard University. https://iop.harvard.edu/fellows/symone-sanders

Thompson, L. F., Cramton, C. D., & O'Connor, K. M. (2016). Subgroups of newcomers and socialization outcomes: How organizations can leverage informal groups. *Academy of Management Journal, 59*(3), 802–822.

Time Staff. (2015). 12 New Faces of Black Leadership. *Time Magazine*. https://time.com/3668782/12-faces-of-black-leadership/

Trier-Bieniek, A. (2016). *The Beyonce's Effect: Essays on Sexuality, Race, and Feminism*. Farland & Company Inc. Publishers.

Tulgan, B. (2009). *Not everyone gets a trophy: How to manage Generation Y*. Jossey-Bass.

Tulgan, B. (2016). *Not everyone gets a trophy: How to manage the millennials*. Wiley. doi:10.1002/9781119215073

Tursunova, D. T., Abobakirova, O. N., Buzrukova, D. M., Mahmudova, O. T., Ubaydullayeva, Z. H., & Kholmatova, N. N. (2022). Principal Principles And Important Factors Of Student Women's Social Activity. *Journal of Positive School Psychology*.

Tuzovic, S., & Kabadayi, S. (2018). The influence of social distancing on employee well-being: A conceptual framework and research agenda. *Journal of Service Management, 32*(2), 145–160. doi:10.1108/JOSM-05-2020-0140

Twenge, J. (2006). *Generation me: Why today's young Americans are more confident, assertive, entitled – and more miserable than ever before*. Free Press.

U.S. Bureau of Labor Statistics. (2020, September 22). *Employee tenure summary*. U.S. Bureau of Labor Statistics. https://www.bls.gov/news.release/tenure.nr0.htm

Uhl-Bien, M., & Arena, M. (2018). Leadership for organizational adaptability: A theoretical synthesis and integrative framework. *The Leadership Quarterly, 29*(1), 89–104. doi:10.1016/j.leaqua.2017.12.009

Ukpokodu, O. (2016). *Ubuntu Pedagogy- A humanistic approach to engaging and empowering students' active learning in urban schools*.

Vaccaro, S., & Marcotte, N. (2019). [JCSCORE]. Insights into the Sense of Belonging from Women of Color Interconnections of Cultural Competence, Expectations, Institutional Diversity, and Counterspaces. *Journal Committed to Social Change on Race and Ethnicity, 5*(2), 33–65.

Valenti, A. (2021). LGBT employment rights in an evolving legal landscape: The impact of the Supreme Court's decision in Bostock v. Clayton County, Georgia. *Employee Responsibilities and Rights Journal, 33*(1), 3–23. doi:10.100710672-020-09359-7

Van Zyl, L. E., Roll, L. C., Stander, M. W., & Richter, S. (2020). Positive Psychological Coaching Definition and Models: A Systematic Literature Review. *Frontiers in Psychology, 11*, 793. doi:10.3389/fpsyg.2020.00793 PMID:32435218

Vasilopoulos, N. L., Ng, K. Y., Xanthopoulou, D., Chasiotis, A., van der Heijden, B. I., & de Witte, H. (2020). Work-related needs and job crafting: A longitudinal study among employees in Greece. *European Journal of Work and Organizational Psychology, 29*(4), 569–582.

Vera, A. (2019). *Colin Kaepernick's Nike ad wins emmy for outstanding commercial.* CNN. https://www.cnn.com/2019/09/15/entertainment/nike-ad-emmy-win-trnd

Vincent, A., & Seymour, J. (1995). Profile of women mentors: A national survey. *S.A.M. Advanced Management Journal, 60*, 4–10. https://www.freepatentsonline.com/article/SAM-Advanced-Management-Journal/17765188.html

Wanzo, R. (2022). Resisting the Revolutionary Call. *New Political Science, 44*(3), 450–456. doi:10.1080/07393148.2022.2119331

Watson, E. (2007). Tupac Shakur, 1971-1996. *BlackPast.org*

Webb, S. A., Bruyere, B., Halladay, M., & Walker, S. (2021). A framework for conceptualizing leadership in conservation. *Oryx*, 1–7.

Weber, M. (1986). Världsreligonernas ekonomiska etik (The economic ethics of the world religions). *Ratio.*

Wei-Li, Y.-C. L. (2017). Empowering group leaders encourages knowledge sharing: Integrating the social exchange theory and positive organizational behavior perspective. *Journal of Knowledge Management, 21*(2), 474–491. doi:10.1108/JKM-08-2016-0318

Weill, P., & Woerner, S. (2013). Thriving on digital ecosystems. *MIT Sloan Management Review, 55*(1), 27–34.

West, M., & Sacramento, C. A. (2012). Creativity and innovation implementation in work groups: The paradoxical role of demands. *Journal of Organizational Behavior, 33*(6), 704–724.

What about men. (2022, March 14). Impostor Syndrome Institute. https://impostorsyndrome.com/what-about-men/

Wilford, L. (2020). *Leadership Strategies and Millennial Organizational Commitment.* [Dissertation, Walden University].

Wilkins, S. (2017). Ethical issues in transnational higher education: The case of international branch campuses[[DOI:]. *Studies in Higher Education, 42*(8), 1385–1400. doi:10.1080/03075079.2015.1099624

Williams, D. A., & Wade-Golden, K. C. (2006). What is a Chief Diversity Officer? Inside Higher Ed.

Williams, D. A., & Wade-Golden, K. C. (2007). The Chief Diversity Officer. *College & University Professional Association for Human Resources*, 38–48.

Wilson, D., & Williams, V. (2013). Ubuntu: Development and Framework of a Specific Model of Positive Mental Health. *Psychology Journal, 10.* www.psychologicalpublishing.com

Wilson, J. L. (2013). Emerging Trend: The Chief Diversity Officer Phenomenon within Higher Education. *The Journal of Negro Education, 82*(4), 433–445. doi:10.7709/jnegroeducation.82.4.0433

Winkle-Wagner, R., & Locks, A. M. (2020). *Diversity and inclusion on campus: Supporting students of color in higher education*. Routledge.

Wolfe, B. L., & Dilworth, P. P. (2015). Transitioning normalcy. *Review of Educational Research, 85*(4), 667–697. doi:10.3102/0034654314565667

Wong, C. S., & Gardiner, E. (2017). Leadership and creativity: A meta-analytic review. *Psychological Bulletin, 143*(4), 367–409.

Woodward, R. (2020). *5 Skills millennials can develop to become better leaders*. Simon Sinek. https://simonsinek.com/discover/5-skills-millennials-can-develop-to-become-better-leaders/

Worthington, R. L., Stanley, C. A., & Lewis, W. T. (2014). National Association of Diversity Officers in Higher Education Standards of professional practice for chief diversity officers. *Journal of Diversity in Higher Education, 7*(4), 227–234. doi:10.1037/a0038391

Wright, E. (2001). *Why Black People Tend To Shout! An Earnest Attempt To Explain The Sociological Negation Of The Atlanta Sociological Laboratory Despite Its Possible Unpleasantness*. Taylor & Francis.

Wright, J., & Vazquez, M. (2021). *Symone Sanders, Harris' chief spokesperson, to leave White House*. CNN. https://www.cnnphilippines.com/world/2021/12/2/Symone-Sanders-Kamala-Harris-spokesperson-White-House-US.html

Wylonis, C. (2021). *Millennials are all in on transparency, and companies need to follow suit*. BenefitsPRO. https://www.benefitspro.com/2021/05/26/millenials-are-all-in-on-transparency-and-companies-need-to-follow-suit/?slreturn=20220707101647

Yohannes, S. (2014). *DON'T TOUCH MY HAIR A Qualitative Study on Professional Norms and Meanings of Black Female Hair in Swedish Public Administration*. University West.

Young, D. (2019). Impostor Syndrome is Having a Massive Effect on the Black Middle Class. *Independent.co.uk*.

Youssef, C. M., & Luthans, F. (2007). Positive organizational behavior in the workplace: The impact of hope, optimism, and resilience. *Journal of Management, 33*(5), 774–800. doi:10.1177/0149206307305562

Yukl, G. (2023). Effective Use of Power and Influence Tactics in Organizations. Principles of Organizational Behavior: The Handbook of Evidence-Based Management, 311.

Yukl, G. (1989). Managerial leadership: A review of theory and research. *Journal of Management, 15*(2), 251–290. doi:10.1177/014920638901500207

Yukl, G. (2006). *Leadership in organizations*. Pearson-Prentice Hall.

Yukl, G. (2012). Effective leadership behavior: What we know and what questions need more attention. *The Academy of Management Perspectives, 26*(4), 66–85. doi:10.5465/amp.2012.0088

Yukl, G., & Gardner, W. (2020). *Leadership in organizations (Global)*. Pearson Education Limited.

Yukl, G., & Lepsinger, R. (2004). *Flexible leadership: Creating value by balancing multiple challenges and choices*. Jossey-Bass.

Yu, M., Wen, J., Smith, S. M., & Stokes, P. (2022). Building-up resilience and being effective leaders in the workplace: A systematic review and synthesis model. *Leadership and Organization Development Journal, 43*(7), 1098–1117. doi:10.1108/LODJ-09-2021-0437

Zackery, S. (2021). *Influence of STEM mentor race and cultural competency on racial and ethnic minority mentees.* [Masters thesis]. Oklahoma Baptist University. https://hdl.handle.net/11244/333649

Zakharov, N., Tate, S. A., Law, I., & Bernardino-Costa, J. (2023). South Africa and the Struggle for Racial Equality: Debating Deracialization, Non-racialism, Decolonization, and Africanization. In Futures of Anti-Racism: Paradoxes of Deracialization in Brazil, South Africa, Sweden, and the UK (pp. 15-67). Springer.

Zaman, S., Ansari, A. H., & Chaturvedi, S. (2021). Work-life enablers for job satisfaction in healthcare: Moderating role of organization type. *Industrial and Commercial Training*. doi:10.1108/ICT-05-2020-0060

Zemke, R., Raines, C., & Filipczak, B. (2000). *Generations at work: Managing the clash of veterans, boomers, Xers, and nexters in your workplace*. AMA.

Zen, A., Yanti, S., Hutomo, M. R., Kraugusteeliana, K., & Arisutama, H. Y. (2023). The Role of Leadership in Managing Organisational Culture Change in the Context of Information Technology Implementation. *Jurnal Minfo Polgan, 12*(1), 1247–1255. doi:10.33395/jmp.v12i1.12697

Zenger, J. (2012, December 17). We wait too long to train our leaders [Blog post]. *Harvard Business Review*. https://hbr.org/2012/12/why-do-we-wait-so-long-to-trai/

Ziegler, M. G. (2022). *Web 2.0 and knowledge sharing. A literature review*. AI, Computer Science and Robotics Technology. doi:10.5772/acrt.03

About the Contributors

Tymon M. Graham serves as Associate Vice President of Student Success and Engagement at Edward Waters University. As a scholar-practitioner, Dr. Graham has joined his administrative career with traditional academics by serving as a classroom professor, publishing scholarship, and presenting research both nationally and internationally related to student success, millennial leadership, educational leadership, and historically black colleges and universities. Dr. Graham earned his Bachelor of Science degree in Family & Consumer Sciences: Business with a concentration in Child Development from SC State University, a Master of Education in Professional Counseling with an emphasis in College Student Affairs from University of West Georgia and his Doctor of Education in Higher Education and Organizational Change from Benedictine University.

***

Neeta Baporikar is currently Professor/Director(Business Management) at Harold Pupkewitz Graduate School of Business, Namibia University of Science and Technology, Namibia. Prior to this, she was Head-Scientific Research, with the Ministry of Higher Education CAS-Salalah, Sultanate of Oman, Professor (Strategy and Entrepreneurship) at IIIT Pune and BITS India. With a decade-plus of experience in the industry, consultancy, and training, she made a lateral switch to research and academics in 2000. Prof Baporikar holds D.Sc. (Management Studies) USA, Ph.D. (Management), SP Pune University, INDIA with MBA (Distinction) and Law (Hons.) degrees. Apart from this, she is an external reviewer, Oman Academic Accreditation Authority, an Accredited Management Teacher, Qualified Trainer, FDP from EDII, Doctoral Guide, and Board Member of Academic Advisory Committee in accredited B-Schools. She has to her credit many conferred doctorates, 300+ scientific publications and authored 30+ books in the area of Strategy, Entrepreneurship, Management and Higher Education. She is also a member of the international and editorial advisory board, reviewer for Emerald, IGI, Inderscience, Wiley, etc.

July P. Carrillo, a native of Bogotá, Colombia, is the Director of the Virginia College Affordability Network (VCAN) & Strategic Initiatives at Virginia State University, an HBCU founded in 1882. July has nearly a decade of experience in higher education, managing programs meant to enhance institutional student success, retention, and graduation efforts. July has devoted particular attention in her career to creating transformational programs for minority, first-generation and underserved students. July holds a Bachelor of Arts and a Master of Education from the University of West Georgia. She completed her dissertation on the college experiences of Latino males, earning an Ed.D. in the Higher Education Administration and Leadership program at the University of Wisconsin-La Crosse. She is a proud member of Alpha Kappa Psi Professional Business Fraternity, Incorporated and Alpha Kappa Alpha Sorority, Incorporated.

Curtis L. Coleman was born and raised in Savannah, Georgia. He earned his bachelor's degree at South Carolina State University and his master's degree from the University of West Georgia. Dr. Coleman completed his doctoral studies in Student Affairs Administration and Leadership at the University of Wisconsin Lacrosse. Currently, Dr. Coleman serves as Assistant Director of Admissions Operations at Life University in Marietta, GA. He is a proud member of Kappa Kappa Psi Honorary Band Fraternity, Alpha Kappa Psi Professional Business Fraternity, and Kappa Alpha Psi Fraternity Incorporated.

Thea Dirton is an Instructional Coach in Greenville, SC. She taught middle school math for 14 years prior to moving into this position. She is a leader in her community, serving on the Board of Directors for two non-profit organizations that serve underserved populations and she is the youth coordinator for the local chapter of her sorority. She is also a life-long learner and researcher who has authored several peer-reviewed publications.

Ranson Sifiso Gwala holds a Doctor of Business Administration (DBA) from the University of KwaZulu Natal (UKZN). He has co-published several peer-reviewed articles. He also attended and presented papers at the international conferences starting in 2022. His interests are corporate governance, marketing, leadership, and leadership development in both the public and private sectors. He believes that academia should be an integral part of supporting the public sector to deliver services and improve the lives of people. Academia is at a vantage point to provide meaningful developmental imperatives for all sectors of society. He was born in Ndwedwe, KwaZulu-Natal, but now resides between Durban and Pietermaritzburg, South Africa

Velicia Hawkins-Moore studies the Global Knowledge Economy and the role of HBCUs in African Diasporic academic initiatives. She attended an International Branch Campus at the University of Maryland in Bad Kreuznach, Germany. She was selected to participate in a Ford Foundation funded, Social Demography Seminar in Xi'an, China in 2008. She taught through an NGO in a rural village (Marfokrom) in Ghana, West Africa in 2008. She taught as a part of the comprehensive education reform in Abu Dhabi from 2013-16. She became a member of Zeta Phi Beta in the United Arab Emirates in 2015. She began working with the Youth auxiliaries in Lambda Zeta in 2017. Velicia has presented her research at: TX-A&M Pathways-2008, International Center for Innovation in Education-Prairie View A&M-2019, Year of Return Conference-Ghana, West Africa-2019, UNLV-2020, Columbia University-2020, The Qualitative Report-Nova Southeastern University-2021. Velicia is a third year PhD student (Educational Leadership) at Prairieview A&M University (an HBCU). She currently serves as the Lead Reviewer for AERA: GSC-Division A. Velicia has published a commentary in the Spring 2021 Issue (Volume 13, Issue 1) of NEOS entitled "In the Pursuit of Racial Justice in Child & Youth Studies."

Jasmine K. S. has 23 years of teaching experience. Published 70+ journals/ conference publications . Published / Edited 10 Book chapters. Received many national /International awards.

Kathryn Towe Littleton, PhD, is the Director of Human Resources for ThyssenKrupp, a materials and metal distributor in Southfield, Michigan. Dr. Littleton grew up in South Carolina and received an undergraduate degree from Hampton University and a Masters degree from Michigan State University. She was employed by General Motors for 30 years and became the first African American woman in the arbitration sector of the General Motors Corporate Relations staff. Inspired by her interactions with and observations of the growing number of millennials on her staff, Dr. Littleton completed her PhD in Organizational Leadership in 2015, including a phenomenological study focusing on mentoring millennial employees and retention in organizations.

Nandini M. H. is an HR Practitioner, Consultant, and Researcher Master's degree in HR and Finance Management, SAP-HR Certified Professional, Performing Research in accordance with the effects of Positive Social Psychology on Employee Behavior and performance. Over Twelve years of consummate human resource management experience, served as HR Head, HRBP, Handled Pan India and overseas HR Operations for various Fortune 500 companies. Effectively Implementing human resources programs by providing human resources services, including talent acquisition, staffing, employment processing, compensation, health and welfare benefits, training and development, Payroll, Legal and compliance, safety and health, succession planning, employee relations and retention. Similarly, proficiency in Collaborating with the various HR Centers of Expertise like Benefits, Compensation, Talent Acquisition, Learning & Development, HRIS, Legal, Finance to streamline processes and provide best in class HR service delivery. Developing human resources solutions by collecting and analyzing information; recommending courses of action. Worked with diverse backgrounds from IT companies to non-IT companies such as Wipro, Adea International, Ascendum, Ultra, Genesis etc. Human resource professional having experience as a consultant, and speaker in addition to being an accomplished practitioner. Presented in various conferences and consulted with various clients across the companies on HR related topics.

Dahleah Moore attended Howard University after graduating high school in Houston, TX. She completed her undergraduate degree (in interdisciplinary Studies) at the University of Houston, Downtown. She operated a Home-School Coop in Abu Dhabi, UAE from 2014-2015. She taught grade school in Tegucigalpa, Honduras in 2017. She completed an Internship with Angela Ryes foundation, Completed the first cohort of HBI (Home Builders Institute) in Houston, and is a member of Zeta Phi Beta Sorority Inc, and National Women of Achievement Inc.

Bhavna Taneja has a doctorate in Management and an MBA specializing in marketing and finance. She has over 18 years of teaching experience In premium institutes like Xiss, Xaviers College Ranchi, Birsa Agricultural University, etc. Presently she is associated with Amity University Jharkhand. She has several publications to her name. Dr. Taneja is an active Rotarian and is presently on the board of directors of the Rotary Club of Ranchi. She is a Pranic healer.

Michael N. Weaver Jr. is an innovative, intriguing, and inspirational scholar. Weaver earned his Bachelor of Arts degree in Music Performance and his Master of Science degree in Educational Leadership and Policy Analysis from The University of Wisconsin-Madison. Currently, he serves as the Associate Director of Donor and External Relations for the Black Studies Department at The University of Texas at Austin. Weaver is also the founder of DreamWeaver Motivation, a speaking, mentoring, and consulting company. He encourages, motivates, and inspires crowds of many to take hold of their dreams, lives, and future. He is best known for speaking on leadership topics, the collegiate experience as a first-generation student, and how to make your dreams come true. Weaver is a proud member of Kappa Alpha Psi Fraternity Incorporated.

Index

P

R

S

T

U

V

W

www.ingramcontent.com/pod-product-compliance
Lightning Source LLC
LaVergne TN
LVHW061538290926
849162LV00004B/836